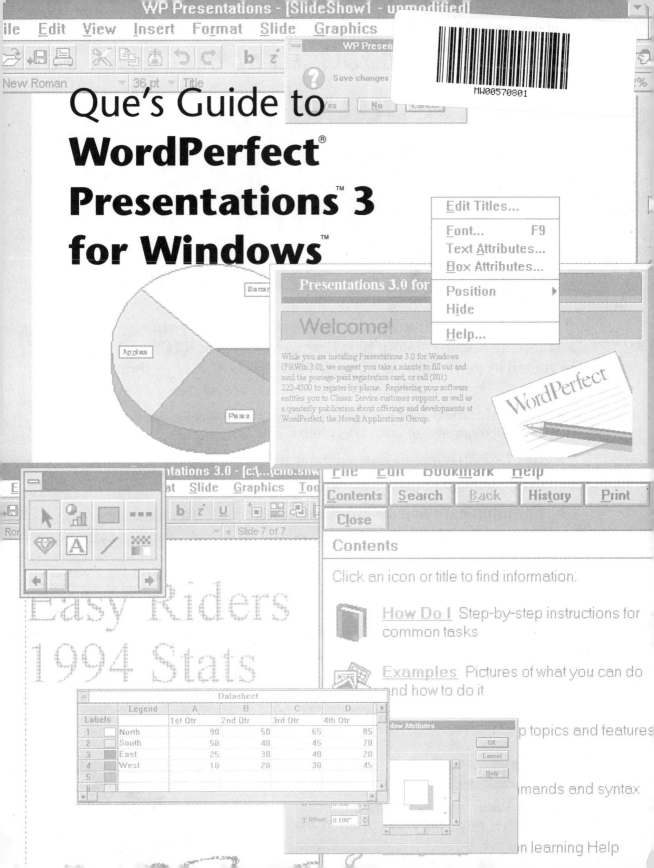

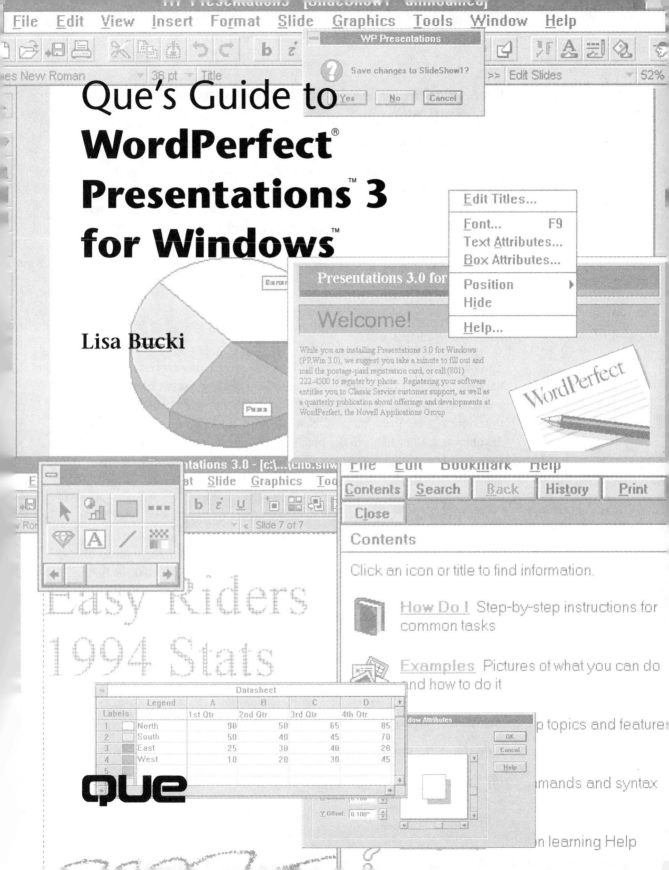

Que's Guide to **WordPerfect® Presentations™ 3 for Windows™**

Lisa Bucki

que

Que's Guide to WordPerfect Presentations 3 for Windows

Library of Congress Catalog Number: 94-74111

ISBN: 1-56529-652-4

97 96 95   4 3 2 1

Interpretation of the printing code: The rightmost double-digit number is the year of the book's printing; the rightmost single-digit number, the number of the book's printing. For example, a printing code of 95-1 shows that the first printing of the book occurred in 1995.

Screen reproductions in this book were created with Collage Complete from Inner Media, Inc., Hollis, NH.

Publisher: David P. Ewing

Associate Publisher: Stacy Hiquet

Associate Publisher—Operations: Corinne Walls

Publishing Director: Brad R. Koch

Managing Editor: Sandy Doell

Credits

Publishing Manager
Thomas H. Bennett

Acquisitions Editor
Cheryl D. Willoughby

Acquisitions Assistant
Ruth Slates

Product Director
Stephanie Gould

Production Editor
Fran Blauw

Editorial Assistant
Andrea Duvall

Operations Coordinator
Patricia J. Brooks

Technical Editors
James Johnston
Mitch Milam

Figure Specialist
Cari Ohm

Book Designer
Sandra Schroeder

Cover Designer
Dan Armstrong

Production Team
Stephen Adams
Stephen Carlin
Maxine Dillingham
Chad Dressler
Judy Everly
Lorell Fleming
DiMonique Ford
Karen L. Gregor
Aren Howell
Bob LaRoche
Elizabeth Lewis
Pete Lippincott
Stephanie Mineart
G. Alan Palmore
Kaylene Riemen
Clair Schweinler
Jon Swain
Michael Thomas
Allan Wimmer
Jody York

Indexer
Michael Hughes

Composed in *Stone Serif* and *MCPdigital* by Que Corporation

About the Author

Lisa Bucki has been involved in the computer book business for more than 4 1/2 years. In addition to *Que's Guide to WordPerfect Presentations 3 for Windows*, she has written the *10 Minute Guide to Harvard Graphics* and the *10 Minute Guide to Harvard Graphics for Windows*, as well as other titles. Bucki resides in Fishers, Indiana.

Trademark Acknowledgments

All terms mentioned in this book that are known to be trademarks or service marks have been appropriately capitalized. Que cannot attest to the accuracy of this information. Use of a term in this book should not be regarded as affecting the validity of any trademark or service mark.

Contents at a Glance

Contents

II Editing and Enhancing Your Slide Show   115

6 Adding and Editing Text   117

III Enhancing Slides with Charts   **187**

14 Working with Bitmap Images   291

V Fine-Tuning and Finishing the Show   313

15 Working with Masters, Templates, and Backgrounds   315

Introduction

Not too long ago, overhead projectors and slide projectors were the only tools available for presentations. Individuals and organizations had to spend large amounts of money having graphics custom-drawn for each presentation, or they had to settle for self-made, less-than-professional results.

Personal computers and presentations graphics programs have changed all that, making truly professional presentations accessible and easy to put together—even for people with limited budgets and artistic skills. This book, *Que's Guide to WordPerfect Presentations 3 for Windows*, teaches you to unleash the powerful features of this latest release from WordPerfect/Novell Corp., preparing clear, colorful graphics that can be presented as printed pages, overheads, 35-mm slides, or even an interactive slide show displayed directly from your desktop or laptop computer.

Features of Presentations like the Slide Show Expert, which guides you step-by-step through the process of creating a new slide show, and the easy-to-use slide templates make this program accessible to novice computer users. More advanced or new features like the capability to scan images directly into Presentations with a TWAIN-compliant scanner and the facility to enhance slide shows with sound accommodate the needs of advanced presenters. The scope of the features of the Presentations program, coupled with its integration in the Novell PerfectOffice Suite and its capability to share data with Suite programs (among others), makes Presentations the right tool for the job—no matter what the job is.

Who Should Use This Book?

Que's Guide to WordPerfect Presentations 3 for Windows suits the needs of anyone trying to take advantage of what Presentations has to offer—including home-office workers, corporate employees, students, teachers, consultants, trainers, and computer support staff. Anyone who wants to get up to speed quickly with Presentations or explore its more advanced features can benefit from *Que's Guide to WordPerfect Presentations 3 for Windows*.

This book assumes that you are familiar with Microsoft Windows but are not necessarily familiar with WordPerfect Presentations for Windows. Whether you're using Presentations on a desktop PC, a networked system, or a laptop, you can benefit from this book.

If you're using Presentations along with the other applications in the PerfectOffice Suite, this book is the perfect companion for *Using WordPerfect 6 for Windows*, Special Edition, *Using Quattro Pro 5 for Windows*, Special Edition, and *Using Paradox 5 for Windows*, Special Edition.

How This Book Is Organized

Que's Guide to WordPerfect Presentations 3 for Windows complements Presentations' on-line Help system and documentation. From step-by-step help to expert advice on designing an effective slide show, both novice users and more experienced users can improve their efficiency. This book is an excellent learning tool and reference for all users.

Que's Guide to WordPerfect Presentations 3 for Windows is organized into five parts:

Part I, "**Understanding the Basics**," explains how to get started with Presentations, including fundamentals like starting and exiting the program. Chapter 2 explains how to start a slide show and pick a look for it by using a master from the Master Gallery. In this part, you also learn how to use Presentations' different slide layout types, how to work in the various views, and how to customize Presentations to work efficiently.

Part II, "**Editing and Enhancing Your Slide Show**," discusses how to add and edit slide text. In addition, this part covers how to apply enhancements and special effects to text, such as choosing a different font or applying Presentations' revolutionary QuickWarp or Quick3-D to text. The last chapter in this part, Chapter 8, explains how to use the QuickArt Gallery to add graphics to your slides.

To discover how to best represent your data on slides, look at **Part III**, "**Enhancing Slides with Charts**." This part explains how to enter and edit chart data and format the appearance of the data chart, changing colors and text styles as you want. Organization charts, including editing and formatting, also are covered in this part.

Part IV, "**Working with Drawings and Graphics,**" covers the Tool Palette drawing tools that enable you to create, save, and edit vector images in Presentations. This part offers detail on working with object outlines and fills, and concludes by explaining how to create bitmap images.

Part V, "**Fine-Tuning and Finishing the Show**," dives into creating the finishing touches for your slide show. Essentials covered here include printing slides, handouts, and speaker notes, and editing the masters, templates, and backgrounds for slides. This part also covers some of Presentations' more advanced features, such as inserting objects into slides, adding transitions and more to create interactive on-screen slide shows, adding sound to a presentation, creating macros, and adding custom menus and toolbars.

Conventions Used in This Book

Presentations enables you to use the keyboard and mouse to select menu commands and dialog box options; you can press a key combination or click with the mouse to make a selection. Letters used in keyboard combinations to open menus, to choose commands from menus, and to select options in dialog boxes are printed in boldface type, as in "Open the **F**ile menu and choose **O**pen."

Names of dialog boxes and dialog box options are written with initial capital letters. Messages that appear on-screen are printed in a special font, as in `Slide Show 1`. New terms are introduced in *italic* type. Text that you are to type appears in **boldface**.

The following example shows a typical command sequence:

Open the **F**ile menu and choose the **O**pen command (or press Ctrl+O).

Uppercase letters are used to distinguish file and directory names.

WordPerfect Presentations 3 for Windows provides toolbars for your convenience. By clicking a button in the toolbar, you can execute a command or access a dialog box. Chapters in this book often contain button icons in the margins, indicating which button you can click to perform a task.

Note

This paragraph format indicates additional information that may help you avoid problems or that should be considered in using the described features.

Tip
This paragraph format suggests easier or alternative methods of executing a procedure.

Caution

This paragraph format warns the readers of hazardous procedures (for example, activities that delete files).

Troubleshooting

This paragraph format provides guidance on how to find solutions to common problems. The problem is presented in the first paragraph.

The following paragraph provides the solution to that problem.

Part I

Understanding the Basics

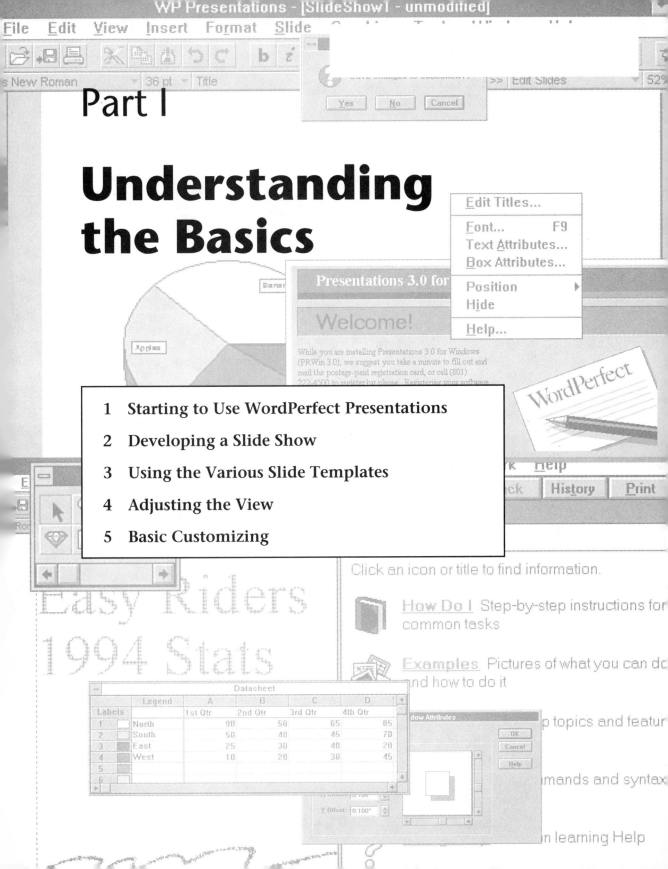

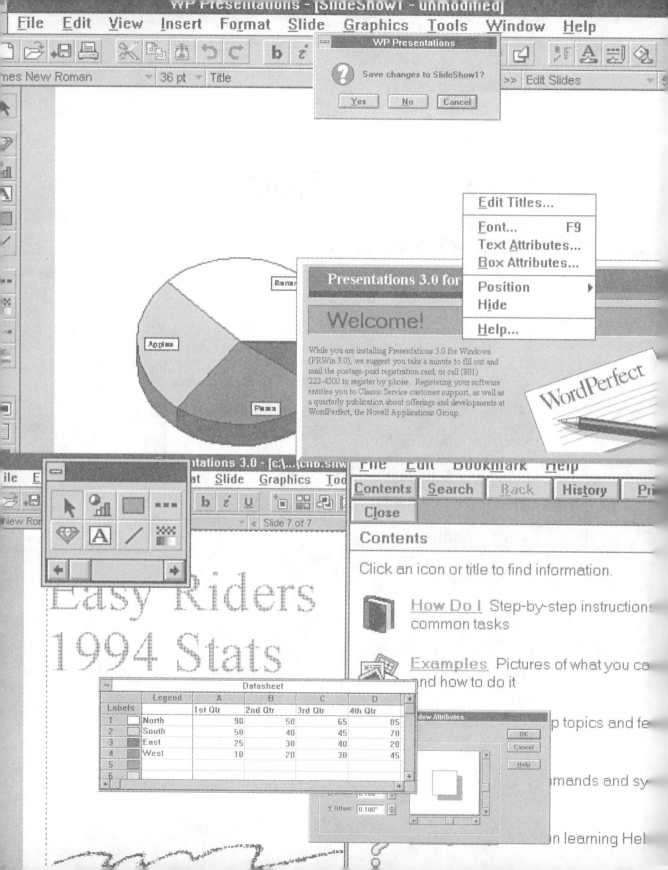

Chapter 1

Starting to Use WordPerfect Presentations

In the last few years, personal computers have transformed the business world, not only providing enhanced capabilities for compiling and analyzing information, but also enhancing every user's ability to communicate with others by providing tools for effectively presenting information. Colorful slides (or printouts) with attractively formatted text and graphics have become essential in presentations and proposals.

Now, the latest version of WordPerfect Presentations for Windows enables you to add punch to sales proposals, company meetings, training sessions, or any other situation where you need to educate or persuade an audience. Presentations enables you to outline and format information easily and quickly. It provides all the capabilities you need to achieve professional results, no matter what your situation—from a gallery of preformatted presentations if you have little time or only need a basic presentation, to tools for drawing, creating a self-running slide show, or adding sounds for an all-out, high-end presentation.

This chapter explains how to get started using WordPerfect Presentations for Windows, so you can be on your way to becoming a more effective communicator. You learn how to perform the following tasks:

- Starting and exiting Presentations

- Identifying parts of the screen

- Selecting commands and using dialog boxes, Toolbars, the Power Bar, and palettes

■ Navigating in Presentations

■ Getting help

Starting WordPerfect Presentations

Before you can start creating flashy slides, you have to start the Presentations program in Windows. Although you initiate the startup procedure in the same way that you would start many other Windows applications, starting Presentations is a bit different because you have to start a new slide show or open an existing slide show as part of the startup process.

Although creating a slide show may sound a bit complicated, it's really a straightforward process. Just use the following steps from the Windows Program Manager to start Presentations:

1. In Program Manager, double-click on the PRWin 3.0 program group icon. This opens the PRWin 3.0 group, as shown in figure 1.1.

Fig. 1.1
The PRWin 3.0 group window opens after you double-click its group icon in Program Manager. From here, double-click the PRWin 3.0 program-item icon.

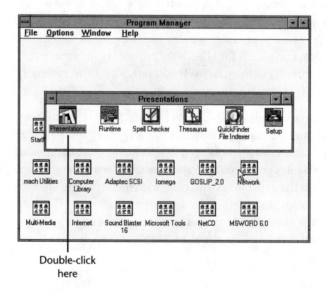

Double-click
here

2. Double-click the PRWin 3.0 program-item icon to display the Document Selection dialog box shown in figure 1.2. This dialog box enables you to specify whether to start a new slide show or open an existing show.

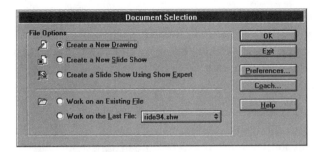

Fig. 1.2
The Document Selection dialog box appears by default when you start WordPerfect Presentations or when you create a new slide show. You can choose whether to start a new slide show or open an existing show.

Note

Using the Coach button in the Document Selection dialog box creates a basic presentation and displays a dialog box asking if you want help on certain topics. You can click a Help topic then click Continue, or click Skip This Coach and move directly to the basic slide show that has been created for you. See "Using Coaches," later in this chapter, to learn more.

Tip
A *slide show* (or *presentation*) is a collection of slides containing text, charts, drawings, and clip art for your presentation. You save each slide show in a separate file with WordPerfect Presentations.

3. Click Create a New **S**lide Show if the button beside that choice isn't selected, and then click the OK button. The New Slide Show dialog box appears, as shown in figure 1.3. This dialog box enables you to specify a default master background and template for the slide show. To learn more about using this dialog box to set up a slide show, see Chapter 2, "Developing a Slide Show."

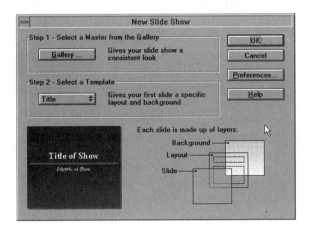

Fig. 1.3
Use the New Slide Show dialog box to specify a master background (gallery) and template for the new slide show.

If you want to open an existing slide show at this point, click the Work on the **L**ast File option, and then click OK to open the file indicated beside that option. Or click Work on an Existing **F**ile, click OK, and choose the file you want using the Open File dialog box. For more information on the Open File dialog box, see Chapter 2.

4. Click the **G**allery button to display the Master Gallery dialog box, which enables you to choose a look for your slide show. For now, just click the Retrieve button to select the first master.

5. Point to the button that says None under Select a Template, and then press and hold the left mouse button to display the pop-up list. Drag down to highlight Title and release the mouse button.

6. Click OK to open the new slide show. WordPerfect Presentations displays the first slide of your slide show.

Setting Startup Preferences

You may have noticed the **P**references button in the Document Selection dialog box. Clicking this button displays the Environment Preferences dialog box (see fig. 1.4). This box enables you to streamline the startup process by choosing to directly display a new **D**rawing or **S**lide Show rather than the **D**ocument Selection dialog box. The **E**rror and Sear**c**h Failure options in the Beep On group enable you to specify whether an audible beep occurs when an error message appears or a search fails. Choosing Use Presentations 3.0 **Q**uick List uses the default QuickList. (A QuickList enables you to assign easy-to-remember names to directories you access frequently.) And, use the Interface **L**anguage pop-up menu to specify a language for menus, dialog boxes, Help prompts, and messages.

Fig. 1.4
Use the Environment Preferences dialog box to set up preferences for how WordPerfect Presentations starts up. You can save time if you tell Presentations always to create a default slide show on startup.

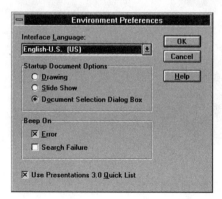

Understanding the Presentations Screen

Figure 1.5 shows the first slide of a new presentation created with the Title template and one of the many backgrounds available from the Gallery. It also illustrates how the default startup screen of Presentations looks, including several key tools with which you need to be familiar.

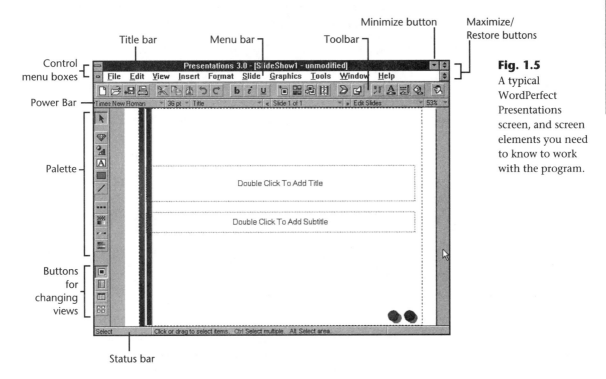

Fig. 1.5
A typical WordPerfect Presentations screen, and screen elements you need to know to work with the program.

Descriptions of each of the items highlighted in figure 1.5 follow:

- *Title bar.* Displays the name of the program and the active slide show. Also displays Help descriptions when you point to a button on the Toolbar, Power Bar, or palette.

- *Menu bar.* Lists the names of all the pull-down menus available in Presentations. This list changes according to the Presentations operation in which you're engaged.

- *Toolbar.* Contains buttons that execute common features. You can display different Toolbars if you create custom ones grouping particular features for performing operations like editing. To identify a Toolbar tool, simply point to it with the mouse cursor, and a small yellow Quick Tip (label) with its name appears.

■ *Control menu boxes.* There's one of these for Presentations itself and one for the current slide show. Click this box (commonly called the *Control menu*) to display a menu of commands. Double-click a Control menu box to close the application or slide show.

■ *Minimize button.* This button is indicated by a triangle pointing downward. Click this button to minimize a window to an icon.

■ *Maximize/Restore buttons.* If the window has been restored (is not maximized), the Maximize button appears on-screen. This button is indicated by a triangle pointing upward. Clicking the button maximizes the window to the largest size available for it. When a window is maximized, you click the Restore button, which is indicated by two triangles; the triangle on top points upward, and the triangle under it points downward. The Restore button returns the window to its previous size.

■ *Power Bar.* This bar offers the most frequently used editing operations, such as changing the size of a font or moving forward or backward to a slide. To identify a Power Bar option, simply point to it with the mouse and a small yellow Quick Tip with its name appears.

■ *Palette.* This box offers tools for drawing objects, creating fill patterns, and so on. To identify a Palette tool, simply point to it with the mouse and a small yellow Quick Tip with its name appears.

■ *Buttons for changing views.* Clicking one of these buttons provides a shortcut for changing to a different working view in Presentations. You can choose Slide Editor, Outliner, Slide List, or Slide Sorter view.

■ *Status bar.* This displays information about the current operation. If you're resizing a drawn object, for example, the status bar will tell you what key to press to size it from the center outward.

Using Menus to Choose Commands

As you saw in figure 1.5, WordPerfect Presentations provides a menu bar listing several menus grouping related commands. Choosing a command is a two-step process. First, point to the menu name with the mouse pointer and left-click to pull down the menu (see fig. 1.6). Then, point to the name of the command you want and left-click it.

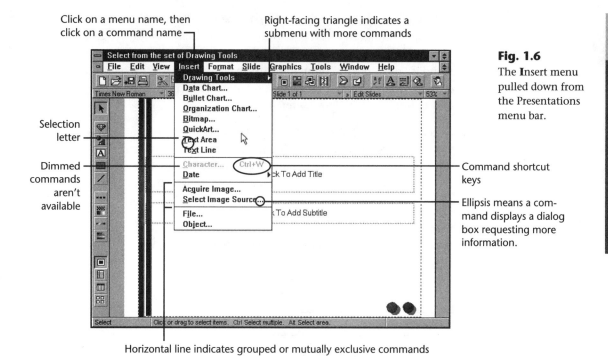

Click on a menu name, then
click on a command name

Right-facing triangle indicates a
submenu with more commands

Fig. 1.6
The Insert menu
pulled down from
the Presentations
menu bar.

Selection
letter

Dimmed
commands
aren't
available

Command shortcut
keys

Ellipsis means a com-
mand displays a dialog
box requesting more
information.

Horizontal line indicates grouped or mutually exclusive commands

Notice in figure 1.6 that there are symbols to the right of several of the menu commands. Learning what these symbols mean can make it quite a bit easier to navigate through Presentations. An explanation of each type of symbol follows:

■ Horizontal lines running across the menu indicate groups of commands or commands that are mutually exclusive. If you pull down the View menu, for example, you see that the top four commands are the differ-ent Presentations views. You can choose only one presentation view at a time.

■ A right-facing triangle beside a command indicates that selecting the command displays a submenu of options. After you choose a command with a triangle beside it by clicking on it, simply point to the submenu command you want and click the left mouse button.

■ An ellipsis (...) beside a command indicates that choosing the com-mand displays a dialog box asking you to supply additional informa-tion to specify how the command will be executed. Selecting Create a New Slide Show in the Select Document dialog box when starting Presentations is an example of making a dialog box choice that tells Presentations what to do next. For more information on dialog boxes, see "Using Dialog Boxes," later in this chapter.

- Some commands have a check mark to the left. (See the **V**iew menu.) The check mark can mean two things: the command simply toggles on and off (with the presence of the check mark indicating that the command is "on"), or the command with the check mark is the selected command in a group of mutually exclusive commands (such as the first four options on the **V**iew menu).

- Other commands have keyboard shortcuts beside them, such as the Ctrl+W beside the **C**haracter command in figure 1.6. You can press the shortcut key combination to choose the command directly, bypassing the process of clicking on the menu name and then clicking on the command name.

- Some menu commands appear grayed out or dimmed, which indicates that the command is not presently available, based on what's selected in the current slide. Presentations will not enable you to choose a command that is grayed out.

Troubleshooting

I opened a menu by accident and don't really want to choose a command.

There are several easy ways to close the menu without executing a command:

- Press the Alt key.

- Click in your document or on another menu.

- Press Esc to close the menu but still display a description of the menu in the title bar. Press Esc again to deactivate the menu bar.

Using the Keyboard with Menus

Although no one should attempt to use any kind of graphics program without a mouse, most computer users today use a combination of mouse and keyboard actions to choose commands and navigate through applications. Using the keyboard to choose commands in WordPerfect Presentations is a straightforward process.

You probably noticed that the name of each menu and command in figure 1.6 also has an underlined letter, which is called the *selection letter*. These letters enable you to choose commands with the keyboard. Start by pressing Alt to activate the menu bar. Then press the selection letter shown in the name of the menu you want to open. To select a command from the menu that appears, simply press the selection letter in its name.

Using QuickMenus

One of the most helpful new aspects of Presentations is that it adapts to the operation you're currently executing, putting key commands or help just a mouse click away. *QuickMenus* are a new Presentation feature that enables you to point to an item on-screen—such as a Toolbar, the status bar, or an object on a slide—and click the right mouse button to display a pop-up menu of commands available for the item to which you're pointing. To select a command from a QuickMenu after you displayed it, simply point to the command and click the left mouse button, as if you were selecting a command from a regular menu.

Figure 1.7 shows the QuickMenu that would appear if you pointed to a text placeholder area and pressed the right mouse button.

Tip
To close a QuickMenu without selecting a command from it, click elsewhere on-screen or press Esc.

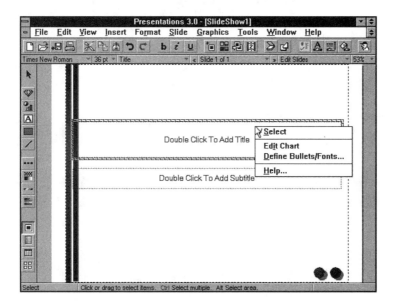

Fig. 1.7
To display a QuickMenu, point to an item and click the right mouse button.

Using Dialog Boxes

As noted earlier, choosing a command followed by an ellipsis displays a dialog box requesting additional information needed to complete the command. There are several kinds of options in dialog boxes, as shown in figure 1.8. The elements that are common to virtually all Presentations dialog boxes include the title bar and Control menu boxes, which are virtually identical in function to those of the main Presentations screen, as well as OK, Cancel, and Help buttons.

Understanding the Basics I

Fig. 1.8
Dialog boxes like these enable you to give Presentations more specific information for executing a command.

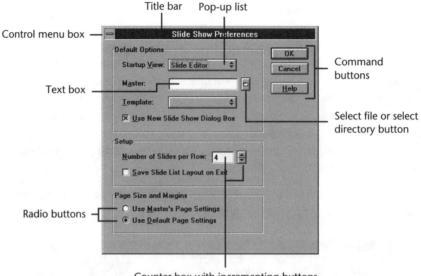

Control menu box

Title bar   Pop-up list

Command buttons

Text box

Select file or select directory button

Radio buttons

Counter box with incrementing buttons

List box

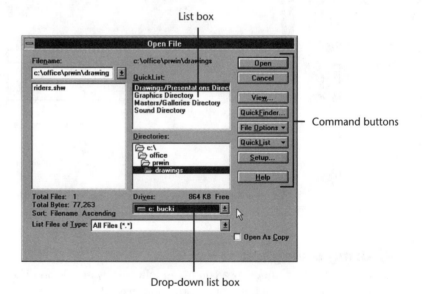

Command buttons

Drop-down list box

After a dialog box is displayed, you point-and-click with the mouse or press Alt+*selection letter* to move to an option, and then select or change the value, if needed. In general, you have the option of clicking a selection, typing to change a value, or choosing from a list, but some of the options can be quite specialized. A more complete description of dialog box options and how to choose them with the mouse follows:

■ *Command button.* Simply click on a command button to execute the command. Clicking Cancel closes the dialog box without doing anything. Clicking OK (the same as pressing Enter) generally closes the dialog box and executes the options specified elsewhere in the dialog box. Some command buttons, such as the View button in the second dialog box in figure 1.8, have an ellipsis and display another dialog box when selected.

■ *Text box.* Double-click on a text box to select all its contents and then type new contents, which overwrite the original contents. Or, you can click to place an insertion point in a text box and use the keyboard (including the Backspace and Delete keys) to edit the text box contents.

■ *Check box.* Left-click on a check box to select or deselect it. When a check box is selected, an x appears in the box.

■ *Radio buttons.* These generally appear in groups and are used to indicate mutually exclusive options; when one in the group is selected, the others are deselected automatically. Click on a radio button to select it.

■ *Pop-up list.* Click on the button for a pop-up list, and Presentations displays a list of choices. When there's just a down-pointing triangle on the pop-up list button (like the QuickList button in the Open File dialog box in fig. 1.8), clicking the button displays a menu that stays open; click a command to select it. When the pop-up list button has two triangles (like the Slide Editor button in the Slide Show Preferences dialog box in fig. 1.8), you have to point to the button and press and hold the left mouse button to keep the options visible, drag up or down to highlight the command you want, and release the mouse button to finalize your choice.

■ *Drop-down list.* For many drop-down lists, you can enter a selection in a text box or click the down triangle beside the box to display a list of choices. Clicking a choice selects it and closes the list. Click outside the list to roll the list back up without making a change.

■ *List box.* This box lists your choices for an option. Click on a choice to select it. Double-click a choice to select it and close the dialog box.

■ *Select file or select directory button.* These buttons appear to the right of certain text boxes. Clicking the button displays a Select File or Select Directory dialog box (depending on the nature of the option in the original dialog box) so you can specify a file or directory name to automatically be inserted into the original text box.

Tip
You can move a dialog box around on-screen by pointing to its title bar, pressing and holding the left mouse button, and dragging the box to a new location on-screen.

After you make the dialog box selections you want, click OK to accept them. To close a dialog box without activating the choices you made in it, click the Cancel button, press Esc, or double-click the Control menu box.

Using the Toolbar and Power Bar

WordPerfect Presentations makes you more efficient by putting as many features as possible within a mouse click and by adapting (as you've already learned) to whatever operation you're presently performing. If you're formatting text on a slide, for example, a text Toolbar replaces the main Toolbar. The Toolbar and Power Bar are first-class examples of Presentations' enhanced ease of use.

Simply click on a Toolbar button to execute a command. Or, click one of the pull-down lists on the Power Bar and click again to apply the option of your choice. Either way, these tools enable you to bypass the process of selecting a menu and then selecting a command.

Using the Toolbar Tools

You saw the Toolbar for the main Presentations screen in figure 1.5. Table 1.1 lists the buttons on this Toolbar and explains the function of each.

Table 1.1   The Main Presentations Toolbar

Tool	Equivalent Command	Description
	File **N**ew	Opens a new slide show
	File **O**pen	Opens an existing slide show
	File **S**ave	Saves a slide show in a file on disk; opens the Save As dialog box if the file hasn't been saved before
	File **P**rint	Opens the Print dialog box so you can print a file
	Edit Cu**t**	Deletes the selected object and inserts it into the Windows Clipboard
	Edit **C**opy	Copies the selected object and inserts the copy into the Windows Clipboard
	Edit **P**aste	Pastes the Clipboard contents onto a slide

Tool	Equivalent Command	Description
	Edit **U**ndo	Reverses the preceding command or action
	Edit **R**edo	Redoes the last undone action
b	Format **F**ont **B**old	Applies bold to selected text
i	Format **F**ont **I**talic	Applies italic to selected text
U	Format **F**ont **U**nderline	Applies underline to selected text
	Slide **A**dd Slides	Adds a new slide into the presentation
	Slide **M**aster Gallery	Displays the Master Gallery dialog box so you can choose a new master
	Slide Transi**t**ion	Assigns a transition to a slide
	Slide **P**lay Slide Show	Plays the slide show
	Insert Ac**q**uire Image	Scans an image directly into a show
	Format **S**hadow Attributes	Applies a shadow to the selected object
	Format **D**efine Bullets/Fonts	Sets the bullet type and font type for the selected text placeholder
A	Format **F**ont **A**ttributes	Sets attributes like Fill Type for selected text or new text
	Format Li**n**e Attributes	Sets attributes for selected or new lines
	Format F**i**ll Attributes	Sets the fill color, pattern, and so on for selected or new objects
	Help **C**oaches	Turns on or off coaching help

Displaying a Toolbar

Presentations automatically displays different Toolbar tools based on the operation at hand. If you've created a custom Toolbar, you can display it instead of the default Toolbar, <slide>.

Tip
You can display only one Toolbar at a time. When you display the QuickMenu for the Toolbar, a check mark appears beside the name of the current Toolbar.

You can use one of two methods to display a particular Toolbar when you need it. The easiest way to make a change is to use the QuickMenu. Simply move the mouse pointer over the Toolbar and press the right mouse button to display the QuickMenu. Click on a Toolbar name to display it, or click on **H**ide Toolbar to display no Toolbar (you can redisplay it with the **V**iew menu). If you prefer not to use the QuickMenu, use these steps to change the Toolbar displayed:

1. Open the **E**dit menu and choose Preferences. Presentations displays the Preferences dialog box, as shown in figure 1.9.

2. Double-click on the icon for Toolbar, or click that icon and then click OK. This displays the Toolbar Preferences dialog box, shown in figure 1.10.

Fig. 1.9
Choose Toolbar from the Preferences dialog box.

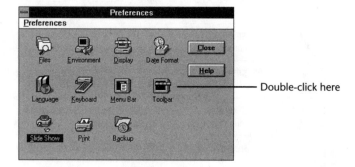

Fig. 1.10
Use the Toolbar Preferences dialog box to select and customize Toolbars. This figure shows a custom Toolbar called Lisa's Tools.

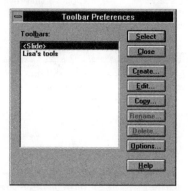

Note

You also can use the Toolbar Preferences dialog box to customize Toolbars and create unique new Toolbars. See Chapter 20, "Customizing with Macros, Toolbars, and Menus," for more information.

3. In the dialog box, double-click a Toolbar name in the Toolbars list, or click a Toolbar name and then click OK. This returns you to the Preferences dialog box.

4. Click Close to close the Preferences dialog box.

Using the Power Bar Options

The Power Bar provides pull-down menus that offer numerous choices, such as a list of fonts you can choose to apply to text. To use a Power Bar choice, simply click to select an object; if necessary, click on a Power Bar button to open the menu it contains and then click a choice on the menu.

As with the Toolbar, you can point to a Power Bar button, and a yellow QuickTip label pops up to explain what the button is used for. Table 1.2 lists the Power Bar buttons and what each is used for.

Table 1.2   The Presentations Power Bar

Button	Equivalent Command	Description
Times New Roman	Format Font Font Face	Specifies a new font for selected or new text
36 pt	Format Font Font Size	Specifies a new size for selected or new text
Title	Slide Apply Slide Template	Changes the basic template for a slide
<<	Slide Go To	Moves to the preceding slide
Slide 1 of 1	Slide Go To	Displays a list of slide titles; click a title to go to that slide
>>	Slide Go To	Moves to the next slide
Edit Slides	Edit Slides Edit Layouts Edit Backgrounds	Changes to the specified view for editing (on Slides, the slide Layouts, or Backgrounds menu)
52%	View Zoom	Specifies how large or small the current slide show appears in Presentations

Using Palettes

Along the left side of the Presentations screen is a palette of tools for various operations, such as adding clip art or a chart to the slide, or changing the color and fill pattern for objects. The available tools depend on the operation underway. These tools work a bit differently than the tools on the Toolbar. Generally, choosing one of these tools displays a palette of additional options to choose from (see fig. 1.11). You have to click one of the choices. Then some tools require you to drag on the slide to create the object.

Although later chapters give you more specific information about using individual Tool Palette tools, table 1.3 introduces you to each of these tools and their functions.

Fig. 1.11
Choosing most
Tool Palette tools
displays several
other choices.

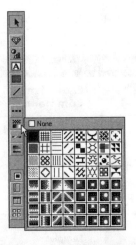

Table 1.3 The Initial Tool Palette	
Tool	**Function**
![select tool]	Selects objects. Click this tool and then click an object to select it.
![art tool]	Places drawn or QuickArt images on a slide; point to this tool and hold down the left mouse button, drag to select the appropriate tool, and then drag to create a box for the art on the slide. Then draw the image or select a piece of clip art.
![chart tool]	Inserts a chart into a slide; click the tool, drag on the slide to define the chart area, and then use the dialog box and Datasheet window to create the chart itself.

Tool	Function
A	Places a text box, text line, or bullet text on the slide. Point to this tool and hold down the left mouse button, drag to select the appropriate tool, drag or click to create a location for the text on the slide, and then type the text.
▣	Draws squares, ellipses, and other closed shapes on the slide. Point to this tool and hold down the left mouse button, drag to select the appropriate tool, and then drag to create the shape on the slide.
⁄	Draws lines on a slide. Point to this tool and hold down the left mouse button, drag to select the appropriate tool, and then drag to create the line on the slide.
---	Specifies attributes for a selected or new line. Click to display the choices, and then click on a choice.
▤	Specifies fill for a selected or new object. Click to display the choices and then click on a choice.
▱	Specifies a line color for a selected or new object. Click to display the choices and then click on a choice.
▤	Specifies a fill color for a selected or new object. Click to display the choices and then click on a choice.
▣	Changes to Slide view.
▤	Changes to Outline view.
▥	Changes to List view.
▦	Changes to Slide Sorter view.

Tearing Off the Toolbar or Palette

Different people have different working styles. You may find you're most comfortable working on a pristine desk, with as few items as possible on the work surface. Other people are comfortable with a bit of clutter, and would rather have everything they may need a short reach away. Similarly, Presentations enables you to put away on-screen items (more on that in Chapter 4, "Adjusting the View") or shift some items around on the screen—in this case, the Toolbar and palette.

You can move the Toolbar or palette to a new location by pointing to a *spacer area* (a plain area between buttons) so that the mouse pointer changes to an open hand, pressing and holding the left mouse button, and dragging it to a new location. As you drag, the Toolbar or palette "tears off" from the location where it's typically anchored and snaps into the shape of a rectangular window that you can drag to a new location (see fig. 1.12). To return the Toolbar or palette to its original location, simply drag it toward its original location; when its dotted outline resumes its original shape, release the mouse button.

Fig. 1.12
When you tear off the Toolbar, it snaps into its own window that you can reposition on-screen and resize as needed.

Drag the Toolbar from here...

...to here.

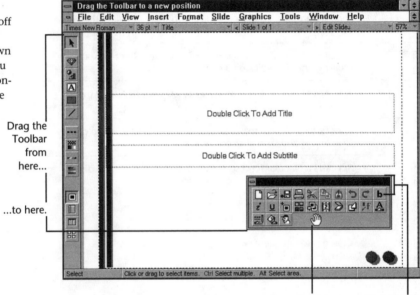

Open hand means you can left-click and drag Toolbar or palette.

To resize the window, point to the border or corner until a double-headed arrow appears, then drag.

Troubleshooting

I don't have enough room to display the whole Toolbar where I want it. How can I make it smaller but still have access to all the tools I need?

If you want to display the Toolbar or palette in a fairly small area, simply drag the item to the location you want and resize the window to a smaller size. When you make the window so small that it can't display all the available buttons, a scroll bar appears to enable you to scroll to the icon you need.

Using Scroll Bars

Scroll bars enable you to move through a list or move the screen around to display an area not previously visible. Figure 1.13 shows a few examples of where scroll bars are encountered. These bars also appear for the main window when you zoom in on a slide so that all its contents can't fit in the window (Chapter 4 gives more information on zooming).

You can use a few techniques to use scroll bars. There are small arrows, called *scroll arrows*, at either end of a scroll bar. To move by a small increment in one direction (up or down, for example) click a scroll arrow once. To move more quickly in a direction, drag the square scroll box. You also can click on the area between a scroll box and scroll arrow to move in a larger increment.

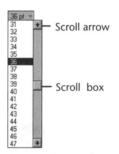

Scroll arrow

Scroll box

Fig. 1.13
Scroll bars appear in Power Bar lists, dialog box list boxes, and even palette windows.

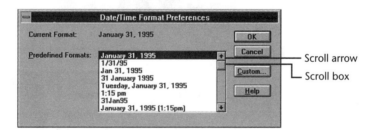

Scroll arrow
Scroll box

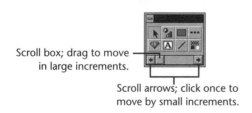

Scroll box; drag to move in large increments.

Scroll arrows; click once to move by small increments.

Getting Help When You Need It

WordPerfect Presentations offers plenty of help when you need it. Not only can you get context-sensitive help at any time, but you also can use Presentations' extensive Help features, including *Coaches*, which walk you step-by-step through particular operations by displaying an instruction for each step.

Before you learn about the help available through the **H**elp menu of Presentations, you should know about a couple of easy ways to get help, particularly if you get stuck. You can get context-sensitive help from anywhere in Presentations by simply pressing F1. This action provides help on the item currently selected or the operation currently underway. If you haven't selected anything or want detailed help on a button somewhere on-screen, press Shift+F1 to display a question-mark balloon, and then click on the object you want help with to display the Help window.

The **H**elp menu provides general help, help on specific features, and more. In general, choosing a command from the **H**elp menu displays a special Help window (see fig. 1.14). You can use a few special techniques to navigate through Help windows.

Fig. 1.14
A Help window.

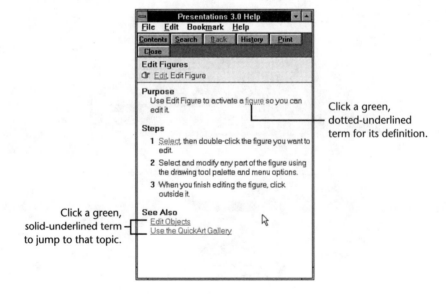

Click a green, dotted-underlined term for its definition.

Click a green, solid-underlined term to jump to that topic.

The Help window has its own menu bar and several command buttons at the top that enables you to navigate through Help. Clicking **C**ontents or **S**earch is the equivalent of choosing the **C**ontents or **S**earch command from the **H**elp menu. The **B**ack button returns you to the preceding Help window. His**t**ory displays a list of all the Help topics you've viewed during the current Presentations work session; double-click a topic to return to it. Finally, click **P**rint to print the current Help topic or C**l**ose to leave the Help system.

In addition, some topics in the Help window are green, indicating that they lead you to additional help. Clicking a topic with a dotted underline displays a definition of that topic. Clicking a topic with a solid underline jumps to another Help window on that topic.

Several icons indicate specialized help:

- Clicking a small Light Bulb icon displays a hint.

- Clicking an icon that looks like a small hand pointing right (a *Route* icon) displays menus and buttons for accessing a feature.

- Exclamation Point icons indicate important information.

- An icon that looks like a group of books (*Reference* icon) refers you to the printed documentation.

- Click other unique icons for additional help on the topic the icon represents.

More information follows about each of the **H**elp menu options and how to use the Help windows that appear.

Using the Contents Help Window

Opening the **H**elp menu and choosing **C**ontents or pressing F1 displays the Help window shown in figure 1.15. Clicking a topic (indicated with green solid-underlined text) displays an additional Help window on the left side of the screen or jumps to the specific Help window for that topic.

Tip

Some Help windows contain a small Light Bulb icon. Clicking this icon displays a hint.

Understanding the Basics

Fig. 1.15
The Help Contents
screen.

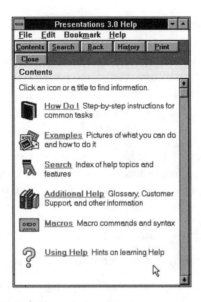

Searching for Help on a Specific Topic

Although navigating the Help system is easy and painless, you can skip the
interim steps by opening the **H**elp menu and choosing **S**earch for Help On or
by clicking the **S**earch button from another Help window, which displays the
dialog box shown in figure 1.16.

Fig. 1.16
You use the Search
dialog box to
search for and
jump directly to
the topic you want
help about.

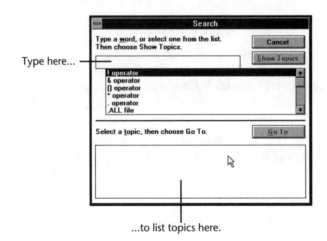

To start a search from this dialog box, simply start typing the name of the term you want to look for (the insertion point should already be in the right position). As you type each letter, Search scrolls the terms list to the group of terms most closely matching the letters you typed. When you finish typing the term, click **S**how Topics or double-click a term from the list that appears. This action displays a list of topics in the bottom list box. To go to the Help window for one of those topics, double-click it, or click to select it and then click **G**o To.

Using the Procedures Window

Opening the **H**elp menu and choosing the **H**ow Do I command, or choosing the How Do I button in most Help windows displays a Help window that's rather unique to WordPerfect Presentations. This window groups specific tasks into logical groups, called *Books*. Choosing a book enables you to get to the procedures for that book quickly. Figure 1.17 shows an example procedures window. Click a Book to open it, click on one of the pages that appears, and then click a procedure to display a Help window giving step-by-step instructions for the procedure. To close the procedures window, click the Close button.

Using Macros

Creating macros can save you a lot of time. This book covers macros in Chapter 20, but it by no means gives exhaustive coverage of the topic. If you really want to delve into macros and learn about advanced macro topics like writing and editing Presentations macros using WordPerfect for Windows, you can use the extensive Help system about macros to learn more.

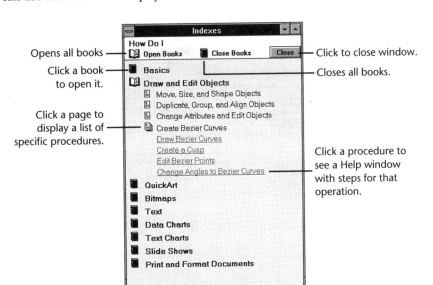

Fig. 1.17
Presentations gives you a whole "Book" of help on specific procedures.

If you open the **H**elp menu and choose **M**acros, you see the Help screen shown in figure 1.18. You can navigate through the Macro Reference Help just as you would through any other Help screens.

Fig. 1.18
From this Help screen, you can learn about macro basics such as recording macros, or even advanced macro topics like creating and editing macros command by command.

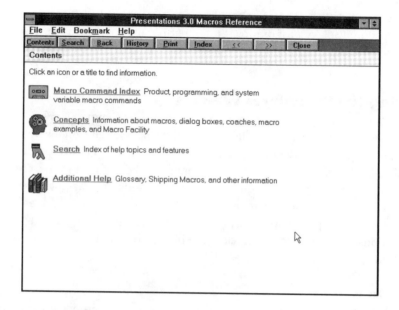

Using Coaches

WordPerfect Presentations for Windows coaches you through a variety of operations. When you need to use its Coaches, just click the Coaches icon at the far right end of the Toolbar, or open the **H**elp menu and choose C**o**aches. You see the Coaches dialog box, shown in figure 1.19.

Fig. 1.19
Coaches guide you through particular operations until you get the hang of what you're doing.

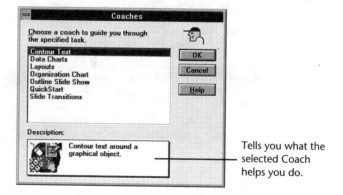

Tells you what the selected Coach helps you do.

Click a Coach in the list, and then click OK to continue. A dialog box appears with a description of the operation you're performing, and some radio buttons that enable you to be more specific in telling the Coach what you want to do (see fig. 1.20). Click an option to select it, and then click Continue. The Coach displays the first step of the operation, telling you exactly what to do and highlighting key screen elements, as shown in figure 1.21.

Fig. 1.20
You can tell the Coach a bit more about what your goal is—what you want to do specifically.

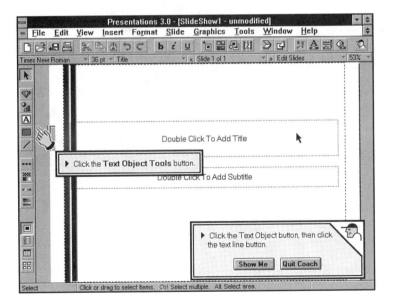

Fig. 1.21
The Coach explains how to perform every step, and shows you where on-screen to find tools you need.

Simply execute the step as described by the Coach. Or, click the Show Me button, and the Coach executes the step for you, showing you clearly how it's done. Completing all the steps completes the Coach. Or, you can click the Quit Coach button at any time to leave the Coach.

Using the Upgrade Expert

The Upgrade Expert gives you special help if you're switching to WordPerfect Presentations for Windows from another presentation graphics program. Open the **H**elp menu and choose **U**pgrade Expert to access the Upgrade Expert. Open the **P**revious Presentation Package drop-down list and click on the name of your old software. Then, in the Presentation Package **F**eatures list, click the name of the task for which you want to find the equivalent Presentations command. At this point, your screen looks something like figure 1.22.

Then, you can click a command button at the bottom of the dialog box for help on the task you selected. **S**how Me demonstrates how to perform a feature. Click **D**o It and Presentations applies the feature for you. The **C**oach button activates the Coach for the feature, and More **H**elp displays additional details about the task.

Fig. 1.22

You can choose a task from your old package to learn how to perform the same action in Presentations.

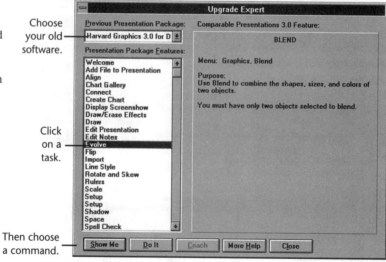

Exiting Presentations

Among commands for performing other operations, the File menu offers a command you can use to exit WordPerfect Presentations. During the exit process, Presentations asks you whether you want to save any unsaved changes you've made to open slide shows. As a general computing practice, you always should exit an application before shutting down your computer, to prevent data loss.

> **Note**
>
> Although Presentations does prompt you to save before exiting, it's best not to wait that long to save, because you could lose your slide show if there's a power outage or a computer failure and you haven't saved yet. As a rule, you should save your work every five minutes. Saving is explained in Chapter 2, "Developing a Slide Show." You also can have Presentations automatically back up a slide show file at an interval you specify. For more information on backing up your slide shows, see Chapter 5, "Basic Customizing."

Tip
To quickly exit Presentations, double-click on its Control menu box in the upper left corner of the Presentations window.

Use these steps when you're ready to exit WordPerfect Presentations:

1. Open the **F**ile menu and choose E**x**it. If you've saved your slide show, WordPerfect Presentations immediately closes. If there are unsaved slide-show changes, Presentations displays the dialog box shown in figure 1.23.

Fig. 1.23
When you exit Presentations, it asks you whether you want to save any unsaved changes.

2. Click **Y**es to save changes. If you've saved the file before, Presentations saves and exits. If you haven't saved and named the slide show before, Presentations displays the Save As dialog box.

3. To do a bare minimum save, simply type a file name of up to eight characters in the File**n**ame box and then click **S**ave. Presentations saves the file and closes. For additional information on using the Save As dialog box, see Chapter 2.

You can add an exit button to any Toolbar. To learn how to customize Toolbars, see Chapter 20, "Customizing with Macros, Toolbars, and Menus."

From Here...

Now that you've taken a look around Presentations and have learned to work with some of its basic features, you're ready to move on and begin to put together your first slide show. For in-depth discussions of the fundamental techniques for building a slide show, see these chapters:

- Chapter 2, "Developing a Slide Show," explains how to create a new slide show file; open an existing slide show; navigate in Presentations; add slides, text, and charts; and save, view, and print the slide show.

- Chapter 3, "Using the Various Slide Templates," reviews the preset slide templates, how to use them efficiently for new slides, and how to apply them to existing slides.

- Chapter 4, "Adjusting the View," explains how to use the various choices on the View menu.

- Chapter 5, "Basic Customizing," explains how to set WordPerfect Presentations preferences and customize Toolbars.

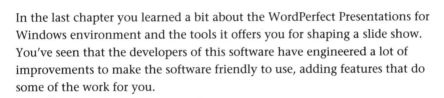

Chapter 2

Developing a Slide Show

In the last chapter you learned a bit about the WordPerfect Presentations for Windows environment and the tools it offers you for shaping a slide show. You've seen that the developers of this software have engineered a lot of improvements to make the software friendly to use, adding features that do some of the work for you.

You learn about some of those ease-of-use features in this chapter as you start a new slide show or work with an existing show. You see how the Show Expert can make the process of setting up the slide show—and even creating its content—anxiety-free. Another useful feature you explore, among others, is the QuickFinder, which can cut down the time it takes you to find and open a slide show file, even if you're not sure exactly where on your hard drive you saved it.

Keep in mind that this chapter offers a "once over lightly" look at creating slide shows. Because Presentations is such a rich program, many of the features introduced here are covered in more depth in later chapters. But, this chapter is a useful and necessary introduction to the following topics:

- Opening new and existing slide shows

- Using Show Expert—the hassle-free way to create a slide show

- Navigating in a slide show

- Changing the page layout and adding slides

- Saving, printing, and viewing a slide show

Creating a New Slide Show

When you start Presentations, or at any time while using it, you have the option of creating a brand-new slide show. As you learned in the last chapter, starting WordPerfect Presentations for Windows displays the Document Selection dialog box, which offers Create a New Slide Show as one of its options. Clicking that option and clicking OK displays the New Slide Show dialog box, which enables you to choose a master for your slide from the Gallery (described next) and select a slide template. To select a template, you click on the button for the pop-up list (this button says Default by default), and then click a slide type. Clicking OK opens a slide show with one slide (yes, only one) using the master and slide template you selected, with placeholders for text or charts. From here, it's up to you to fill in the placeholders and add mores slides as described in "Adding a New Slide," later in this chapter.

 Creating a new slide show after Presentations is running is very similar to the process just described. Open the File menu and choose New, press Ctrl+N, or click on the New icon in the Toolbar. The New Document dialog box appears, shown in figure 2.1. As you can see, this dialog box also offers Create a New Slide Show as one of its options; clicking it and then clicking OK displays the New Slide Show dialog box, which you work in as just described (see fig. 2.2).

Fig. 2.1
Display the New Document dialog box by choosing New from the File menu or clicking the New icon. Choose one of the second two options to continue with creating a slide show.

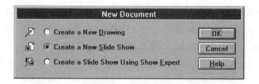

Although you can start a completely blank slide show by not changing either of the options in the New Slide Show dialog box by simply clicking OK to close the dialog box, if you want to change the look of your presentation or select a different layout for the first slide, you have the option of doing so. Changing the slide show master and selecting a slide type in the New Slide Show dialog box are described next.

Working with the Master Gallery

A *slide show master* is a collection of formatting settings that makes all the slides in a show look consistent, even when the slides are different types (have different layouts). Even though the different slide types will have different elements (a chart, a bullet list, or a title and subtitle, perhaps) all the slides types will look consistent, sharing the same background colors and graphics, and using the same text styles. One of the master types is called MARBLEW, for example. When you add new slides to a show with this master, all the new slides have a background with a marble-texture bar running down the left side; the slide title text for all slides is black and is in a font called Times New Roman.

Click here to display the Master Gallery.

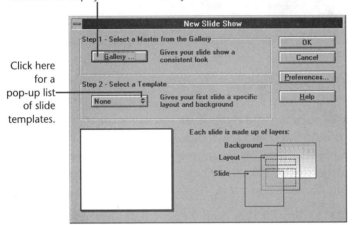

Click here for a pop-up list of slide templates.

Fig. 2.2
From the New Slide Show dialog box, you can select a master for your presentation and a type of layout for the first slide.

Understanding the Basics

> **Note**
>
> If you create a slide show and you're really pleased with its appearance, you can use it to create a new master, and even add your new master to the Master Gallery. (See Chapter 15, "Working with Masters, Templates, and Backgrounds," for more information.)

Clicking the **G**allery command button in the New Slide Show dialog box displays the Master Gallery, shown in figure 2.3. By default, the Master Gallery displays eight different masters, including its name (which corresponds to a file for it in the C:\OFFICE\PRWIN\GALLERY directory) and a thumbnail showing the master's appearance. You can view additional masters by using the scroll bar to display them.

Use these steps to choose a master for your slide show:

1. Point to the thumbnail for the master you want and click to select it.

2. Click Retrieve. This selects the master, closes the Master Gallery dialog box, and returns you to the New Slide Show dialog box.

Tip
In place of steps 1 and 2, you simply can point to a master thumbnail and double-click it to select it and close the dialog box.

Click a master to choose it...

Fig. 2.3
Use the Master Gallery to select from the preset masters provided with Presentations. With these masters, you don't have to be an art whiz to create an attractive presentation.

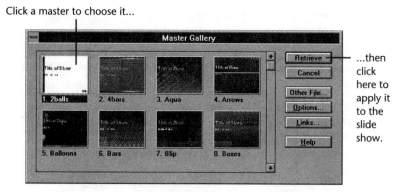

...then click here to apply it to the slide show.

Selecting Slide Templates

WordPerfect Presentations for Windows offers six predefined *slide templates* that make it easy to place text and charts. Each slide template offers pre-defined and preformatted text and chart areas, which you simply fill in. Chapter 3, "Using the Various Slide Templates," provides more detail on each of the slide templates and how to add text and data to them after you select them.

To select a template for the first slide from the New Slide Show dialog box, use these steps:

1. Point to the pop-up list button in the Step 2 - Select a Slide Template box. By default, this button says None.

2. Press and hold the left mouse button to display the list of slide templates, as shown in figure 2.4.

3. Drag to highlight the slide type you want, and then release the left mouse button. The pop-up list closes, and the slide template you chose now appears as the button name.

Using Show Expert

Presentations has expert help built-in, not only for slide show design, as you've just learned, but also for slide show content. The Show Expert provides starter content outlines for slide shows that enable you to inform, persuade, teach, or recognize a special person before your audience. Table 2.1 lists the slide shows that are offered by the Show Expert.

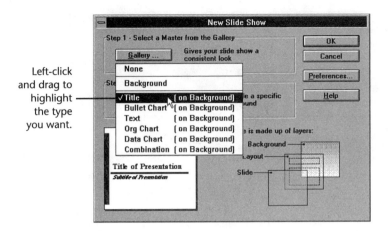

Fig. 2.4
A pop-up list in
the New Slide
Show dialog box
enables you to
choose a template
for the first slide in
the new show.

Left-click
and drag to
highlight
the type
you want.

Understanding the Basics

Table 2.1   Starter Presentations Offered in Show Expert

Presentation Name	Description
Inform Tab	
Describe Alternatives	Enables you to tell your audience about a situation where they have choices or options
Present Idea(s)	Helps you explain one or more new concepts
Report Results	Communicates about results or progress
Persuade Tab	
Doubting Audience	Enables you to sell a plan change, product, or service to a skeptical audience
Negative Audience	Helps you sell a plan change, product, or service to a resistant audience
Neutral Audience	Helps you sell a plan change, product, or service to an unresponsive audience
Positive Audience	Sells a plan change, product, or service to a positive audience
Teach Tab	
Explain a Concept or Method	Enables you to explain how to handle a method or process a situation

(continues)

Table 2.1 Continued	
Presentation Name	**Description**
Teach Tab	
Teach a Skill	Enables you to train audience members to perform a skill and evaluate their performance
Special Tab	
Present an Award or Tribute	Enables you to recognize an achievement
Welcome or Introduce	Use this slide show to introduce a speaker or kick off a meeting

Whether you're starting a new slide show on program startup or are creating a new show after the program is running, you can use the Show Expert to structure the content of the presentation. To use the Show Expert, follow these steps:

1. Start Presentations to display the Document Selection dialog box. Or, if Presentations already is running, open the **F**ile menu and choose **N**ew (or press Ctrl+N) or click the New icon to display the New Document dialog box.

2. Click the Create a Slide Show Using Show **E**xpert option and click OK. The New Slide Show dialog box appears.

3. (Optional) Click the **G**allery button to display the Master Gallery, click the master of your choice, and then click Retrieve.

4. Click OK to close the New Slide Show dialog box. Presentations loads the Show Expert.

5. Click OK at the Welcome to Show Expert screen. This action displays the Show Expert dialog box, shown in figure 2.5.

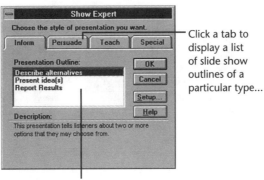

...then click to choose
an outline from the list.

Click a tab to
display a list
of slide show
outlines of a
particular type...

Fig. 2.5
Use the Show
Expert dialog box
to select outlines
for specific pre-
sentations and to
display a descrip-
tion of the cur-
rently selected
slide show outline.

Understanding the Basics

Note

You can change two display options for Show Expert by clicking the **S**etup
button in the Show Expert dialog box to display the Show Expert Setup dialog
box. In this dialog box, you can specify whether you want to display the
Welcome to Show Expert screen and the additional Help screen after Show
Expert sets up the slide show.

6. Click one of the tabs near the top of the dialog box to choose a slide
show to Inform, Persuade, Teach, or recognize a Special person or
achievement (see table 2.1 for a listing of which show outlines are
found on which tab).

7. Click a choice from the Presentation Outline list. When you make a
choice, the Description line at the bottom of the dialog box changes to
provide you with information about your choice.

8. Click OK to accept your choice. The Show Expert dialog box closes, and
Presentations changes to Outline view, displaying a starter outline like
the one shown in figure 2.6.

9. Replace the example outline text with your own text. For help on doing
this, see the Show Expert Additional Help box (if you haven't turned off
this display) or see Chapter 4, "Adjusting the View." Change to Slide
Editor view to view the actual slides in your new show.

Fig. 2.6
Slide Expert
provides an
example outline
that you can
replace with the
actual text for
your slide show.

Example outline; replace this text with your own.

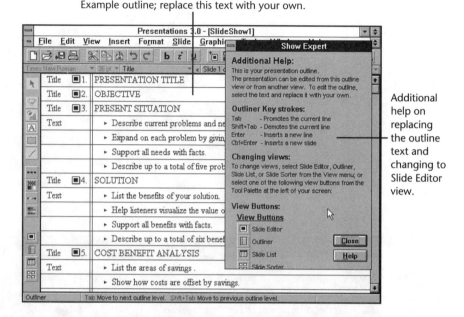

Additional
help on
replacing
the outline
text and
changing to
Slide Editor
view.

Opening an Existing Slide Show

As you probably have deduced by now, you have the option at any time to
not only create new slide shows but also to open a slide show you created
and saved to disk so that you can display, print, or update it. (To learn how
to save, see "Saving and Closing a Slide Show," later in this chapter.) Like
saving in other computer applications, saving a slide show creates a file for
the show on disk, stores the contents of that slide show in the file, and
assigns the file the name you specify. When you save a slide show, Presentations adds the SHW extension to the end of the show name, so if you're
trying to open a slide show rather than another file type, look for a file with
the SHW extension.

By default, Presentations displays the names of slide show files you created
recently at the bottom of the **F**ile menu. To open one of these slide shows,
simply click on **F**ile, and then click on the name of the slide show you want
to open.

Use these steps to open a previously created slide show that doesn't appear at
the bottom of the **F**ile menu:

1. Start Presentations to display the Document Selection dialog box. Click
the Work on an Existing **F**ile option and click OK. If Presentations

already is running, open the **F**ile menu and choose **O**pen (or press Ctrl+O), or click the Open icon to display the Open File dialog box (see fig. 2.7).

Click to display a list of previously viewed files.

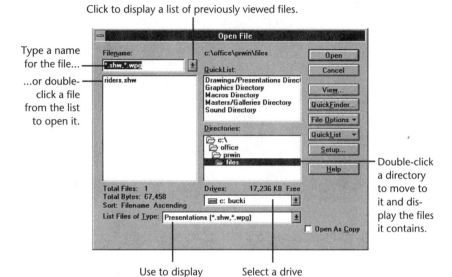

Type a name for the file...

...or double-click a file from the list to open it.

Double-click a directory to move to it and display the files it contains.

Use to display different file types.

Select a drive

Fig. 2.7
Use the Open File dialog box to open a slide show you previously saved.

2. (Optional) Click the down arrow beside the Dri**v**es drop-down list to display its choices and choose another drive, if necessary.

3. (Optional) Use the **D**irectories list box to move to the directory where the file is stored, if needed. To select a directory and display the files it contains in the list at the left side of the dialog box, double-click the directory's name in the list. To move backward through the **D**irectories list, double-click a directory name above the currently open directory.

4. In the File**n**ame text box, type the name of the file you want to open (including the full drive and path name if you skipped steps 2 and 3 and if the file you want to open is on another drive and directory). Or, you can click on the file to select it from the list below the File**n**ame text box. Make sure that you select a file with the SHW extension, which indicates that it is a Presentations slide show file.

If you're unsure that a file is the one you want to open, select it and then click the Vie**w** button to display a Viewer window with small thumbnails of the show slides. Double-click the window's Control menu box to close it.

Tip
Clicking Work on the **L**ast File in the Document Selection dialog box and then clicking OK opens the slide show displayed on the pop-up list button next to that option.

Tip
To immediately
select a file and
close the Open
File dialog box,
double-click the
file in the list
below the
File**n**ame text
box.

5. Click the Open command button. This closes the Open File dialog box and places the slide show in the Presentations application window so that you can view, print, or edit it.

Using QuickList

The QuickList is a new Presentations feature available in dialog boxes where you work with files (such as saving, opening, and so on). As you can see in figure 2.7, the QuickList displays a list of plain-English names for directories (rather than the full DOS path name for a directory). The QuickList enables you to create user-friendly alternate names for directories. Then, you can select the new directory name from the QuickList to access the files in the directory without entering the full path every time. To use the QuickList to display a list of files in a directory, follow these steps:

1. In the Open File dialog box or any other dialog box for working with files where the **Q**uickList appears, double-click on the desired directory name in the **Q**uickList. Notice that the list of files shown below the File**n**ame text box changes to reflect the contents of the new directory you have selected.

2. (Optional) If you want to view only files of a selected type, use the List Files of **T**ype drop-down list to choose a different file type.

3. Select the file you want from the File**n**ame list.

4. Click OK (or Open, and so on) to close the dialog box and perform the specified operation on the file you selected.

For more information about working with and customizing the QuickList so that you can use it effectively, see Chapter 5, "Basic Customizing."

Troubleshooting

I've tried to execute a file operation command, but the dialog box I get doesn't let me go to the directory containing the file I want to work on. Have I lost the file?

No, your file is probably still there. You've simply changed your display so that you're seeing only the **Q**uickList, which may or may not enable you to get to the directory and file you need. To display the **D**irectories list as well, point to the **Q**uickList in the dialog box and click the right mouse button to display the QuickMenu. Then click Show **D**irectories or Show **B**oth to reinstate the **D**irectories list to the display.

Using QuickFinder

If you have saved a file and cannot recall where you saved it to or exactly what you named it, don't worry. WordPerfect Presentations offers *QuickFinder*, a feature that enables you to search for slide show files by a particular pattern in the file name, words or phrases in the slide show, summary fields (such as descriptive name, abstract, or typist), the dates a file was saved or a range of dates, or the QuickFinder (full-text) index.

You can use QuickFinder from any file operation dialog box. Follow these steps:

1. From a file operation dialog box like the Open File dialog box, click the QuickFinder command button to display the QuickFinder dialog box, shown in figure 2.8. You also can start the QuickFinder by double-clicking the QuickFinder File Indexer icon in the PRWin 3.0 group window from the Program Manager.

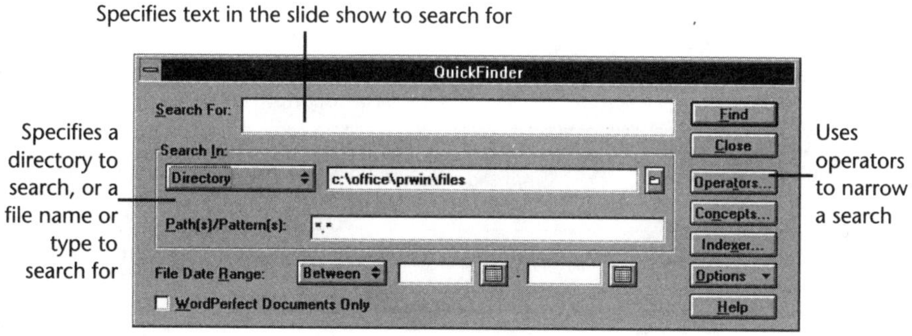

Specifies text in the slide show to search for

Specifies a directory to search, or a file name or type to search for

Uses operators to narrow a search

Fig. 2.8
The QuickFinder dialog box enables you to search for a file if you can't recall its exact name or where you saved it.

2. In the **S**earch For text box, type a word or phrase contained in one of the slides (if it's a slide show) in the slide show you're searching for. Note that you can skip this step if you're searching for a file that doesn't contain text, such as a graphics file.

You can use certain operators or switches to specify more sophisticated search text, such as searching for one word AND another, or searching for a word that only appears on the FIRST PAGE of a document. Clicking the Operators button displays the Search Operators dialog box, which enables you to insert an operator into the **S**earch For text (see fig. 2.9). Once you reach the point in the **S**earch For text where you want to insert the operator or switch (which always must be inserted before the word it's to operate on), click Operators. Click a radio button to select a category, such as **O**perators or **M**atch. A list of operators or switches appears at the right side of the dialog box. Click the operator you want, and then click **I**nsert to insert it into the **S**earch For string. Then you can choose another operator before closing the dialog box. If you choose Insert **a**nd Close rather than **I**nsert, this inserts the operator and closes the dialog box. Double-clicking an operator is the equivalent of using **I**nsert.

Fig. 2.9
The Search
Operators dialog
box enables you to
insert operators in
search strings.

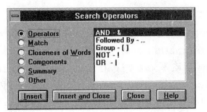

Example **S**earch For strings with operators follow:

Lisa ! Jim	Searches for "Lisa" but not "Jim".
/Text_only Bikes	Searches for the word "Bikes" in the text areas of slides only—not in titles, subtitles, charts, or graphics.
/Case /First_pages BIKES	Searches for "BIKES" in all uppercase on the first page only of the slide show.

Note

There are numerous operators and switches that you can use to greatly narrow a search, but describing each and every one of them is beyond the scope of this book. For help about a particular operation, click the **H**elp button in the Search Operators dialog box.

3. To search by file type or file name, or to search a particular directory, use the Search **I**n options on the QuickFinder dialog box. Use the Directory pop-up list to specify whether you want to search a particular **D**irectory, **S**ubtree, Di**s**k, or **Q**uickFinder Index (see Chapter 5 for more information about these). If you choose **D**irectory or **S**ubtree, you can edit the directory path shown in the text box to the right or use the File

Folder icon beside it to display the Select Directory dialog box, and use the lists in that dialog box to change the path. In the **P**ath(s)/Pattern(s) text box, type a specific file name to search for, or use *wild-card characters* to search for files with a particular name or a particular type. Here are the wild cards and examples of how to use them:

*	Enables you to search for a file or files with a group of unknown or variable characters. For example, ***.AVI** returns all files with the AVI extension, and **BIKE*.SHW** returns all files with the name starting with "BIKE," having one to four characters after "BIKE," and having the SHW extension.
?	Enables you to search for a file with a specific number of unknown or variable characters. For example, **QTR?.SHW** returns files beginning with "QTR," having one character next, and ending with SHW. Thus QTR1.SHW and QTR4.SHW would match, but QTR194.SHW would not.

4. Use the File Date **R**ange option if you want QuickFinder to return files that were last saved on dates matching the dates you specify here. Start by clicking the pop-up list button and choosing **A**fter, **B**efore, Be**t**ween, or **O**n. (Choosing one of these options changes the dialog box so it displays only one date text box.) Specify the necessary date(s) by typing a date in the format m/d/y or by clicking the Calendar icon beside the text box to display a calendar (see fig. 2.10). Use the triangles at the top of the calendar to move to the month and year you want, and then click a particular date to insert it into the text box.

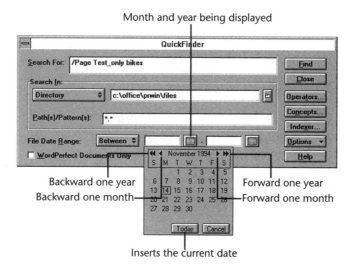

Month and year being displayed

Backward one year
Backward one month

Forward one year
Forward one month

Inserts the current date

Fig. 2.10
A pop-up calendar helps you insert dates when you want to search for file(s) by the last save date.

5. Turn on the **W**ordPerfect Documents Only check box to limit the search to documents in WordPerfect 5.0/5.1/5.2/6.0 format.

6. Click **F**ind. Presentations displays the Search Results List dialog box, with a list of files that match the criteria you specified in the QuickFinder dialog box (see fig. 2.11).

Fig. 2.11
Presentations displays the files that match the criteria you specified in the QuickFinder dialog box.

Click a file to select it.

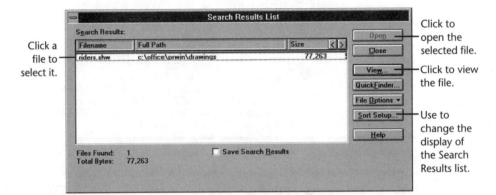

Click to open the selected file.

Click to view the file.

Use to change the display of the Search Results list.

7. Click a file in the list to select it, and then click Ope**n** to open it in Presentations or Vie**w** to display it in the Viewer window. Simply double-clicking a file name opens the file. If you want to change the order of the files in the Search Results list, click the **S**ort Setup button to display the Search Results Sort Setup dialog box, use the **B**y and **O**rder pop-up lists to specify new sort settings, and click OK. Use the QuickFinder button to refine your search if the file you wanted isn't displayed, repeating steps 2 through 6 of this procedure to display a new list of files.

You can further customize your QuickFinder searches using QuickFinder Indexes and the **O**ptions button in the QuickFinder dialog box. These features are discussed in Chapter 5.

Using Other Open File Options

The Open File dialog box and several other file-oriented dialog boxes offer a File **O**ptions pop-up list that enables you to perform other operations from the dialog box, such as copying or renaming a file (see fig. 2.12). You also can display these options by pointing to the File**n**ame list box and pressing the right mouse button. Simply select the file on which you want to perform the operation from the File**n**ame list box, and then display the File **O**ptions pop-up list to choose a command.

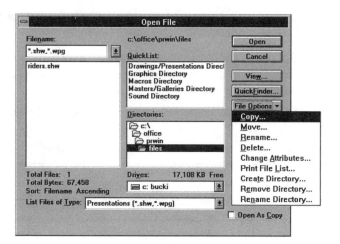

Fig. 2.12
This pop-up menu lists other operations you can perform from any file-related dialog box in Presentations.

Table 2.2 describes each of the File Options commands and what they enable you to do. Most of these commands display a straightforward dialog box. Just specify the options you want and click OK to close the dialog box and perform the operation. Note that you can perform many of these operations on more than one file at a time; simply select many files in the Filename list box by dragging to highlight contiguous files or by pressing and holding Ctrl while clicking to select noncontiguous files.

Table 2.2   File Options Commands

Command	Function
Copy	Copies a file from one drive or directory to another, or opens a copy of an existing file so you can save it under a new name.
Move	Moves selected file(s) from one drive or directory to another.
Rename	Renames the selected file(s). Use wild cards when working with multiple files. Entering ***.SHW** in the Rename Selected Files **T**o text box, for example, changes the extension on all selected files to SHW without altering the preceding portion of the file name.
Delete	Deletes the selected file(s).
Change **A**ttributes	Specifies the selected files as **A**rchive, **R**ead-Only, Hidde**n**, or **S**ystem files.
Print File **L**ist	Prints a list of the file names for all or selected files in a directory.

(continues)

Table 2.2 Continued	
Command	**Function**
Create Directory	Displays the Create Directory dialog box so that you can enter the path for a new directory.
Remove Directory	Deletes the directory currently selected in the **D**irectories list.
Rename Directory	Changes the name of the current directory.

Troubleshooting

*I tried to make changes to a file with one of the File **O**ptions commands, and Presenta-tions displayed an error message telling me it couldn't do what I'd requested. What's wrong?*

For the most part, you cannot rename, move, delete, or perform a similar operation on an open file. Close the dialog box to return to the open slide show, close the show with the File **C**lose command or its Control menu, and retry the File **O**ption command.

Moving Around in Presentations

Whether you're opening a new slide show or an existing one, the show opens to the first slide of the presentation, shown in Slide Editor view (Chapter 4, "Adjusting the View," provides more information about this view and others). Figure 2.13 shows how the screen looks after opening an example show created for this book. Notice that Presentations adds the name of the slide show to the title bar.

Tip
Pressing PgUp moves to the preceding slide, and PgDn moves to the next slide. Ctrl+Home displays the first slide in the show, and Ctrl+End displays the last slide of the show.

If the slide show contains more than one slide, you may need to move to other slides to view or edit them. Navigating to different slides in the slide show is a simple matter of pointing and clicking. The power bar offers a few buttons that you use to move through the show, as identified in figure 2.13. Clicking the left-pointing double arrow moves back one slide; clicking the right-pointing double arrow moves forward one slide. Clicking the Slide *x* of *x* button (where the first *x* is the current slide number), displays a list of slides like the one shown in figure 2.14. Simply click one of the listed slides to jump directly to it.

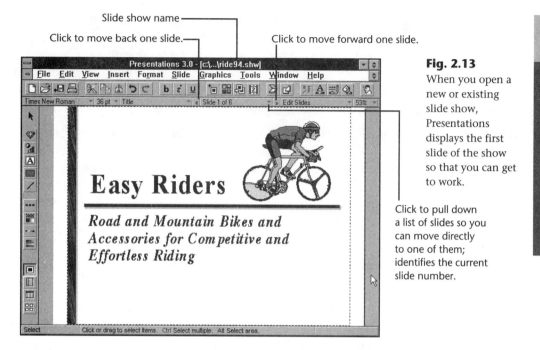

Slide show name ⎯⎯

Click to move back one slide. ⎯

Click to move forward one slide.

Fig. 2.13
When you open a new or existing slide show, Presentations displays the first slide of the show so that you can get to work.

Click to pull down a list of slides so you can move directly to one of them; identifies the current slide number.

Fig. 2.14
You can pull down a list of all the slides in the current show from the Power Bar, and then click a slide to jump directly to it.

Click a slide to jump to it.

You also can choose the **S**lide **G**o To command (or press Ctrl+G) to display the Go To Slide dialog box. Use the scroll bar in that box to display the name of the slide you want to go to, and then click OK to jump to that slide.

Changing Page Format

Most slides are laid out in a *landscape* (wider than it is tall) format, because that's the common format of 35-mm slides. Also, the default for most slide shows is to be printed on standard 8 1/2-by-11-inch (letter) paper. As a result, the default format for each "page" or slide in a slide show is letter-sized and landscape. But what if you're creating a slide show that will never be displayed on-screen, as overheads, or as slides? Or what if you prefer to use a *portrait* (taller than it is wide) format when you're creating overheads? You have the option of adjusting the layout of the slide show pages—including orientation, margins, and background color—to meet whatever needs you may have based on how the presentation will be delivered.

Tip

Although you can change the slide show page format at any time, it's best to do so right after you start a slide show so that you always will have an accurate look at how much information really can fit on each slide and what the finished slide will look like.

When you change the page format, Presentations reformats the layouts of individual slides to conform to the new orientation, margins, and so on. Figure 2.15 compares how a slide looks with a landscape page layout (the default) to how a slide looks with a portrait page layout. Notice that when it changed the slide show to the taller layout, Presentations changed the background gradient to make it vertical, and made the boxes holding text narrower.

To adjust the page layout for your slide show, use these steps:

1. Open the Format menu and choose **P**age **S**ize/Margins or press Ctrl+F8. Or, point to an open area of the slide, press the right mouse button, and choose **S**ize/Margins. Presentations displays the Page Format dialog box, shown in figure 2.16.

2. Click the Size pop-up list and click one of the default page sizes listed. (Note that **S**tandard/**S**tandard Landscape, **L**egal/Legal La**n**dscape, and **A4**/A**4** Landscape are the portrait/landscape versions of paper of the specified size. Choosing one of these options sets the correct paper orientation.) If you choose **O**ther from the bottom of the list, use the Wi**d**th and He**i**ght text boxes below the Size pop-up list to enter the actual page dimensions you want (type a value or click the incrementor arrows to increase or decrease the values).

3. Specify new margin widths, if needed, in the Margins area. Type a value for each margin or click the incrementor buttons to increase and decrease the values.

4. Turn on the Size View to Fit **G**raphic option by clicking the check box to place an x in it to change the amount of white space surrounding an object when you save it. This setting is important to use if you plan to save a drawing or slide as a WPG file and then retrieve it into WordPerfect to reduce the amount of white space that appears in the WordPerfect Viewport. After turning on this check box, change the value in the Displa**y** Border box to control how much white space surrounds the graphic.

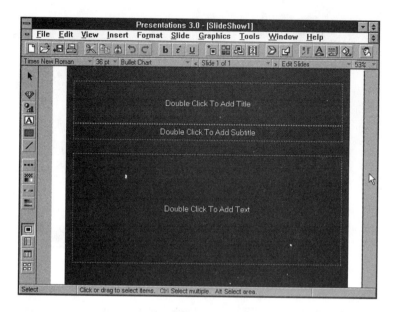

Fig. 2.15
You can change the page layout from wide to tall, as shown here. Presentations reformats slide contents to fit the new layout.

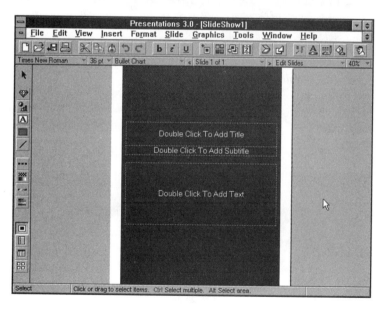

Fig. 2.16
Use the Page
Format dialog box
to adjust the page
format for your
slide show.

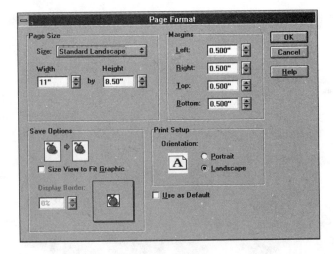

5. Choose **P**ortrait or **L**andscape orientation, if needed.

6. Place an x in the **U**se as Default check box if you want Presentations to use your new page format settings as the default for all new slide shows.

7. Click OK to close the dialog box and apply the new settings. As already noted, Presentations reformats all slides in the open slide show to conform with the new settings.

Changing the background color for your current slide show is just as easy. Use these steps:

1. Open the Fo**r**mat menu and choose **P**age **C**olor to display the Page Color Settings dialog box (see fig. 2.17).

Fig. 2.17
Use the Page Color
Settings dialog box
to change the
background color
for your slide
show.

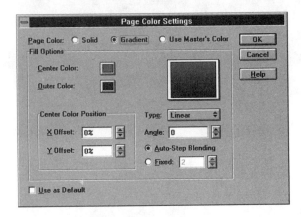

2. From the **P**age Color area, choose Solid or Gradient. You should choose Use Master's Color only if you have changed the background color and want to return to the master's background color. This option disables all the other choices in the dialog box.

3. If you chose Solid in step 2, the only option available is to choose a new background color. Click the **C**olor button to display a palette of colors, and then click a new color. Skip to step 9 to finish this procedure.

If you chose Gradient in step 2, all the dialog box options become available, and two Color buttons appear: one for **C**enter Color (which also represents the top color in a top-to-bottom gradient) and one for **O**uter Color. Click on each of these buttons, and then click the palette that appears to select a new color.

4. If you want the gradient to originate from somewhere other than the upper left-hand corner of the screen, enter new values in the **X** Offset (controls left-to-right position) and **Y** Offset (controls top-to-bottom position) boxes. Legal values range from 0 to 100, with 50 being the screen midpoint.

5. Click the Typ**e** pop-up list to indicate a new fill type: **L**inear, **C**ircular, or **R**ectangular. This setting dictates whether the colors blend along a straight line, in a curve, or at an angle.

6. Enter an An**g**le value of 1 to 359 to rotate the gradient.

7. Leave **A**uto-Step Blending selected if you want Presentations to specify the number of blending steps between the gradient colors. Or, click **F**ixed and enter a value to specify the desired number of blending steps.

8. Turn on the **U**se as Default check box if you want Presentations to use your new Page Color settings as the default for all new slide shows.

9. Click OK to apply your changes to the open presentation.

Troubleshooting

My printer cuts off the edges of my slides when I print out my slide show. What can I do to fix this?

Most printers cannot print all the way to the edges of the paper, and if you lay out your slide to print all the way to the edge, some elements are cut off. Check your printer manual to see what its minimum margins are. To avoid this problem, change the layout to use margins wider than the minimum margins for your printer.

My slide background prints out black rather than the color it appears on-screen. It's not very attractive, and I know it uses a lot of toner to print. Is there a workaround?

Yes. You can use the **P**age **C**olor command from the Fo**r**mat menu to change the background of the slide to a lighter value, so the slide prints with a background, but not one that's too dark.

*I changed my background with Fo**r**mat **P**age **C**olor, and now when I print my slide the text is hard to read or missing. What did I do and how can I fix it?*

Not all printers can handle very subtle differences in colors, so if you set a background color that's too close in value to the color of the text, the text blends into the background and is unreadable. To fix this problem, change the text or the background (with **P**age **C**olor from the Fo**r**mat menu) to a color that is a few shades darker.

Adding a New Slide

Once you've started a slide show, you build on it by adding new slides. The process of adding a new slide involves telling Presentations where you want to insert the new slide(s), specifying how many slides to insert, and specifying a type for the new slide(s). (For more on choosing and inserting the text and data for the various slide types, see Chapter 3, "Using the Various Slide Templates.") Here are the steps for adding one or more new slides to your slide show:

1. Go to the slide after which you want to insert one or more new slides (see "Moving Around in Presentations," earlier in this chapter).

2. Open the **S**lide menu and choose **A**dd Slides or click the Add Slides icon on the Toolbar. The Add Slides dialog box appears, shown in figure 2.18.

3. Enter the Number of **S**lides you want to add.

Fig. 2.18
Use the Add Slides
dialog box to add
one or more slides
of the same type
after the currently
displayed slide in
your slide show.

4. Click the **T**emplate pop-up list button and choose a new slide template
   from the list.

5. Click OK. Presentations adds the new slide(s) and displays the first (or
   only) slide inserted.

Saving and Closing a Slide Show

Your slide show isn't a masterpiece yet, but until you save it to a file on a
hard or floppy disk, you risk losing your work if a computer or power failure
occurs. The first time you save, you also create a name for your slide show;
Presentations adds a three-letter extension, SHW, to the file name you
specify. To save a slide show file for the first time, follow these steps:

1. Open the **F**ile menu and choose **S**ave, click the Save icon, or press
   Ctrl+S. Presentations displays the Save dialog box (see fig. 2.19). Notice
   that this dialog box is very similar to the Open File dialog box.

Use a QuickList entry to quickly set
the drive and directory to save to.

Type a name
for the file
(up to eight
characters).

Specify a
directory to
save to.

Specify a drive to save to.

Fig. 2.19
When you save a
file the first time,
you have to
specify a location
and name for the
file in the Save
dialog box.

2. Use the Drives drop-down list to specify another disk drive to save the file to, if necessary.

3. Double-click a directory in the **D**irectories list to specify that the file will be saved in that directory. (If you need to move backward through the **D**irectories list, double-click the directory above the presently open, or bottom, directory.)

4. Type a file name of up to eight characters in the File**n**ame text box. Note that you don't have to type the SHW extension, and that special characters (including * / & ?) cannot be used in file names. It's a good idea to come up with a logical naming system. If you create several slide shows for each of your clients, for example, you might include the client billing number at the start of each file name, as in 030show1, 030show2, and so on.

5. Click the **S**ave button. Presentations saves the slide show in a file with the name you specified and closes the Save As dialog box so that you can continue working on the slide show.

Troubleshooting

I tried to save my file and got a message that there wasn't enough disk space. What can I do?

Try saving the file to an empty floppy disk. Insert the floppy into drive A or B, and use the Drives list in the Save As dialog box to choose the drive where you inserted the floppy. Working with a floppy prevents you from losing your work, for now. Working from a floppy drive is much slower than working from the hard drive, however, so when possible, you should delete unneeded files from your hard disk and copy the slide show file from the floppy to the hard disk.

When I try to save my file, I get a Save dialog box telling me that I have items selected. What do I do?

You can save the entire slide show rather than the selected items by clicking on the **E**ntire File radio button and clicking OK.

After you name and save a file, clicking the Save icon simply resaves the file under its current name and location, which is the equivalent of opening the **F**ile menu and choosing **S**ave.

If you want to save an existing file with a new name, open the File menu and choose Save As to redisplay the dialog box and save the file with a new name, leaving the old file with its original name intact on disk. (You also can use the File Options Copy command within a file-related dialog box to create and name a copy of an existing file, although the file you're copying cannot be open at the time.)

Closing a Slide Show

If you've finished working on one slide show and want to put it away without leaving Presentations, you can close the slide show. As a rule, you should close slide show files you're not using, because this frees up RAM (random-access memory) for your present work. You can close a file tw•o ways:

- With the slide show you want to display on-screen, open the File menu and choose Close or press Ctrl+F4.

- Double-click the Control menu box for the slide show.

From Here...

If you've applied the techniques described in this chapter, you've gotten your first slide show off to a running start, and may have a few slides all ready for your text and data. Although parts II, III, and IV of this book focus on the detail work for finishing your slide show, you first may want to check out some of these chapters for additional basic techniques and for elaboration on some of the features presented in this chapter:

- Chapter 3, "Using the Various Slide Templates," explains how to choose the best slide template for the message you want to convey. You also learn how to substitute your own text, charts, and graphics for the placeholders that appear on new slides.

- Chapter 4, "Adjusting the View," explains how to use the different design views offered in Presentations, as well as handy features like the grid and zooming.

- Chapter 5, "Basic Customizing," expands on some of the concepts introduced in this chapter, including setting Preferences and customizing the QuickList and QuickFinder.

Chapter 3

Using the Various Slide Templates

Most users don't have time to design a slide show from the ground up, let alone make decisions about where to place every word, what font to make it, what color it should be, what charts should be used to illustrate it, and more. If you did have to make all those decisions (in addition to writing the content for your slide show), you would be shackled to your computer for days just to complete a 10-slide presentation.

Well, the good news is that the slide *templates*—predefined layouts for text and data—offered in WordPerfect Presentations 3.0 for Windows make all the nitty-gritty decisions for you after you use the Master Gallery to pick a look and feel for the slide show. Even better, the slide template layout areas partially automate the procedure for getting data into your slide show. Simply double-click an area and enter text, or use a dialog box to select a chart type.

This chapter reviews the different slide templates and what kinds of information each best presents, and also gives you some creative ideas for using different slide templates in a slide show. In addition, this chapter helps you master the following tasks:

- Working with the layout-area placeholders
- Creating a slide of each type, including Title, Text, Bullet Chart, Org Chart, Data Chart, and Combination
- Applying a new type to an existing slide

Identifying the Various Slide Templates and Their Uses

Chapter 2 showed you briefly how to select a slide template in the New Slide Show dialog box or in the Add Slide dialog box. As you learned in that chapter, each slide template is a predefined format that specifies where the text and charts for the slide are placed and sized, and how they are formatted by default. Within the selected master, all the slide types use consistent backgrounds, text fonts and colors, and layout of all the elements, so that no matter what slide template you select, all the slides in the slide show look consistent.

Presentations offers six predefined slide templates custom built for displaying particular types of data. Table 3.1 reviews the slide templates, what elements each offers, and when to choose each template.

Table 3.1 Using the Six Predefined Slide Templates in Presentations		
Template	**Areas (Placeholders)**	**Use It To**
Title	Title text, Subtitle text	Introduce the slide show or make simple assertions
Bullet Chart	Title text, Subtitle text, Bullet text	Discuss a major topic and outlines supporting points or steps
Text	Title text, Subtitle text, Narrative text	Present long support statements or paragraphs in the title topic; also useful for presenting quotes
Organization Chart	Title text, Subtitle text, Org chart	Present an organizational structure, hierarchy, or process
Data Chart	Title text, Subtitle text, Data chart	Present a point and supporting data, representing data as a pie, bar, area, line, table, radar, surface, scatter, or high/low chart to visually communicate patterns or relationships
Combination	Title text, Subtitle text Bullet text, Data chart	Present a topic and supporting data in chart form and main points about the data in bullet format

Working with Layout Areas

Figure 3.1 shows a new slide created with the Title template. Notice that the figure shows two boxes bounded by dotted outlines: one for the slide title and one for the slide subtitle. Each of these dotted outlines is referred to as a *layout area*. You can think of these as placeholders for the real text and data you're going to add.

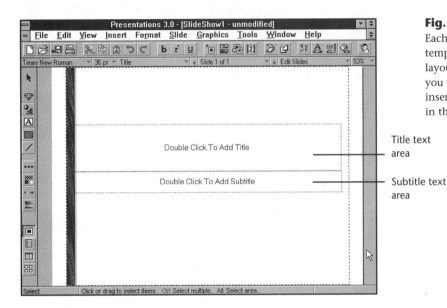

Fig. 3.1
Each slide template offers layout areas telling you where to insert charts and, in this case, text.

Title text area

Subtitle text area

There are two ways to work with or select layout areas. The first method, sometimes called *activating* the layout area, is for filling in or editing the text or data in the layout area. When you want to add the actual text or chart into its designated layout area, point to the layout area with the mouse and double-click. After you double-click data- and org-chart layout areas, you see a dialog box that leads you through the chart-creation process; simply make your selections to create the kind of chart you want. When you double-click to activate a text layout area, the area becomes surrounded with a hatched outline, and a flashing insertion cursor appears in the area. Simply begin typing the text you want. As you see in figure 3.2, the text appears in an attractive, preselected font. Figure 3.2 also shows the mouse pointer, which changes to an I-beam for editing text. You learn more about using this cursor in Chapter 6, "Adding and Editing Text." When you're finished typing the text, simply click outside the layout area to deactivate it.

Tip

If you don't "fill in" a layout area with text or data, don't worry. The dotted lines surrounding the area and the text telling you to double-click don't print or appear when you play the slide show on-screen.

Fig. 3.2
Double-click a text layout area and type the text you want into it.

Hatched outline   I-beam pointer

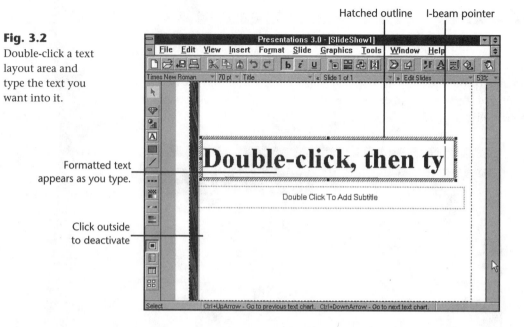

Formatted text appears as you type.

Click outside to deactivate

Tip
Presentations automatically wraps text to a new line when needed. If you want to specify a line break while typing, press Enter.

You don't really need to know the second way of working with layout areas until you start editing slides, but it's good to understand the difference now, so that you know what you're doing at all times. You can select a layout area (whether or not it contains text) to make changes to its size, position, colors, and even contents. To select a layout area, simply point to it or one of its boundaries and click. Black selection handles appear around the layout area, as shown in figure 3.3. You can use these handles to resize the layout area, as well as to perform other tasks. You learn more about formatting and changing selected layout areas in later chapters. To deselect the layout area, simply point to a blank area and click.

> **Note**
>
> You can activate the next layout area on a slide (and leave the one you're presently in) by pressing Ctrl+Down arrow. Activate the preceding layout area by pressing Ctrl+Up arrow.

The next several sections of this chapter focus on adding the text and data for each of Presentations' six slide templates. To perform the procedures described in this chapter, you mainly need to activate layout areas rather than select them.

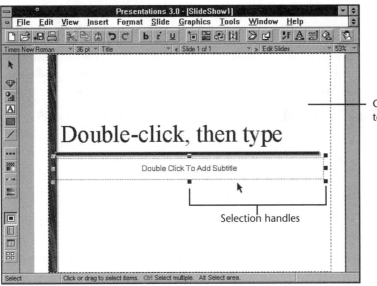

Fig. 3.3
Select a layout area
if you want to
change its position
or formatting.

Creating a Title Slide

The first slide in every slide show is traditionally a title slide, offering the title of the presentation or company name; and a subtitle that can be the company name, presenter's name, motto, or other statement. Many presenters also add an attractive graphic or company logo to jazz up the title slide. In addition to using the title slide to kick off your slide show, you can use it to do the following:

■ Isolate or emphasize a key point

■ Introduce an important new topic, followed by a bullet chart slide

■ Close the presentation with a parting thought

To create a title slide in your slide show, use these steps:

1. Open the **S**lide menu and choose **G**o To or use the Power Bar button to move to the slide after which you want to insert the new title slide.

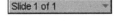

2. Open the **S**lide menu and choose **A**dd Slides or click the Add Slides button on the Toolbar to display the Add Slide dialog box.

3. (Optional) Specify the Number of **S**lides to add by typing a new number or clicking the incrementor buttons.

4. If the **T**emplate pop-up list button doesn't say Title, click and hold the left mouse button to display the choices, and then drag to select Title.

5. Click OK to close the dialog box and insert the new slide into the slide show. Its look follows the show's master. For title slides, the layout consists of two layout areas (one for a title and one for a subtitle).

6. Double-click the layout area labeled `Double Click to Add Title` to activate it. A hatched outline appears around the layout area, and a blinking vertical insertion cursor appears in the layout area.

7. Type the title text, letting it wrap automatically to new lines or pressing Enter if you want to manually start a new line after a particular word.

8. Double-click the layout area labeled `Double Click to Add Subtitle` to activate it. A hatched outline appears around the layout area, and a blinking vertical insertion cursor appears in the layout area.

9. Type the subtitle text, letting it wrap automatically to new lines or pressing Enter if you want to manually start a new line after a particular word.

10. Click in a blank area of the slide to deactivate the subtitle layout area. The slide now features title and subtitle text, as shown in figure 3.4.

Fig. 3.4
A newly created title slide, complete with title and subtitle text.

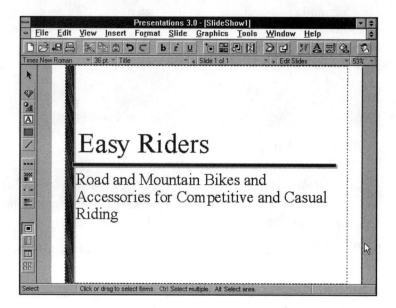

Making a Bullet Chart Slide

A bullet chart is a traditional format that enables you to present a major topic, followed by three or four points supporting the topic or steps leading to the conclusion. One dramatic way to use this type of chart is to create a *build sequence*—revealing the first bullet point, then the second bullet point, and so on. (Chapter 18, "Creating and Viewing the On-Screen Show," explains how to create the build effect.)

Caution

Bullet slides work best if you limit them to three or four points—not just due to design considerations, but also for clarity's sake. Packing too many bullet points onto a single slide clutters it up, and may tempt you to resize the text to a tiny size that's not readable and grossly inconsistent with the text in the rest of the slide show. In addition, you may lose your audience's attention, particularly when displaying a live slide show, if you linger on one slide too long because you've included too many bullet points. Audience attention—and retention—improves if you keep your lists short and snappy.

Other novel ways to apply a bullet chart in your slide show could include

- Using a bullet list to identify top products or performers on which to focus the discussion.

- Using a list of attention-grabbing questions near the beginning of the presentation to pique your audience's curiosity and segue into the main discussion points.

- Identifying succinctly the top three or four actions the audience members need to take.

- Creating a concluding take-away list for your audience, along the lines of, "If you remember nothing else that I've said, don't forget blah-blah, ta-da, ta-da, or um-humn."

To create a bullet chart slide in your slide show, use these steps:

1. Open the **S**lide menu and choose **G**o To or use the Power Bar button to move to the slide after which you want to insert the new bullet chart slide.

2. Open the **S**lide menu and choose **A**dd Slides or click the Add Slides button on the Toolbar to display the Add Slide dialog box.

3. (Optional) Specify the Number of **S**lides to add by typing a new number or clicking the incrementor buttons.

4. If the **T**emplate pop-up list button doesn't say Bullet Chart, click and hold the left mouse button to display the choices, and drag to select Bullet Chart.

5. Click OK to close the dialog box and insert the new slide into the slide show. Its appearance follows the show's master. For bullet chart slides, the layout consists of three layout areas (one for a title, one for a sub-title, and one for bullets), as shown in figure 3.5.

Fig. 3.5
Bullet chart slides have three layout areas: Title, Subtitle, and Bullets.

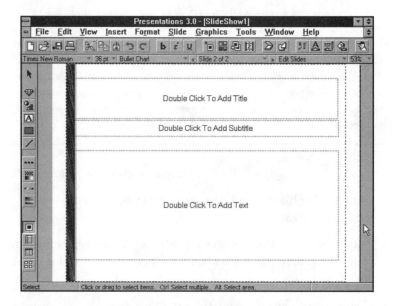

6. Double-click the layout area labeled `Double Click to Add Title` to activate it.

7. Type the title text, letting it wrap automatically to new lines or pressing Enter if you want to manually start a new line after a particular word.

Tip
You also can press the down arrow to move to the next layout area.

8. Double-click the layout area labeled `Double Click to Add Subtitle` to activate it.

9. Type the subtitle text, letting it wrap automatically to new lines or pressing Enter if you want to manually start a new line after a particular word.

10. Double-click the layout area labeled `Double Click to Add Text` to activate it. A hatched outline appears around the layout area, and a blinking vertical insertion cursor appears in the layout area. In addition, the first bullet appears at the left side of the layout area.

11. Type the text for the first bullet entry. To create additional lines, start a new line with one of the methods described next, and then type the text for the new line. Your text might resemble figure 3.6.

   ■ Press Enter to create the next bullet entry at the same level.

   ■ Press Enter to create a new bullet entry, and then press Tab to indent one level (demote the entry).

   ■ Press Enter to create the next bullet entry, and then press Shift+Tab to promote it one level (remove one level of indention).

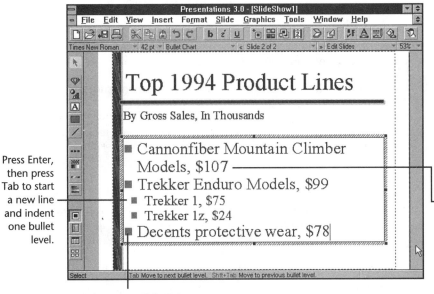

Press Enter, then press Tab to start a new line and indent one bullet level.

Press Enter to create a new bullet entry.

Press Enter, then press Shift+Tab to start a new line and promote one bullet level.

Fig. 3.6
Entering text in a bullet list layout area. Presentations inserts attractive bullet characters, which are preformatted based on the selected master for the slide show.

12. Click in a blank area of the slide to deactivate the bullet layout area. The slide now features title and subtitle text, along with any bullet entries you created in the bullet layout area.

Troubleshooting

Arghh! I typed a bullet entry and pressed Enter, but then realized I needed to indent the line by one bullet level. How can I fix it?

Click anywhere in the line you want to demote, and then press Tab to demote the line. Likewise, you can click in any bullet entry and press Shift+Tab to promote it, unless it's at the highest (farthest left) level.

Creating a Text Slide

Text slides enable you to deliver slightly longer thoughts to your audience, such as long sentences or paragraphs, excerpted information from printed sources, famous quotations, and more. Keep in mind that you shouldn't cram too much text on a text slide. The same cautions given earlier for bullet chart slides apply here, among others:

- Keep the text short and snappy. If you have to make it too small, it will be too hard—and too time-consuming—for your audience to read.

- If you need to, break the information into more than one slide.

- As always, copyright and courtesy rules apply. Make sure that you credit sources appropriately or obtain permission for reprinting material if your slide show is to be distributed commercially.

To create a text slide in your slide show, use these steps:

1. Open the **S**lide menu and choose **G**o To or use the Power Bar button to move to the slide after which you want to insert the new bullet chart slide.

2. Open the **S**lide menu and choose **A**dd Slides or click the Add Slides button on the Toolbar to display the Add Slide dialog box.

3. (Optional) Specify the Number of **S**lides to add by typing a new number or clicking the incrementor buttons.

4. If the **T**emplate pop-up list button doesn't say Text, click and hold the left mouse button to display the choices, and drag to select Text.

5. Click OK to close the dialog box and insert the new slide into the slide show. Its look follows the show's master. For text slides, the layout consists of three layout areas (one for a title, one for a subtitle, and one for text), as shown in figure 3.7.

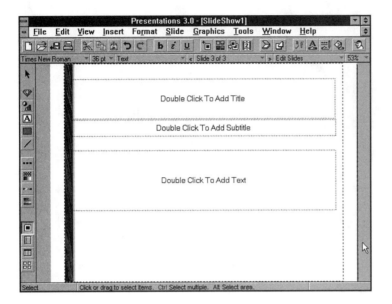

Fig. 3.7
The skeleton of
layout areas that
you use to start
your text slide.
Remember to keep
the contents as
short and snappy
as possible.

Understanding the Basics

6. Double-click the layout area labeled `Double Click to Add Title` to activate it.

7. Type the title text, letting it wrap automatically to new lines or pressing
   Enter if you want to manually start a new line after a particular word.

8. Double-click the layout area labeled `Double Click to Add Subtitle` to
   activate it.

9. Type the subtitle text, letting it wrap automatically to new lines or
   pressing Enter if you want to manually start a new line after a particular
   word.

10. Double-click the layout area labeled `Double Click to Add Text` to acti-
    vate it.

11. Type your text. Presentations wraps the text to the next line when you
    reach the end of a line. Press Enter to manually create a line break or to
    add a blank line (see fig. 3.8).

12. Click in a blank area of the slide to deactivate the final layout area and
    finish the slide.

Fig. 3.8
Simply type the
blocks of text you
want to appear on
your text slide.

Press Enter to
create a new
or blank line.

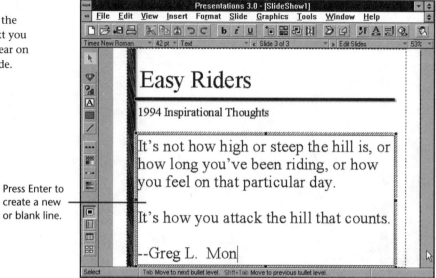

Adding an Organization Chart Slide

Computer programs that generate organizational charts have been a welcome
purchase for many companies, especially those that reorganize frequently
and rapidly. Now there are even programs created exclusively for generating
organizational charts! Like its more specialized cousins, the organization
chart slide template in Presentations enables you to quickly and painlessly
create an organization chart in the format you choose. You don't have to
waste time drawing boxes or connecting annoying lines.

When you consider the organization chart slide template, don't just think
about charts that show who reports to whom. Also consider these uses for
organization charts in your slide show:

- Showing how different departments or processes relate

- Showing what categories (such as product categories) particular items
  fall into

- Examining a list of branching choices, or possible divergent paths a
  company or industry could take in the future

- Looking at the pros and cons of an issue in a more graphical format

- Previewing several different seminar speakers and the topics each is
  planning to discuss

Without further ado, here are the steps for adding an organization chart to your slide show:

1. Open the **S**lide menu and choose **G**o To, or use the Power Bar button to move to the slide after which you want to insert the new organization chart slide.

2. Open the **S**lide menu and choose **A**dd Slides or click the Add Slides button on the Toolbar to display the Add Slide dialog box.

3. (Optional) Specify the Number of **S**lides to add by typing a new number or clicking the incrementor buttons.

4. If the **T**emplate pop-up list button doesn't say Text, click and hold the left mouse button to display the choices, and drag to select Org Chart.

5. Click OK to close the dialog box and insert the new slide into the slide show. Its look follows the show's master. For organization chart slides, the layout consists of three layout areas (one for a title, one for a sub-title, and one for the organization chart), as shown in figure 3.9.

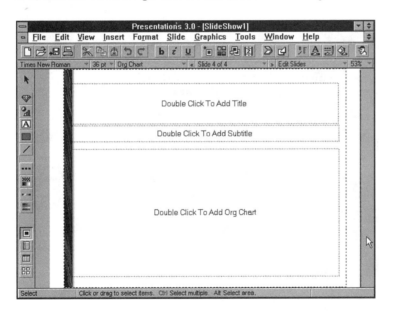

Fig. 3.9
The layout areas for the org chart template resemble the layout areas for other chart templates. However, adding data to the org chart layout area is a process that is unique to this slide type.

6. Just as you did for the slide types described earlier in this chapter, complete the title and subtitle layout areas by double-clicking to activate each, entering its text, and then clicking on a blank slide area to deactivate it.

7. Double-click in the area labeled `Double Click to Add Org Chart`. This action displays a special gallery in the Organization Chart dialog box (see fig. 3.10).

Fig. 3.10
Choose a thumbnail that resembles the structure you want for your chart from the Organization Chart dialog box.

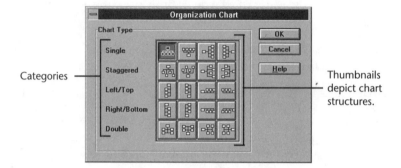

Categories

Thumbnails depict chart structures.

8. Click a chart thumbnail to select it and then click OK, or simply double-click a chart thumbnail. This closes the Organization Chart dialog box and displays a screen similar to the one shown in figure 3.11. Notice that this screen shows an Outline window for the new organization chart. The Power Bar and Toolbar also have changed; several Toolbar icons are gone and three new ones have appeared.

Manually redraws chart
Shows/hides the Outline window
Automatically redraws chart based on outline changes

Fig. 3.11
When you create an organization chart, Presentations displays an Outline window to use to enter the chart data.

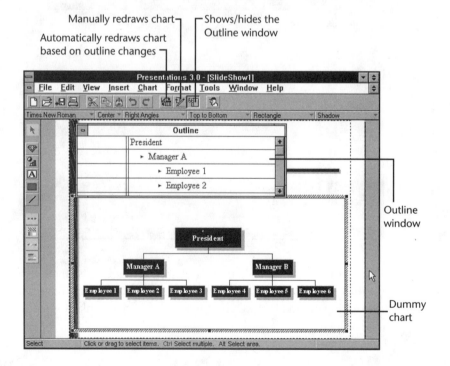

Outline window

Dummy chart

9. To change an entry in the Outline window, drag over its text to select it, and type new text. Edit all the entries as needed, using these techniques (see fig. 3.12):

- Press Enter to create a new entry at the same level.

- Press Tab to indent an entry one level.

- Press Shift+Tab to promote an entry one level.

- Use the Backspace key or open the **E**dit menu and choose **D**elete to remove an entry.

Tip

You can cut, copy, and paste information in the Outline window. For more information on using these techniques, see Chapter 6.

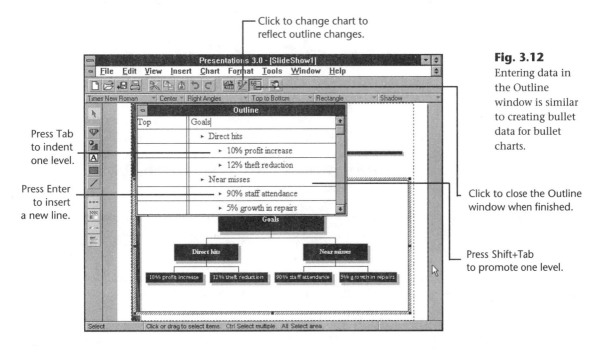

Fig. 3.12
Entering data in the Outline window is similar to creating bullet data for bullet charts.

10. Click the Manual Redraw button on the Toolbar to display your changes in the chart.

11. Double-click the Outline window's Control menu box to close it, or click on the Toolbar icon that shows and hides the outline window.

12. Click in a blank area away from the organization chart layout area to deactivate it. This step returns you to the normal Slide Editor view and redisplays the default Toolbar and Power Bar.

Understanding the Basics

Troubleshooting

*Every time I make a change in the Outline window, the screen flickers and my
computer pauses for a few seconds before I can enter more data. Is there any way
to stop this?*

Yes. The problem is that the Automatic Redraw feature is toggled on, causing
Presentations to redraw the chart every time you make an edit—no matter
how slight it is. To turn off this feature, click the Automatic Redraw button on
the Toolbar to deselect it. (It should have looked "pressed" when the tool was
toggled on.)

Creating a Data Chart Slide

The data chart slide is a fixture of the modern slide show. There is quite a bit
of emphasis on graphing data in different formats to compare numbers in
a visually appealing way. Presentations enables you to graph your data in
several data chart formats. There are numerous chart types in WordPerfect
Presentations, and an introduction to each of them and how to edit them
is presented in Chapter 9, "Working with Data Chart Data." For now, just
use these basic steps to create a data chart slide:

Slide 1 of 1

1. Open the **S**lide menu and choose **G**o To or use the Power Bar button to
   move to the slide after which you want to insert the new data chart
   slide.

2. Open the **S**lide menu and choose **A**dd Slides or click the Add Slides
   button on the Toolbar to display the Add Slide dialog box.

3. (Optional) Specify the Number of **S**lides to add by typing a new number
   or clicking the incrementor buttons.

4. If the **T**emplate pop-up list button doesn't say Data Chart, click and
   hold the left mouse button to display the choices, and drag to select
   Data Chart.

5. Click OK to close the dialog box and insert the new slide into the slide
   show. Its look follows the show's master. For data chart slides, the layout consists of three layout areas (one for a title, one for a subtitle, and
   one for the data chart).

6. Just as you did for the slide templates described earlier in this chapter,
   complete the title and subtitle layout areas by double-clicking to activate each, entering its text, and then clicking on a blank slide area to
   deactivate it.

7. Double-click in the area labeled `Double Click to Add Data`. This action displays a special gallery in the Data Chart dialog box (see fig. 3.13).

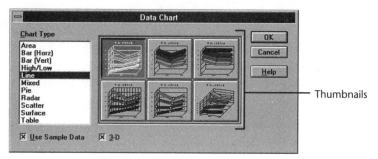

Fig. 3.13
You can select from a whole gallery of slide types when you create a data chart.

Thumbnails

8. Click a **C**hart Type from the list (these are described in Chapter 9, if you're not familiar with them), which changes the thumbnails displayed at the right. Click the thumbnail that offers the formatting features you want. Click OK to close the dialog box and display the Datasheet window and dummy chart (see fig. 3.14). Note that, as when creating an organization chart, there are several changes to your screen.

Automatic Redraw

Manual Redraw

Click on a cell, then type to change its entry.

Show/Hide the Datasheet

Click to highlight a whole row, then press Delete to clear it.

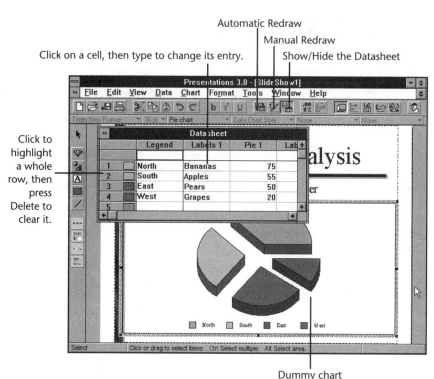

Fig. 3.14
Presentations displays a Datasheet window, where you enter the actual data for your chart.

Dummy chart

9. To change an entry in the Datasheet window, click to select its cell and type new text or a new value. Figure 3.14 illustrates some other editing techniques; editing techniques are covered fully in Chapter 9.

10. Click the Manual Redraw button on the Toolbar to display your changes in the chart.

11. Double-click the Datasheet window's Control menu box to close it, or click on the Toolbar icon that shows and hides the outline window.

12. Click in a blank area away from the data chart layout area to deactivate it. This step returns you to the normal Slide Editor view and redisplays the default Toolbar and Power Bar.

Making a Combination Slide

A combination slide template combines title, subtitle, bullet chart, and data chart elements. These slides are useful for displaying data that may need a few descriptive points to be clear to the viewer. Add a combination slide to your slide show using the steps described for the other five slide types, and then activate the layout areas one by one and enter the text or data for them as described earlier in this chapter.

Applying New Templates to Existing Slides

If you enter data into a slide—particularly a slide with a chart—and are unhappy with the resulting chart, you can apply another slide template to the slide without having to delete the slide and start from scratch. This feature is useful especially because it enables you to apply a new template to several slides at once, saving you time and aggravation. To apply new slide templates, use these steps:

1. With any slide in the show visible, open the **S**lide menu and choose Apply **T**emplate to display the Apply Template dialog box (see fig. 3.15).

2. Use the left and right arrows to choose the slide to change, if its name isn't displayed.

3. In the Apply To area, specify whether changes should apply to **A**ll Slides, the C**u**rrent Slide, or a Slide **R**ange (for which you should specify **S**tart and **E**nd slide numbers).

Use to select the slide to change.

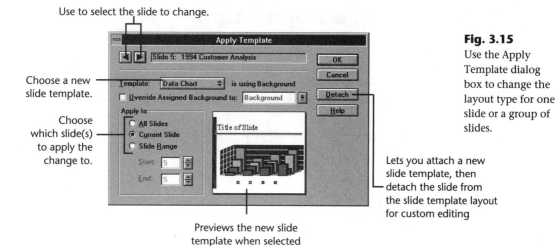

Fig. 3.15
Use the Apply
Template dialog
box to change the
layout type for one
slide or a group of
slides.

Choose a new
slide template.

Choose
which slide(s)
to apply the
change to.

Lets you attach a new
slide template, then
detach the slide from
the slide template layout
for custom editing

Previews the new slide
template when selected

4. Choose a new slide **T**emplate. Notice that the preview slide reflects the new format you just selected.

5. (Optional) If you want to detach the slide from its slide type layout for custom editing but want to retain the new formatting, click **D**etach, and then click **Y**es. When you change the slide show master, the detached slides do not adapt the new master formatting for the slide type.

6. Click OK to close the Apply Template dialog box. This returns you to the slide, inserting new layout areas (reflecting the new slide type) in place of certain layout areas for the original slide type. If you started with an organization chart, for example, and applied the bullet chart as a new type, the organization chart layout area is replaced with a bullet chart layout area.

7. Double-click the new layout area to activate it and enter the data as you would for a normal slide of the new type.

Troubleshooting

*I used **S**lide, Apply **T**emplate and accidentally chose the wrong type. Presentations won't let me undo the operation. Do I have to start over?*

No, you don't. Luckily, Presentations retains the data you entered in the original slide. Just choose Apply **T**emplate from the **S**lide menu again, and choose the original **T**emplate. When you click OK and return to the slide, your data appears in its original format.

Understanding the Basics

Undoing an Operation

You can undo many of the steps and changes involved in creating slides. You also can undo nearly all the menu commands and editing and drawing changes. The key to effective use of Undo is to *undo an action immediately*, before you make any additional changes or commands. To undo an action, open the **E**dit menu and choose **U**ndo or click the Undo icon on the Toolbar. You also can redo an action immediately by opening the **E**dit menu and choosing **R**edo or by clicking the Redo icon.

From Here...

Adding slides to a slide show is a very basic procedure, as you've seen in the procedures for adding different slide types as described in this chapter. The effectiveness of your presentation may depend, however, on how wisely and creatively you use the various slide templates; this chapter provided some guidance in those areas, too. If you're looking forward to enhancing your slide show and feel comfortable enough to skip some of the basic data-entry and editing information, check out these chapters:

- Chapter 7, "Enhancing Text," provides you with the tools for changing the formatting of text and text-layout areas, and even discusses some text special effects.

- Chapter 8, "Adding QuickArt to a Slide," explains how to add a graphic touch to any slide using the QuickArt provided with WordPerfect Presentations 3.0 for Windows. The chapter also gives you the basic steps for importing other types of graphics files.

- Chapter 10, "Formatting the Data Chart," explains how you can customize the prefabricated chart layouts in the Data Chart dialog box. Learn here about controlling legends and scaling, adding 3D, and more.

- Chapter 18, "Creating and Viewing the On-Screen Show," explains what you need to do to create a presentation to run on a computer screen.

Chapter 4

Adjusting the View

Even though the slide template layouts greatly streamline the slide-creation process, it's still a little tedious to have to double-click every single area to type text. You also may have noticed that your computer seems to run a bit more slowly when it's drawing all that nicely formatted text on-screen.

WordPerfect Presentations 3.0 for Windows offers different views of your slide show to help you work more effectively. You may be more comfortable typing all the text for your slide show in Outliner view. Or, you may be wondering if there's an easy way to move slides around within your show (there is). Presentations also enables you to set other viewing options based on your preferences, such as whether you like to work with a background grid, whether you like to zoom in on the details, and more.

In this chapter, you learn about the following topics:

- Using the Slide Editor, Outliner, Slide List, and Slide Sorter views

- Displaying and using a grid

- Zooming in and out

- Using a crosshair pointer

- Working in Draft mode

- Viewing multiple slide shows

Choosing a View

In the preceding chapters, all slides were shown in the default view of Presentations—Slide Editor view. Although this view is useful for taking a look at the whole slide to see whether it's pleasantly formatted and whether all the elements are in place, it's not the best view for other operations such as changing the order of slides or entering data quickly. To help you use your time as best as possible, Presentations offers several views, as described in table 4.1.

Table 4.1	The Views Provided in Presentations	
Palette Icon	**View**	**Description**
	Slide Editor	Displays the full slide, so that you can see the overall look and content. Use to add charts and graphics.
	Outliner	Lists the slides in the show and their contents. Useful for quickly entering and editing slide text.
	Slide List	Lists the slides by number and title, and indicates the transition and advance settings (used when displaying the show on-screen) for each slide. Useful for arranging slides and editing the transitions.
	Slide Sorter	Shows thumbnails of multiple slides, in order. Use to quickly rearrange slides in a show.

The next several sections explain not only how to switch to each view when you need to, but also how to use all the features offered in the view.

Working in Slide Editor View

Slide Editor view shows the full slide on-screen. This is the view you have to use when you want to add charts and graphics (such as QuickArt) to a particular slide. This is also the view you need to use if you want to change the look and feel of the slide, from repositioning and reformatting layout areas to changing the color or font for text. Although you can change the slide show master and apply slide type layouts from other views, it's best to handle those operations from Slide Editor view so that you immediately can see and evaluate the results of a change.

 To change to Slide Editor view from any other view, open the **V**iew menu and choose Slide **E**ditor, or click the Slide Editor View icon in the tool palette. Because most of the other chapters in this book, such as Chapter 3, explain how to perform operations from Slide Editor view, those details aren't provided here. For help on performing a particular operation in Slide Editor view, see the chapter that covers that operation.

Structuring the Show in Outliner View

When you change to Outliner view, the Presentations screen changes to look like a piece of lined notebook paper, as shown in figure 4.1. To change to Outline view, open the **V**iew menu and choose **O**utliner or click the Outliner View icon in the tool palette. Use Outliner view to quickly add, edit, and arrange slide show text. Because Presentations doesn't have to draw fancy fonts to the screen in this view, it can be much faster than using Slide Editor view. Furthermore, Outliner view enables you to see the text for several slides at once so you can evaluate the logical flow of the information you're presenting. Figure 4.1 illustrates some of the basic techniques for working in Outliner view.

Tip

To quickly return to Slide Editor view for any slide, double-click on the slide while in any other view.

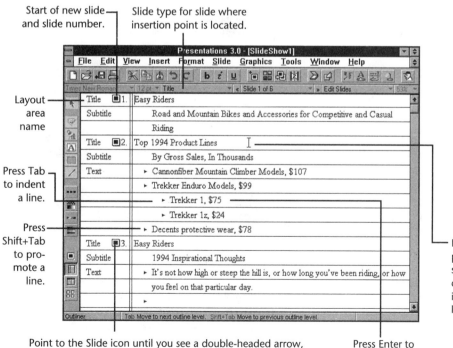

Start of new slide and slide number.

Slide type for slide where insertion point is located.

Layout area name

Press Tab to indent a line.

Press Shift+Tab to promote a line.

Fig. 4.1
Just as you would plot out a slide show on a piece of notebook paper, you can use Outliner view to plan and arrange the information you want to present.

Drag the I-beam pointer over text to select it, or point and click to position the insertion point in a line.

Point to the Slide icon until you see a double-headed arrow, then click to select all slide text. Click-and-drag up or down to move the slide to another location in the show.

Press Enter to add a new line.

Adding a new slide in Outliner view is a slightly different process than adding a slide in Slide Editor view, so it's worth examining here:

1. Click to place the insertion point anywhere in the text of the slide after which you want to insert the new slide.

2. Open the **S**lide menu and choose **A**dd Slides or click the Add Slides icon in the Toolbar to display the Add Slide dialog box.

3. (Optional) Specify the Number of **S**lides to add by typing a new number or clicking the incrementor buttons.

4. Click and hold the left mouse button on the **T**emplate pop-up list button and drag to choose a slide template.

5. Click OK to close the dialog box and insert the new slide into the slide show. This inserts a Slide icon and a blank line, the slide title layout area, as shown on the left side of figure 4.2.

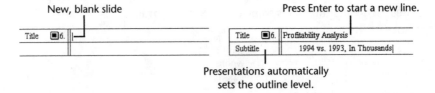

Fig. 4.2
Adding a new slide
in Outliner view.

6. Type the slide title and press Enter. Presentations indents the next line to the appropriate outline level, which in the example shown in figure 4.2 is for the subtitle layout area.

7. You should be finished with data entry at this point if you're creating a title slide. If you're creating a text, bullet, or combination slide, press Enter to add the rest of your text. Presentations automatically indents for bullets.

> **Caution**
>
> Even if you're not creating a text, bullet, or combination slide, Presentations enables you to add more text for bullets. When you change back to Slide Editor view, however, that text disappears. Make sure that you're using the text or bullet chart template if you want that kind of text on your chart. It's best to start with the text, combination, or bullet chart slide type, and then insert a chart later, if needed. Chapter 16, "Inserting Objects into Slides," covers inserting a chart into any slide.

If, on the other hand, you're creating a combination, data, or organization chart slide, and you're finished entering text at this point but aren't finished with your slide, use the next step.

8. Change to Slide Editor view to enter the data for all chart layout areas.

The top outline level for each slide and all the supporting levels are sometimes called the *outline family*. To select all the text for a slide or outline family, point to the icon for that slide (beside its slide number) until the pointer becomes a double-headed arrow, and then click. This highlights all the slide's text. To drag the slide and all its contents to a new location in the outline, select the slide as just described, point to the Slide icon, and click-and-drag the slide up or down to its new location. As you drag, a red horizontal bar indicates where the slide will be positioned when you release the mouse button. Similarly, you can point to any smaller chunk of selected text and drag it to a new location.

To delete one or more slides, simply position the cursor in the slide and choose **S**lide **D**elete Slide(s). Then click **Y**es when Presentations asks you to confirm the deletion.

When editing an outline, you can use all the normal text-editing techniques (described in more depth in Chapter 6, "Adding and Editing Text"), including cutting, copying, and pasting information; and dragging and dropping selected text. In addition, Outliner view is an ideal place to perform spell checking and find-and-replace operations (described in Chapter 6 as well), because Presentations can move through the text quickly. Pressing the right mouse button while in Outliner view displays a QuickMenu listing some of these operations.

To delete an entire line in Outliner view, highlight the contents of the line and press Backspace. Presentations deletes the line entirely, including the slide layout area name at the left. The insertion point jumps up to the end of the preceding line.

Troubleshooting

I deleted some text or an entire line from my outline, but now I want it back and Undo isn't available. Have I lost my work?

You can get the text back. Rather than using the Undo feature, open the **E**dit menu and choose Undelete. In the dialog box that appears, click **R**estore.

Setting Outline Levels

You easily can promote and demote outline levels within the outliner—not only within a bullet list, but for all parts of the slide. Look at slide 3 in figure 4.1, for example. Suppose that you want the Subtitle line "1994 Inspirational Thoughts" to be promoted to a title. Simply click on that subtitle line and press Shift+Tab to promote the line; Presentations changes the layout area name at the far left side of the line to Title. Press the Tab key to demote (indent) any selected line or line containing the insertion point, and press Shift+Tab to promote any line.

Working in Slide List View

Opening the **V**iew menu and choosing Slide **L**ist or clicking the Slide List View icon in the palette moves to Slide List view, shown in figure 4.3. By default, this view lists the slides by number and title, and indicates the transition and advance settings (used when displaying the show on-screen) for each slide. You can customize this view to also show the settings for slide type, Go To keys (which enable you to specify a key to jump to a particular slide), speaker notes, and sounds.

Right-click to display a dialog box that enables you to change a setting (determined by the heading) for the current slide.

List heading bar

Fig. 4.3
You can use the Slide List to quickly view and change several settings for slides—in particular, the settings for automating a slide show.

Current slide

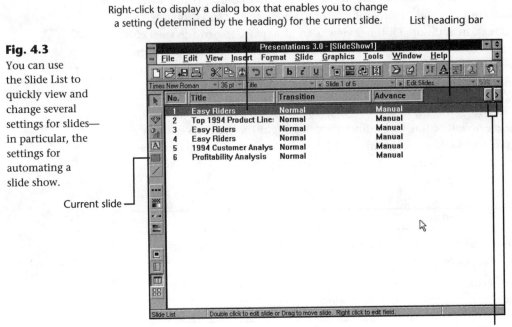

Use to scroll left and right through the list headings.

Basically, you use the Slide List view much like other views. Click a slide to select it (make it the current slide). Drag a slide to a new location. Use the **A**dd Slides and **D**elete Slide(s) commands from the **S**lide menu as needed to add and delete new slides to the lineup.

This view's unique feature it that it enables you to right-click to display a dialog box for changing certain settings (you can't change the slide number or title). Here's an example of how this feature works:

1. Click a slide in the list to make it the current slide.

2. Point to the column for the setting you want to change. The heading for that column (in the list heading bar) indicates the setting. You could point to the Transition column, for example.

3. Right click on the column to display a dialog box for changing that setting. Figure 4.4 shows the dialog box that appears when you right-click the Transition column.

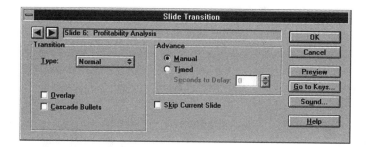

Fig. 4.4
Right-clicking a column in the Slide List displays a dialog box so that you can change that setting. This is the dialog box for setting Transitions.

4. Adjust the dialog box settings as needed and click OK to return to the Slide List and display your change. (Later chapters deal with the details of using these dialog boxes.)

By default, the Slide List shows No., Title, Transition, and Advance headings. To add a Slide List heading, point to the gray spacer area on the list heading bar (you have to scroll to the right with the buttons on the right side of your screen if the spacer area isn't visible) and click the right mouse button to display the pop-up menu. Click one of the other headings to add it to the list heading bar. By default, you can add headings for SlideType, Go To Keys, Notes, and Sounds; if one of the default headings has been deleted, it also appears on the QuickMenu so that you can add it back to the list.

To delete a heading from the list heading bar, simply point to it, press and hold the left mouse button, and drag it down off the bar. Release the mouse button, and the heading (and all the column entries) disappear. To move a list heading to another location, simply drag it left or right. Suppose that you want to move the title heading in figure 4.3 to the left of the No. heading. Simply point to the title heading and click-and-drag the No. heading.

Rearranging the Show with Slide Sorter

The Slide Sorter view presents thumbnails of each slide to give you a visual overview of the slide show. It is most frequently used to rearrange the order of the slides. To change to Slide Sorter view, open the **V**iew menu and choose Slide **S**orter or click the Slide Sorter View icon in the palette. You see a view of your slide show that resembles figure 4.5.

Fig. 4.5
The Slide Sorter view shows thumbnails of your slide to give you a visual overview of how the show will progress.

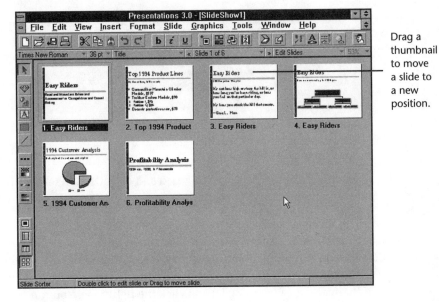

Drag a thumbnail to move a slide to a new position.

Using the Slide Sorter view is very straightforward. Simply drag a thumbnail to a new position. As you drag, a red bar indicates where the slide will be inserted when you release the mouse button. As for other views, you can add and delete slides, add notes, change masters, and more from this view. To select a slide, click on its thumbnail; then issue the menu command you want. Or, right-click on a slide thumbnail to display a QuickMenu.

Making Other View Adjustments

There are several other options on the **V**iew menu that enable you to control the screen appearance in Slide Editor view for more efficient editing. Displaying a grid can be very helpful when you're trying to precisely line up objects on a slide, for example. The next few sections describe the remaining **V**iew menu options.

Using a Grid

As just mentioned, a grid is an effective tool in enabling you to align objects, particularly when you're moving and resizing layout areas and graphics on the slide. You even can use a feature that makes objects "snap to" the grid for perfect alignment. Gridlines appear on-screen only; they don't print.

To toggle the grid display on and off, open the **V**iew menu and choose **G**rid/ Snap **G**rid or press Alt+Shift+F8. Figure 4.6 shows a slide with the grid displayed. To specify that objects should "snap to" or align against the nearest gridlines when you move or resize the object, use the Snap To feature. To toggle this feature on and off, open the **V**iew menu and choose **G**rid/Snap, **S**nap to Grid or press Alt+F8. The grid does not have to be displayed to snap objects to it.

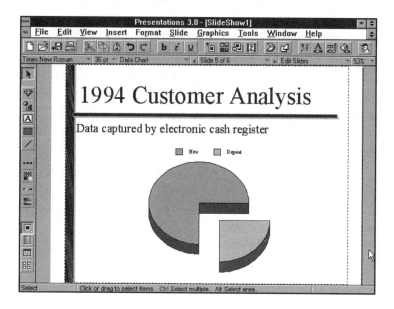

Fig. 4.6
A grid can help you align objects in Slide Editor view.

Understanding the Basics

You can customize the settings for grids, changing the spacing of gridlines and more. Use these steps to customize the grid:

1. Open the **V**iew menu and choose **G**rid/Snap, Grid/Snap **O**ptions. The Grid/Snap Options dialog box appears (see fig. 4.7).

Fig. 4.7

Setting the Grid/ Snap options.

Sets the spacing for the actual gridlines, whether or not they're displayed.

Specifies how many gridlines are actually displayed. For example, 4 denotes that every 4th gridline is displayed

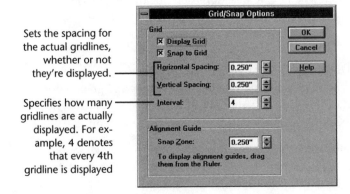

2. If desired, use the Displa**y** Grid and **S**nap to Grid check boxes to turn on and off those options.

3. Change the H**o**rizontal Spacing and **V**ertical Spacing settings, if desired, by clicking the text boxes and typing new values or using the incrementor buttons. These settings determine the spacing between the actual gridlines, whether or not all of them are displayed.

4. Use the **I**nterval setting to determine how many of the gridlines actually display when you choose to view the grid. Choosing 6, for example, means that one out of every 6 gridlines is displayed. To change this setting, click in the text box and type a new value or use the incrementor buttons.

5. Change the Snap **Z**one for alignment guides if you've created any with the ruler (see "Displaying the Toolbar and Ruler," later in this chapter). Click in the text box and type a new setting or use the incrementor buttons to change the value.

Zooming

The zoom settings control how large or small the slide appears on-screen. By default, the zoom is set at about 53 percent (it may be more or less depending on the page layout for the slide) so that the full slide fits in the drawing area in Slide Editor view. *Zooming in* increases the zoom percentage so that the slide contents look larger on-screen. *Zooming out* decreases the zoom percentage so that slide contents look smaller on-screen. Figure 4.8 shows a slide show that's zoomed in to 150 percent size.

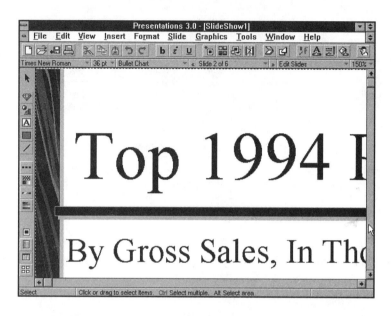

Fig. 4.8
Zooming in
to 150 percent.
In contrast, zooming out to a lower
percentage makes
all the screen
contents look
smaller rather
than larger.

There are two ways to zoom: you can use the options on the **V**iew menu or you can use the Power Bar. The zoom options available through each of these methods are similar, but not all options are available through either method. Table 4.2 lists the available zooming options.

Table 4.2   Zooming Options

Menu (Power Bar)	Description
(%)	Zooms to the specified percentage.
Zoom Area (Zoom To Area)	Select, then drag magic wand pointer over an area to zoom in only on that area.
Full Page	Displays the whole page of the document in the drawing area. Even the margins are visible. Whether this makes the page appear larger or smaller depends on the page layout.
Margin Size	Displays all of the slide contents (except for margin areas that don't fit) in the available drawing or work area.

(continues)

Table 4.2 Continued	
Menu (Power Bar)	**Description**
Selected Objects (Selected)	If you've selected any objects such as layout areas on-screen, zooms in on them.
Actual Size	Zooms to the size the slide would print at, as specified by the page setup.
Screen Size	Zooms to the size the slide would be if displayed on-screen in a show. Does not display the slide without the Presentations window.
Previous View	Returns you to the view before you last used zoom.
Zoom In	Zooms in the view 20 percent.
Zoom Out	Zooms out the view 20 percent.

Tip

To really preview your slides, use the **P**lay Slide Show command from the **S**lide menu, described in Chapter 18, "Creating and Viewing the On-Screen Show."

To use the **View** menu to adjust the zoom percentage, choose **Z**oom from the **View** menu, and then click the option you want from the submenu that appears. To use the Power Bar, click the button displaying a percentage at the far right end of the Power Bar, and then click the zoom option you want.

Displaying the Toolbar and Ruler

The **View** menu enables you to toggle the display of the Toolbar and ruler on and off. The ruler, shown in figure 4.9, is useful for precisely positioning objects on a slide because it provides vertical and horizontal units of measurement; the rulers start numbering at zero from the actual edge of the page (determined by the page setup), not from the margin. A moving mark on each ruler indicates the current pointer (or object) position.

To turn on the Toolbar or ruler display (if they're not already displayed, open the **View** menu and choose Tool**b**ar or **View R**uler (or press Alt+Shift+F3). To turn off the display for the Toolbar or ruler, choose the **View** menu command again, or right click the Toolbar/ruler to display a QuickMenu and choose the QuickMenu option to hide or toggle off the Toolbar/ruler display.

Note that you can use the ruler to set up alignment guides for precisely aligning objects; the objects "snap to" the guides, as they would to the grid. Suppose that you want to print a slide on letterhead so that the top two inches of the page must be blank. Set up an alignment guide at the two-inch mark so that you have a boundary. To create an alignment guide, point to the horizontal or vertical ruler, press and hold the left mouse button, and drag the alignment guide to the position you want on the slide, as shown in figure 4.10. Because you cannot turn off the "snap to" feature of alignment guides, it's often best simply to delete an alignment guide if it's no longer needed. Do so by dragging it off the slide. To clear all guides, right-click the ruler to display its QuickMenu and choose **C**lear Guides or use the **G**rid/Snap **C**lear Guides command from the **V**iew menu.

Moving marks indicate the
current pointer position.

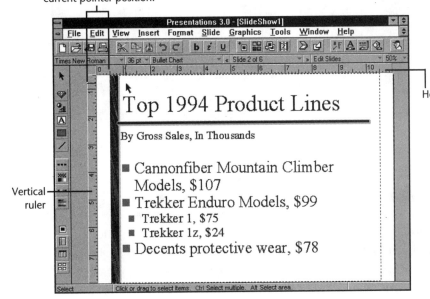

Vertical
ruler

Fig. 4.9
Use the rulers to
precisely position
objects.

Horizontal ruler

Troubleshooting

I turned on the ruler, and it appeared with some really weird measurement units that I don't even recognize and can't use. How can I change it to inches?

The default ruler measurement is a preference. To change this particular preference, open the **E**dit menu and choose Preferences; then double-click the **D**isplay icon. In the Display dialog box, click on the Display and **E**ntry of Numbers pop-up list and drag to choose inches. For more on setting preferences, see Chapter 5, "Basic Customizing."

Fig. 4.10
You can use the
ruler to add
alignment guides
that help you
precisely position
objects at desig-
nated measure-
ments.

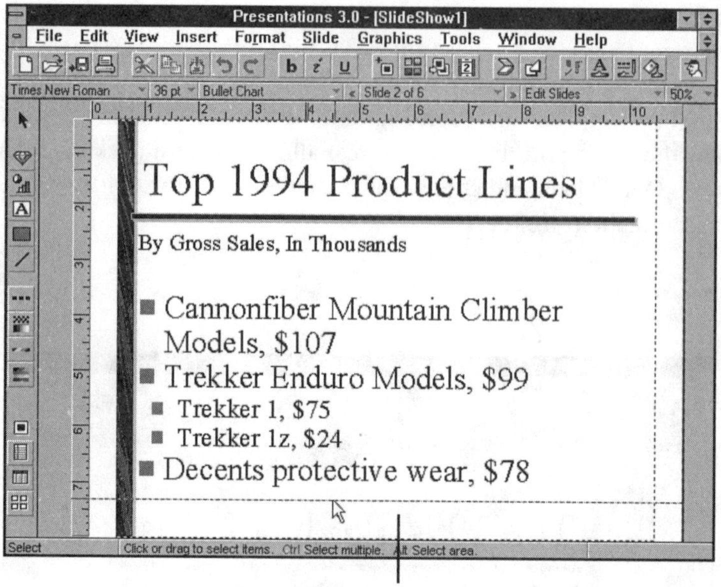

Dragging an alignment guide down
from the horizontal ruler.

Working in Draft Mode

If your computer doesn't have a lot of RAM (random-access memory) or just
plain slows down when you're working with charts and graphics, consider
working in Draft mode. This mode suppresses the display of colors, fills, and
patterns, yielding a "wireframe" view of your slide that redraws quickly on-
screen when you make a change (see fig. 4.11). Don't worry. Even if you've
selected this view on-screen, your slide still will print correctly. To turn on
and off Draft mode, open the **V**iew menu and choose **D**raft Mode (or press
Ctrl+F5).

Turning the Crosshair On and Off

You can display a crosshair pointer that clearly indicates the mouse position
and extends to the edges of the drawing area (see fig. 4.12). The crosshair
pointer, especially when used with the ruler, increases your precision when
you're drawing and aligning objects. Suppose that you want to draw an object that aligns at the left with the indented bullets in figure 4.12. You would
click the tool you need to draw the object and then position the crosshair
pointer as shown in that figure (so that the vertical guideline aligns with the
bullets). Next, you would draw your object. To turn on and off the crosshair
pointer, open the **V**iew menu and choose Cross**h**air.

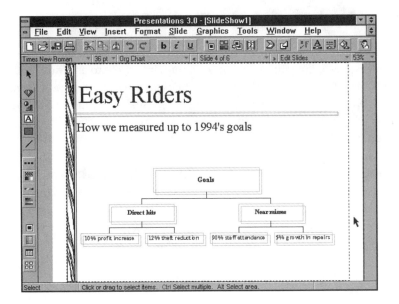

Fig. 4.11
Draft mode displays only a "wireframe" view of your slide, speeding up the capability to make changes.

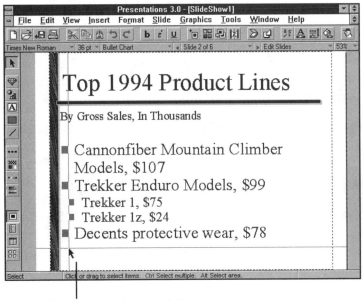

Fig. 4.12
Use the crosshair pointer to align new objects with existing ones.

Positioning the crosshair pointer so that a new object aligns at the left with the indented bullet text.

I

Understanding the Basics

Viewing Multiple Slide Shows

At times you may need to have access to more than one slide show at once. You may want to copy information from one slide show to another, for example. To open a new slide show without closing those that already are open, use the **O**pen command from the **F**ile menu as usual. Opening a slide show makes it the current or active slide show (the show displayed on-screen). You can work in only one slide show at a time—the current slide show.

Changing the Current (Displayed) Slide Show

If you have more than one slide show open at a time, you need to move between slide shows. Click to pull down the **W**indow menu and then click on the name of the slide show you want to go to. Presentations makes your selection the active slide show and displays it on-screen.

Cascading and Tiling

When you have multiple slide shows open in Presentations, you have two options for displaying them simultaneously: *cascading* and *tiling*. Choosing **C**ascade from the **W**indow menu resizes and "stacks" the slide show windows, as shown in figure 4.13, placing the active slide show on top of the stack. Choosing **T**ile from the **W**indow menu resizes the open slide show windows and shapes them so that they line up against one another and fill the drawing area, as shown in figure 4.14. To make a different slide show active in cascaded or tiled view, click its window title bar.

Fig. 4.13
Cascading windows stacks them on-screen and places the window for the active slide show on top of the stack.

The colored title bar is the active show; click another show's title bar to make it active.

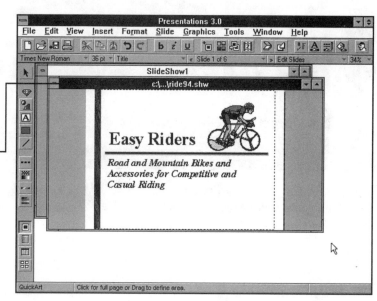

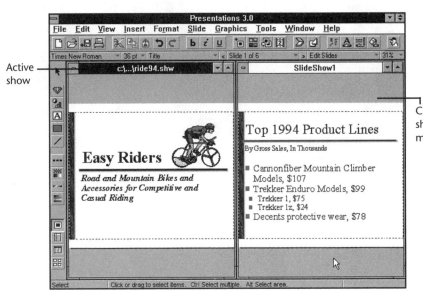

Active show

Fig. 4.14
Tiling open slide shows fills the drawing area with the slide show windows.

Click another show window to make it active.

Understanding the Basics

From Here...

This chapter showed you how using Presentations' viewing options can increase dramatically the speed with which you create a slide show. Using the Outliner dramatically simplifies the process of entering and organizing the text for your presentation, for example, before you even have to worry about setting up the slide charts and graphics. For more information about other ways to view your slide show or change the view, refer to these chapters:

■ Chapter 15, "Working with Masters, Templates, and Backgrounds," describes how to change to the view for each of those elements and set them up to meet your own preferences. The chapter also describes how to save unique masters, templates, and backgrounds.

■ Chapter 17, "Printing and Saving Your Slide Show: Basics and Other Considerations," tackles the information you need to know to get your slide show to look as good on overhead film or paper as it does on-screen.

■ Chapter 18, "Creating and Viewing the On-Screen Show," explains what you need to do to create a presentation to run on a computer screen, including how to adjust some of the options found in Slide List view (described in this chapter).

■ Chapter 20, "Customizing with Macros, Toolbars, and Menus," describes not only how to automate repetitive or complicated procedures with macros, but also how to create and display personalized Toolbars and menus.

Chapter 5

Basic Customizing

Early computer programs were one size fits all, for the most part. If you were using a word processor to write a letter in Spanish and wanted to have the program check the letter's spelling, forget it! All the program could deal with was U.S. English.

WordPerfect Presentations 3.0 for Windows, in contrast, offers so many customizing options that this book needs a whole chapter about them! This chapter introduces you to all the choices you have when setting up Presentations to run just the way you want it to, including the following:

- Setting default file directories, startup display options, date formats, language, printing, backup options, and more

- Changing the entries in your QuickList

- Printing or hiding the QuickList

- Setting up and using QuickFinder Indexes for searches

- Working with QuickFinder options

Setting Preferences

Preference settings control how Presentations behaves. You can change any or all of these settings to tailor Presentations so that it fits you like a well-made suit. Presentations offers 11 categories of preferences, and each is described in turn in this chapter.

To display the preferences categories and to begin the process of setting preferences, open the **E**dit menu and choose Prefere**n**ces to display the Preferences dialog box (see fig. 5.1). To choose a preferences category, double-click

Tip

Every preference category dialog box contains a **H**elp button you can click for more help on the options in that dialog box.

its icon or open the **P**references menu and choose its name. Choosing a preferences category displays a dialog box where you can change the settings for that category. Determine the settings for that category, and then click OK to return to the Preferences dialog box. When you finish setting all the categories, click **C**lose to close the Preferences dialog box. The next several sections describe each of the categories.

Fig. 5.1
The Preferences dialog box displays an icon for each of the 11 preference categories.

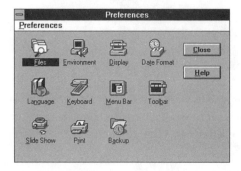

Files

File preferences tell Presentations where to look for files of a particular type when it needs to access them, or where you're likely to want to store files of a particular type. If you create a new slide show file and save it, for example, Presentations saves it to the **D**rawings/SlideShows directory specified in the File Preferences dialog box, unless you choose another directory while saving. To set file preferences, double-click the **F**iles icon in the Preferences dialog box or open the **P**references menu and choose **F**iles. The File Preferences dialog box appears (see fig. 5.2).

Fig. 5.2
Use the File Preferences dialog box to specify where Presentations stores or accesses files of the specified types.

Type a path name...   ...or click to use
                             the Select Directory dialog box.

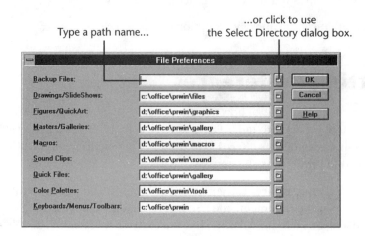

To change the default directory for a particular file type, type or edit the path name in the text box beside it, or click the File Folder icon to use the Select Directory dialog box to change the directory. When you're finished, click OK to return to the Preferences dialog box.

Environment

Environment preferences determine the default beep options, the language your computer uses, whether the QuickList is displayed by default, and what kind of document Presentations displays when you start it. To set environment preferences, double-click the **E**nvironment icon in the Preferences dialog box or open the **P**references menu and choose **E**nvironment. The dialog box shown in figure 5.3 appears. Choose the options you want and click OK to finish.

Choose a new language for menus, etc., if you've installed another language module.

Choose whether you want to display a blank drawing or document instead of the Document Selection dialog box on startup.

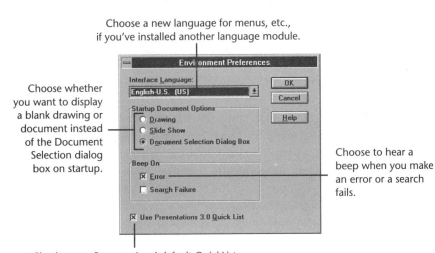

Choose to hear a beep when you make an error or a search fails.

Fig. 5.3
Setting preferences for startup files, beeping, and language.

Check to use Presentations' default QuickList.

Display

Use the Display preferences to determine the default option settings for numerous screen, menu, editing, and measurement options. From the Preferences dialog box, double-click the **D**isplay icon or open the **P**references menu and choose **D**isplay to open the Display Preferences dialog box (see fig. 5.4). The Screen Options group enables you to display the ruler, grid, or pointer position by default. The Menu Options group turns shortcut-key display on and off, and enables you to choose whether to display the last few open file names at the bottom of the **F**ile menu. You use the Editing Options group to choose whether to use handy editing tools, such as Draft mode, by default.

And the Units of Measure pop-up lists enable you to specify a unit of measure used to display measurements (such as on the ruler) or the units Presentations uses when it asks you to enter a measurement value. You also can specify the measurement units used in the status bar display. Make your changes in this dialog box and then click OK.

Fig. 5.4
Use the Display Preferences dialog box to control the defaults for several on-screen features.

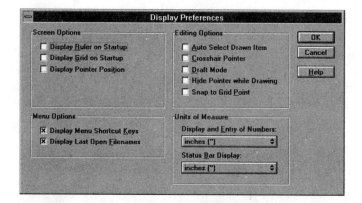

Date Format

Double-clicking the Date Format icon or opening the Preferences menu and choosing Date Format displays the Date/Time Format dialog box. This dialog box controls the default format Presentations uses whenever you insert the current date and time into slide text with the Insert Date command. The current format is shown at the top of the dialog box. To change that format, choose another format from the Predefined Formats list or click the Custom button to display the Custom Date/Time Format dialog box (see fig. 5.5). To create the custom code, use the Edit Date Format text box, which contains date codes enclosed in brackets []. To remove a date code, highlight it in the Edit Date Format text box and press Delete. To add a new data code, click in the Edit Date Format text box to position the insertion point where you want to insert the new code, and then double-click the name of the code you want to insert in the Date Codes or Time Codes list. Click OK to close this dialog box, and click OK again to return to the Preferences dialog box.

Language

If you installed a separately purchased language module, you can use the Language Preferences setting to use that language when entering and editing text. In the Preferences dialog box, double-click the Language icon or choose Language from the Preferences menu. In the Language dialog box that appears, click a choice in the Current Language list and then click OK.

Previews your custom format

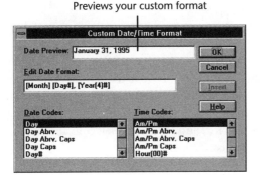

Fig. 5.5
You can create
a custom date
format that will be
used whenever you
choose **I**nsert **D**ate.

Keyboard

Many WordPerfect applications enable you to create and save custom keyboard setups, where you can assign shortcut keys to particular functions. Presentations enables you to assign keyboard shortcuts to execute functions, *keyboard scripts* (a sequence of keystrokes), and macros; it also enables you to launch other programs. If you have a client named "Rocky Road Mountain Bikes," for example, and you know you will be creating numerous slide shows for that client, you can create a script and assign it to the F6 key so that pressing F6 types Rocky Road Mountain Bikes at the cursor location. Chapter 20, "Customizing with Macros, Toolbars, and Menus," explains how to create custom keyboard setups. To use preferences to load a custom keyboard, double-click the **K**eyboard icon in the Preferences dialog box or open the **P**references menu and choose **K**eyboard. The Keyboard Preferences dialog box appears. Click the name of the keyboard you want to use in the **K**eyboards list and choose **S**elect to close the dialog box and activate it.

Menu Bar

Just as you can create custom keyboard setups, you can create custom menu bars and pull-down menus (described in Chapter 20), and use preferences to load the menu setup of your choice. The custom menus can activate features, run macros or scripts, or launch a program. To load a custom menu bar, double-click the **M**enu Bar icon in the Preferences dialog box or open the **P**references menu and choose **M**enu Bar. In the Menu Bar Preferences dialog box, click on a menu name in the **M**enu Bars list and click **S**elect to accept your change and return to the Preferences dialog box.

Toolbar

Last but not least, you can create your own Toolbars and display them in Presentations using the Preferences dialog box. Custom Toolbar icons (which you learn to create in Chapter 20), can activate features, run macros or scripts, or launch a program. To load a custom Toolbar, double-click the Toolbar icon in the Preferences dialog box or open the **P**references menu and choose Tool**b**ar. In the Toolbar Preferences dialog box, click on a menu name in the Tool**b**ars list, and then click **S**elect to accept your change and return to the Preferences dialog box.

Slide Show

You can set several preferences for starting a new slide show and for the default master gallery by double-clicking the **S**lide Show icon in the Preferences dialog box or by choosing **S**lide Show from the **P**references menu to display the Slide Show Preferences dialog box (see fig. 5.6). Simply set the options you want, and then click OK to close the Slide Show Preferences dialog box. The options you can set in this dialog box follow:

- *Startup View.* Specifies which design view in which to display the new slide show.

- *Master.* Lets you choose the default master for a new slide show. Click the File icon beside this text box to display the Select File dialog box so that you can choose a different master file.

- *Template.* Sets the default slide Template that appears on the template pop-up button in the New Slide Show dialog box, or the default type for the first slide in the show if you're not using the New Slide Show dialog box.

- *Use New Slide Show Dialog Box.* Specifies whether to display that dialog box when creating a new slide show or to just open the show to the first slide, applying the default master and slide type.

- *Number of Slides per Row.* Specifies the number of slide thumbnails shown in each row in Slide Sorter view.

- *Save Slide List Layout on Exit.* If you changed the layout of the Slide List view for a slide show as described in Chapter 4, "Adjusting the View," turning on this option saves that new layout when you exit the slide show.

■ *Page Size and Margins.* Specifies whether new slide shows use the master's page setup settings (margins, for example) or Presentations' default page settings.

Fig. 5.6
Use the Slide Show Preferences dialog box to set defaults for new slide shows.

Print

To save yourself some time when printing, you can change a few default settings in the Preferences dialog box so that those settings already are selected when you initiate printing. From the Preferences dialog box, double-click Print or open the **P**references menu and choose P**r**int to display the Print Preferences dialog box (see fig. 5.7). Change the settings you want and click OK.

Default number of copies to print.

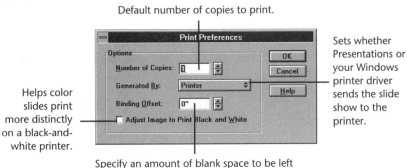

Helps color slides print more distinctly on a black-and-white printer.

Sets whether Presentations or your Windows printer driver sends the slide show to the printer.

Specify an amount of blank space to be left at the left edge of all pages for binding.

Fig. 5.7
Choosing preferences for printing.

Backup

Use the Backup preferences to save specialized copies of your slide show files to increase the chance that you'll be able to recover your work if a power or equipment failure occurs. In the Preferences dialog box, double-click the Backup icon or open the **P**references menu and choose **B**ackup to display the Backup Preferences dialog box (see fig. 5.8).

Fig. 5.8
Using Backup Preferences features creates specialized copies of your slide show files that you can retrieve later if needed.

Tip
If you need to use a backup file, open the **F**ile menu, choose the **O**pen command, and choose a TMP or BK! file from the File**n**ame list. Then click Open to open it.

Turning on **T**imed Document Backup and adjusting the **E**very Minutes setting creates an automatic backup file at the specified interval. These files are named in the format ~{PRn.TMP, with n representing the slide show window number. Turning on **O**riginal Document Backup creates an automatic backup every time you save a slide show file. With this option enabled, saving renames the previously saved file with the BK! extension, and names the new file with the SHW extension. After you set your Backup preferences, click OK.

Customizing the QuickList

Chapter 2, "Developing a Slide Show," explained how to use the QuickList in file-related dialog boxes to quickly display a prenamed file or directory in the dialog box. You may recall that Presentations comes with some predefined QuickList entries such as a Drawings/Presentations directory (which is C:\OFFICE\PRWIN\DRAWINGS). The QuickList name certainly is friendlier and easier to remember than the full directory path name.

The next few sections explain how you can modify your QuickList display. You learn how to add new QuickList entries, as well as how to change or remove existing entries. In addition, you see how to print the QuickList names and how to choose whether to display the QuickList in dialog boxes.

Adding, Editing, or Deleting a QuickList Entry

Clicking the Quick**L**ist pop-up list button in any dialog box where it appears (such as Open File or Save As) or pointing to the QuickList and clicking the right mouse button displays a list of options for working with the QuickList entries.

Use the **A**dd Item choice to display the dialog box shown in figure 5.9. To specify the directory or file you want to add a QuickList entry for, you can type the directory path and file name (if any) including wild-card characters to specify files of a certain type (*.SHW, for example, shows all slide show files) in the Directory/**F**ilename text box. An example entry might be **c:\client1\sept*.shw**, which would display all slide show files that begin with *sept* in the \CLIENT1 directory on drive C. If you can't recall the full path name, click the File Folder icon beside the Directory/**F**ilename text box to display the Select Directory dialog box, which is nearly identical to the Open File dialog box. Use the Dri**v**es, **D**irectories, and File**n**ame lists as de- scribed for opening a file to select the directory (and file) that you want to add to the QuickList. Click OK to return to the Add QuickList Item dialog box. In the **D**escription text box, type the name for the selected directory/file that you want to appear in the QuickList. Click OK to close the dialog box and add the entry you just created.

Enter the name of the entry as you want it to appear in the QuickList.

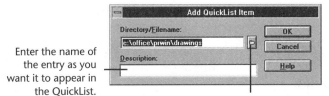

Click to display the Select Directory dialog box.

Fig. 5.9
The Add QuickList Item dialog box enables you to specify the directory or file you want to add to the QuickList, as well as a plain- English description that will actually appear in the list.

To change the directory, file name, or description of any QuickList entry, click the Quick**L**ist pop-up list button or point to the QuickList and click the right mouse button, and then click **E**dit Item. The Edit QuickList Item dialog box appears, which is virtually identical to the Add QuickList Item dialog box in figure 5.9. As described for adding a QuickList entry, use the Directory/ **F**ilename and **D**escription options to make your changes, and then click OK.

Deleting a QuickList entry is even more brief. Click the entry you want to delete in the QuickList to highlight it. Right-click or click the Quick**L**ist pop- up list button and click De**l**ete Item. Presentations displays a dialog box ask- ing whether you really want to delete the entry. Click **Y**es to complete the deletion.

Printing the QuickList

You can print the QuickList. To print the whole list, click the QuickList pop-up list button or point to the QuickList and click the right mouse button, and then click **P**rint QuickList. The Print QuickList dialog box appears. Change the printer setup or font if desired, and then click **P**rint to continue.

Displaying or Hiding the QuickList and Directories List

You can specify whether dialog boxes for file operation display the QuickList only, the Directories list only, or both—depending on how you prefer to work and depending on the degree to which you have customized your QuickList. To change the display in this way, click the QuickList pop-up list button or point to the QuickList and click the right mouse button. Then click Show **Q**uickList, Show **D**irectories, or Show **B**oth to make your selection. Note that when you right-click the QuickList, there's an option called **C**hange Default Directory as well. This option enables you to use the QuickList to specify the default directory that will be displayed whenever you open a file dialog box. Simply double-click a QuickList entry to select it, right-click, and then click to ensure that **C**hange Default Directory is checked.

Using QuickFinder Indexes for Custom Searches

Presentations now offers a special feature that compresses the contents of a group of files you specify into a highly compressed, alphabetical list of terms and file information (an *index*), which QuickFinder can search quickly to identify a file for which you're looking. Indexes are so specialized that they can be used only by QuickFinder; you cannot view or print them.

Creating a QuickFinder Index

To create the QuickFinder index, follow these steps:

1. From a file operation dialog box such as Open File or Save As, click the QuickFinder button to display the QuickFinder dialog box, and then click Inde**x**er. Or, in the PRWin 3.0 program group window in Windows Program Manager, double-click the QuickFinder File Indexer icon. Either of these actions opens the QuickFinder File Indexer dialog box shown in figure 5.10.

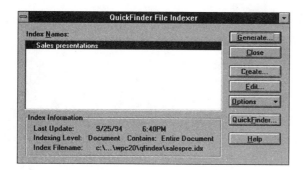

Fig. 5.10
Use this dialog box to create and edit QuickFinder indexes for faster QuickFinder searches.

2. Click Create and the Create Index Name dialog box appears. Type a name for the Index in the **N**ame box (such as **Sales presentations**) and choose OK. The Create Index dialog box appears. This dialog box enables you to specify what directories contain the files that you want to have indexed in the QuickFinder index of the name you just specified, or what specific files to add to that QuickFinder index.

3. To specify each directory or file name, type the name or the directory or file you want to add in the Add **D**irectory (and File Pattern) text box, and then click **A**dd. Repeat to add as many directories or files as you want to the list. Figure 5.11 shows the Create Index dialog box with a list of several selections in the Directories **t**o Index list.

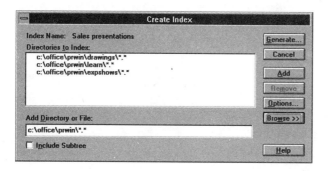

Fig. 5.11
Specifying several directories to add to a QuickFinder Index.

4. (Optional) Click the **O**ptions button to display the Individual Index Options dialog box. This dialog box enables you to exclude files with certain file-name extensions, include only WordPerfect files, index the entire document or only parts of it, choose whether to index numbers, and choose how to treat extended characters. Click OK to close this dialog box after you specify the options you need in it.

Tip
Clicking the
Browse button
extends the Create
Index dialog box,
displaying Drives,
Directories, and
Filenames lists so
that you can
point-and-click to
find directories
and files. Display
each directory or
file, and then click
Add. Click Browse
again to return the
dialog box to
normal.

5. Click Include Subtree to also index the files in all subdirectories under the directories contained in the Directories to Index list.

6. Click Generate. QuickFinder creates the index file of the files and directories you listed and gives it the name you specified.

7. Click OK to close the Index Completed dialog box and return to the QuickFinder File Indexer dialog box, which now displays the name of the new index in the Index Names list.

Searching with a QuickFinder Index

To perform a search with a QuickFinder index file, follow these steps:

1. From a file operation dialog box such as Open File or Save As or from the QuickFinder File Indexer dialog box, click the QuickFinder button to display the QuickFinder dialog box.

2. In the Search For text box, type the text string to search for (such as **Easy Riders**), inserting operators and switches with the Operators button as needed.

3. Under Search In, point to the pop-up list button and click-and-drag to highlight QuickFinder Index. This action tells QuickFinder to search in the QuickFinder Index file specified in the drop-down list box to the right (see fig. 5.12). Click the down arrow to the right of the current index names to display the drop-down list, and then click to select another index.

Fig. 5.12
Choosing
QuickFinder Index
in the Search In
area enables
you to specify
the name of a
QuickFinder index
file to search.

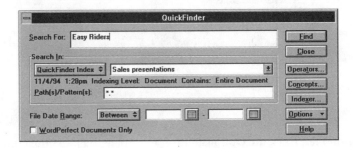

4. Fill out all the other QuickFinder dialog box options as usual, and then click Find to begin the search. Rather than searching numerous slide show files on your hard drive looking for the search text, QuickFinder searches through the specified QuickFinder index file only.

5. QuickFinder displays the results of the search when finished. Click OK to close this dialog box.

Editing a QuickFinder Index

You can select an index file from the Index **N**ames list in the QuickFinder File Indexer dialog box and make changes to it. Use the **O**ptions pop-up list button to perform such operations as deleting, importing, renaming, and moving QuickFinder index files.

> **Note**
>
> Because the index contains only the data that was in the files on the day the index was created, you may need to edit your indexes periodically just to refresh them. Simply use the following procedure without changing any settings in the Edit Index dialog box. In the Index Method dialog box, choose to **U**pdate Index with New or Modified Files (scan only for changes to files), and then click OK. This procedure refreshes your index file.

It's a little bit more complicated to change the list of files and directories compressed in the index file. To edit a QuickFinder index, follow these steps:

1. From a file operation dialog box such as Open File or Save As, click the Quick**F**inder button to display the QuickFinder dialog box, and then click Inde**x**er. Or, in the PRWin 3.0 program group window in Windows Program Manager, double-click the QuickFinder File Indexer icon. Either of these actions opens the QuickFinder File Indexer dialog box.

2. Click to select an index file in the Index **N**ames list, and then click **E**dit. The Edit Index dialog box appears. It's virtually identical to the Create Index dialog box; you choose all the options in the same way.

3. To specify new directories or files to index, type the name of the directory or file you want in the Add **D**irectory (and File Pattern) text box, and then click **A**dd. (You also can use the Bro**w**se button to browse for directories through point-and-click lists.) Repeat to add as many directories or files as you want to the list.

4. To remove a directory from the index, click to select it in the Directories **t**o Index list and click Re**m**ove.

5. (Optional) Click the **O**ptions button to display the Individual Index Options dialog box. Set the options contained there and click OK.

6. Click **In**clude Subtree to also index the files in all subdirectories under the directories contained in the Directories **t**o Index list.

7. Click **G**enerate. The Index Method dialog box appears.

8. Choose whether to **U**pdate Index with New or Modified Files (scan only for changes to files) or **I**ndex All Files (re-index all files in the specified directories, whether or not they have changed). Click OK.

9. Click OK to close the Index Completed dialog box and return to the QuickFinder File Indexer dialog box.

Using QuickFinder Options for Custom Searches

The Options button in the QuickFinder dialog box (displayed by clicking the QuickFinder button in any file operation dialog box) provides even greater flexibility in setting up a search. If used effectively, the options also can save you time by enabling you to recycle your search results. To use these options from the QuickFinder dialog box, simply click the **O**ption button to display the pop-up list of options, and then click the option you want. Use Options to display *summary fields* (key information about a document that's not part of the text of the document but is saved with WordPerfect documents) and the results of the last search, and to reuse search criteria to save time. If you created a slide show that has your company mission statement and you know you frequently will need to reuse that information, for example, you can set up the search criteria to let QuickFinder find that file, and then save those search criteria as a query that you can load again to quickly find the file. Table 5.1 displays the available QuickFinder options.

Table 5.1   The QuickFinder Dialog Box Options and How to Use Them

Option	Description
Estimated Relevance Ranking	Ranks found files based on the estimated number of times per 1,000 words in which the search text appears.
Full Word Count Relevance	Ranks found files based on the number of times the search text appears in each file.
No Summary Fields	Doesn't display any WordPerfect 5.0/5.1/5.2/6.0 document summary fields in the QuickFinder dialog box.

Option	Description
Default Summary Fields	Expands the QuickFinder dialog box to display five default WordPerfect 5.0/5.1/5.2/6.0 document summary fields such as file-creation date. You can enter items to search for in any summary field to have QuickFinder search for files with matching summary field entries.
All Summary Fields	Expands the QuickFinder dialog box to display a scroll box with all WordPerfect 5.0/5.1/5.2/6.0 document summary fields. Use the scroll bar to display the summary fields you want, enter items to search for, and QuickFinder searches for files with matching summary field entries.
Last Search **R**esults	Displays the Search Results list, so you can see the files found during the last QuickFinder search.
Clear	Clears all search criteria that you've entered in the QuickFinder dialog box.
Load Search Query	Loads a previously saved search query (see the next entry).
Save Search Query	Saves all the QuickFinder search options as a query that you can load later, saving you the time of entering all the search criteria again.
Delete Search Query	Deletes a previously saved search query.

From Here...

This chapter explained how to fine-tune WordPerfect Presentations for Windows so that you can use it more efficiently. You learned how to set the preferences in 11 categories—from setting defaults for new slide shows to choosing a different language to use in Presentations. You also learned how to create custom QuickFinder Index files to perform faster searches, and how to use QuickFinder options. At this point, you should have set up everything you need to continue creating your slide shows. You can look forward to these chapters for more information about creating a slide show:

■ Chapter 6, "Adding and Editing Text," explains how to work with text in slide-type layout areas and how to add text wherever you want on a slide. The chapter also explains how to use built-in proofreading features such as the Spell Checker, QuickCorrect, and more.

■ Chapter 7, "Enhancing Text," provides you with the tools for changing formatting of text and text layout areas, and even discusses some text special effects.

■ Chapter 8, "Adding QuickArt to a Slide," explains how to add a graphic touch to any slide using the QuickArt provided with WordPerfect Presentations 3.0 for Windows, and also gives you the basic steps for importing other types of graphics files.

■ Chapter 20, "Customizing with Macros, Toolbars, and Menus," explains how to create custom keyboard, Toolbar, and menu files that you load via the **P**references option on the **E**dit menu, as described earlier in this chapter.

Part II

Editing and Enhancing Your Slide Show

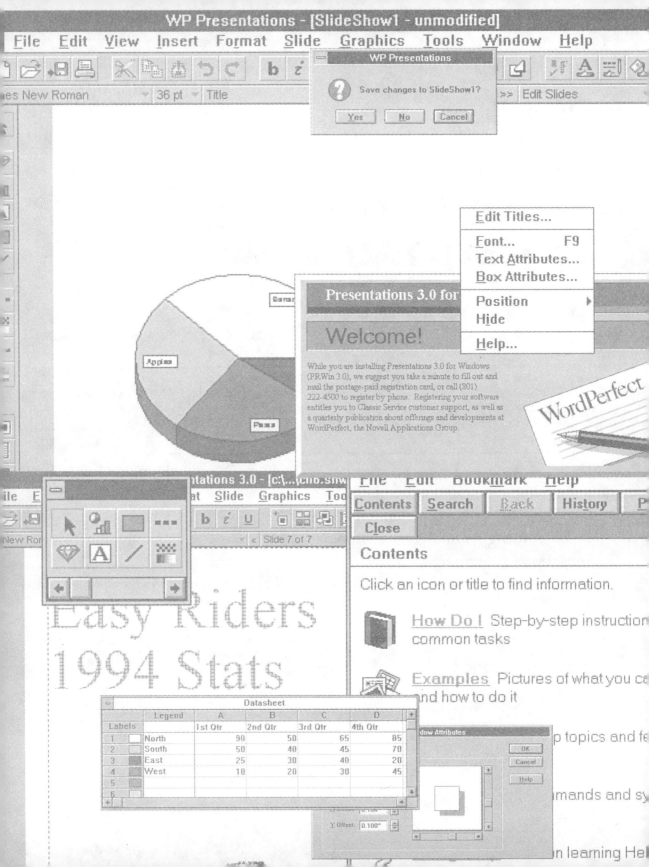

Chapter 6

Adding and Editing Text

Boilerplate designs—that is, preformatted designs you can just plug your data into—such as those provided by the Master Gallery and Slide Types in WordPerfect Presentations 3.0 for Windows can save a lot of time, but they also can impose a lot of limitations. What if you need to add text to explain a particular position on an organization chart slide? What if your printer prints text in a color that's hard to distinguish from the background, and you need to change the color of the text? What if you need to move the text a little to have room for your company logo on a slide? A boilerplate layout doesn't help you in any of these situations.

Presentations offers a great deal of text-handling flexibility. You can position text virtually anywhere you want on a slide, reformat it to change its line spacing, copy it, and more. This chapter explains how to work with slide text and introduces you to the following concepts:

- Understanding the difference between text areas and text lines, and adding each to a slide

- Adding new bullet lists to a slide

- Selecting and changing the contents of text containers

- Changing the formatting of selected text, including kerning, line spacing, fonts, and more

- Repositioning text on a slide

- Enhancing and correcting text with the Spell Checker, Thesaurus, Find and Replace, and QuickCorrect

- Inserting the date and text from other sources

Looking at Text Containers

Think of text areas and text lines as different kinds of containers for the text you add to a slide. Each type of container (or *object*, the term used by WordPerfect) has unique characteristics you should be aware of to use that type effectively. You can add new text in any format to slide types that already have layout areas for text. You also can create completely custom slides in which you design all the text from scratch.

You should add text in a *text area* when you want to add multiple lines of text (such as a paragraph) to a slide, especially if you think you may need to change the way the text wraps (where it breaks) at the end of each line. Text areas enable you to quickly reshape a block of text to fill a particular area without changing the size of the text.

In contrast, add text in a *text line* when you want to add only a single line of text and you later may want to quickly resize the text size and adjust the letter width and spacing between letters so that the text fits in a given area. Figure 6.1 shows an example of each type of text container.

Fig. 6.1
You use text areas to resize blocks of multiple lines of text, and you use text lines to quickly change the font size and letter spacing in a single line of text.

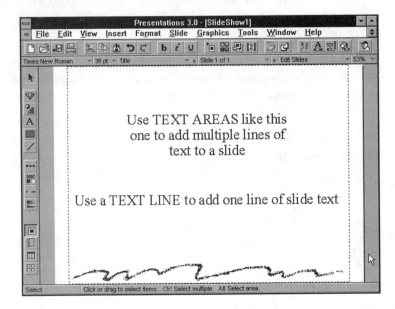

Another type of text container is the bullet chart, which is similar to a text area. Use the bullet chart feature to quickly add lists of data anywhere on the slide. As with text areas, you have complete control over how the text wraps in the bullet chart.

> **Note**
>
> To create a new slide with completely custom text, add a new slide, choosing Background for the Slide **T**ype. A slide is created with the master background but no layout areas. Add the text areas, text lines, and bullet charts you want, along with any other elements such as QuickArt, data objects, or organization charts.

Adding New Text Areas

Choose a text area whenever you have several lines of text to add to a slide, such as a long paragraph cited from another resource or a quotation. Adding new text areas is a simple operation, as the following steps demonstrate:

1. Choose **T**ext Area from the **I**nsert menu or click the Text Object icon in the palette. The mouse pointer changes to a hand holding a dotted-outline box.

2. Point on the slide to the location where you want the upper left corner of the text area to be.

3. Press and hold the left mouse button, and drag to start creating the text area (see fig. 6.2). When the area reaches the width you want, release the mouse button.

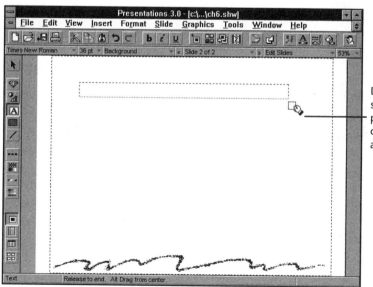

Fig. 6.2
Dragging to create the text area.

Drag this special mouse pointer to create the text area.

4. When you release the mouse button, a hatched outline appears around the area you've drawn, and a blinking vertical insertion cursor appears in the box. Begin typing your text.

5. To let Presentations wrap the text for you, simply continue typing when your first line of text approaches the right border of the text area. When the text fills the line, Presentations makes the text area longer and jumps the insertion point to the beginning of the next line.

6. To wrap a line manually as you're typing, press Enter wherever you want a line to end. Figure 6.3 shows a comparison of lines that were wrapped automatically and manually.

Fig. 6.3
Type the text you want into your text area. Presentations makes the text area longer to accept all the text you enter.

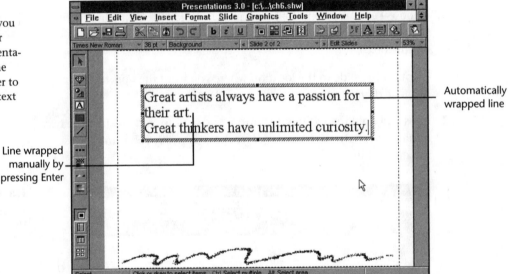

Automatically wrapped line

Line wrapped manually by pressing Enter

7. When you're finished typing, click on a blank area of the slide to make the hatched border disappear, and then click on the Selection tool in the Tool Palette to make the cursor return to normal.

Adding New Text Lines

Choose to add a text line when you want to add a single line of text, such as your company name or a short tag line. The procedure for adding a text line is very similar to the procedure for adding a text area.

Use these steps:

1. Choose Te**x**t Line from the **I**nsert menu. Or, point to the Text Object icon in the palette and hold down the left mouse button to display additional text tools. Drag to the right to move the red selector to the Text Area tool, as shown in figure 6.4. Release the mouse button, and the mouse pointer changes to a cross-hair.

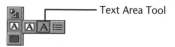
— Text Area Tool

Fig. 6.4
Selecting the
Palette tool to
create text areas.

2. Click on the slide in the location where you want the left side of the text area to start. This places the blinking insertion point on the slide.

3. Begin typing, as shown in figure 6.5.

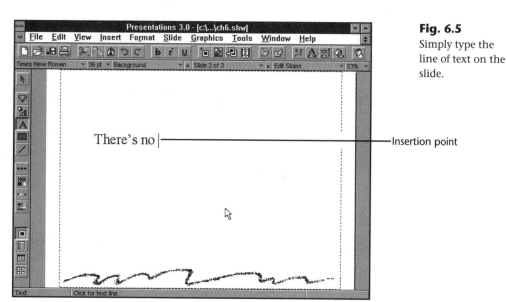
Insertion point

Fig. 6.5
Simply type the
line of text on the
slide.

4. When you're finished typing, click on a blank area of the slide, and then click on the Selection tool in the Tool Palette to make the cursor return to normal.

> **Note**
>
> After you select the Text Line tool, it remains displayed on the palette. To reselect the Text Area tool, point to the Text Line tool and click-and-drag the red selector back to the Text Area tool.

Adding Bullet Lists

If you want to add an additional bullet list (bullet chart) to any slide, the Text Object tool enables you to do so. Suppose that you want to create a text slide with a small list of footnotes at the bottom. To add a new bullet chart to any slide, use these steps:

1. Choose Bullet Chart from the Insert menu. Or, point to the Text Object icon in the palette and hold down the left mouse button to display additional text tools. Drag to the right to move the red selector to the Bullet Chart tool, as shown in figure 6.6. Release the mouse button. The mouse pointer changes to a hand holding a dotted-outline box.

Fig. 6.6
Selecting the
Bullet Chart tool
to add a bullet list
to a slide.

 ———— Bullet Chart Tool

2. Point on the slide to the location where you want the upper left corner of the text area to be.

3. Press and hold the left mouse button, and drag to start creating the bullet-chart area. When the area reaches the width you want, release the mouse button.

4. When you release the mouse button, a hatched outline appears around the area you've drawn, and a bullet character followed by a blinking vertical insertion cursor appears in the box (see fig. 6.7). Begin typing your first bullet item.

Fig. 6.7
Inserting a bullet.

5. Add bullet items and adjust the indention levels by doing the following:

   ■ Press Enter to start a new bullet item.

- Press Tab with the insertion point anywhere in a line to indent it one level.

- Press Shift+Tab with the insertion point anywhere in a line to promote it (move it left) one level.

6. When you're finished typing, click on a blank area of the slide to make the hatched border disappear. Then click on the Selection tool in the Tool Palette to make the cursor return to normal.

> **Note**
>
> After you select the Bullet Chart tool, it remains displayed on the palette. To reselect the Text Area tool, point to the Text Line tool and click-and-drag the red selector back to the Text Area tool.

Selecting and Modifying Text

One of the beauties of creating slides electronically is that you can make improvements to the slides at any time. After you add a text area, text line, or bullet chart to your slide—or fill in a layout area on a slide type—you can select the text within the text container or layout area and edit it, change its font (style), and more. The next several sections describe the modifications you can make to text within the text container.

Selecting Text-Container Contents

The boundaries containing a text area, text line, or bullet chart still exist after you click elsewhere on the slide. The boundaries simply are invisible temporarily. To change the text within a boundary, you have to reinsert the flashing vertical insertion cursor within the boundary. When you do so in a text area or bullet chart, the hatched border reappears. To place the insertion cursor within a text container, simply double-click on the text on the slide. You also can click the text container once, right-click to display the QuickMenu or Open the **E**dit menu, and then choose Ed**i**t Chart. Press Ctrl+Up Arrow and Ctrl+Down Arrow to move the insertion point to the preceding and next text container, respectively.

After you have placed the insertion point in the text container, you may need to select specific text. Suppose that you have a slide with a title containing your company name, *Easy Riders*, and you want to change the slide title to

Tip
You also can use the editing techniques described in the next few sections in Outliner view.

Tip
Text areas, text lines, and bullet charts are *text containers*, or slide areas, that hold text.

II

Enhancing Your Show

1995 Goals. You need to select *Easy Riders* to replace it. When you select text, a reverse highlight appears over the text (see fig. 6.8).

Here are the methods you can use to select text:

- Press and hold down Shift, and then use the arrow keys to extend the selection highlight.

- Point to the start of the text you want to select and click the mouse. Then press and hold Shift, and click just to the right of the last character in the group you want to select.

- Drag over the text to select it.

- Double-click on a word to select that word.

Editing Text

Editing text in Presentations is similar to editing text in word processors (like WordPerfect for Windows). You can position the insertion point and then type to insert more characters, or you can use other editing keys such as the following:

- *Backspace.* Deletes the character to the left (or selected text).

- *Delete.* Deletes the character to the right (or selected text). Choosing **D**elete from the **E**dit menu is the equivalent of this key.

- *Arrow keys.* Moves the insertion point one character or line in the direction specified.

- *Insert.* Toggles between inserting typed characters at the insertion point and having typed characters overwrite text to the right.

- *Home.* Moves the insertion point to the start of a line.

- *End.* Moves the insertion point to the end of a line.

- *PgUp.* Moves the insertion point to the top line.

- *PgDn.* Moves the insertion point to the bottom line.

Moving and Copying Text

You can move selected text within the text container or from one text container to another on the slide. You can use one of two methods—dragging or cutting and pasting—to move text within a container. You're limited to cutting and pasting only if you want to move or copy text from container to container. These two text-editing methods are described next.

Dragging Text to Copy or Move It

To give you even more ways to work efficiently with the mouse, numerous software designers are building *drag-and-drop* editing capabilities into their programs. With drag-and-drop, you can quickly move or copy selected text to a new location within a text area. This is a great technique for rearranging words or moving a bullet-chart entry up or down in the list. To move or copy text with drag-and-drop, use these steps:

1. Within the text container, select the text you want to move or copy as described earlier in this chapter.

2. Point to the text with the mouse. Press and hold the left mouse button. To copy the text instead of moving it, also press and hold the Ctrl key. The mouse pointer changes to a pointer with overlapping outlines of two rectangles. If you're only moving the text, the back rectangle appears as a dotted outline. If you're copying the text, the back rectangle appears as a black filled area.

3. Drag to move or copy the text to a new location, as shown in figure 6.9. When the vertical insertion point reaches the position where you want to place the copied or moved text, release the mouse button.

Troubleshooting

I moved or copied a bullet-chart entry, and the bullet didn't move with it. There's no bullet where the text was inserted, and there is a bullet left behind where the text originally was. Did I forget to do something?

No. You cannot move or copy a bullet along with the text, either in Slide Editor view or Outliner view. You have to add or delete the bullets manually. To delete a bullet, click to place the insertion point just to the right of the bullet and press Backspace. To add a bullet, click to place the insertion point at the end of the preceding line and press Enter.

Fig. 6.9

Dragging-and-dropping enables you to use the mouse to move and copy text. Notice that the mouse pointer looks as if it's carrying sheets of paper with it.

The vertical insertion point shows where the text will be moved to.

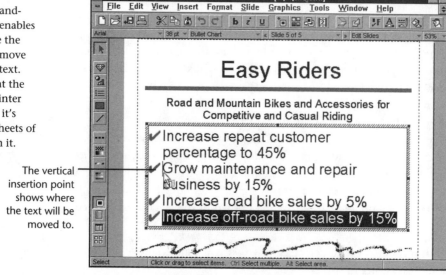

Using Cut, Copy, and Paste

Menu commands and Toolbar icons enable you to cut, copy, and paste selected text. *Cutting* removes the text from its current location on the slide and places the text on the Windows *Clipboard*—a temporary holding area. *Copying* duplicates the selected text and places the copy on the Clipboard. *Pasting* pastes the contents of the Clipboard at the insertion point.

Caution

Note that whenever you perform a new cut or copy operation, the newly cut or copied material replaces whatever was previously in the Clipboard. If you have text that you will use frequently in numerous slide shows, you may want to create a separate slide show that contains boilerplate text to use over and over (just type the text into the slide show and save it), or create a keyboard script to insert frequently used text (see Chapter 20, "Customizing with Macros, Toolbars, and Menus").

As noted earlier, you can use Cut, Copy, and Paste to edit text within a text container; or to copy and move text between text containers. You even can use these techniques to copy or move text between slides in the same slide show or between open slide shows.

To copy text to another location, follow these steps:

1. Place the insertion point in a text container and select the text to be copied.

2. Choose **C**opy from the **E**dit menu (or press Ctrl+C) or click the Copy icon on the Toolbar to copy the selected text to the Clipboard.

3. Position the insertion point where you want to insert the copied text. If you want to copy the text to another text container, double-click that container and position the insertion point appropriately within it. You also can move to another slide or another open slide show (using the **W**indow menu), and then position the insertion point.

4. Choose **P**aste from the **E**dit menu (or press Ctrl+V) or click the Paste icon on the Toolbar to paste the text from the Clipboard.

To move text to another location, follow these steps:

1. Place the insertion point in a text container and select the text to be copied.

2. Choose Cu**t** from the **E**dit menu (or press Ctrl+X) or click the Cut icon on the Toolbar to remove the selected text from its present location and place it on the Clipboard.

3. Position the insertion point where you want to insert the cut text. If you want to move the text to another text container, double-click that container and position the insertion point appropriately within it. You also can move to another slide or another open slide show (using the **W**indow menu), and then position the insertion point.

4. Choose **P**aste from the **E**dit menu (or press Ctrl+V) or click the Paste icon on the Toolbar to paste the text from the Clipboard.

Changing Fonts, Sizes, and Styles

A font consists of a full set of letters that have a consistent *typeface* (appearance), *weight* (relative boldness), and *posture* (upright or italic). For a traditional feel, choose fonts with *serifs* (cross strokes at the ends of letters); *sans-serif* fonts (those with no serifs) have a more modern feel. Special fonts, such as script fonts, should be used sparingly in slide shows because they can be difficult to read—and your business presentation shouldn't resemble a wedding invitation anyway.

> **Note**
>
> Presentations comes with several of its own TrueType fonts (mostly designated by
> -WP at the end of the font name). TrueType fonts are ideal for designing slide shows,
> because what you see on-screen is exactly what prints.

Presentations, like other computer programs, specifies the size of text in
points. There are 72 points per inch, so 12-point text, for example, is one-
sixth of an inch tall. The styling you attach to your text can include such
things as bold, italics, underlining, superscript, subscript, and relative sizing.

The slide show masters preselect all these text settings for a consistent, readable appearance. Although Presentations gives you unlimited options for
styling and sizing your text, there are a few guidelines to keep in mind to
ensure that you're choosing formatting that's attractive and effective:

■ Stick with only one to three fonts per slide. Too many fonts on a page
  or slide give it a "ransom note" feel.

■ The same applies for slide styling; don't use too much of it. If you try
  to emphasize all the words by using different styling, you will end
  up emphasizing nothing. Carefully choose which lines or words to
  emphasize with styling.

■ The title font should be the largest on the slide, to give the slide a bal-
  anced appearance.

■ All slide text should be 20 points or more (with the possible exception
  of footnotes at the bottom of a slide). This helps ensure that you avoid
  the temptation to pack too much text onto a single slide.

The Power Bar enables you to quickly change the font and size of selected
text. You will use these tools often as you create slide shows because they're
very convenient. To change the font or size of text with the Power Bar, select
the text in the text container, click on the font or size buttons in the Power
Bar to display its options, scroll through the list, and then click on your selection. The Toolbar provides tools that enable you to make selected text bold,
italic, and underline. Simply select the text you want to change and then
click the appropriate tool. Clicking one of these tools when the text already
has a particular style (such as bold) removes the style.

Using the Font dialog box to change the font, size, and style gives you a few
more options than the Power Bar and Toolbar, and enables you to choose the

default font for new text containers. To use the Font dialog box to change text font, size, and style, use these steps:

1. Select the text in the text containers.

2. Choose **F**ont from the Fo**r**mat menu or press F9. The Font dialog box appears (see fig. 6.10).

Previews your selections

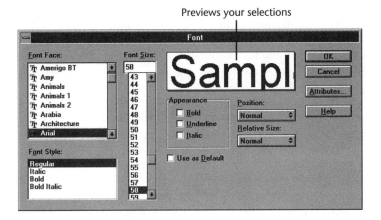

Fig. 6.10
You use the Font dialog box to change text font, size, and style all at once.

3. Choose a font for the text from the **F**ont Face list.

4. Make a selection from the F**o**nt Style list. Some fonts are available in bold and italic. When a font has those options available, choose an option from this list.

5. Choose a Font **S**ize from the list or type a size in the text box.

6. Choose a font appearance if you couldn't make all your specifications using F**o**nt Style.

7. If you want superscript or subscript text, use the **P**osition pop-up list to choose one of these options.

8. If you have one or two words selected within a text container and want to change the size of those words relative to the size of all the other words in the container, make a selection from the **R**elative Size pop-up. Using this option saves you trouble later if you resize all the text in the text container. In this case, Presentations maintains the relative sizing.

9. To use your settings as the default for new text, turn on the Use as **D**efault check box.

10. Click OK to close the dialog box.

II

Enhancing Your Show

If you want to change the font for text in a text line or area you added to the slide, just click the areas to select them and then use the Power Bar to select a font.

Changing Line Formatting

The options on the Format Line submenu enable you to control the positioning of selected text within the text container. Here's how to use each of these options:

- *Changing line spacing.* Select one or more lines of text to format in a text container. Open the Format menu and choose **Line Spacing**. In the Line Spacing dialog box, type or select a new **S**pacing setting, and then click OK.

- *Center-aligning a line.* Select the line you want to center in the text container (use **J**ustification on the Format menu to change more than one line). Open the Format menu and choose **Line Center** or press Shift+F7.

- *Right-aligning a line.* Select the line you want to align to the right in the text container (use **J**ustification to change more than one line). Open the Format menu and choose **Line Flush Right** or press Alt+F7.

Changing Paragraph Formatting

The Format Paragraph submenu commands enable you to change indentions of any paragraph (any line or more of text followed by pressing Enter) in a text container. These commands are different from using Tab and Shift+Tab to create bullet items. Using these choices does not insert bullet characters; it simply indents the text by five-character indention increments. You can use any of these options in new text as you create it, or you can position the insertion point in a paragraph where you want to change the paragraph formatting. Position the insertion point, open the Format menu, choose **P**aragraph, and choose a submenu option. Here's how each of these options works:

- *Indent (F7).* Inserts a half-inch indent to the right at the insertion-point position. Placing an indent within a paragraph indents all subsequent lines of a paragraph.

- *Hanging Indent (Ctrl+F7).* Indents all but the first line of a paragraph by a half-inch.

- *Double Indent (Ctrl+Shift+F7).* Inserts a half-inch indention at the left and right margins.

■ *Back **T**ab (Shift+Tab).* Moves the insertion point to the preceding tab stop.

To remove an indent, position the insertion point where you inserted the indent (most likely at the beginning of the paragraph, unless you placed it within the paragraph) and press Delete.

Justifying Text

Open the Fo**r**mat menu and choose **J**ustification to display submenu options that enable you to specify whether multiple lines of text in a paragraph align to the text container boundary you specify. Figure 6.11 illustrates the result when you choose **L**eft (or press Ctrl+L), **R**ight (or press Ctrl+R), or C**e**nter (or press Ctrl+E) from the Fo**r**mat **J**ustification submenu.

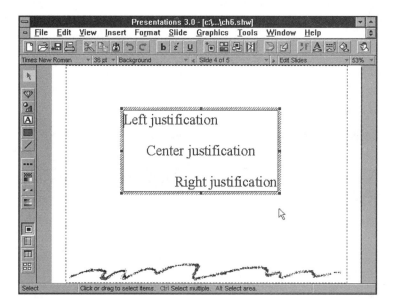

Fig. 6.11
How justification positions paragraph text within a text container.

To justify all the paragraphs in a text container, simply position the insertion point anywhere within the container. Open the Fo**r**mat menu, choose **J**ustification, and then choose the option of your choice from the submenu. To justify only part of the text in a text container, simply select the paragraph(s), open the Fo**r**mat menu, choose **J**ustification, and then choose an option from the submenu.

Troubleshooting

I tried to left-justify some indented text, but it wouldn't align all the way to the left edge of the text-container boundary. What did I do wrong?

You need to manually delete the indents first. Position the insertion point on the indent (usually the beginning of the paragraph), and press Delete.

I want to right-justify the text in my bullet chart, but I can't.

The justification for the bullet levels overrides your capability to re-justify bullet charts. Try using another kind of text instead.

Changing Kerning (Letter Spacing)

Kerning (also called *letter spacing*) indicates how much or little spacing there is between letters within words. Because of the varying letter shapes, some narrow letters such as *l* and *i* typically need less space around them, as do letter couples with complementary shapes like *AW*. Also, some letters or letter couples with tails or serifs (*t, rn, we*) may need additional spacing between them so that letters don't run together. Figure 6.12 shows some examples of bad kerning.

Fig. 6.12
If kerning is too tight, letters run together. When kerning is too loose, the words seem to float apart on the slide.

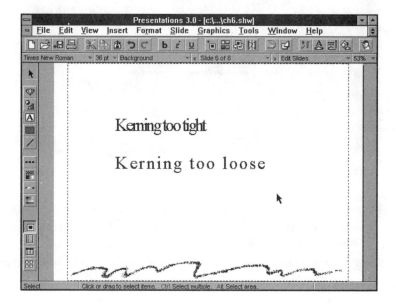

To adjust kerning, select the text you want to kern, open the Format menu, and choose Manual Kerning. In the Manual Kerning dialog box, specify a kerning Amount. Negative values make the kerning tighter (bring letters together), and positive values spread out the letters. Click OK when you're finished. After you set an Amount, you can apply kerning directly by pressing Ctrl+Plus (+) to expand kerning and Ctrl+Minus (-) to contract kerning.

Undoing Changes (Undo versus Undelete)

If you realize that you have made an error while editing or formatting text, you can reverse your error. You need to be aware of the different methods for undoing changes and how to use them.

If you accidentally delete text while editing, and you're still working inside the text container where you deleted the text, you can get the text back immediately by opening the Edit menu and choosing Undelete. You have to use Undelete rather than Undo because Undo is unavailable while you're editing. When the Undelete dialog box appears, click Restore to insert your text back into the text container. If you've made several deletions, you can use the Next and Previous buttons before clicking Restore to view the appropriate text to reinsert.

If you've made an editing change and have clicked outside the text container or have made a formatting change you don't like, use Undo. First make sure you click outside the text container so that Undo becomes available. Then open the Edit menu and choose Undo (or press Ctrl+Z) or click the Undo icon on the Toolbar. You can choose the Redo option from the Edit menu (or press Ctrl+Shift+Z) or click the Redo icon on the Toolbar to reverse any undo action.

Sizing and Moving Text Containers

After you place a text container on the slide or fill text into a layout area, the placement of the text isn't set in stone. You can resize the boundaries of any text container to fit the area you want, or even move the text container around anywhere on the slide. To do so, you first must select the text container, as described next.

Selecting Text Containers

Selecting a text container is like selecting any other object in a graphics program. Simply click once on the area so that black selection handles appear around it, as shown in figure 6.13.

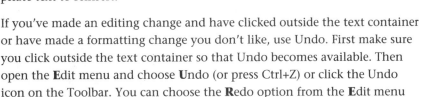

Fig. 6.13
Black selection
handles appear
around a selected
text container.

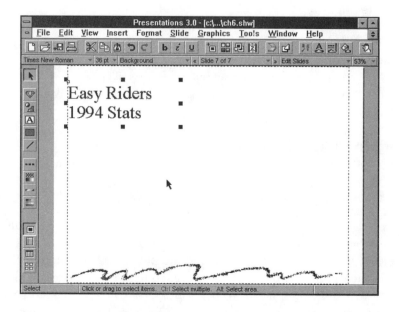

Sizing Text Containers

Sizing a text container is a simple matter of dragging a selection handle.
However, you should be aware of a couple of issues:

- Sizing a text container also resizes the text it contains. If you want to
  add more text to a container, don't make it larger first. Simply double-
  click it to place the insertion point in it and edit it to add more text.

- If you want to reshape the text area without changing the font size and
  you want to rewrap the text, double-click the text area to make the
  hatched outline appear, and then drag to resize the hatched outline.

- Drag a corner handle to resize both the height and width of a text area;
  drag a side or top handle to skew the shape of the text in the box.

Tip
You quickly can
invert text by
dragging its bot-
tom border above
its top border.

- Pressing Ctrl when you drag to resize creates a copy of the text area and
  resizes the copy.

- When you resize the text by dragging the text-container boundaries,
  the display size of the text changes. The text may look disproportion-
  ately narrow or short, for example.

To resize a selected text area, point to one of the selection handles until it turns into a double-headed arrow. Then click-and-drag until the container outline is the size you want. Dragging a corner selection handle enables you to resize vertically and horizontally at the same time.

Moving Text Containers

You can move a text container around on the slide. You can move a title in the upper left corner of the slide to the lower right corner of the slide, for example. Simply select the text container and click-and-drag it to the new location.

Troubleshooting

When I try to move a text container, it jerks around and won't let me place it precisely where I want to. It jerks either left or right when I release the mouse button. What's going on?

Your text container is aligning to a grid that Presentations enables you to use to line up multiple objects. You need to turn off Presentations' Snap to Grid feature. Open the **V**iew menu, choose **G**rid/Snap, and then choose **S**nap to Grid from the submenu; or press Alt+F8 to toggle off this feature.

I dragged my text container to the edge of the page, and now some text is cut off.

Presentations does not display any text positioned beyond the margin areas. Reset the margins to 0 by opening the Fo**r**mat menu and choosing **P**age and then choosing **S**ize/Margins from the submenu. Or, drag the text container back within the dotted margin boundaries.

Correcting Text

Proofreading and checking word choice are often a user's last concerns when creating a slide show. You tend to focus on the appearance of the text, because you're creating graphical layouts; you may lose sight of the importance of having accurate, clearly presented content. Luckily, Presentations now offers features to make last-minute tasks like proofing your presentation painless, so that you don't skip crucial steps. These tools include the Spell Checker, Thesaurus, QuickCorrect, and Find and Replace—all of which are described next.

Tip
You can spell check a single text container by double-clicking it and then pressing Ctrl+F1 or by opening the **T**ools menu and choosing **S**pell Check.

Using the Spell Checker

The Spell Checker proofreads your slide show for typos, including misspelled words, double words, and incorrect capitalization. You can check an entire slide show or portions of it by using the options on the **C**heck menu in the Spell Checker window. To perform a spell check, follow these steps:

1. Open or create the slide show to spell check. Double-click to select the text area to spell check, or change to Outliner view to check the whole slide show.

2. Choose **S**pell Check from the **T**ools menus (or press Ctrl+F1). The Spell Checker dialog box appears.

3. Choose appropriate options from the Che**c**k, Dictio**n**aries, and O**p**tions menus in the Spell Checker dialog box to adjust the scope of the spell check. When Spell Checker finds the first word it doesn't recognize, it displays a dialog box much like figure 6.14.

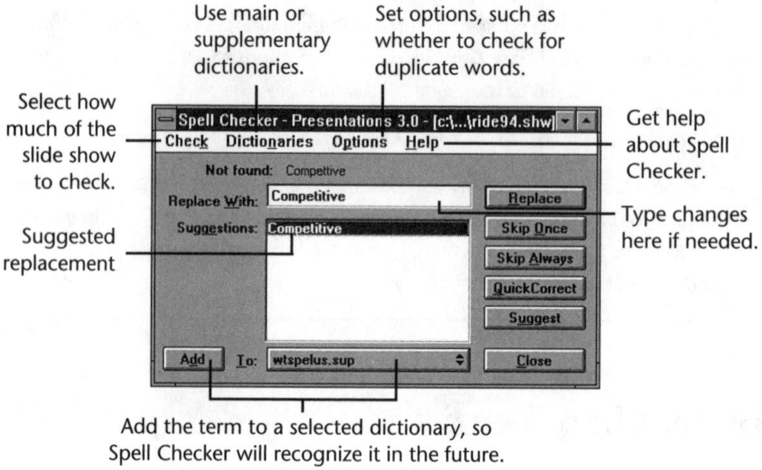

Fig. 6.14
You use the Spell Checker to perform very detailed or limited proofreading passes.

Use main or supplementary dictionaries.

Set options, such as whether to check for duplicate words.

Select how much of the slide show to check.

Suggested replacement

Get help about Spell Checker.

Type changes here if needed.

Add the term to a selected dictionary, so Spell Checker will recognize it in the future.

4. The word is displayed in the Not Found field at the top of the dialog box. The Sugge**s**tions list box lists possible corrections for the word, and the Replace **W**ith text box initially displays the most likely suggestion. At this point, you have the following options:

    ■ *Replace.* Substitutes the Not Found word with the word shown in the Replace **W**ith text box. Edit the text in the Replace **W**ith text box, if necessary, before clicking the **R**eplace button.

- *Skip **O**nce.* Does not replace the word, but alerts you if the word is found again.

- *Skip **A**lways.* Tells Spell Checker that the word is spelled correctly and it should assume that the word is correct for the rest of the spell check.

- ***Q**uickCorrect.* Corrects the term and adds the correction to the **To** dictionary so that it's corrected automatically during future spell checks.

- *Su**g**gest.* Recommends alternative spellings if you type a word in the Replace **W**ith text box.

- *Close.* Terminates the spell check.

5. After Spell Checker completes the spell check, it displays a message asking whether you want to close Spell Check. Click **Y**es.

Using the Thesaurus

If you're creating a slide show and cannot quite think of the word that exactly communicates your meaning, the Thesaurus can lend you a hand. The *Thesaurus* is a dictionary of synonyms and antonyms for words. To use the Thesaurus, follow these steps:

1. Double-click the text container to place the insertion point in it.

2. Double-click the word for which you want to find a synonym or antonym. This selects the word.

3. Open the **T**ools menu and choose **T**hesaurus (or press Alt+F1). Presentations displays the Thesaurus dialog box (see fig. 6.15).

Choose another
Thesaurus dictionary.

Use to edit the Word text
box contents.

Headwords
appear at the
top of each
column.

Double-click
terms with
bullets to list
additional
terms in the
next column.

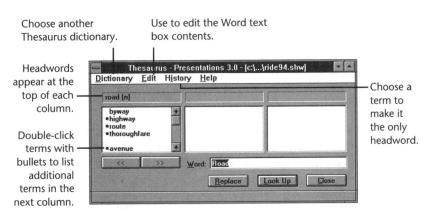

Choose a
term to
make it
the only
headword.

Fig. 6.15

The Thesaurus
enables you to find
synonyms and
antonyms for the
words in your slide
show.

4. Use the menus at the top of the dialog box to set options as appropriate. The **D**ictionary menu offers the **C**hange Dictionary command, which enables you to choose another dictionary of synonyms. The **H**istory menu displays other words you have viewed synonyms for, so you can go back to a word.

5. To view antonyms, scroll to the bottom of the list of words.

6. Double-click a term with a bullet beside it to make that term the headword for the next column and to display synonyms for it.

7. To select a replacement for the original term, click it in the list where it appears, and then click **R**eplace. The Thesaurus dialog box closes and the original word is replaced by the word you selected in the Thesaurus.

Tip
To see synonyms for a different word while the Thesaurus dialog box is open, type the term in the **W**ord text box, and then click **L**ook Up.

Using QuickCorrect

Touch typing is based on your ability to recall patterns of movement so you can type quickly. Occasionally, however, the wrong pattern programs itself into your mind and fingers. You may have a tendency to type "beging" instead of "begin," for example. You can use a Presentations feature called *QuickCorrect* to fix common spelling errors, mistyped words, and capitalization errors.

QuickCorrect also can save typing time. If you have a long word that you will need to use repeatedly in a slide show, such as "perchloroethylene," for example, typing it every time could be tedious and create quite an opportunity for errors. Instead of typing that term every time, you could simply type **perc** into the slide show where needed and use QuickCorrect to go through the slide show and expand every occurrence of "perc" to "perchloroethylene." QuickCorrect also performs other custom grammar corrections; you can typeset certain characters such as the copyright symbol, or you can specify other grammar changes with the **O**ptions button, such as replacing double spaces typed into the end of sentences with single spaces.

To use QuickCorrect, follow these steps:

1. Open the **T**ools menu and choose **Q**uickCorrect (or press Ctrl+Shift+F1). The QuickCorrect dialog box appears.

2. Click the **O**ptions button, and set any grammar correction options you want. You can specify corrections at the beginning and end of sentences and replace single and double prime marks with typeset curly quotes. Click OK to close the QuickCorrect Options dialog box when you're finished with it.

3. In the **R**eplace text box, type a misspelling or abbreviation.

4. In the **W**ith text box, type the full, correct spelling that you want to expand the typo or abbreviation to.

5. Click the **A**dd Entry button. This step adds the **R**eplace and **W**ith entries to the listings below the text boxes.

6. Repeat steps 3 through 5 to add as many corrections as you want to make.

7. Highlight an entry in the list box and click **D**elete Entry to cut it from the list so that QuickCorrect will not correct it.

8. Place an x in the **R**eplace Words as You Type check box to have QuickCorrect replace typos or abbreviations as you type.

9. Click **C**lose.

Finding and Replacing

Although the QuickCorrect feature is useful for replacing numerous typos and making many corrections simultaneously, choose **F**ind/Replace from the **E**dit menu to replace single words or phrases in a text container with the word or phrase you specify. Find/Replace finds the search text wherever it appears.

To use Find/Replace, follow these steps:

1. Double-click a text container to place the insertion point in it.

2. Open the **E**dit menu and choose **F**ind/Replace (or press F2). The Find and Replace dialog box appears (see fig. 6.16).

3. In the **F**ind text box, type the word or phrase to find, such as **and**.

Enter a word or phrase to find.

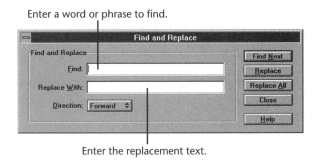

Enter the replacement text.

Fig. 6.16
Use Find and Replace to change a single term or phrase at a time, rather than replacing multiple terms with QuickCorrect.

Tip
Pressing the space
bar before and after
the word you are
searching for ensures
that **F**ind/Replace
treats the entry you
want to **F**ind as a
whole word, such as
"hat" rather that
finding words that
contain your find
entry, such as "that."

4. In the Replace **W**ith text box, type the word or phrase to replace the found text with "or."

5. Use the **D**irection pop-up list to change the direction of the search.

6. Start the Replace procedure. Choose Find **N**ext to locate the first occurrence of the **F**ind text, and then click **R**eplace. Repeat this step until the Find/Replace operation is complete. Otherwise, simply click Replace **A**ll.

7. When the Find/Replace operation is finished, a dialog box tells you that the search text isn't found. Click OK.

8. Click Close to close the Find and Replace dialog box.

Importing Text

You can import data directly into a text container or into an outline view of your slide show. Import enables you to import various types of ANSI (Windows), ASCII (DOS), and RTF text, as well as text created in WordPerfect. To import text into your slide show, follow these steps:

1. Position the pointer where you want to insert the text, either in Outline view or in a text container. Or, to automatically create a slide show from an outline, simply set up the new slide show and don't position the insertion point.

2. Open the **I**nsert menu and choose F**i**le. The Insert Text dialog box appears. It resembles the Open File dialog box and other file-related dialog boxes you have seen before.

3. Use the Dri**v**es and **D**irectories lists to specify the location of the text file you want to import.

4. Click the name of the file from the File**n**ame list, and then click **I**nsert. If your document is a WordPerfect file, its text is placed directly into the slide show. Otherwise, the Convert File Format dialog box appears.

5. In the Convert File Format dialog box, use the Convert File Format From drop-down list to specify the format of the file you're inserting.

6. Use the pull-down list to select the type of file you're importing, and then click OK.

When the Import procedure is finished, the text appears in the area you selected in the slide show. If you imported an outline, multiple slides are created automatically.

Inserting the Date

You may want a slide to show the date on which you created a slide show, or you may want to have a date entry automatically updated each time you open and resave a slide show. Presentations uses your computer system's internal date and time when creating date entries. You can create static date or changing date entries easily by using the **D**ate command from the **I**nsert menu. Follow these steps:

1. Create the text container and position the insertion point in it where you want to insert the date.

2. (Optional) Set up the date format by opening the **E**dit menu and choosing Preferences, as described in Chapter 5, "Basic Customizing." Or, open the **I**nsert menu and choose Date **F**ormat.

3. Open the **I**nsert menu and choose **D**ate. From the submenu that appears, choose **T**ext (or press Ctrl+D) to insert the current date, which will not change, or choose **C**ode (or press Ctrl+Shift+D) to insert a date code that will update itself each time you open and save the file.

From Here...

Adding text to a slide is a key operation in putting together an effective slide show. This chapter covered the key techniques you need to be aware of, and explained how to edit and correct your text to ensure that it's accurate as well as attractive. To learn more about text and text shortcuts, see the following chapters:

■ Chapter 7, "Enhancing Text," explains how to add colors and patterns to text, as well as how to create numerous special effects that lend a professional appearance to your slide show.

■ Chapter 15, "Working with Masters, Templates, and Backgrounds," describes, among other things, how to edit the text-container layout areas on slide templates to create custom slide templates.

■ Chapter 20, "Customizing with Macros, Toolbars, and Menus," teaches you how to custom automate several Presentations features, and even attach keyboard scripts to Toolbar tools or specified keystrokes, for faster, more convenient text entry.

Chapter 7

Enhancing Text

The text formatting applied to the slide masters certainly yields attractive, professional-looking slide shows. You learned in the last chapter how you can customize text formatting by changing text fonts, styles, sizes, and more. You don't have to stop there.

WordPerfect Presentations 3.0 for Windows provides a variety of attributes and special effects you can apply to text to emphasize particular words, set a different mood in your slide show, or even add a little levity or comic effect to keep your audience interested and entertained. Whether or not you're a graphic designer, you can use Presentations' tools to create interesting and effective text effects. This chapter explains how to use these tools to accomplish the following tasks:

- Changing the color, outline, and fill for text

- Designing the text chart; and adding borders, fills, patterns, and drop shadows

- Redesigning bullet charts to add new bullets and more

- Applying warping and 3D effects to text, curving text, and including special characters

Working with the Various Text Attributes

The color and appearance of text can say a lot about the words they're representing. Think of the significance of reporting financial results when your company is "in the red," for example. You can alter the appearance of text to emphasize or de-emphasize it, to add decorative effects, or to adjust text colors and patterns so that text prints more distinctly on your printer. Presentations enables you to change these attributes:

- The color filling the body of the text

- Whether the text has an outline, and whether the outline has color

- The fill pattern or gradient in the body of the text

As was recommended for choosing new fonts and font sizes, you shouldn't go overboard in applying text attributes. Don't do anything too wild or too fancy. As a good rule of thumb, if you cannot easily read the text, undo the attribute. Your main concern in creating a slide show is to communicate—not to decorate—the information.

Note that to apply certain attributes to text created in a template layout area, you have to override the colors and other attributes defined by the slide-show master. To do so, you have to actually select the text within the text container, not simply select the text container. For text containers that you add to a slide, you usually can simply click to select the container, and then choose commands to apply attributes. The only exception is bullet charts that you add. For these, you have to select the text within the text container.

After you change the attributes settings, those settings are used for any new text you create. You can change the settings before typing. Simply position the insertion point, set the attributes as described in this chapter, and begin typing.

Setting the Text Attributes

You can change all the text attributes at once by using the Text Attributes dialog box. The steps for using this dialog box follow:

1. If you're changing the attributes for a text container you added, click the text container to select it.

> **Note**
>
> If you want to change the attributes for text created by one of the slide templates, only selected words, or a bullet chart, double-click to place the insertion point within the text and then select the text you want to change. No QuickMenu command is available to help you change attributes for text selected in this way.

2. Choose **T**ext Attributes from the Fo**r**mat menu, or right-click and choose **A**ttributes from the QuickMenu. You also can click the Text Attributes tool on the Toolbar. The Text Attributes dialog box appears (see fig. 7.1).

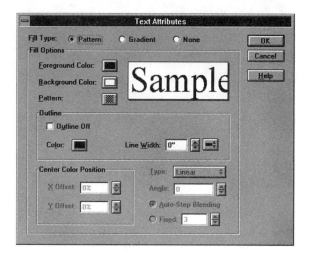

Fig. 7.1
You can change all the text attributes by using this dialog box.

3. Choose a Fill Type. Pattern enables you to create letters with a solid color or patterned centers. Gradient enables you to fill letters with a blend of two colors. None fills the letters with nothing.

4. Click on the **F**oreground Color button to display a palette of colors. Click a color to select it. For Pattern fills, this color is the color the pattern or hatch marks will have. For Gradient fills, this color is one of the colors that will be blended.

5. Click on the **B**ackground Color button to display a palette of colors. Click a color to select it. For Pattern fills, this color is the color behind the pattern or hatch marks. For Gradient fills, this color is the second of the colors that will be blended.

6. If you chose Pattern in step 3, click the **P**attern button to display the palette shown in figure 7.2. Click the pattern you want to select it and close the palette.

Enhancing Your Show

II

Fig. 7.2
Displaying a
palette of
patterns. Click a
pattern to select it.

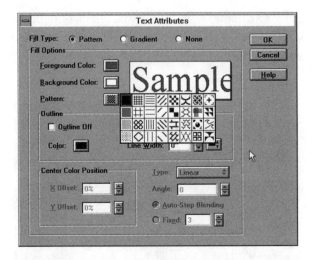

If you chose Gradient in step 3, several settings became available at the bottom of the dialog box. If you want the gradient to originate from somewhere other than the upper left-hand corner of the screen, enter new values in the **X** Offset (controls left-to-right position) and **Y** Offset (controls top-to-bottom position) boxes. Legal values range from 0 to 100, with 50 being the screen midpoints. Click the **T**ype pop-up to indicate a new fill type: **L**inear, **C**ircular, or **R**ectangular. This setting dictates whether the colors blend along a straight line, in a curve, or at an angle. Enter an An**g**le value of 1 to 359 to rotate the gradient. Leave **A**uto-Step Blending selected if you want Presentations to specify automatically the number of blending steps between the gradient colors, or click Fix**e**d and then enter a value to specify the desired number of blending steps.

7. Use the Outline area to adjust the outline. Use the Co**l**or pop-up to change the color. Enter or choose a new Line **W**idth, if needed, using the text box, incrementor buttons, or pop-up. If you want no outline, click to place an x in the O**u**tline Off check box.

8. Click OK to close the dialog box. Presentations displays your newly formatted text. Figure 7.3 shows an example of text with new attributes.

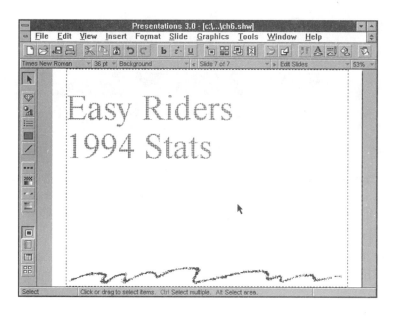

Fig. 7.3
This text has a dark green foreground color, a light green background color, a pattern, and no outline.

Adding a Drop Shadow

A drop shadow lends the illusion that text is floating above the background. Although this is an attractive effect, you should use it sparingly because it can make the text difficult to read. You should avoid adding drop shadows to text that has a small font size or to long sentences or lists; stick to using drop shadows for large, title text. Figure 7.4 shows text with a drop shadow.

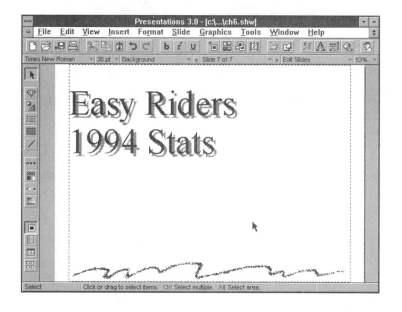

Fig. 7.4
Adding a drop shadow makes text appear to be floating over the background.

II

Enhancing Your Show

To add a drop shadow to text, follow these steps:

1. Click the text container for the text you want to change to select it.

> **Note**
>
> The masters don't enable you to add a drop shadow for text created by one of the template layout areas.

2. Choose **S**hadow Attributes from the Fo**r**mat menu, or right-click and choose **S**hadow Attributes from the QuickMenu. You also can click the Shadow button on the Toolbar. The Shadow Attributes dialog box appears.

3. Click the **S**hadow On check box to place an x in it (see fig. 7.5). This displays a preview of the shadow.

Fig. 7.5
The Shadow Attributes dialog box enables you to add drop shadows to text and customize them.

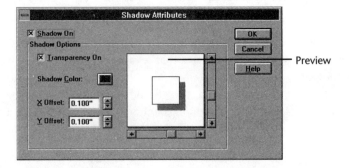

Preview

4. To make the shadow opaque rather than transparent, click to deselect the **T**ransparency On check box.

Tip
Use opaque drop shadows only if you choose a much lighter color for the shadow; otherwise, you get a "seeing double" effect rather than a shadowed effect. In general, lighter colors create more subtle drop shadows.

5. Click the Shadow **C**olor button to display a palette of colors. Click a color to select it for the drop shadow.

6. If you want to reposition the drop shadow, enter new values in the **X** Offset (controls left-to-right position) and **Y** Offset (controls top-to-bottom position) boxes. Legal values range from -0.500 to 0.500. You also can change the drop-shadow position by using the scroll bars at the bottom and right side of the drop-shadow preview.

7. Click OK to close the dialog box and apply the drop shadow.

To remove a drop shadow, follow steps 1 through 3. Clicking the **S**hadow On check box toggles it off in this case. Click OK once again to close the Shadow Attributes dialog box.

Changing the Fill Color

If you prefer to change the color of the text only, or you want to quickly try out other text colors for solid, gradient, or pattern fills, you can do so quickly and easily using the Fill Color tool on the Tool Palette instead of choosing **T**ext Attributes from the Fo**r**mat menu. If you're changing the attributes for a text container you added, click the text container to select it. If you're changing the attributes for text created by one of the slide templates or want to change only selected words, double-click to place the insertion point within the text, and then select the text you want to change.

After the text is selected, click the Fill Color tool to display the palette shown in figure 7.6. To change the foreground color (as shown in the foreground chip), point to a color and click the left mouse button. To change the background color (as shown in the background chip), point to a color and click the right mouse button. Each time you click, Presentations applies the new color and closes the palette.

Foreground chip

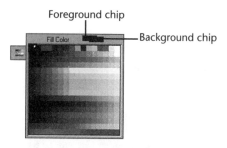

Background chip

Fig. 7.6
The Tool Palette enables you to quickly select foreground and background colors for the selected object.

II

Enhancing Your Show

Note

You also can change the selected text color by opening the Fo**r**mat menu and choosing **C**olor Attributes. Click the **T**ext Color choice, and click a new color in the C**u**rrent Palette.

Troubleshooting

I changed the foreground color to white so that I could create outline text, but my outline disappeared.

Changing the foreground color automatically changes the outline color as well. Use the Line Attributes tool on the palette (as described later in this chapter) to adjust the outline color.

After you apply a color other than black or white to text, the Format Image Settings submenu offers a few options to quickly alter that text if you select it:

■ *Outline*. Changes the text fill to white, leaving the outline in the object's current color.

■ *Silhouette*. Changes the text to black.

■ *Black and White*. Changes the fill to white and the outline to black, unless the fill already was black.

■ *Invert*. Changes the line and fill colors to the opposite color on the color wheel. Blue changes to yellow, and vice versa, for example.

Changing the Fill Pattern or Gradient

Similarly, there's a tool for quickly applying a new or changing an existing fill pattern or gradient to the selected text. Select the text as described earlier, and then click the Fill Attributes tool on the palette to display the palette shown in figure 7.7. Simply click a new pattern or gradation to select it. Figure 7.8 shows text with a gradation that goes from a dark foreground color at the upper left to a light background color at the lower right.

> **Note**
>
> Any color palette you see in Presentations is organized conveniently to help you easily pick complementary gradient colors. Each horizontal line in a palette (except for the top line) contains different tones of the same color, from darker on the left to lighter on the right. Click a darker value on one palette line for the background color and a lighter value on the same palette line for the foreground color.

Fig. 7.7
This tool on the Tool Palette enables you to add or change the pattern or gradation applied to selected text and objects.

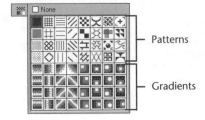

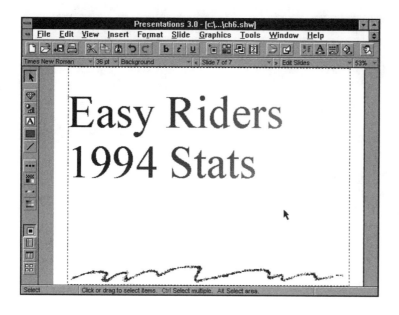

Fig. 7.8
Text with a new
gradation applied
to it.

Changing the Outline Color and Style

Making changes to the text outline color and outline style can be accomplished with a simple mouse click. Changing the outline color to a color that is different from the fill color gives your text a contrasting outline. Unless your slide show has a dark background, you probably should stick with outlines that are darker than the fill color. If the outline is too light, it will tend to fade into the background.

To change the outline color, select the text container or text, and then click the Line Color tool on the Tool Palette. Click the color you want for your outline.

You also can change the outline of text to have a different pattern. Figure 7.9 shows some text with a dotted outline. Use custom outline styles sparingly with text, because funky outlines can be difficult to read. To apply a new outline style, select the text area or text, and then click the Line Attributes tool on the palette to display the palette shown in figure 7.10. Click a line width, style, or the None check box. Clicking closes the palette and applies your choice to the selected text.

Fig. 7.9
You can apply
different outline
styles to text.

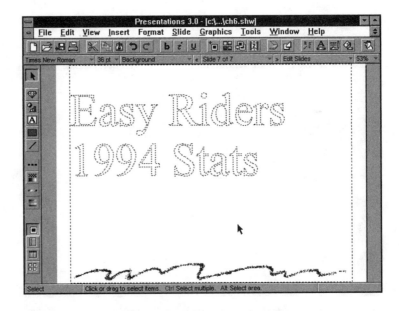

Fig. 7.10
The palette for
selecting outline
attributes.

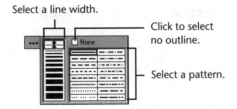

Troubleshooting

I tried to apply attributes to my slide title, but nothing happened.

Because you need to override the slide master formatting choices, you need to actually select the text within the text container to make changes to it. Double-click on
the title to place the insertion point within it, drag to select the text, and then choose
the attributes you want.

*I tried adding a new text area to my slide, and it used the attributes I last selected. Did I
do something wrong?*

No, these settings remain until you change them back. Make sure that you have the
correct settings selected before you add new text.

Copying Attributes with Get Attributes

If you have a long slide show and add a lot of custom text areas and text lines, you could spend a lot of time custom-formatting them. Fortunately, you don't have to select text containers one by one to format them. The **G**et Attributes and Appl**y** Attributes commands on the Fo**r**mat menu enable you to copy the text attributes you select and apply those attributes to other text. Here's how to use those commands:

1. Create the text area or text line and apply the attributes you want to the text.

2. Click the text container to select it.

3. Open the Fo**r**mat menu and choose **G**et Attributes. The Get Attributes dialog box appears.

4. Choose whether you want to copy the attributes for **G**raphics Only, **T**ext Only, or Gr**a**phics and Text by clicking the appropriate option. Click OK.

5. Select the text area or text line to which you want to copy the attributes.

6. Choose Appl**y** Attributes from the Fo**r**mat menu.

Creating a Text Box Fill and Border

You can add a border and background to any text container defined by the slide template, or to bullet charts that you add to a slide. Borders and backgrounds enable you to add accent colors to a slide, to highlight an important piece of text, or simply to add a decorative accent to a slide. Figure 7.11 illustrates a couple of fill and border options.

Note

For some reason, Presentations does not enable you to add a background or border for text lines and text areas you add to a slide.

Graduated fill

Double, octagonal border

Fig. 7.11
Borders and fills are useful for decorating and accenting text.

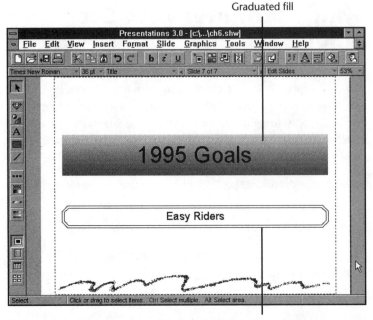

To add a border or fill to a text container (except for text areas and text lines you have added to a slide), follow these steps:

1. Click the text container to select it. Selection handles appear around it.
2. Open the Format menu and choose **D**efine Bullets/Fonts, or right-click to display the QuickMenu and choose **D**efine Bullets/Fonts. The Define Bullets/Fonts dialog box appears, with the Fon**t** radio button selected (see fig. 7.12).

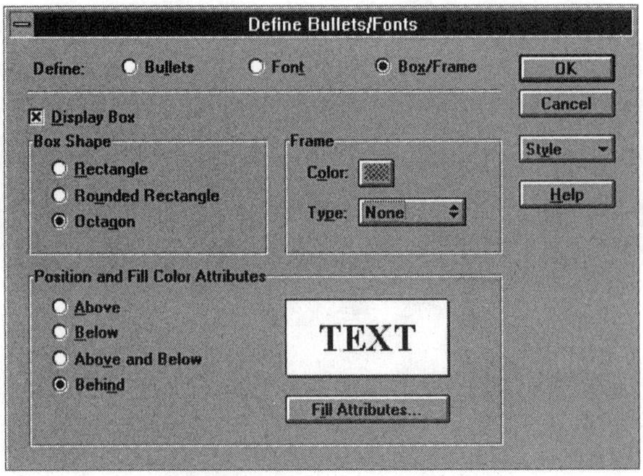

Fig. 7.12
The options for adding a border and fill to a text container.

3. Click the Box/Frame radio button. This alters the dialog box so that it shows the options for adding frames and fills.

4. Click the **D**isplay Box check box to enable the options for adding borders and fills.

5. Click to select **R**ectangle, Ro**u**nded Rectangle, or Octa**g**on from the Box Shape area.

6. To add an outline to the box, click the Ty**p**e pop-up list and drag to select a type, such as **S**ingle.

7. Click the C**o**lor button in the Frame area to choose a color for the Frame Ty**p**e.

8. Choose a position for the frame in the Position and Fill Color Attributes area. **A**bove compresses the frame at the top of the box, much like a bar. **B**elow compresses the frame at the bottom of the box. Abo**v**e and Below places a compressed frame above and below. Behi**n**d outlines the text container.

9. Click the F**i**ll Attributes button to display the Fill Attributes dialog box (see fig. 7.13).

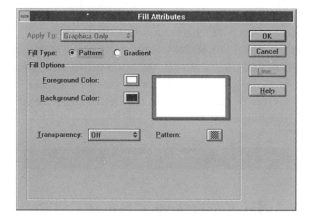

Fig. 7.13
Specifying a fill appearance.

10. Choose a Pattern or Gradient Fill T**y**pe. Choose a **F**oreground Color, **B**ackground Color, **T**ransparency, or **P**attern. Choosing these options works the same as the other dialog boxes you've seen. Click OK when you're done to close the Fill Attributes dialog box.

> **Note**
>
> You can use the Style pop-up list from the Define Bullets/Fonts dialog box to save the frame and border settings, and to retrieve the saved formatting later.

11. Click OK to close the Define Bullets/Fonts dialog box. Your new frame appears on the slide.

Troubleshooting

I tried to display the Define Bullets/Fonts dialog box, but that option wasn't available for the selected text. What's wrong?

For some reason, Presentations does not enable you to add a fill or box to text lines or text areas you have added to a slide. Try adding a bullet chart instead, and then use the methods described later in this chapter to delete the bullets. Then you can format the chart with a fill or box.

Creating Reversed Text

You can use the Define Bullets/Fonts dialog box to create *reversed text*, which is light or white text on a dark background, as shown in figure 7.14. When you first open the dialog box and the Font radio button is selected, use the Font Color button to display the Text Attributes dialog box. Set a white or light Foreground Color, click the Outline Off check box, and then click OK. Then use the Box/Frame radio button in the Define Bullets/Fonts dialog box to add a dark background fill.

Fig. 7.14
Reverse text is light text on a dark background.

Customizing Bullet Charts

In some instances, you may need to change or delete the kinds of bullets used in a bullet chart. Or, you may want to quickly change the font for all the text for a certain bullet level without having to highlight individual lines and manually change their font or size. You accomplish all this with the Define Bullets/Fonts dialog box, as described next.

Changing the Text Attributes

Imagine that you have a bullet chart on a slide. You type three bullets of text, only to find that you don't have enough room for the fourth (and last) line. Or, the bullets on the slide might be check marks, when you would rather have a simple bullet. To change the text attributes globally in a bullet chart, use these steps:

1. Click the text container to select it. Selection handles appear around it.

2. Open the Format menu and choose **D**efine Bullets/Fonts, or right-click to display the QuickMenu and choose **D**efine Bullets/Fonts. The Define Bullets/Fonts dialog box appears, with the Fon**t** radio button selected, as shown in figure 7.15.

Start by selecting the chart level you want to change.

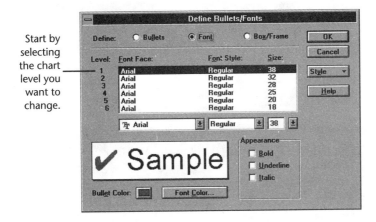

Fig. 7.15
Defining a new font for the text in each level of a bullet chart.

3. Click on the level of the text you want to change to select it.

4. Use the **F**ont Face, F**o**nt Style, and **S**ize pull-down lists below the Level list to change those attributes for the selected bullet text level.

5. Specify any Appearance attributes you want for the selected level.

6. Click the Bull**e**t Color button, and then click a color from the palette that appears to change the color of the bullets for that level.

7. Click the Font **C**olor button to display the Text Attributes dialog box. Then change the colors and outline as needed, and click OK to return to the Define Bullets/Fonts dialog box.

8. Repeat steps 3 through 7 to change these specifications for other chart text levels.

9. Click OK to close the dialog box and make your changes.

Changing the Bullets

Changing the bullets used for different chart levels also is simple. You even can select a custom bullet from those available within Presentations. Use these steps to change the bullets used in your bullet chart:

1. Click the text container to select it. Selection handles appear around it.

2. Choose **D**efine Bullets/Fonts from the Fo**r**mat menu, or right-click to display the QuickMenu and choose **D**efine Bullets/Fonts. The Define Bullets/Fonts dialog box appears, with the Fon**t** radio button selected.

3. Click the Bu**l**lets radio button to display the options shown in figure 7.16.

Fig. 7.16
Options for changing the bullets in a chart.

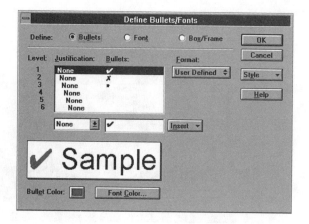

Tip
You can insert a few different bullet types using the I**n**sert button in the WordPerfect Characters dialog box. When you close and return to the Define Bullets/ Fonts dialog box, you can view all your choices in the preview area and delete the bullet(s) you don't want from the **B**ullets text box.

4. Click on the level of the text containing the bullet you want to change to select it.

5. Use the **J**ustification pull-down list and the I**n**sert pop-up list to specify different alignment or to choose a new bullet style.

6. Click the **F**ormat pop-up list to select automatic bullet formats. **U**ser-defined is the format that appears when you specify custom bullet choices. **C**hart assigns decorative bullets, with no bullet specified for the top level. **P**aragraph assigns report paragraph designations (1., a., i., and so on), and **O**utline assigns formal outline levels (I., A., 1., and so on) to the chart levels. **L**egal assigns legal outline levels (1., 1.1, 1.1.1, and so on) to the chart text. **B**ullets applies formal bullet styles to the chart levels.

7. Use the Bull**e**t Color button to display a palette, and then click to choose the color of the new bullet you selected.

8. Repeat steps 4 through 7 to edit other bullets.

9. Click OK to close the dialog box and apply your changes to the selected bullet chart.

If you want to specify a specialized bullet for a particular chart level, delete the bullet style from the **B**ullets text box below the Level list. Then click the **In**sert pop-up list and choose WP Characters (or press Ctrl+W). The WordPerfect Characters dialog box appears (see fig. 7.17). Click the Character **S**et button to access the pop-up list and select a symbol type. Scroll through the Cha**r**acters list and click the character you want. Click the Insert **a**nd Close button to close the dialog box and make your selection. Figure 7.18 shows a slide where red check mark bullets have been changed to stars.

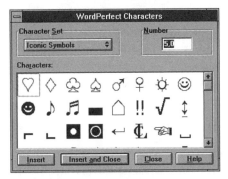

Fig. 7.17
Choosing a special bullet character.

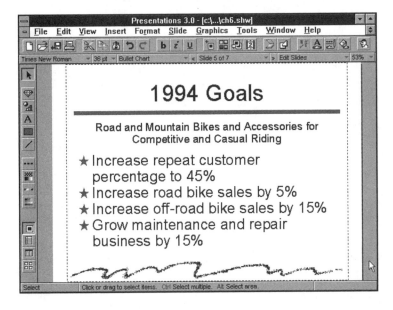

Fig. 7.18
The stars in this bullet chart are custom bullets.

II

Enhancing Your Show

Adding Special Effects

Previously, only the most expensive, high-end programs used by graphic artists enabled users to create fancy effects like rotating or curving text. Now, Presentations offers easy commands so that you can accomplish these special effects in moments. The text effects available to you are described and illustrated next. As for other text-formatting options, use special effects sparingly. You always need to ensure that your audience will be able to easily read and comprehend your text, no matter how it's formatted.

After applying these special effects (with the exceptions of QuickWarp and Quick3-D), you can apply attributes to or otherwise format the text as usual.

Contouring Text to a Curve

Curving text requires you to create two elements: a text line (which you learned about in Chapter 6) and a drawn line or object (see Chapter 12, "Using the Presentations Drawing Tools"). You cannot curve text in other forms of text containers or curve it around a bitmap object. Use the following steps to curve text around a drawn element:

1. Create a text line and enter the text you want, or select a text line. Apply any text attributes you want.

2. Draw the object you want to curve the text around. You can use the Filled Object tool on the palette to draw an ellipse, for example. If you plan to display the object as well as the text, set the fill, color, and pattern for the object.

3. Click the Pointer tool on the Tool Palette.

4. Click the text line to select it. Press and hold Shift, and click the drawn object. The selection handles should surround both objects, as shown in figure 7.19.

5. Choose Contour **T**ext from the **G**raphics menu. The Contour Text dialog box appears.

6. Use the **P**osition pop-up list to determine where on the object the text will start from, such as the Top Right or Bottom Left corner.

7. Turn off the Displa**y** Text Only check box if you want the object to appear, as well as the text.

8. Click OK. The text curves around the object and, if you specify, the object is removed. Figure 7.20 shows the result of curving the text around the object.

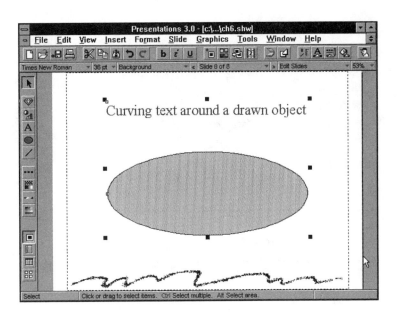

Fig. 7.19
Selecting the text
line and object.

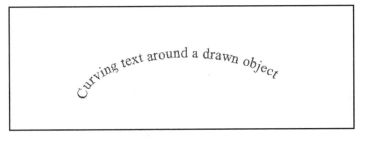

Fig. 7.20
The result of
curving the text
around the ellipse.
In this case, the
ellipse isn't
displayed.

Rotating Text

Instead of having perfectly horizontal text, you can rotate it or skew it to change its position. You can rotate text lines and text areas that you add to charts, but not bullet charts or layout areas that are part of a slide template. Figure 7.21 illustrates rotated and skewed text. *Rotating* text simply turns it around an axis; the letters remain perpendicular to the axis. *Skewing* text turns it around an axis and simultaneously tilts the text relative to the axis.

To rotate or skew text, follow these steps:

1. Select the text line or area you want to rotate.

2. Right-click to display the QuickMenu and choose R**o**tate, or open the **E**dit menu and choose R**o**tate. The object changes to have rotation handles and a rotation axis, as shown in figure 7.22.

Fig. 7.21
Comparing
rotated and
skewed text.

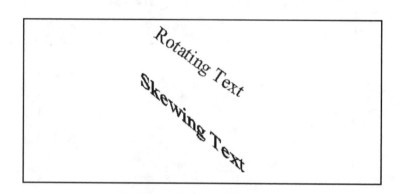

Skew handles on top, bottom, and sides

Fig. 7.22
The rotation and
skewing handles
appear when you
choose Rotate.

Rotation axis

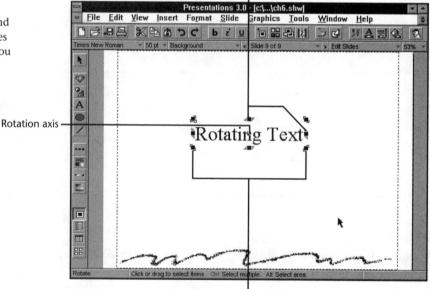

Rotation handles on corners

3. Drag the rotation axis to a new location if needed.

4. Drag a rotation or skew handle to a new location. Pressing Ctrl while dragging creates a copy of the text and rotates or skews it.

> **Note**
>
> To rotate or skew text by precise intervals, point to a rotate or skew handle and right-click. Use the settings in the Rotate or Skew dialog box that appears and then click OK.

Flipping Text

You can flip an added text area or text line vertically or horizontally. Click to select the text area. Then open the **G**raphics menu and choose **F**lip **L**eft/Right or **F**lip **T**op/Bottom.

Adding Special Characters

Another effect you can use to jazz up text is to insert special bullet characters anywhere in the text. Simply double-click to place the insertion point within a text container. Click or use the arrow keys to position the mouse pointer where you want to insert the special character. Open the **I**nsert menu and choose **C**haracter (or press Ctrl+W) to display the WordPerfect Characters dialog box (refer to fig. 7.17). Make your choices from the dialog box and click OK.

Using QuickWarp

To shape a text line or text area to fill a specialized curve or wave, Presentations offers the QuickWarp feature. Here's how to use it:

1. Click on the text line or text area you want to warp.

2. Open the **G**raphics menu and choose Quick**W**arp to display the QuickWarp dialog box (see fig. 7.23).

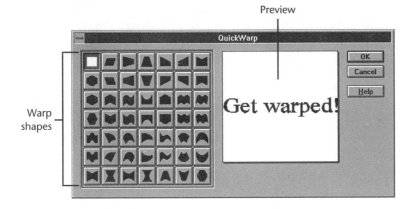

Fig. 7.23
Choosing a shape to warp text to.

3. Click the shape you want from the choices at the left side of the dialog box. The preview area shows what effect that choice will have on your text.

4. Click OK. Your text warps on the slide, as shown in figure 7.24.

Fig. 7.24
Your warped text.

Using Quick3-D

As opposed to adding perspective to an entire line of text, Quick3-D adds 3D depth and shading to individual letters within the words, and also tilts the text. Here's how to use Quick3-D:

1. Click on the text line or text area you want to make 3D.

2. Choose Quick**3**-D from the **G**raphics menu. The Quick3-D dialog box appears (see fig. 7.25).

Preview

Fig. 7.25
Creating a 3D effect.

Predefined rotations

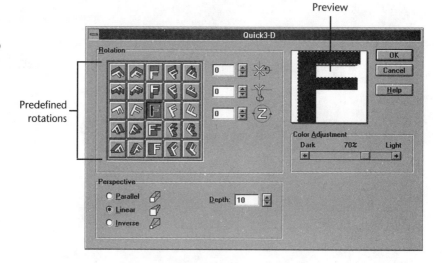

3. Click to choose a predefined rotation from the **R**otation area; or change the X, Y, and Z rotation values.

4. From the Perspective area, click a type of perspective and change the **D**epth, if needed.

5. Drag to change the Color **A**djustment for the depth area of the graphic.

6. Click OK to inspect your results (see fig. 7.26).

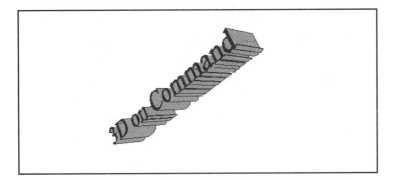

Fig. 7.26
Text formatted
with Quick3-D.

From Here...

This chapter explained how to enhance text that you have added to a slide. Text is only one essential feature of any slide show, however. From here, you need to look at adding graphics, charts, and drawings to your slide shows. These chapters can help:

■ Chapter 8, "Adding QuickArt to a Slide," teaches you to quickly add predrawn art to your slides to make them more attractive.

■ Chapter 9, "Working with Data Chart Data," and Chapter 11, "Editing Organization Charts," lead you through the process of manipulating chart data for those chart types.

■ Chapter 10, "Formatting the Data Chart," explains how to enhance the chart design by changing colors, text formatting, and more.

■ Chapter 12, "Using the Presentations Drawing Tools," enables you to draw your own custom lines and shapes on a slide, and to manipulate and edit them like a professional.

Chapter 8

Adding QuickArt to a Slide

Enhancing a slide show with artwork can make it more attractive, enhance your message, and impress your audience with the professional touches you've added. Presenting your company logo on a slide can make it more memorable. Showing a photo of how to perform a particular action is more effective than simply explaining it. And, including other images that lend humor or that your audience can identify with will make your message hit home and keep your audience awake.

WordPerfect Presentations 3.0 for Windows offers *QuickArt*, a selection of predrawn images you can insert on any slide. This chapter explains how you can add predrawn artwork to a slide, including the QuickArt and images from other sources. After reading this chapter, you will know how to perform the following tasks:

- Inserting QuickArt into a slide

- Selecting, moving, resizing, and modifying QuickArt

- Using other QuickArt options, such as choosing another QuickArt file or creating a category in the QuickArt Gallery

- Inserting graphics from other sources into slides

- Saving a QuickArt image as a WPG file for use with WordPerfect

Understanding Bitmap versus Vector Images

Before you start randomly inserting graphics into your slides, you need to understand different types of graphics and why using the QuickArt gallery provides many advantages. A fundamental distinction to understand when working with graphics is the difference between bitmap and vector images.

Bitmap images are created with colored pixels, and typically are created by paint programs or paint tools. Scanning also typically yields bitmap images. Although bitmap images are common because the tools for creating them are widely available, there are some disadvantages to using bitmaps. First, they're difficult to edit, because you have to change individual pixels. Every shape you draw becomes part of the whole image itself, and the shapes cannot be separated. Second, resizing bitmap images—especially enlarging them—distorts them and can cause them to have the jaggies. When you use the Insert Bitmap palette tool or choose **B**itmap from the **I**nsert menu in Presentations, you're switched to a drawing screen where you can create your own bitmap.

All other images you create or insert in Presentations, including QuickArt and shapes you draw directly on the slide with the Tool Palette tools, are *vector images* (also known as *object-oriented images*). Each object you draw is defined not by coloring on-screen pixels, but by storing a mathematical formula. Because each object is discreet, all the objects used to create the vector image can be resized independently. Also, the whole image can be resized easily without creating a jaggie look. Because QuickArt images are vector images, you easily can resize and edit them after you place them on a slide.

Inserting QuickArt

Presentations stores the QuickArt images you can insert in the slide in QuickArt Gallery files stored in \OFFICE\PRWIN\GALLERY. The QuickArt Gallery organizes the images in categories so that you quickly can find the image you need. Categories of QuickArt include Animals, Business, Graphics (such as special borders for text), Flowchart (for creating flow charts), and more. To place a QuickArt image on the current slide, use these steps:

 1. Open the **I**nsert menu and choose **Q**uickArt, or click the Insert Graphic tool on the palette, ensuring that you drag to select the icon for inserting figures (it looks like a diamond), if needed.

2. Point to the slide background. The mouse pointer changes to a hand holding a dotted outline.

3. Drag to create a box to hold the QuickArt. Or, to insert the QuickArt image at full-page size, click on the center of the slide. The QuickArt Gallery dialog box appears, as shown in figure 8.1.

Double-click a category to display its figures.

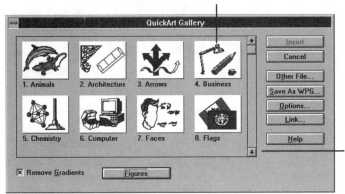

Fig. 8.1
The QuickArt Gallery displays the different categories of images you can insert into a slide.

Scroll to see other categories.

4. If necessary, use the scroll bar to display the category you want.

5. To select a category, double-click on the thumbnail for it, or click its thumbnail and click the **F**igures button at the bottom of the dialog box. Selecting a category displays the images it contains. Figure 8.2 shows the images that appear when you select category 1—Animals.

Double-click a category to display its figures.

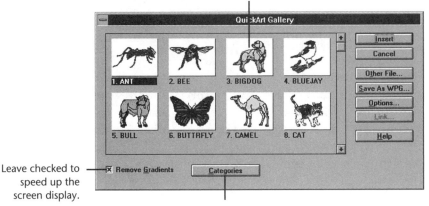

Fig. 8.2
Choosing a category displays the images you can choose from that category.

Leave checked to speed up the screen display.

Returns you to the categories.

II

Enhancing Your Show

6. Use the scroll bar, if needed, to scroll to the image you want to insert.

7. To insert the image, double-click its thumbnail, or click its thumbnail and then click **I**nsert. Selecting the image closes the QuickArt Gallery and inserts the image into the box you had dragged to create on the slide. Figure 8.3 shows image 3, BIGDOG, from figure 8.2 inserted into a slide.

Notice that the background of the image is transparent, even though the image itself is opaque.

Fig. 8.3
A QuickArt image inserted into a slide.

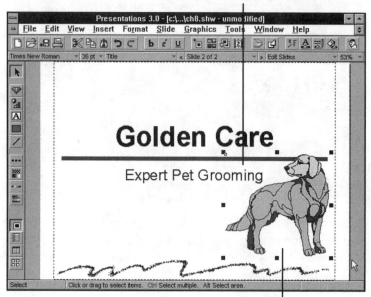

The image is placed in the box you created.

8. Click outside the image to select it.

The background of the QuickArt image is transparent, because the image actually is composed of many grouped shapes. This feature gives you great flexibility in placing QuickArt around text and even enables you to combine text with the image on the slide. Figure 8.4 shows one of the frame images from the Graphic category placed on a slide with a bullet chart, so that the image frames the bullet chart text. When you use the Flowchart graphics to create a slide, you need to combine text with each of the flowchart images you add. Chapter 12, "Using the Presentations Drawing Tools," explains how to combine drawn objects. The same techniques described in that chapter can be used to combine QuickArt with text.

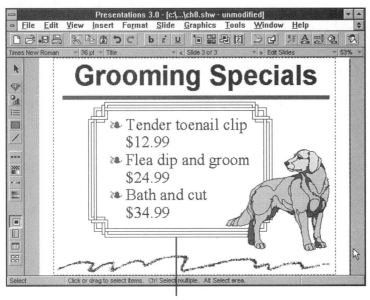

Fig. 8.4
Combining QuickArt with text gives you even more options for framing and dressing up the slide.

Transparent graphics let the bullet chart text
show, so the graphic frames the text.

Selecting, Moving, and Resizing QuickArt

You use basically the same techniques when moving and resizing QuickArt images that you use to move and resize text containers. Simply click an image to select it; selection handles appear around the image. To move the image after it has been selected, move the mouse pointer to it, press and hold the left mouse button, and drag the image to a new location. Figure 8.5 shows an image being dragged to a new location; note that a dotted outline and "ghost" of the image appear as you drag to indicate where the image will be repositioned. When the image reaches the position you want, release the mouse button. Pressing Ctrl while dragging creates a copy of the image and moves the copy.

Fig. 8.5
Moving QuickArt
to a new location
is a simple matter
of dragging.

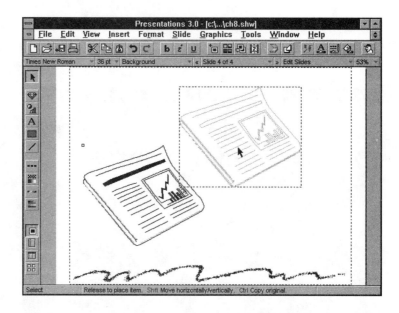

When resizing the QuickArt image, you have a few options, depending on whether you want to resize the image proportionally or whether you want to change the relative height or width of the image (stretch it).

To resize an image proportionally, use these techniques:

■ Point to one of the four corners of the image until the mouse pointer turns to a double-headed arrow. Press the left mouse button and drag to resize the image. Pressing Alt while dragging resizes the object from the center so that all four sides of the image's boundaries expand or contract. Pressing Ctrl while dragging creates a copy of the image and resizes the copy.

Tip
Use the **A**round
Center option in
the Size dialog box
to better predict
where the resized
image will appear.

■ Point to one of the four corners of the image until the mouse pointer turns to a double-headed arrow. Right-click to display the Size dialog box (see fig. 8.6). Select a **M**ultiplier by typing it or using the incrementor buttons. For example, 2 doubles the size of the image, and .5 reduces the image to half its size. Choose **A**round Center to size from the center out, or choose **C**opy object(s) to create a copy of the image and resize the copy.

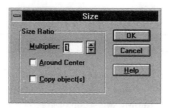

Fig. 8.6
The Size dialog box enables you to proportionally resize an image in specified increments.

To resize an image and stretch its height or width (change them in proportion to each other), use these techniques:

■ Point to one of the four corners of the image until the mouse pointer turns to a double-headed arrow. Press the left mouse button and drag to resize the image. Pressing Shift while dragging enables you to resize the horizontal and vertical size simultaneously. Pressing Ctrl while dragging creates a copy of the image and resizes the copy.

■ Point to one of the resize handles on the top, bottom, or side of the image until the mouse pointer turns to a double-headed arrow. Press the left mouse button and drag to resize the image. Pressing Ctrl while dragging creates a copy of the image and resizes the copy.

■ Point to one of the resize handles on the top, bottom, or side of the image until the mouse pointer turns to a double-headed arrow. Right-click to display the Stretch dialog box (see fig. 8.7). Select a **M**ultiplier for the selected dimension by typing it or using the incrementor buttons. For example, 2 doubles the size of the width or height, and .5 reduces the dimension by half. Choose **A**round Center to size from the center out, or choose **C**opy object(s) to create a copy of the image and resize the copy.

Fig. 8.7
Use the Stretch dialog box to change the proportions of an image.

Troubleshooting

When I try to move a QuickArt image, it jerks around and will not let me place it precisely where I want to. It jerks left or right when I release the mouse button. What's going on?

Your image is aligning to a grid that Presentations enables you to use to line up multiple objects. You need to turn off Presentations' Snap to Grid feature. Open the **V**iew menu and choose **G**rid/Snap, and then choose **S**nap to Grid from the submenu. Or, press Alt+F8 to toggle off this feature.

I dragged my QuickArt image to the edge of the page, and now some text is cut off.

Presentations does not display any image positioned beyond the margin areas. Reset the margins to 0 by opening the Format menu and choosing **P**age **S**ize/Margins, or drag the text container back within the dotted margin boundaries.

Cutting, Copying, and Pasting QuickArt

In addition to copying a QuickArt image as you resize it, you may want to make a copy of it to place on another slide, move it to another slide, or delete it altogether from your slide show. You can accomplish all these operations with the Cu**t**, **C**opy, and **P**aste commands on the **E**dit menu, or the corresponding icons on the Toolbar.

   To cut a piece of QuickArt from the slide and place it on the Clipboard, select it and then choose Cu**t** from the **E**dit menu (or press Ctrl+X) or click the Cut icon. To copy a piece of QuickArt, leaving the original in its present location and placing the copy on the Clipboard, choose **C**opy from the **E**dit menu (or press Ctrl+C) or click the Copy icon. To place the contents of the Clipboard in a new location, move to the slide you want and choose **P**aste from the **E**dit menu (or press Ctrl+V) or click the Paste icon.

Modifying QuickArt

As noted earlier in this chapter, one of the advantages to using QuickArt is that you easily can modify it to suit your needs. This capability is possible because each piece of QuickArt is made from a collection of drawn objects.

The specific techniques for editing the objects that compose a piece of QuickArt are described in Chapter 12, "Using the Presentations Drawing Tools," and 13, "Working with Outlines and Fills." Before you jump to those chapters to learn more, read on to learn how to select a figure for editing.

Before you make changes to the objects in a QuickArt image, you need to switch to the mode for editing it. When you do so, a hatched outline appears around the image. That hatched outline indicates that you can select and edit the objects in the QuickArt image. To display the hatched outline, double-click the QuickArt image or click it and choose Edit Figure from the Edit menu. You can stretch the hatched outline to make room to add more objects to it. To removed the hatched outline, click outside it, or right-click to display the QuickMenu and then choose Close Figure Editor.

You also can apply numerous special effects to a QuickArt image, just as you can to text. These features are described next; the steps for all these procedures are the same as the steps used in Chapter 7 for adding special effects to text; for more detail about any procedure, refer to Chapter 7.

Rotating the Image

You can rotate or skew a QuickArt object to change its position. *Rotating* it simply turns it around an axis; the image remains perpendicular relative to the axis. *Skewing* the image turns it around an axis and simultaneously tilts it relative to the axis.

To rotate or skew the image, first click on it to make the selection handles appear. Point to the image and right-click to display the QuickMenu and choose Rotate; or open the Edit menu and choose Rotate. The object changes to have rotation handles and a *rotation axis* (a black circle with a plus in the center of the image). Drag the rotation axis to a new location if needed. Drag a rotation or skew handle to a new location. Pressing Ctrl while dragging creates a copy of the image and rotates or skews it.

Note

To rotate or skew by precise intervals, point to a rotate or skew handle and right-click. Use the settings in the Rotate or Skew dialog box that appears, and then click OK.

Flipping the Image

You can flip QuickArt you add vertically or horizontally. Click to select the
QuickArt. Then open the **G**raphics menu and choose **F**lip **L**eft/Right or **F**lip
Top/Bottom.

Applying QuickWarp or Quick3-D to the Image

To shape QuickArt to fill a specialized curve or wave, or to add 3D depth to it,
use the QuickWarp and Quick3-D features.

Here's how to use these features (both of which were described in greater
detail in Chapter 7):

1. Click on the QuickArt image to select it.

2. Open the **G**raphics menu and choose Quick**W**arp or Quick**3**-D. Presen-
    tations displays the appropriate dialog box for the selected option.

3. Select the dialog box options of your choice. The preview area shows
    what effect that choice will have on your image.

4. Click OK. Your image warps on the slide. Figure 8.8 shows an image
    with QuickWarp added.

Fig. 8.8
A warped QuickArt
image.

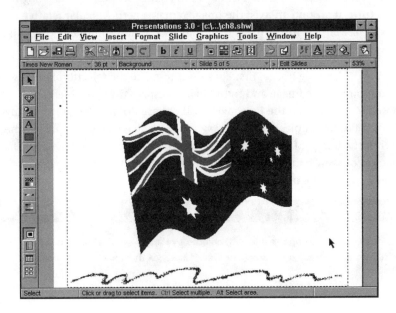

Using Other QuickArt Options

With QuickArt, you don't just have to take it or leave it. You can customize some aspects of the QuickArt Gallery in order to suit your particular purposes (such as saving a QuickArt image in a special format that's easy to place in WordPerfect documents). The rest of this chapter focuses on other features of the QuickArt Gallery.

Inserting Other Graphics

If you have been using computers for a while, it's likely that you have worked with other programs that offered clip-art collections. You also may have art you need to use frequently, such as a scanned logo. Or, you may have image files in various formats that you created yourself or collected from other sources, such as online services like CompuServe or the Internet—even if those images are in bitmap formats like PCX instead of vector formats. The QuickArt Gallery enables you to import graphics files of several types. Table 8.1 lists the types of graphics files you can import with the QuickArt Gallery.

Table 8.1   Graphic File Formats You Can Import

Extension	Type
BMP	Bitmaps
CGM	Computer Graphics Metafiles
DRW	Micrografx Designer
DXF	AutoCAD
EPS	Encapsulated Post Script
HPG	HP Graphics Language
PCT	Macintosh PICT
PCX	PC Paintbrush
PIC	Lotus PIC
TGA	Truevision Targa
TIF	Tagged Image Format
WMF	Windows Metafile
WPG	WordPerfect Graphics

II Enhancing Your Show

Keep in mind that when you import bitmap images like BMP, PCT, PCX, and TIF images, there may be limits to the amount of resizing you can do. Sizing the image to a size that's too large gives it the jaggies look. Inserting graphics files of another format is a straightforward procedure that resembles inserting QuickArt or opening a slide show file. Follow these steps:

1. Open the **I**nsert menu and Choose **Q**uickArt, or click the Insert Graphic tool on the palette, ensuring that you drag to select the icon for inserting figures (it looks like a diamond), if needed.

2. Point to the slide background. The mouse pointer changes to a hand holding a dotted outline.

3. Drag to create a box to hold the QuickArt. The QuickArt Gallery dialog box appears.

4. Click the O**t**her File command button. The Insert Figure dialog box appears (see fig. 8.9).

Fig. 8.9

You use the Insert Figure dialog box to insert figures in other graphics file formats.

Insert Figure		
File**n**ame:	c:\olfhelp	**Insert**
🖼	**QuickList:**	**Cancel**
239007.pcx	Drawings/Presentations Direc	
ch6.bk!	Graphics Directory	**View...**
ch6.shw	Macros Directory	
ch8.bk!	Masters/Galleries Directory	**QuickFinder...**
ch8.shw	Sound Directory	
readme.net		File **O**ptions ▾
readme.prw		
readme.shp	**D**irectories:	Quick**L**ist ▾
ride94.bk!	📂 c:\	
ride94.shw	📁 olfhelp	**S**etup...
riders.bk!	📁 gal2	
riders.shw		**Help**
samp.doc		
samp2.doc		
Total Files: 14	D**r**ives: 3,424 KB Free	
Total Bytes: 1,196,310	💾 c: bucki ▾	
Sort: Filename Ascending		
List Files of **T**ype: All Files (*.*) ▾		

Select the type of graphics file to retrieve.

Tip

Clicking on a file in the File**n**ame list and then clicking on the Vie**w** button enables you to preview a graphics file with the Viewer. Double-click the Viewer Control menu box to close it when you're done.

5. Start by using the List Files of **T**ype pull-down list to select the type of image to import.

6. Use the Dri**v**es and **D**irectories lists or QuickLists, if needed, to display files in other directories.

7. Click the name of the file you want in the File**n**ame list and then click **I**nsert, or simply double-click the file name. Presentations closes the Insert Figure and QuickArt Gallery dialog boxes and imports the file you

selected, inserting it into the area you drew in step 3. Figure 8.10 shows an example of a slide created for a seminar using an imported PCX image.

Fig. 8.10
You can import a variety of image types, including scanned photos like the one shown in this slide; this image is from a Corel Professional Photos CD-ROM.

Using QuickArt in Other Applications

The QuickArt Gallery enables you to save single or multiple QuickArt images as WPG (WordPerfect graphics) files to use with other PerfectOffice applications such as WordPerfect and Quattro Pro. You can convert a single QuickArt image, an entire category of images, or all the images. The Gallery converts the images and copies them to the directory you specify (although you should avoid copying them to C:\, your root directory, which can support only a limited number of files).

To convert a single image, display the QuickArt Gallery dialog box (by clicking the Insert Graphic tool on the Tool Palette and dragging to create an area for the QuickArt). Then select a category and click on the image you want to convert. To convert a category of images, display the QuickArt Gallery dialog box and click on a category. (Make sure that you have plenty of hard-drive space available to choose categories of images.) After you specify an image or category, click the **S**ave As WPG command button to display the dialog box shown in figure 8.11. Select whether to convert the Current **I**mage, Current **C**ategory, or **A**ll Categories of images. Type a directory to save to in the **D**irectory text box, or click the File icon beside it to display the Select Directory dialog box to browse to select a directory. After you make your directory specification, click OK to complete the conversion, and then click Cancel to close the QuickArt Gallery dialog box.

Tip
It's best to create a separate directory to store the converted images—especially if you're converting an entire category or more. Use the Windows File Manager to create a directory, and name it something like C:\WPG, so you easily can find your converted graphics.

File name for the converted image corresponds
to QuickArt image name

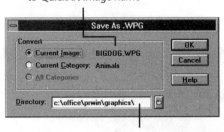

Fig. 8.11
Saving QuickArt in
WPG format.

Specify a directory to save the image(s) to.

Note

You can click to select a QuickArt image on a slide, and then choose Save **A**s from
the **F**ile menu (or press F3) to save it in a completely different graphics format such
as BMP. When the Save As dialog box appears, make sure that **S**elected Items is
selected and click OK. In the Save As dialog box, pull down the Save File as **T**ype list
and choose the file format to save to. Specify where you want to save the new image
in the Dri**v**es and **D**irectories lists, and type a name for the file in the File **n**ame text
box. Then click OK to finish the conversion. Chapter 17, "Printing and Saving Your
Slide Show: Basics and Other Considerations," gives additional information on saving
files to different formats.

Setting Gallery Options

You can customize the QuickArt Gallery display by clicking the **O**ptions button in the QuickArt Gallery dialog box to the Gallery Options dialog box
shown in figure 8.12. Change the **N**umber of Columns setting to determine
how many columns of thumbnails to display in the QuickArt Gallery. You
can display one to nine columns. The Create **Q**uick Files option is a bit more
complicated. When this option is enabled, Presentations saves the images in
any QuickArt category you view in special bitmap files on the hard drive,
which speeds up the display of the QuickArt images. There is a down side to
enabling this option, however. Doing so takes up more hard-drive space and
memory (RAM), so if you're low on either of those commodities, turn off this
option. Click OK after you make your choice to close the Gallery Options
dialog box.

Fig. 8.13
Changing
QuickArt display
options.

Creating a Gallery Category

As you may have noticed by now in your travels with Presentations, each category of QuickArt is actually a Presentations slide show saved in the \OFFICE\PRWIN\GALLERY directory on your computer. If you were to open one of the gallery slide show files, you would see that each image appears on a separate slide, and that each image is sized to fill the whole slide.

Those are almost all the facts you need to know to learn how to create your own QuickArt Gallery category. Suppose that you have a series of PCX images that show outdoor scenes, and you think you might want to use some of these scenes as slide backgrounds. Or, you have a few drawings you created with the Presentations palette tools, and you want to use them again. To make these drawings easy to access, you want to save them in a QuickArt Gallery category. You can do so if you want. The general process involves creating and saving the slide show holding the images you want to group in a category, adding a cover slide for the new category to the list of title slides, and then linking the title slide in the gallery to the slide show files holding your images.

Follow these steps to add a new QuickArt Gallery category:

1. Create a new slide show. Open the **F**ile menu and choose **N**ew (or press Ctrl+N) or click the New icon to create a new slide show. In the New Document dialog box, choose Create a New **S**lide Show and click OK. When the New Slide Show dialog box appears, do not select a master with the **G**allery button, and make sure that None is selected as the Slide Type. You want to start a slide show with no master and no slide layouts.

2. Add the images to the slide show, one image per page, with each image sized to the full page. To insert the image on each slide, open the **I**nsert menu and choose **Q**uickArt, or click the Insert Graphic tool on the palette, ensuring that you drag to select the icon for inserting figures (it looks like a diamond), if needed. Point to the center of the slide and click to insert the image at full size. Use the O**t**her File button in the

QuickArt Gallery dialog box to specify the file you want to insert and its format as described in "Inserting Other Graphics," earlier in this chapter. Add a new slide, and repeat the insert procedure. After you add all your slides, switch to Outliner view, if desired, and type a title for each slide.

3. After you have added all the slides (images) you want, save the slide show to the \OFFICE\PRWIN\GALLERY directory. You could save your collection of scenes as SCENES.SHW, for example. Do not close the slide show.

 4. Open the **F**ile menu and choose **O**pen (or press Ctrl+O) or click the Open icon on the Toolbar, and open the FIGURGAL.SHW slide show from the \OFFICE\PRWIN\GALLERY directory.

 5. Now you need to copy the cover slide for your slide show to the FIGURGAL.SHW slide show, which organizes the cover slides for all the slide show categories. With FIGURGAL.SHW open, press Ctrl+End to move to the last slide in the show, and then choose **A**dd Slides from the **S**lide menu or click the Add Slides button on the Toolbar. This inserts a new, blank slide into FIGURGAL.SHW.

  6. Use the Window menu to switch to the slide show you created for your gallery category. Press Ctrl+Home to move to the first slide, if it's not already displayed. You want to copy this graphic to the new slide you inserted in FIGURGAL.SHW in step 5. Choose Se**l**ect **A**ll from the **E**dit menu (this is preferable to clicking, especially if you're copying a drawing consisting of many objects). Then choose **C**opy from the **E**dit menu (or press Ctrl+C) or click the Copy icon. Use the **W**indow menu to move back to FIGURGAL.SHW, making sure that the new, blank slide is the current slide, and open the **E**dit menu and choose **P**aste (or press Ctrl+V) or click the Paste icon. This action pastes your image into FIGURGAL.SHW. Click a margin to deselect the image.

 7. Open the **V**iew menu and choose **O**utliner or click the Outliner View tool on the palette. This action changes to Outliner view, so that you can add a title for your cover slide, which you just copied to FIGURGAL.SHW (see fig. 8.13). There should be an icon for your cover slide, with a blank Title line beside it. Click in the Title line and enter a name for your QuickArt category. If you skip this step, your cover slide will be named "Untitled" in the QuickArt Gallery.

Using Other QuickArt Options

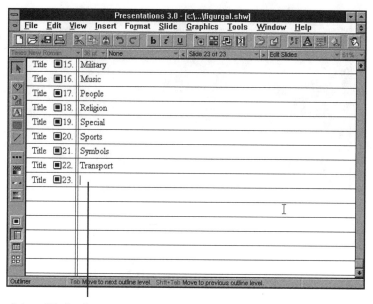

Enter a title for the new category.

Fig. 8.13
You use
Outliner view in
FIGURGAL.SHW
to add a title for
your cover slide.

8. Save FIGURGAL.SHW by opening the **F**ile menu and choosing **S**ave (or pressing Ctrl+S), and choosing **C**lose from the **F**ile menu (or pressing Ctrl+F4) to close the file. Also save and close your slide show.

9. With another slide show open, choose **Q**uickArt from the **I**nsert menu, or click the Insert Graphic tool on the palette, ensuring that you drag to select the icon for inserting figures (it looks like a diamond), if needed. Point to the slide margin and click once to display the QuickArt Gallery dialog box without defining an image area. Make sure that the categories are displayed (clicking the **C**ategories button in the QuickArt Gallery dialog box, if needed), and scroll to the cover slide for your new category. Click the slide to select it (see fig. 8.14).

10. Click the **L**ink button in the QuickArt Gallery dialog box. Presentations displays the Edit Gallery dialog box. You need to specify the file name of the slide show for your new category of images, as shown in figure 8.15. Type the name in the **F**ilename list box or use the File icon beside the text box to browse for the file. Click OK after you specify the file name to link the image file to the cover slide.

11. Double-click the cover slide to display the figures it contains (see fig. 8.16).

Tip
While you're in Outliner view, you also can drag cover slides to new locations to change the order that the categories appear in within the QuickArt Gallery.

Enhancing Your Show

Fig. 8.14
The cover slide you added to FIGURGAL.SHW now appears in the QuickArt Gallery. You need to link the cover slide to the slide show you created for the category.

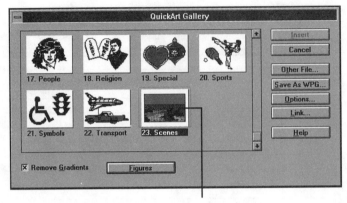

New cover slide

Fig. 8.15
Linking the slide show file with your images to the cover slide title.

Your cover slide title

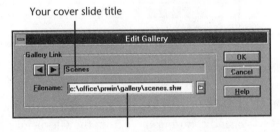

The slide show file with your images

Fig. 8.16
This slide is in a new, custom QuickArt category.

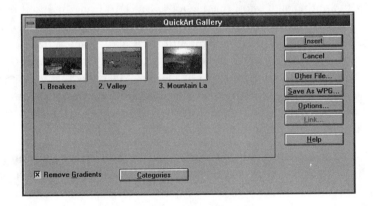

Troubleshooting

I changed a slide show that contains a QuickArt Gallery category, but when I clicked its cover slide in the gallery, nothing happened.

You need to relink the cover slide with the slide show that contains the images. Repeat steps 9 through 11 of the preceding procedure to fix this problem.

From Here...

With QuickArt, you can painlessly illustrate your slides to make them appear more attractive and professional. As you learned in this chapter, the QuickArt Gallery makes it easy to insert not only the images that come with Presentations, but also images from other sources that you may need to use frequently, such as your company logo. Once you're comfortable working with QuickArt basics, you may want to move on to topics in these chapters:

- Chapter 12, "Using the Presentations Drawing Tools," explains how to use the tools on the tool palette to draw vector images on a slide and how to edit objects. You can save these kinds of images in your own QuickArt categories.

- Chapter 13, "Working with Outlines and Fills," teaches you to apply attributes to vector objects on a slide. You can use the techniques described here to edit QuickArt images.

- Chapter 14, "Working with Bitmap Images," describes how to create bitmap images in Presentations, and how to scan bitmap images directly into Presentations for use in slides or for saving in a QuickArt category.

- Chapter 17, "Printing and Saving Your Slide Show: Basics and Other Considerations," explains, among other things, how to use Save As to save Presentations slide shows and selected objects such as QuickArt in other formats.

II

Enhancing Your Show

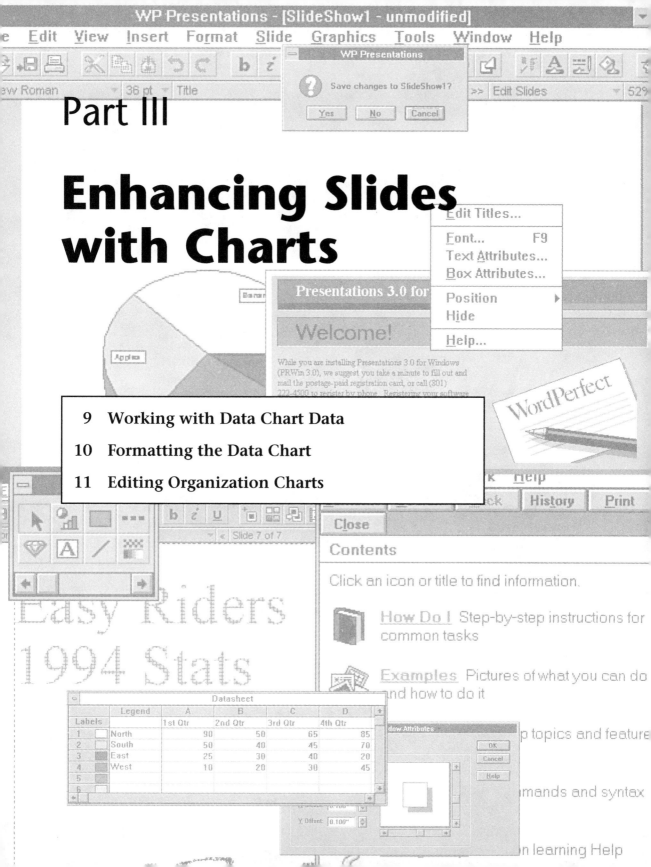

Part III

Enhancing Slides with Charts

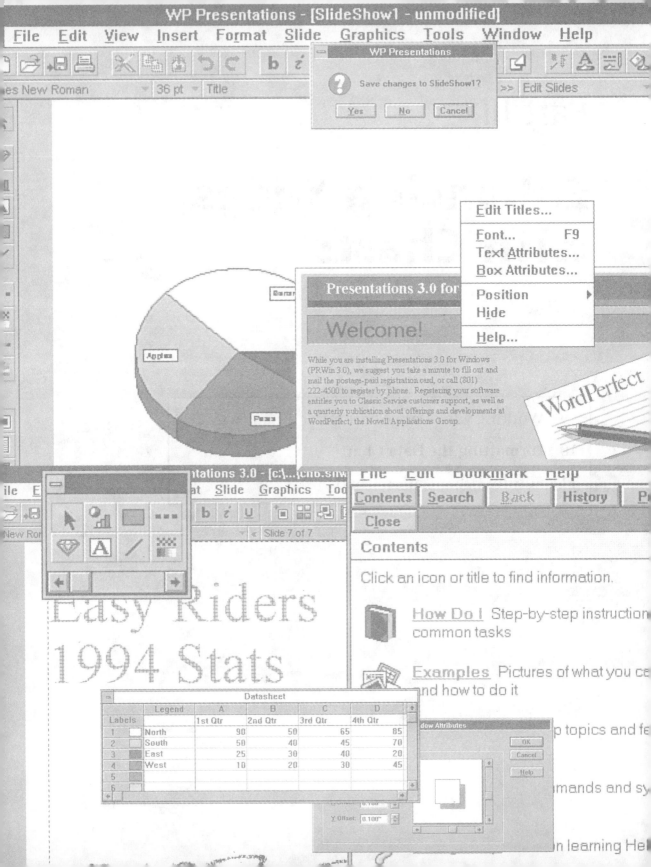

Chapter 9

Working with Data Chart Data

The most traditional use for slides and overheads in a presentation is to display graphs of numerical data to effectively communicate that data to your audience. Displaying the data in this visual way makes the data clearer, enabling viewers to identify trends and anomalies with just a glance.

The Gallery of data charts in WordPerfect Presentations 3.0 for Windows enables you to create a chart for just about any type of numerical data you need to communicate to an audience. The Gallery provides 11 categories of charts, with numerous preformatted variations within each category. All you have to do is make a Gallery selection and enter your data to create a fantastic, full-color chart with 3D effects and more.

You learned the basics for creating a data chart in Chapter 3, "Using the Various Slide Templates." This chapter acquaints you with the various kinds of data charts available in Presentations, and explains how to perform the following tasks:

- Choosing the right chart type for the data you need to display, and selecting a new chart type

- Editing the chart data

- Pasting data into the data sheet or importing it from other applications

- Filling data series

- Analyzing and sorting data

Understanding the Different Data Chart Types

Most people wouldn't try to unscrew a screw with a hammer. Similarly, in Presentations you shouldn't try to show a trend with a pie chart. Choosing the right chart type for your data is as important as choosing the right tool for a home-repair job. Each of Presentations' 11 data chart types best presents a certain type of data and best communicates a certain message. See table 9.1 for a description of each chart type and the type of data it best presents. Use this table to help select the best chart type for your data. Figures 9.1, 9.2, and 9.3 illustrate each data chart type, using sample data that Presentations inserts into the data sheet.

Table 9.1 The Data Chart Types in Presentations	
Date Chart Type	**Shows**
Area	Magnitudes of the values charted, and trends or changes over time.
Horizontal Bar	Variations in discrete values; the bars run horizontally, from left to right.
Vertical Bar	Variations in discrete values; the bars run vertically, from the bottom up.
High/Low	Daily high, low, open, and close values for items like stocks; the ends of the vertical lines indicate the high and low values, and the horizontal lines indicate the open and close values.
Line	Trends over time by connecting values with lines.
Mixed	Two series types for the data, such as lines and bars.
Pie	A circular representation with each value shown as a wedge so that the values can be compared to the whole; you can create up to nine pie charts on each data sheet.
Radar	Data radiating from the center so that you can compare trends and magnitudes.
Scatter	Discrete values where data points coincide along the X and Y axes.

Date Chart Type	Shows
Surface	Data on a blanket-like surface that rises and falls to emphasize peaks and valleys.
Table	Rows and columns of data, much like a spreadsheet.

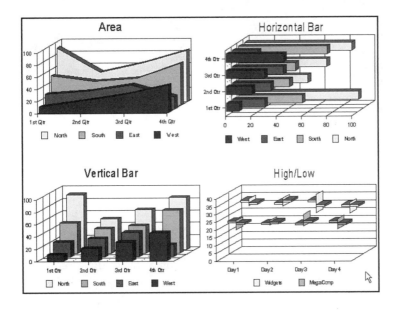

Fig. 9.1
Sample Area, Horizontal Bar, Vertical Bar, and High/Low charts.

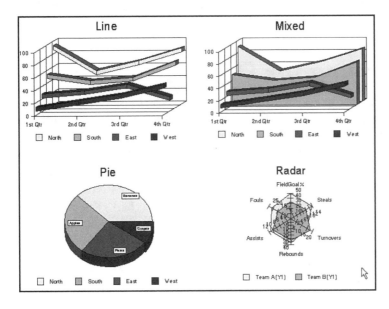

Fig. 9.2
Sample Line, Mixed, Pie, and Radar charts.

III

Using Charts

Fig. 9.3

Sample Scatter, Surface, and Table charts.

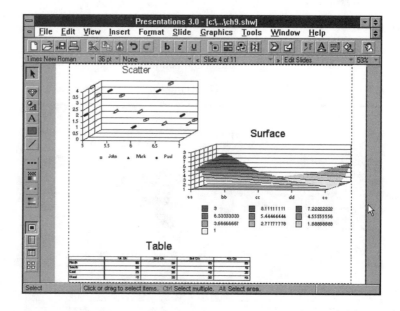

Tip

If you aren't completely sure about how to enter the data for a chart type, examine the sample data for cues.

Data charts compare series of data. A *series* groups all the data points related to one entity. If you have three products and you want to compare their sales each month for four months, a series would consist of the four monthly sales figures for a single product. As you can see from some of the descriptions in table 9.1, in most data charts, data is charted against one or more axes. The X axis is the horizontal axis, and usually is used to indicate time, such as the four months in this example. The vertical axis, or Y axis, usually indicates the units being measured, such as dollars.

Selecting the Chart

As with other items you place on a slide, you can make numerous changes to data charts. As you learned in previous chapters about working with text and QuickArt, you can click on a chart to display selection handles. When a chart is selected in this manner, you can copy or move it by choosing Cu**t** from the **E**dit menu (or pressing Ctrl+X) or **C**opy from the **E**dit menu (or pressing Ctrl+C), and then choosing **P**aste from the **E**dit menu (or pressing Ctrl+V). Or, you can drag the resize handles to change the chart's size and proportion. You even can rotate or add perspective to a chart selected in this way by using the R**o**tate and Perspecti**v**e commands on the **E**dit menu.

To edit the chart, you need to achieve the equivalent of placing the insertion point within a text container. To make changes to the type of data chart, the data within the data chart, or the design of the chart elements, you need to enter the Chart Editor to make the tools for editing charts available. Follow these steps:

1. Click the data chart to display its selection handles.

2. Open the Edit menu and choose Edit Chart, or right-click on the chart to display the QuickMenu and then click Edit Chart. Presentations changes to Chart Editor view (see fig. 9.4).

3. Open the View Menu and choose Datasheet to display the Datasheet Window when editing the chart.

Tip
You also can simply double-click a chart to enter the Chart Editor.

Chart menu   New chart tools

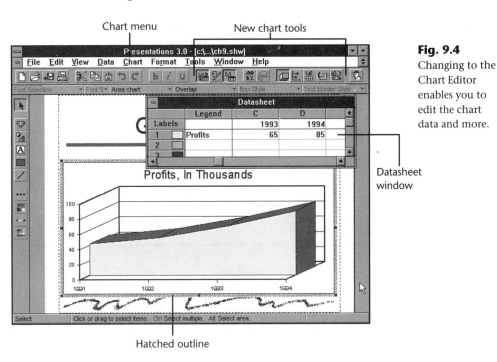

Datasheet window

Hatched outline

Fig. 9.4
Changing to the Chart Editor enables you to edit the chart data and more.

When Presentations enters the Chart Editor, the selected chart is surrounded by a hatched outline, and the datasheet with the chart data appears. Two new menus, Data and Chart, are added to the menu bar. In addition, new icons are added to the Toolbar to facilitate chart editing. Table 9.2 shows the new charting icons and describes the function of each. In addition, the Power Bar changes to offer buttons for adjusting the font and size of chart text, changing the chart type and style, and adjusting borders around chart text. You learn how to use many of the Chart Editor's formatting tools in the next chapter. This chapter concentrates on working with the datasheet, shown in figure 9.4.

III

Using Charts

Table 9.2	The Chart Editor Toolbar Icons
Tool	**Description**
	Automatically redraws the chart when you change datasheet data.
	Turns on manual redraw of the chart based on data changes when you click it.
	Toggles on and off datasheet display.
	Formats datasheet data.
	Sorts datasheet data.
	Toggles on and off 3D appearance.
	Presents chart data in a horizontal format.
	Displays a data table as part of the chart.
	Displays the Layout dialog box so that you can edit chart depth, size, and display.
	Enables you to edit the appearance of the data series.

To leave the Chart Editor, simply click outside the chart on a blank area of the slide, or point to the chart (not the datasheet), right-click to display the QuickMenu (making sure that you haven't selected any items on the chart), and choose Close Chart Editor.

Working in the Datasheet

 The *datasheet* contains a matrix of vertical columns (labeled with letters A, B, and so on) and horizontal rows (labeled with numbers 1, 2, and so on), much like a spreadsheet. The intersection of a row and column is called a *cell*. Each cell has an address consisting of its column letter plus its row number. The cell in the fifth row of column B is cell B5, for example. When working in the Chart Editor, you can toggle on and off display of the Datasheet window by clicking the View Data Toolbar icon or by opening the **V**iew menu and choosing **D**atasheet. Closing the datasheet does not exit Chart Editor view. The Datasheet window behaves like any other window; you can resize it, drag its title bar to move it on-screen, use the scroll bars to view other parts of the data it contains, or close it by double-clicking its Control menu box.

Entering and Editing Data

Figure 9.5 shows the sample data that Presentations gives you when you create a new vertical bar data chart. The top row of the datasheet presents the labels for the X axis—in this case, quarterly time periods. The first column contains the series names, which also are used in the chart legend if you choose to display one. Each row on the datasheet contains the values for one series. The X axis labels and series names can be labels (text) or dates. All the other entries in the datasheet must be numeric.

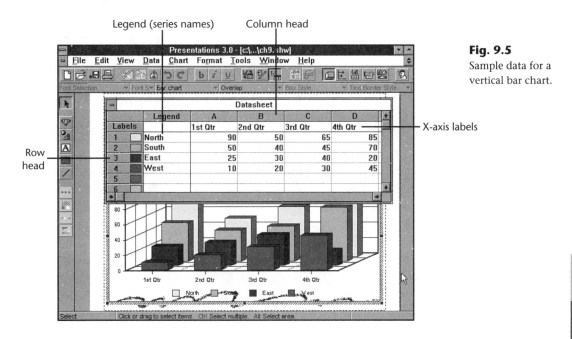

Fig. 9.5
Sample data for a vertical bar chart.

To complete your data chart, you need to replace the sample series names, X axis labels, and values with the information you want to chart. To enter data in a blank cell, simply select it by clicking on it or by moving to it with the arrow keys, and then type a label or value. A rectangular selector tells you when you have selected the cell. You also need to replace existing sample data. You can use a couple of methods to change the labels, series names, and data in data-entry cells in a datasheet:

Tip
To clear all the sample datasheet data, open the **E**dit menu and choose Clear **A**ll, or press Ctrl+Shift+F4.

III

Using Charts

- Double-click a cell to display the Edit Current Cell dialog box. You also can display this dialog box by selecting a cell and pressing F11 (or opening the Edit menu and choosing **E**dit Cell). Enter a new value or label for the cell, and then click OK.

- Use the arrow keys or press Tab to move to the cell you want (or click on the cell), and type the new value.

Selecting Cells

In some instances, you need to move around the datasheet more quickly or select multiple cells at once. You can press Ctrl plus an arrow key to jump quickly to the last cell visible in the direction you specify. If your datasheet window is sized so that 10 rows are fully visible and you press Ctrl+Down arrow, for example, the selector jumps to the cell in row 10 of the column where it's located. If you know the address of the cell you want to go to, choose **G**o To Cell from the **E**dit menu or the Datasheet QuickMenu (or press Ctrl+G) to display the Go To dialog box. Type an address in the **C**ell text box and then click OK to move the selector to it.

Selecting more than one cell puts a special reverse highlight on it. You can use the following techniques to select multiple cells at once:

- Use the mouse to drag over the cells you want to highlight.

- Move the selector to a cell in one corner of the group of cells you want to select, press and hold the Shift key, and use the arrow keys to extend the selection.

- Click a column head or row head to select the whole column or row.

- Select the whole datasheet by choosing **S**elect All from the **E**dit menu or Datasheet QuickMenu, or by clicking the gray box at the upper left corner of the Datasheet window where the column heads and row heads intersect.

Clearing Data

Figure 9.6 shows the datasheet from figure 9.5, with the top two rows edited. To clear the remaining sample data, you can select the rows containing it and use the Cle**a**r (Delete) command, available on both the **E**dit menu and the Datasheet QuickMenu. Choosing this command displays the Clear dialog box, which you can use to clear the cell entries or cell formatting, or both (see fig. 9.7). Make your selection and click OK to delete the data. Note that clearing the data does not place it on the Windows Clipboard, but instead completely discards it.

New data in
these rows

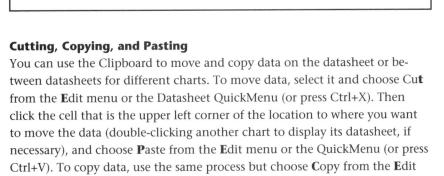

Fig. 9.6
Sample data has
been replaced in
the datasheet.

Fig. 9.7
Clearing data
and formatting
removes it
permanently from
the chart.

Troubleshooting

I mistakenly deleted my chart data, and Undo isn't available. How do I get my data back?

To enable Undo, immediately click outside the chart to leave the Chart Editor, and then click the Undo icon, or open the **E**dit menu and choose **U**ndo (or press Ctrl+Z).

Cutting, Copying, and Pasting

You can use the Clipboard to move and copy data on the datasheet or between datasheets for different charts. To move data, select it and choose Cu**t**
from the **E**dit menu or the Datasheet QuickMenu (or press Ctrl+X). Then
click the cell that is the upper left corner of the location to where you want
to move the data (double-clicking another chart to display its datasheet, if
necessary), and choose **P**aste from the **E**dit menu or the QuickMenu (or press
Ctrl+V). To copy data, use the same process but choose **C**opy from the **E**dit

III

Using Charts

menu (or press Ctrl+C) rather than Cut. Be aware that when you paste your data to the new location, the pasted data overwrites any data that was previously in the cells. If you don't want to lose that data, move it out of the way before you cut or copy other data to paste there.

Transposing Data by Pasting

After you have copied data to the Clipboard, you can perform a special type of paste to transpose the data. *Transposing* converts data rows to columns and vice versa. Thus, the values from row 1 in the original data are placed down column 1 in the pasted (transposed) data, and so on. To transpose data after you have cut or copied it to the Clipboard, click on the datasheet cell where you want the transposed data to start, open the **E**dit menu, and choose Paste Transposed.

Redrawing the Chart

You can specify whether Presentations automatically redraws the chart after you make changes to the datasheet, or whether it waits for you to ask it to redraw the chart. To toggle on and off automatic redraw, use the Automatic Redraw button on the Chart Editor Toolbar, or open the **V**iew menu and choose **A**uto Redraw.

Leaving off the Auto Redraw feature can speed up your data entry, because Presentations doesn't have to stop and redraw the screen every time you change a cell. The down side is that you have to tell Presentations when you want to see the results of your changes. To manually redraw the chart after changing data, click the Redraw button on the Chart Editor Toolbar, or open the **V**iew menu and choose **R**edraw (or press Ctrl+F3).

Changing Datasheet Layout

If you're having a good year and have lots of zeros to display in your data, you may need to increase the width of the datasheet columns to view your data. You can change the widths of all the columns by dragging. Point to the right border of a column head so that the mouse cursor turns into a two-headed arrow intersected by a vertical bar (see fig. 9.8). Drag the column border to make the columns wider or narrower, and release the mouse button. Alternatively, you can open the **D**ata menu and choose **C**olumn Width to display the Column Width dialog box, specify a new width (in characters), and click OK.

Two-headed
arrow

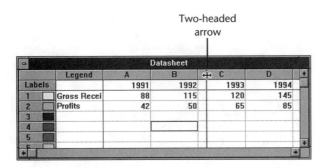

Fig. 9.8
Resizing a column
in the Datasheet
window.

Changing Data Formats

The way data is displayed in the datasheet doesn't affect how it's charted, but it can make it easier for you—and anyone else who's working on a presentation with you—to adjust the precision or meaning of the numbers. You can specify the number of decimal values displayed, whether to display numbers as percents or dollar values, how to display negative numbers, and how to display dates.

Suppose that you're creating a pie chart to compare for your audience the relative values of the cost of goods sold and the margin or profit for your company. You're pasting the data from a spreadsheet program where you already have calculated it into the datasheet for your pie chart. When you paste the data into the datasheet, you're surprised to find that you're getting decimal values (such as .88 and .12) rather than the percentages you saw in the spreadsheet. That's because the actual value of a percentage in a spreadsheet is a decimal value; it is formatted only to eliminate the decimals and include the percentage sign. For clarity, you want to do the same thing in your datasheet—you want to display .88 and .12 as 88% and 12%.

To change the format of data in the datasheet, follow these steps:

1. Select the cells in which you want to change the format.

2. Choose F**o**rmat from the **D**ata menu or QuickMenu (or press Ctrl+F12), or click the Format icon on the Chart Editor Toolbar. The Format dialog box appears.

3. Click to specify a **N**umeric or **D**ate format, based on whether you're formatting numbers or dates. If you chose **D**ate, simply choose a date format from the list and click OK. If you chose **N**umeric, there are a few more choices to make, as shown in figure 9.9.

III

Using Charts

Preview

Fig. 9.9
Defining a format
for numbers
displayed in the
datasheet.

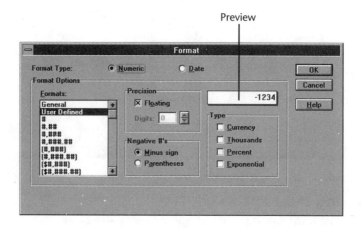

4. To use a predefined format, click one from the Formats list. To specify your own format, click User Defined in the list, which enables the other dialog box options as shown in figure 9.9. Specify the number of decimal points in the Precision area, whether to treat negative numbers with a Minus Sign or Parentheses, and a Type of number such as Percent.

5. Click OK to close the dialog box and apply the formatting.

Inserting and Deleting Rows and Columns

If you realized you omitted some data from your datasheet or would like to omit some data, you can do so easily and quickly by inserting a row or column to accept new data or by cutting a row or column to remove it from the datasheet. Note that when you insert a row, existing data is moved down one row; when you insert a column, existing data is moved right one column. When you delete a row or column, the data in it also is deleted. Use these steps to insert or delete rows and columns:

1. Click on the header for the row or column you want to insert or delete.

2. Choose Insert or Delete from the Edit menu or QuickMenu, as appropriate.

3. If you're deleting a row or column that contains data, click OK at the message that appears to continue the deletion.

Including and Excluding Rows and Columns

Presentations enables you to control whether the data in your datasheet actually displays on a chart, without deleting the data. Removing the data from display is called *excluding* it. To redisplay the data, you *include* it. Figure 9.10 shows an example of data present in the datasheet but excluded from chart display. When data is excluded, it appears grayed out on the datasheet.

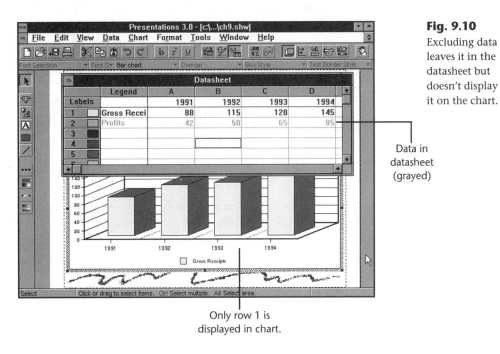

Fig. 9.10
Excluding data leaves it in the datasheet but doesn't display it on the chart.

Data in datasheet (grayed)

Only row 1 is displayed in chart.

To exclude or include rows or columns of data from the chart display, follow these steps:

1. Click on the header for the row or column you want to include or exclude.

2. Choose **I**nclude Row/Col or **E**xclude Row/Col from the **D**ata menu or QuickMenu, as appropriate.

Filling a Series

Data entry can be a tedious task, especially if you're typing dates or a long list of incrementing data. Presentations gives you a shortcut to eliminate the busy work so that you can get down to displaying the results: filling a row or column with a series of numbers. Suppose that you want to look at sales on your two products over four consecutive quarters, but you don't want to type Qtr-1, Qtr-2, and so on. Here are the steps for saving time by filling the series:

1. Select the cells that you want to fill in the row or column.

2. Open the **D**ata menu and choose **F**ill (or press Ctrl+Shift+F12). The Data Fill dialog box appears, as shown in figure 9.11.

Fig. 9.11
Using the Data Fill
dialog box to
automatically
enter series of data
in cells.

Tip
To fill a range
with the same
number, choose
the **G**rowth data-
fill type and
specify a S**t**ep
value of 1.

3. If you didn't select a group of cells in step 1, specify a fill Direction: **R**ows or **C**olumns.

4. Specify a fill Type. **L**inear increases the entry for each cell by adding the specified step value to the value in the current cell. **G**rowth multiplies each cell by the specified step value to create the entry for the next cell. **D**ate is used to increment by days, weeks, quarters, years, and so on. Choose a value from the pop-up list, such as Quarters.

5. Enter a **S**tart value, or the value you want in the first cell of the series. For dates, you need to enter the value in the format of m/d/y. You enter 1/1/94 to start your quarterly dates at the first quarter of 1994, for example.

6. Enter a S**t**ep value. This is the value by which your series is incremented (or multiplied by for **G**rowth fills).

7. Click OK. Presentations closes the dialog box and fills the cells you specified.

The filled numbers you get may not look quite like the values you want to see, especially if you're filling a series of dates. The cell entries you would get if you filled a year by quarters would look like 3/30/94, 6/30/94, and so on. Open the **D**ata menu and choose F**o**rmat (or press Ctrl+F12) to change the display to Q1-94, or whatever format you prefer.

Analyzing the Statistics

Presentations enables you to see at a glance some pertinent information
about a particular row or column of data. Click on a cell in the row or column you want to analyze, open the **D**ata menu, and choose S**t**atistics. The
Data Statistics dialog box appears, which lists the number of data points in
the row/column; minimum, maximum, and average values; standard devia-
tion; and what kind of statistical curve the data fits, if a curve has been defined for that row or column (see fig. 9.12).

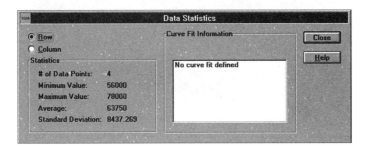

Fig. 9.12
Statistics about a
particular row of
data.

Using Formulas

You can use formulas to automatically calculate data in a datasheet; you can
perform functions such as summing, subtracting, averaging, and more. The
advantage to using formulas comes when you need to edit your data; you can
make the changes and then recalculate the data to view updated results. In
Presentations, you cannot type formulas as mathematical expressions. You
have to use the Row/Column Formulas dialog box to select a formula to insert in a worksheet row or column. Suppose that you are comparing quarterly
sales data for your two products, and you want to add a row that totals the
sales of the products (see fig. 9.13).

Total the
data in this
row.

	Legend	A	B	C	D
Labels		Q1-94	Q2-94	Q3-94	Q4-94
1	Product 1	56000	61000	60000	78000
2	Product 2	43000	50000	57000	63000
3	Total				
4					
5					
6					

Fig. 9.13
Comparing
quarterly sales for
two products.

III

Using Charts

To enter a calculation, follow these steps:

1. Click on a cell in the row or column that you want to hold the results of the calculation.

2. Open the **D**ata menu and choose Form**u**las. The Row/Column Formulas dialog box appears (see fig. 9.14).

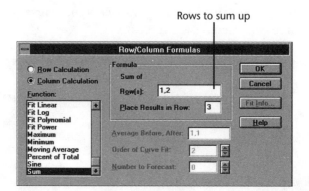

Rows to sum up

Fig. 9.14
These settings sum the row 1 and 2 contents of each column and place the results in row 3.

3. To calculate values across rows and place the results in a column to the right, click the **R**ow Calculation radio button. To calculate values down columns and place the results in a row below, click the **C**olumn Calculation radio button.

4. Click a **F**unction in the list, such as Sum. Scroll to display more functions, if needed.

5. Specify which R**o**w(s) or C**o**lumn(s) of data to calculate. To specify two rows or columns, you can separate the header numbers or letters with a comma, as shown in figure 9.14. To specify even more rows or columns, separate the header numbers or letters with a colon, as in 1:5, which calculates the values in rows 1 through 5.

6. Specify which column or row Presentations should **P**lace Results in, if it's different from the row or column containing the cell you selected earlier in this procedure.

7. Click OK. Presentations places the formulas in the specified row/column, and displays the resulting calculations. Figure 9.15 shows the results of using the Sum function to total two rows of data. Note that the new data also is added to the chart as a separate series that you may need to reformat to suit your tastes. See Chapter 10, "Formatting the Data Chart," to learn how to reformat series display.

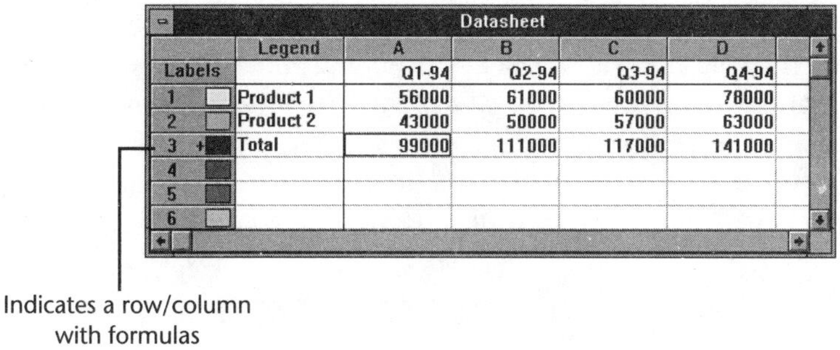

Fig. 9.15
Summing two
rows of data.

Indicates a row/column
with formulas

If you make a change in data that's calculated on the datasheet, you need to tell Presentations to update the calculation. Open the **D**ata menu and choose **R**ecalculate (or press Alt+Shift+F12). Presentations updates the results displayed in the datasheet.

Applying Curve-Fitting Formulas

The Row/Column Formulas dialog box offers several specialized statistical functions, called *Fit* functions, that you can use to analyze how your data compares to certain kinds of trends and project future results based on the kind of curve that your data fits. Fit curves are *regression* curves, meaning that they define a pattern of values. If the values in your datasheet approximate the curve, then you can expect the future data of whatever you're measuring to match the curve as well. You therefore can fit your sales data to a curve and predict approximate future sales figures. You can fit your data to these curve types:

- *Exponential.* Grows exponentially.
- *Linear.* Grows in a straight line, as if values are being added.
- *Log.* Grows logarithmically.
- *Polynomial.* Grows in a fluctuating fashion; choose this fit if your data doesn't match other fit types, but don't rely on this data as a prediction tool.
- *Power.* Fits your data to a power curve.

Figure 9.15 can serve as a basic example. Suppose that you want to take those total sales figures in row 3 and project what your sales will be for the first two quarters of '95. You start out by selecting a cell in row 4, because that's where you want to insert the results of the curve fit. Next, you open the **D**ata menu

III

Using Charts

and choose Form**u**las to display the Row/Column Formulas dialog box (see fig. 9.16). You then click on Fit Exponential from the **F**unction list to start, and ensure that row 3 was entered for Fit Exponential of R**o**w(s) and row 4 was entered for the **P**lace Results in Row. You enter 4 in the **N**umber to Forecast text box, because you want to predict results for four more quarters. At this point, the Row/Column Formulas dialog box resembles figure 9.16.

Fig. 9.16
Preparing to fit the data in figure 9.15 to a regression curve.

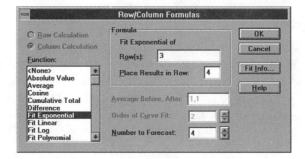

The next step is to use the Fit **I**nfo button in the Row/Column Formulas dialog box to determine what curve type most closely approximates the data in row 3 (the data being fit to a curve). Click this button to display the Curve Fit Info dialog box, shown in figure 9.17. To match the best curve-fit formula to data, select the curve-fit type with the correlation coefficient closest to 1.0. Use the **F**it Type pop-up list to examine each fit in turn. Choose the Polynomial type if none of the other coefficients approach 1.0. In this case, Exponential fits the data best.

Fig. 9.17
Using the Curve Fit Info dialog box to choose the best curve to fit your data to.

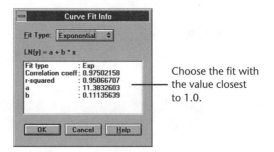

Choose the fit with the value closest to 1.0.

After you make your final selection from the **F**it Type pop-up list, click OK to return to the Row/Column Formulas dialog box. Click OK again to fit your data to the curve and place the fit data in the specified row (in this case, 4). Figure 9.18 shows the results of the example curve fit. Presentations took the values in the Total data in row 3, altered the values slightly so that they fit the Exponential curve-fit formula (109751.397 in cell B4 is an approximation of 111000 in cell B3, for example), and then extended the curve by projecting four more values in columns E through H of row 4.

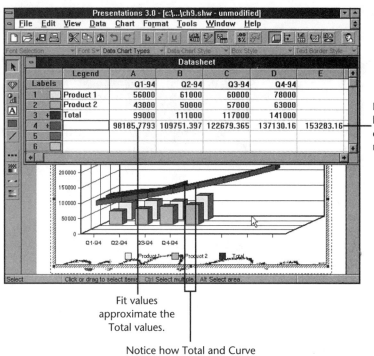

Fig. 9.18
Row 4 contains the Total data, fit to an exponential curve.

Projected values begin here and continue to the right.

Fit values approximate the Total values.

Notice how Total and Curve data follow similar trend.

Sorting Data

For some charts, it makes little difference in what order the data is entered on the datasheet. Because the datasheet order controls the charted display of the data, however, you might encounter situations where you want to change the order of data. Suppose that you have a bar chart comparing sales of products 1 and 2 in rows 1 and 2, respectively. Product 2 always sells more, so the values in row 2 are much higher that the values in row 1. When you view the chart, unfortunately, the bars for product 2 are so large they obscure the bars for product 1, ruining your ability to visually compare the two.

You can fix this situation by sorting the chart data in the datasheet. Presentations enables you to sort selected rows or columns of data.

III

Using Charts

Use these steps to sort datasheet data:

1. Select the cells in the rows or columns to sort, including the column (if you're sorting by column) or row headings.

2. Choose **S**ort from the **D**ata menu or QuickMenu (or press Alt+F9), or click the Sort icon on the Chart Editor Toolbar. The Sort Data dialog box appears (see fig. 9.19).

Fig. 9.19
Preparing to sort data.

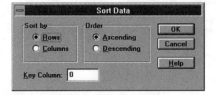

3. Change the Sort by setting, if needed.

4. Enter a **K**ey Column or **K**ey Row to sort by. Leave this setting at 0 to sort alphabetically based on legend or X-axis labels. Otherwise, enter the first row or column that contains the kind of value you want to sort.

5. Specify an **A**scending or **D**escending sort.

6. Click OK to complete the sort.

Importing Chart Data

There's no use in redoing work, so if you already have created data in a spreadsheet program (or another program that enables you to save it as ASCII or ANSI delimited text), you can import that data into your datasheet. You can directly import data from these spreadsheet programs: Quattro Pro for Windows, Quattro Pro for DOS (versions 2.0 through 4.0), Lotus 1-2-3 for Windows, Lotus 1-2-3 for DOS (versions 2.01 through 3.1), Excel (versions 2.1 through 4.0) and PlanPerfect (versions 3.0 through 5.1).

To import data into the open datasheet, follow these steps:

1. Save and close the spreadsheet or other file holding the data you want to import.

2. Go to your Presentations slide show, and display the datasheet for the chart in which you want to insert the data. (If you need to add a new slide, do so first and choose a chart type from the Gallery.)

3. Open the **D**ata menu and choose **Im**port (or press Ctrl+O) to display the Import Data dialog box (see fig. 9.20).

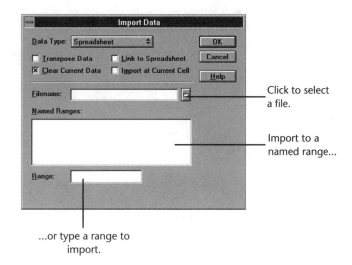

Click to select a file.

Import to a named range...

...or type a range to import.

Fig. 9.20
Use the Import Data dialog box to specify spreadsheet, ASCII, or ANSI data to import into the datasheet.

4. Use the **D**ata Type pop-up list to change the type of data to import, if necessary.

5. Select the following check boxes, if needed:

- ■ *Transpose Data.* Converts columns to rows or vice versa.

- ■ *Clear Current Data.* Deletes all datasheet data before importing.

- ■ *Link to Spreadsheet.* Links the imported datasheet to the spreadsheet data.

- ■ *Import at Current Cell.* Inserts the imported data starting at the last cell you selected in the datasheet instead of the top-left cell.

6. Type the name of the file you're importing in the **F**ilename text box, or click the File icon beside it to display the Select File dialog box, which you can use to select the file.

7. If the selected file has any named ranges and you want to select which one to import, click it in the **N**amed Ranges list. Or, you can type a range in the **R**ange text box. If you make no choices, all the file contents are imported.

III

Using Charts

8. Click OK. Presentations inserts the file data in the datasheet, interpreting the data labels as appropriate.

> **Note**
>
> You can perform the reverse process and export your datasheet data as ANSI (Windows) or ASCII (DOS) text. To do so, open the **D**ata menu and choose E**x**port (or press F3).

From Here...

After reading this chapter, you should have a good feel for working with the datasheet, and how you can change that data to alter the chart display. In addition, you learned how to format the appearance of the data on the datasheet, how to use formulas to calculate data or even perform regression analysis, and more! To build on this knowledge, continue on to the following chapters:

- Chapter 10, "Formatting the Chart Data," explains how to change the appearance of your chart to best present the data you painstakingly entered in the datasheet.

- Chapter 11, "Editing Organization Charts," explains how to work with the last kind of chart available in Presentations.

- Chapter 16, "Inserting Objects into Slides," details how to place additional text, data, and organization charts on slides, as well as how to link other forms of data with your presentation.

Chapter 10

Formatting the Data Chart

Data charts provide a visual interpretation of data, so you can give your audience a clear picture of the point you're communicating with a particular slide. The chart will not be as effective, however, if its appearance detracts from its attractiveness or clarity. If the colors of a series of items are too similar, your audience will have difficulty telling them apart. Audience members might have difficulty distinguishing measurement values if there are too many of them displayed. If you have two charts on a slide and don't have titles distinguishing them, their meanings could be confused.

Although the Chart Gallery provides attractive preformatting for charts, there are numerous situations such as those just described when you will need to customize the formatting for your data charts. This chapter introduces you to the different parts of the chart that you can adjust, and also explains the following procedures:

- Repositioning and resizing the chart
- Changing the chart background and grid
- Working with the chart legend
- Adding chart titles, other text, and arrows
- Modifying the chart axes
- Using 3D and exploded chart effects
- Saving your chart design

Understanding the Parts of Charts

Data charts are composed of numerous elements that you can choose to display or not, or format as you please. Figure 10.1 shows an example of a bar chart with several of these elements labeled.

Fig. 10.1
Identifying the parts of a data chart.

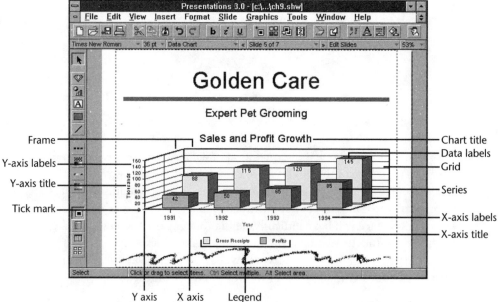

Most charts (with the exception of pie charts and table charts) arrange the data along two axes. The *X axis* normally presents the categories (normally time periods) being compared. The *Y axis* depicts the units being measured. A chart can have two Y axes: one is called the Y1 axis, and the other is called the Y2 axis. Each axis can have its own title and labels. *Tick marks* indicate actual values on an axis. To more clearly indicate how data compares to values, *gridlines* can be drawn from tick marks.

In most data chart types, each *series* is depicted by bars, a line, or symbols of the same color. The *legend* indicates the color used for individual series, and gives the series names. You can choose whether to include a *label* for each series data point to convey the actual data value. At the top of the chart, the *chart title* explains the data being portrayed. A *frame* surrounds the chart to give it dimensions and a boundary; you can choose an even more detailed frame or no frame at all.

Now that you have taken a glimpse at the common features of most charts, it's time to move on to formatting the chart to meet your needs. With the exception of moving and resizing charts, you handle most of the formatting while in the Chart Editor. To enter the Chart Editor, simply double-click a chart. A hatched outline appears around it, the Power Bar changes, and **D**ata and **C**hart menus are added to the menu bar.

Note

The formatting options available depend on the chart type. After you double-click a chart to enter the Chart Editor, you should check the **D**ata and **C**hart menus, the chart QuickMenu, and the Power Bar to examine the different options available.

Moving and Resizing the Chart

The capability to move and resize objects like text and charts enables you to design chart layouts at will. Unlike the default text layout areas on the various slide types, however, you can move and resize data charts in normal Slide Editor view. You don't have to open the **S**lide menu and choose Edit **L**ayouts to move the placeholders around (see Chapter 15 for more information).

You move and resize charts with basic dragging techniques, and you can do so by clicking the chart to make selection handles appear or by entering Chart Editor mode by double-clicking the chart. After the chart is selected in either manner, point to it and drag it to a new location. Or, point to one of the corner handles or side handles and drag to resize.

Tip
To size a chart from the center, press Alt while dragging a handle.

Be aware that there's one advantage to resizing a chart after only clicking it once. In this case, if you drag one of the corner selection handles, the chart resizes proportionally so that none of the text or graphics becomes skewed in appearance. You cannot resize proportionally in the Chart Editor. Also note that dragging a top or side handle when you have used either method to select the chart does skew the chart by resizing only one of its dimensions. Resizing a chart in this manner can cause unpredictable results, especially in how the chart labels and titles appear.

Changing the Series Layout

One of the first and most important changes you may need to make to any chart is to improve the data presentations by editing the appearance of the chart series. Consider figure 10.2, for example. There are a few things wrong with this data chart, but the layout of the series presents the most serious problem. As you can see in the figure, some of the series are obscured by series in the front containing larger values. A couple of the series even seem to be too close in color to be distinguishable. These problems make it difficult to distinguish exact values or even to compare the values in the various series.

Fig. 10.2

A basic bar chart with some serious design problems.

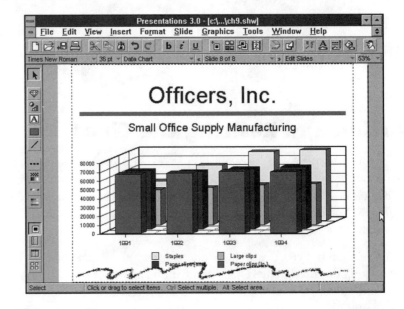

You can edit the series layout and design in the Chart Editor. You have the option of editing all series simultaneously, or of making series-by-series changes to the data. Changing the layout of chart series controls such series features as the 3D appearance of the series, the series style (such as overlapping bars versus clusters of bars), and the sizing of the series markers (such as controlling the width of bars). The options available depend on the chart type. To more clearly understand this process, practice making the changes to the bar chart in figure 10.2.

Tip

To change the layout for a single series, click it to select it (after entering the Chart Editor), and continue with the remainder of the procedure.

To change the layout of all series in a chart, follow these steps:

1. Open the Chart Editor by double-clicking on the chart.

2. Open the **C**hart menu and choose **L**ayout, or click the Layout icon on the Chart Editor Toolbar. The Layout dialog box appears, as shown in figure 10.3.

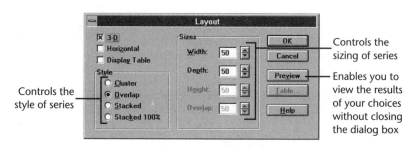

Fig. 10.3
Editing the layout
of bar chart series.

Controls the
style of series

Controls the
sizing of series

Enables you to
view the results
of your choices
without closing
the dialog box

3. To toggle on or off 3D appearance, use the 3-**D** check box.

4. To change the chart display to horizontal, turn on the Horizontal check box.

5. Choose a style for the series by clicking one of the radio buttons in the Style area.

6. Enter new sizes for the series in the appropriate text boxes in the Sizes group. The dimensions you can change depend on whether a chart is 3D, as well as other factors.

7. (Optional) Click the Pre**v**iew button to see whether the changes you specified are appropriate. If not, repeat steps 3 through 6. If you're satisfied, continue to step 8.

8. Click OK to close the dialog box and apply your changes. Figure 10.4 shows two ways that the chart series could be made more readable.

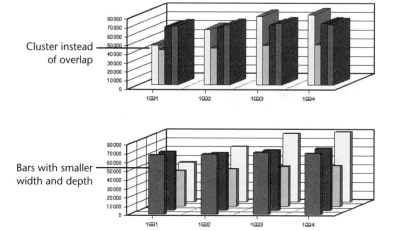

Fig. 10.4
Options for
changing the
layout to make
bars more
readable.

Cluster instead
of overlap

Bars with smaller
width and depth

III

Using Charts

You can toggle on and off 3D and horizontal chart display by using the 3D and Horizontal icons on the Chart Editor Toolbar. In addition, the Power Bar provides a button (the fourth from the left) that enables you to change the series style.

> **Note**
>
> There is not room in this book to discuss each and every layout option for each and every chart type. To explore the effects of the available options for your chart, click the Preview button in the Layout dialog box. You always can change a selection or cancel the layout changes altogether.

In addition to changing the series layout as just discussed, you can change series appearance attributes such as the line and fill color, the shape, and so on, depending on the chart type. The procedure is similar to changing the series layout, but the changes have to be made to each series in turn. Follow these steps:

1. Open the Chart Editor by double-clicking on the chart. If you want to preselect the series to alter, click on it to make selection handles appear.

 2. Open the **C**hart menu and choose **S**eries, or click the Series icon on the Chart Editor Toolbar. The Series Options dialog box appears, as shown in figure 10.5.

Fig. 10.5
Use this dialog box to specify series color, shape, and more.

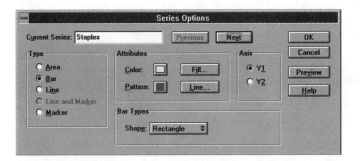

3. Click the **P**revious and Ne**x**t buttons to choose the series to alter if you didn't do so in step 1.

4. Select a new type for the series by clicking one of the radio buttons in the Type group.

5. To change the foreground **C**olor or **P**attern for the series, click the appropriate button and then click your choice. Or, to change both the fill

and pattern or to create a gradient fill, click the F**i**ll button to display the Fill Attributes dialog box. Specify your options and click OK.

6. To specify whether you want the series outlined or to change the outline color or style, click the **L**ine button, which displays the Line Attributes dialog box. Use the **N**o Line check box to turn off line display entirely, or set the other dialog box options to alter the line display. Click OK when you finish.

7. In the case of the bar chart, choose a Shap**e** for the bar types, such as a cone or octagonal shape.

8. (Optional) Click the Pre**v**iew button to see whether the changes you specified are appropriate. If not, repeat steps 3 through 7. If you're satisfied with your changes, continue to step 9.

9. Click OK to finish. Figure 10.6 shows an example of one series formatted with a pattern to make it more distinctive from others.

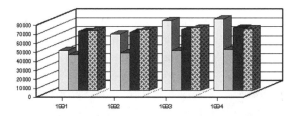

Fig. 10.6
Formatting a series with a pattern can make it stand out from the others.

Note

If you click a series to select it and then right-click to display the QuickMenu, you have the option of choosing to alter the **L**ayout or **E**dit Series, as well as choosing E**x**clude Row to hide the display of that series. Note that you have to use the datasheet to redisplay the series.

Troubleshooting

When I try to preview the changes I've made to a series layout or its attributes, it doesn't do any good because the dialog box is hiding the chart.

Remember that you can drag dialog boxes by their title bars to move them out of the way. Move the Layout or Series Options dialog boxes until they no longer cover your chart.

III

Using Charts

Adding Text to a Chart

Another problem with the basic chart shown in figure 10.2 is that it's not quite clear what's being charted. Other than the legend text, which appeared by default based on the chart selected from the gallery, there's no text on the chart to tell you what the bars mean. This section explains how to add text to a chart to clarify the data for your viewer.

Adding Chart Titles

To clarify the exact meaning of data for your audience, add titles to your charts. Presentations enables you to add a title and subtitle for the whole chart, as well as a title for each axis to identify the units it shows. To add titles to a chart, follow these steps:

1. Open the Chart Editor by double-clicking on the chart.

2. Open the **C**hart menu or the chart QuickMenu and choose **T**itles. The Titles dialog box appears.

3. Click a check box to turn on the display of a particular title, and then enter the text to be displayed, as shown in figure 10.7. Repeat the process for all titles you want to create.

Fig. 10.7
The Titles dialog box enables you to add titles to various parts of the chart.

4. To change the default display of any of the titles (for example, the Y axis title is vertical by default), click the **O**ptions button. The Titles Options dialog box appears. Set the options you want and click OK to close the dialog box.

5. Click OK to close the Titles dialog box and apply your titles to the chart.

Adding Labels

You can think of labels as text that is a bit more specific than titles. Whereas *titles* explain overall parts of a chart, *labels* refer to specific items such as a tick mark on an axis or a data point. To add labels to a chart, use these steps:

1. Open the Chart Editor by double-clicking on the chart.

2. Open the **C**hart menu and choose La**b**els. The Labels dialog box appears.

3. Click to choose a kind of label to apply, such as **D**ata Labels.

4. In the Options area, click Dis**p**lay to turn on the labels. Choose other Options if available for that kind of label.

5. Pick a **P**osition for the label from that pop-up menu. For example, in figure 10.8 you can see that Below is specified, so the data labels appear below the top of each bar.

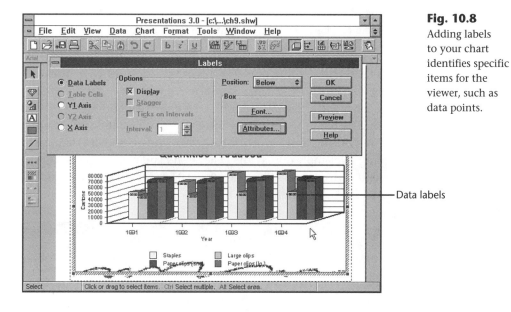

Fig. 10.8
Adding labels to your chart identifies specific items for the viewer, such as data points.

6. Use the **F**ont button to change the font for the labels. Choose the options you want and click OK.

7. To add a box to the selected labels, click the **A**ttributes button. Choose a **B**ox Style, fill, and border. Then click OK.

8. Repeat steps 3 through 7 to create other label types.

9. Click OK to finish.

Troubleshooting

I added boxes to my data labels, but they're just black rectangles. What's wrong?

By default, the boxes are placed with black backgrounds. Click to select one of them, and then use the Fill icon on the Tool Palette to reset it to white.

Formatting Chart Text

In addition to using the Titles and Labels dialog boxes to change the fonts for chart titles and labels, you can change them directly on the chart. You also can reformat the legend text this way (for more information on legends, see "Modifying the Legend," later in this chapter). Note that when you select a single data label and apply new formatting, all the data labels of that type are reformatted.

To change the font, color, or placement of the title or label, first select it by clicking it. When it's selected, you can drag it to a new location. You also can apply a new font, size, or border using the Power Bar buttons or Tool Palette tools. But, perhaps the fastest way to view and change the attributes available for a given title or label is to right-click it to display its QuickMenu, as shown in figure 10.9. Simply display the QuickMenu and choose the appropriate command to display the dialog box for making the change you want. This dialog box greatly resembles those you saw in Chapter 7, "Enhancing Text."

Fig. 10.9
The QuickMenu displays all the attributes you can change for the selected chart text.

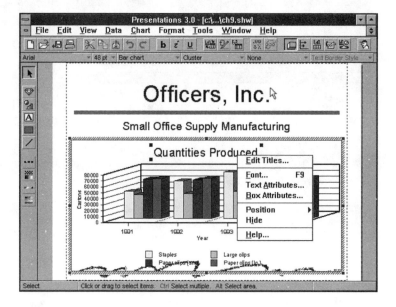

Adding a Data Table

A *data table* lists the actual values on which a data chart is based. In some cases, a data table can be less confusing (and more legible) than adding data labels to your chart. You saw data labels in figure 10.8, for example, and they weren't very readable because there were so many bars in the chart. Figure 10.10 shows a reformatted version of the figure 10.8 chart, including a table at the bottom giving the precise chart values. To add a data table to a chart in the Chart Editor, open the **C**hart menu and choose **L**ayout. Then turn on the Displa**y** Table check box in the Layout dialog box and click OK. Or, simply click the Show Table icon in the Chart Editor Toolbar. Use the same process to turn off data table display.

Tip

To edit the table attributes, click on the table, display the Layout dialog box, and click the **T**able button. Click the **F**ont button if you need to change the table font.

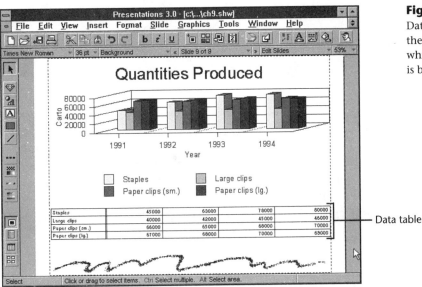

Fig. 10.10

Data tables show the exact data on which your chart is based.

— Data table

Modifying the Legend

The *legend* identifies the chart series and what colors/patterns/outlines depict each series in the chart. Although a legend is useful, there may be instances where it's not needed, or it needs to be reformatted to be more usable. Look at figure 10.11, for example. Because the data labels for this pie chart are very explicit, a legend is unnecessary. In addition to hiding a legend, you might want to move it to another position on a chart, change its font, box it, or add a name to it. You can do all of this very easily.

Fig. 10.11
Explicit data labels make a legend unnecessary in this case.

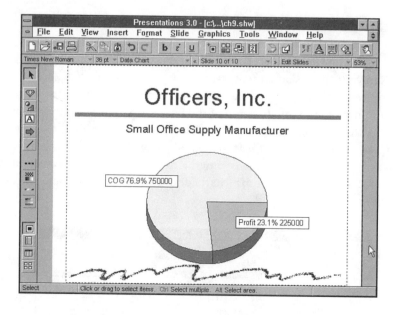

To make changes to the chart legend, open the Chart menu and choose Legend. Or, click the legend, right-click to display the QuickMenu, and choose Edit Legend. In either case, the Legend dialog box appears, as shown in figure 10.12. (Note that you can use the legend QuickMenu to perform several quick-and-dirty legend operations, such as turning off legend display.) Use the Display Legend check box to turn the legend on and off. You can choose to place the legend Inside or Outside the chart, as well as specify a Position for it. Select whether the legend entries have a Vertical (stacked one on top of another) or Horizontal Orientation. You also can specify a Box Option and Title for the legend. Click OK to close the dialog box when you're finished.

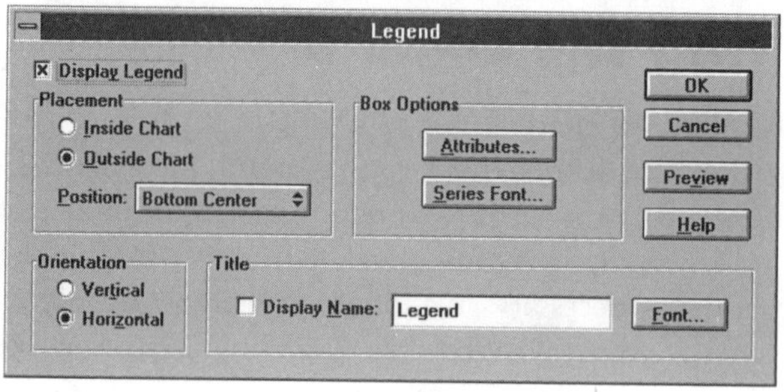

Fig. 10.12
Use the Legend dialog box to control the legend appearance.

Changing the Frame Design

As described earlier in this chapter, the *frame* for the chart is the outline surrounding the back, floor, and so on of the chart. By default, most chart types have a frame on the left side, back, and bottom (floor) of the chart. The frame appears even more prominent on 3D charts, so formatting the appearance of the frame is particularly important. You may need to add color to the frame to make it stand out from the slide background color, or to add contrast between the frame and series. Be careful when editing the frame; you want to make sure that there is enough contrast between the frame and the series, but you don't want a frame color or pattern to overwhelm the series.

To change the frame design, follow these steps:

1. Double-click the chart to enter the Chart Editor. You also can click on the frame after entering the Chart Editor to select it.

2. Open the **C**hart menu and choose **F**rame. Or, if you have selected the frame, right-click and then choose **E**dit Frame/Base from the QuickMenu. The Frame dialog box appears (see fig. 10.13).

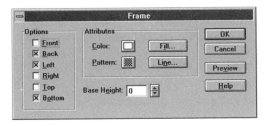

Fig. 10.13

Changing the look of the frame for your chart.

III

Using Charts

3. Specify the frame options to determine where the frame appears.

4. Use the **C**olor button to specify a fill color for the frame background. Use the **P**attern button to specify a fill pattern for the frame background. Or, you can use the F**i**ll button to set both the color and pattern at once, or to create gradient fills.

5. Use the Line button to specify whether to display a frame outline, and what color and pattern it should use.

6. To give the frame base the appearance of 3D thickness, use the Base Height setting. Increase the setting to make the base seem thicker.

7. Click the OK button to accept your changes.

Changing the Grid Design

Unlike the grid in Slide Editor view, the grid in a chart is meant to be viewed. The *chart grid* indicates major and minor increments along (usually) the chart's Y axis. The gridlines run horizontally so that you can more easily see the actual values that each series has. Along the X axis, gridlines separate the increments being compared. You can change the color of the gridlines, their pattern (see fig. 10.14), their placement, and whether they have tick marks. You can display gridlines for major increments and minor increments along the axis.

Fig. 10.14
The grid helps you to identify series values; you can change the color and pattern of the grid.

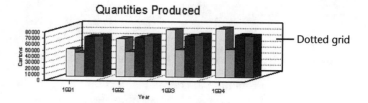

To change the chart grid, follow these steps:

1. Double-click the chart to enter the Chart Editor. You also can click on the grid after entering the Chart Editor to select it.

2. Open the Chart menu and choose Grid/Tick. Or, if you've selected the grid, right-click and then choose Edit Grid/Tick from the QuickMenu. The Grid and Tick Options dialog box appears.

3. Specify the axis you want to change the grid for.

4. For the Major increments, use the Grid button to specify None, Dotted, Solid, or Dashed for the grid appearance. Use the Tick button to control whether tick marks appear outside, inside, both, or not at all. Choose the Color button to specify a color for the major increment gridlines.

5. For the Minor increments, use the **G**rid button to specify **N**one, Do**t**ted, **S**olid, or **D**ashed for the grid appearance. Use the Tic**k** button to control whether tick marks appear outside, inside, both inside and outside, or not at all. Choose the Co**l**or button to specify a color for the major increment gridlines.

6. You can use the **A**xis button to change the axis settings, as described in the next section.

7. Repeat steps 3 through 6 to change the settings for another axis, if needed.

8. Click OK when you finish changing the axis settings.

Modifying the Axes

Look again at figure 10.14. Notice that the Y axis looks rather crowded. There are a lot of values crowded along it. You can change the axis so that fewer values are displayed, adjust the major and minor values displayed, change to a logarithmic rather than linear scale, specify the number of minor gridlines displayed between major increments, and scale the values shown for minor increments.

To adjust the axis settings, follow these steps:

1. Double-click the chart to enter the Chart Editor. You also can click on the axis after entering the Chart Editor to select it.

2. Open the **C**hart menu and choose **A**xis. Or, if you have selected the axis, right-click and then choose **E**dit Axis from the QuickMenu. The Axis Options dialog box appears (see fig. 10.15).

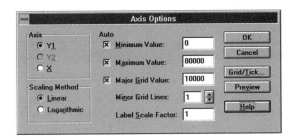

Fig. 10.15
Use the Axis Options dialog box to change the scaling of an axis.

3. If needed, choose which axis you want to adjust by selecting one of the radio buttons in the Axis group.

4. Select a Scaling Method.

5. To change the minimum (starting) value for the axis, deselect the **Mini-mum** Value check box and enter a new value in the text box beside it. If you have a chart and the minimum value in any of the series is 45,000, for example, you might choose to set the minimum Y1 axis value to 40,000.

6. To change the maximum value for the axis, deselect the **Ma**ximum Value check box and type a new value for it.

7. Changing the Major **G**rid Value adjusts the values shown on the axis. In figure 10.14, for example, the major grid value is 10,000, because the axis displays increments of 10,000. Changing this value to 20,000 would make for a more readable axis, showing 20,000, 40,000, 60,000, and 80,000. To change this setting, deselect the Major **G**rid Value check box and type a value in the text box.

8. To display more than one minor grid increment between major gridlines, change the Mi**n**or Grid Lines setting.

9. To scale the values shown on the axis, use the Label **S**cale Factor text box. Referring to figure 10.14 again, the chart shown would look cleaner if the axis were scaled in thousands (10, 20, 30, and so on) instead. To scale the axis values by thousands, you would enter 1000 in the Label **S**cale Factor text box.

10. Repeat steps 3 through 9 to adjust another axis, if necessary.

11. Click OK when you have finished.

Troubleshooting

I specified minor gridlines in the Axis Options dialog box, but none appeared. What happened?

You need to ensure that a grid display is specified for minor increments in the Grid and Tick Options dialog box. To display this dialog box, click the Grid/**T**ick button in the Axis Options dialog box, or use the **C**hart **G**rid/Tick command. Use the **G**rid button to choose a setting other than None.

Specifying Multiple Axes

Sometimes, you may need to compare disparate data on the same chart.
Suppose that you want to show how your company has drastically reduced
shipping times while rapidly increasing production. It may seem like you
could simply show both trends on a line chart; but because you're trying to
compare days with hundreds of thousands of units, you don't get the result
you want, as shown in figure 10.16. The values for the ship time are so small
when compared to the production values that the chart displays them as
zeros.

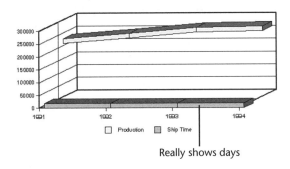

Really shows days

Fig. 10.16
If data values
aren't similar,
trying to show
them on one axis
makes one or more
series meaningless.

To fix this problem, you can create a second Y axis, Y2, to show the values for
the ship time so that you can see a discernible trend. Double-click the chart
to enter the Chart Editor, and then double-click the series you want to
change to display the Series Options dialog box. Click the Y**2** option button
and click OK. Alternatively, you can right-click a series in the Chart Editor
and click Y**2**. In either case, your choice adds a second Y axis at the right side
of the chart, and you now can compare the trends in your chart, as shown in
figure 10.17. To reassign values to the Y1 axis, simply use the same process,
choosing Y1.

III

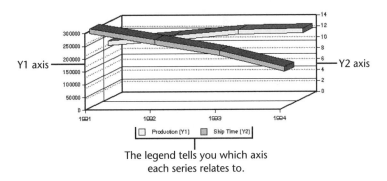

The legend tells you which axis
each series relates to.

Fig. 10.17
Assigning disparate
values (units
versus days) to the
Y2 axis reveals the
data trends for
comparison.

Using Charts

Changing the Perspective

Any 3D chart has perspective or a sense of depth. The default perspective was defined by your selection from the Chart Gallery. You can change this perspective to make a chart appear deeper or shallower, as you choose. To do so, enter the Chart Editor, open the Chart menu, and choose Perspective. Use the **R**ight Angle Axes to specify whether the axes are displayed at right angles. The Hori**z**ontal text box controls the horizontal rotation of the chart. Change this setting to rotate the chart around, so that you can see the chart more from one end or another. The Ver**t**ical text box controls the vertical rotation of the chart—whether you see it more from the side or the top. A preview area shows you the effects of your changes to these two text boxes, and offers scroll bars you can use in place of the text boxes. Check the **W**ire Frame View to preview only series outlines in the preview area, or use the Re**s**et button to change the chart back to its original settings. Click OK when you finish.

Creating Exploded Chart Views

Pie charts offer a special feature called exploding the chart. When you *explode* a slice from a pie chart, you detach it from the rest of the chart to emphasize it (see the bottom of fig 10.18).

Fig. 10.18
An exploded pie slice created with the Pie Layout dialog box.

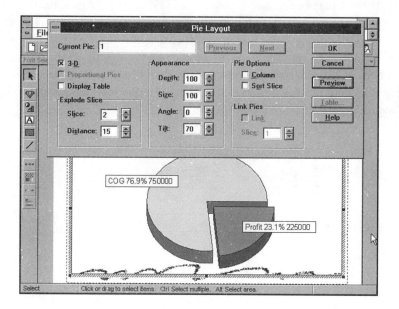

To create an exploded chart, follow these steps:

1. Double-click the chart to enter the Chart Editor.

2. Open the Chart menu and choose Layout, or click the Layout icon on the Chart Editor Toolbar.

3. In the Pie Layout dialog box, choose the Slice to break out in the Explode Slice area.

4. Use the Distance text box to specify how much space appears between the exploded slice and the rest of the pie.

5. Click OK to finish.

Saving Custom Chart Designs

For data, bullet, and organization charts, you can save the styling choices you make to reapply them to other charts you create so that you don't have to retrace all your selections. To save the style for a chart, double-click it to enter the Chart Editor, open the Chart menu, and choose Save Style. The Save Chart Style dialog box appears, as shown in figure 10.19. Specify a drive and directory to save the style to, and then type a name in the Filename text box. Click Save to store the chart styling where you specified.

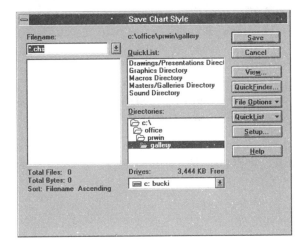

Fig. 10.19
You can use this dialog box to save your chart styling to reapply it to other charts later.

III

Using Charts

To apply the style to the chart of your choice, double-click it, open the **C**hart menu, and choose Ret**r**ieve Style. Choose the file you want from the appropriate drive and directory and click **R**etrieve.

Changing the Chart Type

If at any time you want to change the chart type (from a bar chart to a line chart, for example), you have two options after double-clicking the chart to start the Chart Editor:

- Open the **C**hart menu and choose **G**allery to display the Data Chart dialog box so that you can choose a new master design for your chart. Be aware, however, that changing the chart type this way undoes any design changes you have made to the chart, such as relocating the legend.

- Open the **C**hart menu and choose **Ty**pe. Choose a new chart type from the menu that appears. This changes the chart type, leaving any formatting selections you have made intact.

From Here...

You now have accumulated the skills you need to develop succinct, attractive charts to present data in your slide show. This chapter demonstrated how to move and resize your chart, add and format different kinds of chart text, and redesign the chart series—including changing colors and patterns and assigning series to a new axis. To take advantage of the changes you have made again, you can save the chart style or change the chart type without changing the styling—both of which were described in this chapter. To continue building your slide show, explore these chapters:

- Chapter 11, "Editing Organization Charts," explains how to change the data and styling of organization charts on your slides, much like the techniques described in this chapter.

- Chapter 12, "Using the Presentations Drawing Tools," teaches you skills for drawing directly on a slide, both to add graphics and to highlight text and the data chart contents.

- Chapter 15, "Working with Masters, Templates, and Backgrounds," explains how you can customize not just individual elements like data charts, but the look and feel of an entire slide show.

Chapter 11

Editing Organization Charts

You learned in Chapter 3, "Using the Various Slide Templates," how easy WordPerfect Presentations for Windows makes it to create an organization chart. You simply choose a layout for the chart and enter data in an Outliner window. Presto! You have an organization chart.

This chapter focuses on enhancing and improving your organization, or org, chart. Like the other chart types already covered in this book, you can control the formatting and appearance of your org charts by altering the data, changing the layout, and applying attractive formatting. Read on to learn more about the following:

■ Selecting and editing organization charts

■ Choosing a new chart layout

■ Redesigning the chart text, boxes, and connectors

■ Creating staff positions

■ Choosing what parts of the chart to display

Selecting the Organization Chart

Before you can make any changes to an organization chart, you need to select it in the appropriate fashion. You need to understand two types of selections; the type that you use depends on the operation you want to perform.

Tip

Drag a corner handle when resizing to size the chart proportionally. Pressing Alt while dragging a handle resizes from the center out.

The first type of selection entails selecting the chart as you would select an object. Click the chart once so that black selection handles appear around the chart. When an organization chart is selected in this way, you can drag it to a new location on the slide. You also can resize the chart by pointing to a selection handle and dragging the handle to change the size and shape.

When you use the second method of selecting an organization chart, you can do more than just move or resize the chart. Double-clicking an organization chart surrounds it with a hatched outline and opens the Chart Editor. (Or, you can right-click the chart and choose Edit Chart from the QuickMenu.) When working with data charts, opening the Chart Editor adds a new menu to the menu bar and changes the Toolbar and Power Bar, as shown in figure 11.1.

Fig. 11.1

Double-clicking an organization chart activates the Chart Editor.

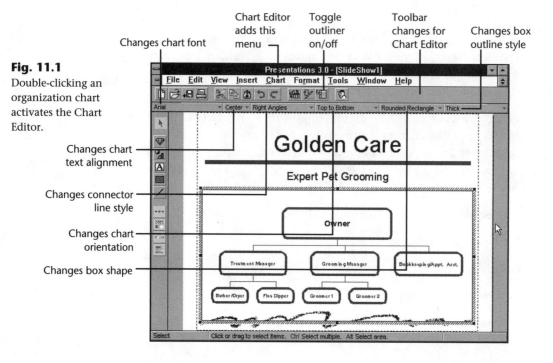

You can resize the chart using the hatched outline; be cautious, because this method doesn't enable you to resize the chart proportionally. The Chart Editor primarily enables you to perform the operations described in the rest of the chapter.

Editing the Entries

You enter and work with the organization chart's contents in an Outline window that greatly resembles Outliner view for the slide show. As noted in figure 11.1, when you enter the Chart Editor, an icon is added to the Toolbar, enabling you to toggle on and off the display of the Outline window. You also can choose the **O**utline command from the **V**iew menu to display and hide the Outline window. Figure 11.2 shows the Outline window, which has been resized (by dragging the window border) to provide ample working space.

Outline	
Top	Owner
	▸ Treatment Manager
	▸ Bather /Dryer
	▸ Flea Dipper
	▸ Grooming Manager
	▸ Groomer 1
	▸ Groomer 2
	▸ Bookkeeping/Appt. Asst.

As you learned briefly, editing in the organization chart outline is similar to editing in applications like word processors. You move the cursor to the position you want by clicking or using the arrow keys, and then type. You can drag over text to select it and then press Del to remove it. You also can use the following special editing keys:

- Press Enter to create a new entry at the same level.

- Press Tab to indent an entry one level. To create the Bather/Dryer position after the Treatment Manager position in figure 11.2, for example, type **Treatment Manager**, press Enter to start the new line, and then press Tab to indicate that the position reports to the preceding position.

- Press Shift+Tab to promote an entry one level. In this case, creating the Grooming Manager position after the Flea Dipper position in figure 11.2 means that you have to press Enter and then press Shift+Tab to create a position back at the manager level.

- Press Backspace or open the **E**dit menu and choose **D**elete to remove an entry.

Tip

You can cut, copy, and paste data in the organization chart Outline window by using the Cu**t**, **C**opy, and **P**aste commands on the **E**dit menu or the Toolbar tools.

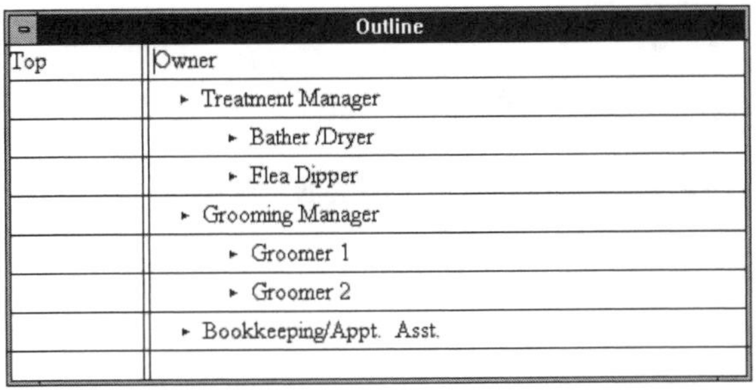

Fig. 11.2
The Outline window enables you to edit the organization chart's contents.

Tip

Pressing Ins toggles on and off the overtype feature. When overtype is on, Presentations replaces letters to the right of the insertion point with new letters being typed, rather than inserting the new letters at the cursor location.

III

Using Charts

Any time you want to view the results of editing or design changes, you can redraw the chart if it isn't set to Automatic Redraw. To manually redraw changes, open the **V**iew menu and choose **R**edraw (or press Ctrl+F3), or click the Redraw icon on the Chart Editor Toolbar.

> **Note**
>
> Keep in mind that organization charts have greater impact when you keep them simple. You should never plan to display more than three or four levels in an organization chart. You can type more levels into your chart outline, but you should hide nonessential levels in the slide display, as described in "Designating the Displayed Part," later in this chapter.

Defining Layout Options

The more levels you have in your organization chart, the more space it takes to display them. Suppose that you create a slide show that has the traditional landscape (horizontal) layout, and you add an organization chart slide to it. Your organization chart has four levels, but there isn't room to display them all correctly. When you try to do so, the text on the lowest level appears microscopic. Your chart would work much better if it were oriented horizontally, like the slide itself, providing more room to display the levels. You have two options for changing the chart orientation. You can work with the Chart Gallery, or you can work with the Layout dialog box. These methods are described next.

When you create your organization chart, the Chart Gallery displays an Organization Chart dialog box presenting you with numerous layout options for your chart—some vertically oriented, some horizontally oriented, and so on. You can use the Gallery again in Chart Editor to change the layout for your chart. You must remember that using this method to change the chart layout applies the master formatting to the chart; any font or color changes you have made to the organization chart are undone. To use the Chart Gallery to choose a new organization chart layout, follow these steps:

1. Double-click the organization chart to open the Chart Editor.

2. Open the **C**hart menu and choose **G**allery. The Organization Chart dialog box appears (see fig. 11.3).

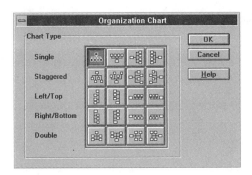

Fig. 11.3
You can use the
Chart Gallery to
display this dialog
box and use it to
select another
layout for your
org chart.

3. Click a new chart layout thumbnail.

4. Click OK to finish making your selection and close the dialog box.

To have more flexibility in specifying your organization chart layout and to make changes without overriding your other organization chart formatting specifications, use the Layout dialog box. Follow these steps:

1. Double-click the organization chart to open the Chart Editor.

2. Open the **C**hart menu or QuickMenu and choose **L**ayout. The Layout dialog box appears, as shown in figure 11.4.

Tip
When the Chart
Editor is open, the
fourth button from
the left on the
Power Bar enables
you to quickly
change the chart
orientation.

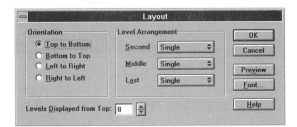

Fig. 11.4
Use the Layout
dialog box to
specify organiza-
tion chart layout
options.

3. Choose an Orientation for the chart by clicking one of the radio buttons in that section.

4. Choose an arrangement for various levels from among the following choices:

■ Single places the boxes for the level in a single-file horizontal or vertical arrangement, depending on the chart's orientation.

III

Using Charts

■ Sta**g**gered places the boxes for the level in an alternating formation.

■ **L**eft or **T**op places the boxes for the level to the left of or on top of a single connecting line, depending on the chart orientation.

■ **R**ight or **B**ottom places the boxes for the level to the right of or below a single connecting line, depending on the chart orientation.

■ **D**ouble places the boxes for the level on either side of a connecting line.

5. Click OK to close the Layout dialog box.

Figure 11.5 shows some examples of the organization chart Layout options in action. The chart on the left in the figure has a **T**op to Bottom orientation, with the **S**econd level arranged to the **L**eft and the **La**st level arranged in a **D**ouble formation. The chart on the right has a **L**eft to Right orientation, with the **S**econd level in a **D**ouble formation and the **La**st level Sta**g**gered.

Fig. 11.5
Specifying different Layout options for your organization chart.

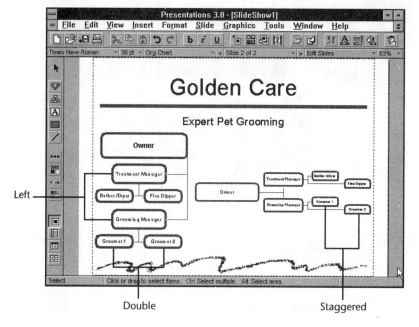

> **Troubleshooting**
>
> *I used the **G**allery command on the **C**hart menu to apply a new layout, and now all my other formatting is gone. What can I do?*
>
> Start by undoing the formatting choices you just made. Or, if you saved the chart styling by opening the **C**hart menu and choosing the Sa**v**e Style command, you can open the **C**hart menu again and choose Retri**e**ve Style to reapply the formatting.

Formatting the Organization Chart

After you define the general layout of your organization chart, you can fine-tune the details to ensure that it has the look you want. The details you can change include the font used in the organization chart text and its color, the box style and fill, and the connecting line style and fill.

When formatting your organization chart, as always, you should keep in mind that the objective is not to use every available bell and whistle. The objective is to create an attractive chart that is easy for your audience to read and understand. Don't choose colors or fonts that clash with the slide show master. Don't choose light or dark colors for both the chart text and boxes; the lack of contrast makes them difficult to read. Do select a font size large enough to read for all chart levels. And do add more color when needed to make the chart more interesting.

Setting Text Attributes

One attribute you may want to change frequently is the organization chart text. If your chart has a sans serif font for the title and subtitle, for example, you may want to choose a font with serifs, such as Times New Roman, for the chart text to add contrast and make it more legible. Note that you can change the font settings only for the entire chart; you cannot choose different fonts and colors for different levels. Therefore, you need to be sure that the font attributes you set work for all levels in your chart.

To change the specified font, color, and fill for your chart, use these steps:

1. Double-click the organization chart to enter the Chart Editor.

2. Open the Fo**r**mat menu or QuickMenu and choose **F**ont (F9). The Font dialog box appears. It resembles the Font dialog box you've seen in other chapters, as shown in figure 11.6. You also can display this dialog box by clicking the **F**ont button in the Layout dialog box.

III

Using Charts

Fig. 11.6
Choosing a new font for your chart.

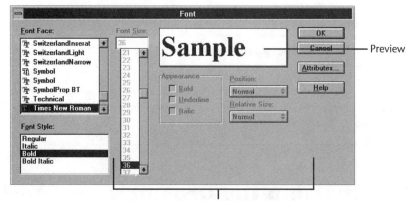

Preview

These options are disabled because they vary depending on the chart level.

Tip
Display the Text Attributes dialog box directly by displaying the organization chart's QuickMenu and choosing Font Attributes.

3. Choose a Font Face and Font Style.

4. Click the Attributes button if you want to change the font color or fill. The Text Attributes dialog box appears, as shown in figure 11.7.

Fig. 11.7
Use the Text Attributes dialog box to change attributes for text, including color, line, and fill.

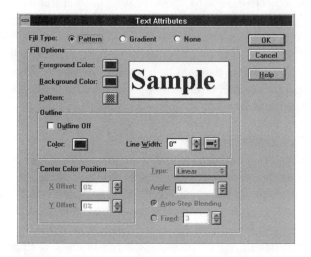

5. Choose the attributes you want. Using the Text Attributes dialog box is described in detail in Chapter 7, "Enhancing Text." Click OK to close this dialog box.

6. Click OK to close the Font dialog box and apply your changes.

The Power Bar offers two buttons containing pull-down menus for changing text attributes. The first button, at the far left end of the Power Bar, displays a pull-down menu of fonts, enabling you to change the organization chart font with just a couple of mouse clicks.

The second Power Bar button changes an attribute you haven't examined yet—the alignment of the organization chart text within the boxes. Click this button to choose Right, Center, or Left alignment.

Defining the Box Design Attributes

Changing the appearance of the position boxes has perhaps the greatest impact on the look of your organization charts. Presentations enables you to choose whether to display boxes, to specify the shape of the boxes, and to set the fill and outline colors and patterns. You should let readability and function guide you in making your formatting choices for the organization chart boxes. You may run into occasions where the title contained in an organization chart box is particularly long and looks crowded, for example. In such a case, removing the boxes from the positions on that level frees up a bit of space so that the longer titles don't look crowded.

Two dialog boxes present the options for formatting organization chart boxes. The Box Options dialog box enables you to choose which levels to display boxes for and to set the height, width, and text justification for the chart boxes. The Box Attributes dialog box, in contrast, enables you to set the box shape, color, fill, and outline. To start out by choosing the Box Options dialog box, use these steps:

1. Double-click the chart to enter the Chart Editor.

2. Open the **C**hart menu or the QuickMenu and choose Box **O**ptions to display the Box Options dialog box (see fig. 11.8).

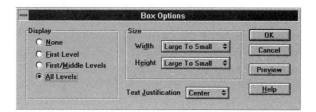

Fig. 11.8
Use the Box Options dialog box to specify whether to display boxes on an organization chart and to determine the box size and text alignment.

III

Using Charts

3. Choose a Display option. **N**one removes boxes from all chart levels. **F**irst Level displays a box around the first (top) level only. First/**M**iddle Levels displays boxes around all levels but the very bottom (this is a very traditional organization chart look). Finally, **A**ll Levels ensures that you see boxes for all chart levels.

4. Choose the options in the Size area. The Wi**d**th and **H**eight pop-up menu lists offer the same options. **L**arge to Small uses the largest width/height for the top level boxes and decreases the width/height for each successive level. **A**ll the Same sizes the boxes identically for all levels. The last option, **F**it to Text, adjusts boxes individually to fit the length of the box text.

5. Use the Text **J**ustification pop-up menu to specify **L**eft, **C**enter, or **R**ight alignment for the box text.

6. Click OK to close the Box Options dialog box and implement your changes.

After you specify which boxes to display and how to size them, you can fine-tune their look by using the Box Attributes dialog box.

> ### Note
>
> You cannot select individual boxes and change their attributes. The changes you make apply to the entire organization chart.

Follow these steps:

1. If necessary, double-click the chart to enter the Chart Editor.

2. Open the **C**hart menu or the QuickMenu and choose Box **A**ttributes to display the Box Attributes dialog box (see fig. 11.9).

Fig. 11.9
Designing box colors and fills is easy with the Box Attributes dialog box.

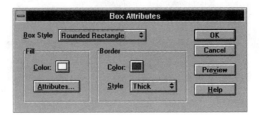

3. Choose the **B**ox Style you want. The pop-up menu choices are **R**ectangle, Roun**d**ed Rectangle, **O**ctagon, and **N**one.

4. In the Fill area, click the **C**olor button to display a palette, and click a color from the palette to specify a solid color fill. Or, to specify a pattern, click the **A**ttributes button to display the Fill Attributes dialog box (see fig. 11.10).

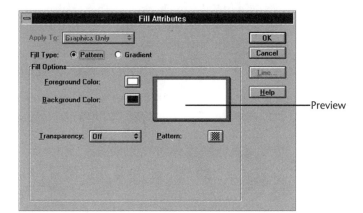

Fig. 11.10
Choosing Fill Attributes for the organization chart boxes.

Preview

5. Choose whether you want a Pattern or Gradient F**i**ll Type. Use the **F**oreground Color and **B**ackground Color pop-up palettes to choose the colors you want. Specify **T**ransparency: **O**ff, **B**ackground, or **F**oreground. Choose a Pattern or Gradient type, plus any of the gradient options you want to change. Click OK to return to the Box Attributes dialog box.

6. To change the Border, click the C**o**lor button to display a pop-up palette, and click a color in the palette. Click the **S**tyle pop-up menu to choose from several line styles.

7. Click OK when you finish specifying your changes.

Figure 11.11 shows an example of some of the design changes you can make to your organization chart. The Box Options dialog box was used to resize the boxes to the same width, and the depth has been fit to the text. A new fill and outline color has been chosen, as well as a bevel outline style.

III

Using Charts

Fig. 11.11

Even simple design changes like these can enhance the attractiveness and readability of an organization chart.

Designing Connecting Lines

The connecting lines, or *connectors*, are the last element of an organization chart that you can design. You can choose whether to display connectors, change their color, add arrows to them, and more. Use these steps to redesign the connectors for an organization chart:

1. If necessary, double-click the chart to enter the Chart Editor.

2. Open the **C**hart menu or the QuickMenu and choose **C**onnectors to display the Connectors dialog box (see fig. 11.12).

Fig. 11.12

Edit the organization chart connectors in the Connectors dialog box.

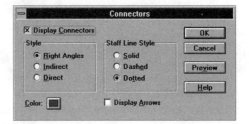

3. Choose whether to Display **C**onnectors using that check box. If you choose to display connectors, continue with the rest of the steps to format them; otherwise click OK.

4. Choose a Style for the connectors. **R**ight Angles is a squared-off style. **I**ndirect modifies the connectors by angling the horizontal lines. **D**irect eliminates any joint in the connectors and draws lines directly from an upper level box to all boxes containing positions reporting to or flowing into the upper level box.

5. Click the **C**olor button to display a pop-up palette; click a color from the palette to select it.

6. Choose a Staff Line Style. This setting controls the display of connectors to staff positions.

7. Turn on the Display **A**rrows check box if you want to add arrows to the connectors.

8. Click OK to confirm these changes and close the dialog box.

Figure 11.13 shows an organization chart with new connecting lines. The connector style is **D**irect, and arrows have been added to the connectors.

Fig. 11.13
The connectors on this organization chart have been modified with the Connectors dialog box.

Adding Staff Positions

Staff positions generally are independent, administrative, or special-projects positions that are specially represented on organization charts. A common example of a staff position is the executive assistant to the president of a company; the executive assistant reports to the president and must be charted as such, and because no position reports to the executive assistant, it receives special treatment on the chart.

In Presentations, you designate staff positions using the organization chart Outline window. The following steps lead you through this process:

1. Double-click a chart to open the Chart Editor.

2. Display the outline, if needed, by opening the **V**iew menu and choosing **O**utline, or by clicking the View icon on the Chart Editor Toolbar.

3. Ensure that the position you want to change is at the correct outline level. It must be one level below the position that it reports to. If needed, position the insertion point on it by clicking it and pressing Tab or Shift+Tab to adjust its level.

4. Select the position to make a staff position by clicking it.

5. Open the **C**hart menu or QuickMenu and choose **S**taff. This designates the position as a staff position. Figure 11.14 shows a staff position drawn on the organization chart and in the chart Outline window.

Tip
Repeat these steps to remove the staff position designation from an Outline window entry.

III

Using Charts

Fig. 11.14
Use the Outline
window to create
a staff position.

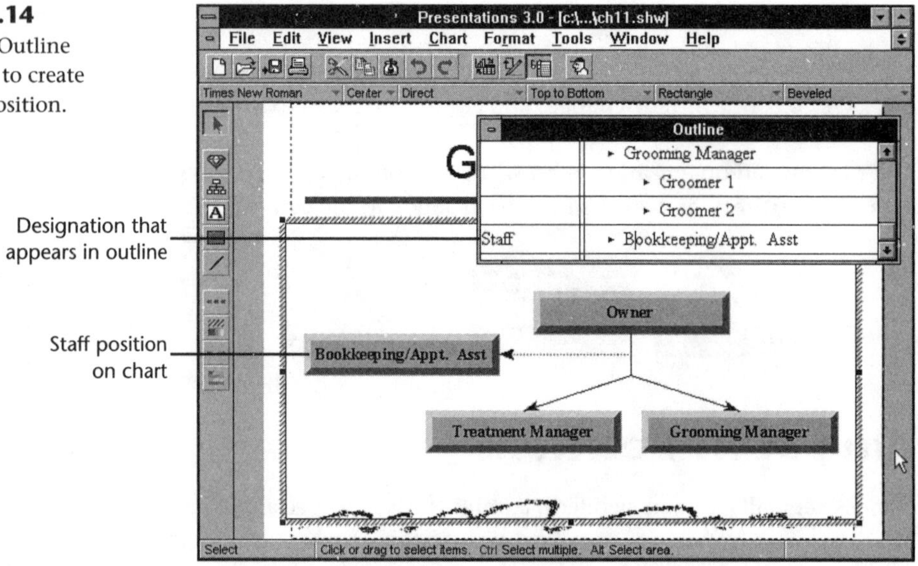

Designation that
appears in outline

Staff position
on chart

Designating the Displayed Part

As noted earlier in this chapter, it's not prudent to display more than four
levels of an organization chart on a slide, even if you enter more levels in the
Outline window, such as if you copied the data from another application or
are using Presentations to store the entire organizational structure for a large
company (because you easily can move positions around). The good news is
that even when you enter many levels in the Outline window, you don't
have to display all of them on the chart.

You have two options for controlling what parts of the Outline window's
contents are displayed on the organization chart:

■ You can choose how many levels of the outline contents to display,
starting from the top level. In the Chart Editor, open the **C**hart menu
or QuickMenu and choose **L**ayout. The Layout dialog box appears.
Change the Levels **D**isplayed from Top setting to control how many
of the levels appear on the chart.

■ You can change the level designated as the top level of the chart. To
show only a certain manager and the positions reporting to that
manager, for example, you would designate that manager as the top
level of the chart. To do so in the Chart Editor, display the outline, if
needed, by opening the **V**iew menu and choosing **O**utline or by
clicking the View icon on the Chart Editor Toolbar. Select the position

to make the top position by clicking it. Open the **C**hart menu or QuickMenu and choose Set **T**op. This designates the position as the top position, noting that in the left margin of the Outline window. When you want, use these steps to redefine the first line in the Outline window as the top position.

From Here...

Using the techniques described in this chapter, you can create clear and attractive organization charts to communicate structures and processes to your audience. This chapter discussed how to edit organization chart contents, as well as how to change the chart layout and formatting for chart text and the boxes containing the chart text. The next challenge to consider is enhancing and finishing your WordPerfect Presentations 3.0 for Windows slide show with drawings and more. Consider these other chapters:

- Chapter 3, "Using the Various Slide Templates," first introduced organization charts. Jump back to that chapter if you need to learn how to get started with these charts.

- Chapter 12, "Using the Presentations Drawing Tools," explains how to draw vector objects directly on a slide.

- Chapter 13, "Working with Outlines and Fills," provides information on editing the fills for vector images and more.

- Chapter 17, "Printing and Saving Your Slide Show: Basics and Other Considerations," explains details for saving your slide show and creating output.

- Chapter 18, "Creating and Viewing the On-Screen Show," explains how to tie the various chart types together into a finished presentation that you can display on your computer.

III

Using Charts

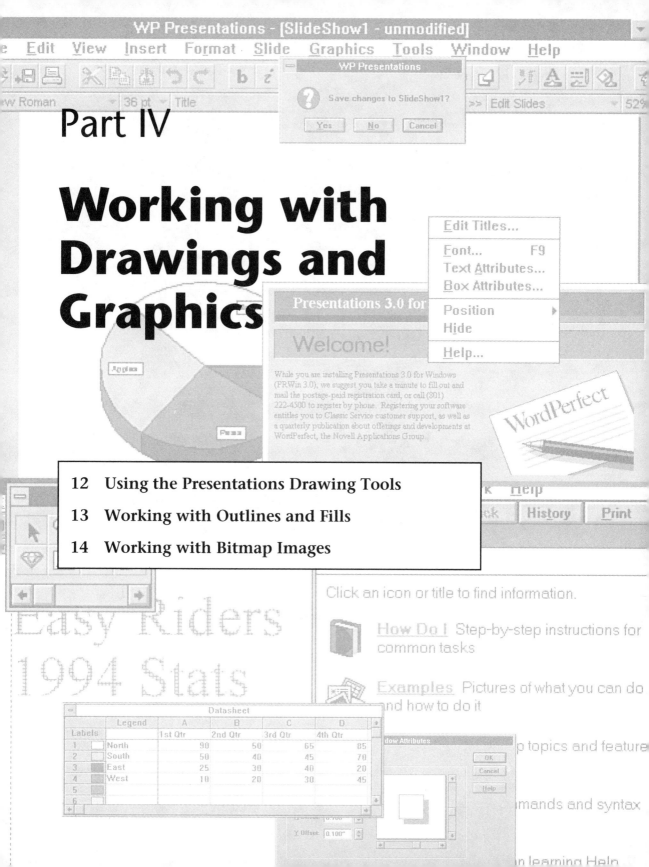

Part IV

Working with Drawings and Graphics

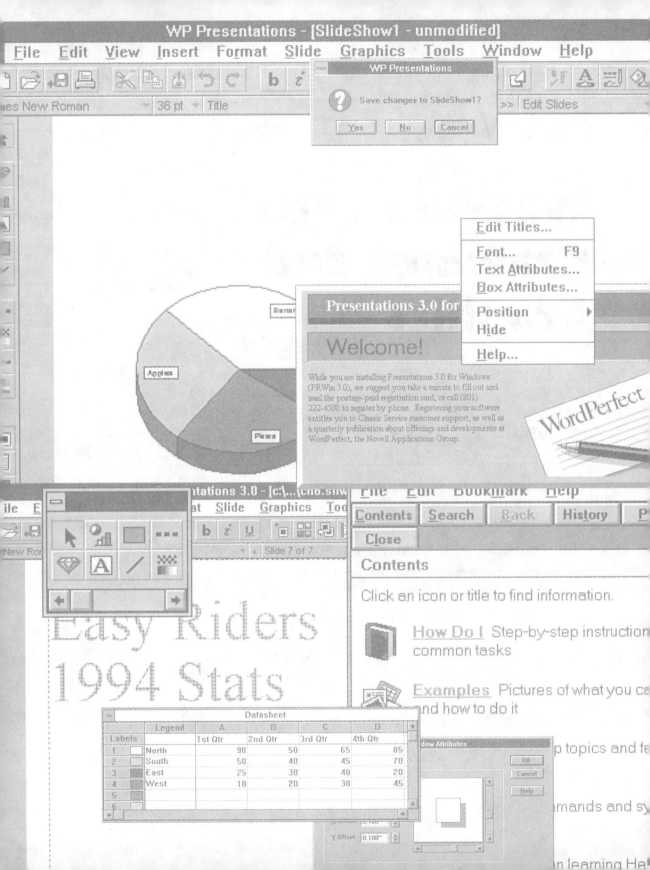

Chapter 12

Using the Presentations Drawing Tools

Even though WordPerfect Presentations 3.0 for Windows provides you with a versatile collection of predrawn QuickArt as well as the capability to use predrawn art from other sources, graphics are never one size fits all. Adding custom-made art to a slide show enables you to tailor the enhancements for any situation.

The Tool Palette along the left-hand side of the Presentations screen provides numerous tools to make drawing vector images simple and accessible—even for the nonartist. This chapter introduces you to each of these tools and how to use them. You also learn how to combine the objects you draw and use special effects with them to create attractive drawings without investing in a graphic arts degree.

With your creativity and the following techniques, you can create nearly any kind of drawing you need for your slide show:

- Drawing basic lines and shapes

- Using the grid as a drawing tool

- Altering objects by moving, sizing, duplicating, rotating, and flipping them

- Reordering, grouping, and combining objects

- Working with perspective, 3D, and QuickWarp

- Using Bezier curves in objects

Comparing Drawings to QuickArt

Chapter 8, "Adding QuickArt to a Slide," covered the QuickArt Gallery and the images it contains. You learned there that the QuickArt images are *vector* drawings; because they are defined mathematically, they are easy to edit and resize. The lines and shapes you create with the Tool Palette tools also are vector images. After you draw the images on a slide, you easily can resize them, change their colors, and more. In this chapter and the next, an *object* is any line or shape (or even text) drawn with the Tool Palette tools.

QuickArt images actually consist of numerous drawings, layered on top of each other to provide the illusion of depth and to add detail. Consider figure 12.1, for example. The top image in the figure shows a dolphin from the QuickArt Gallery. The bottom image is the same dolphin, with all the top drawing layers stripped off to reveal a simple outline drawing of the dolphin. It's clear on the top dolphin that the additional layers and their careful placement and coloring (dark to light) provide realism. Although it's clear that the bottom image is also a dolphin, it looks much less realistic and attractive.

Fig. 12.1
Compare the top QuickArt image with the bottom image, which is a simple outline drawing.

Text Object tool
Closed Shape Object tool
Line Object tool

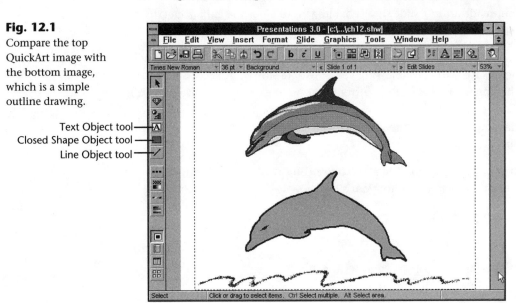

You can use the techniques that the Presentations software developers used in creating QuickArt to create your own drawings. To learn how a particular QuickArt image was put together, place it on your slide show, open the **G**raphics menu and choose the **Se**parate command, and examine the individual pieces.

Starting the Drawing

Drawings in Presentations, as in professional drawing programs, are composed of simple lines and shapes. To begin creating your own drawings, use the drawing tools on the Tool Palette in Slide Editor view (see fig. 12.1). Next, this chapter discusses how to draw basic lines and shapes, which you primarily accomplish by dragging with the mouse. Then, you learn techniques for combining and working with the objects you create.

Although the shapes shown in this chapter may use different fill and line colors and patterns, you will not learn how to change those here. Working with colors and fills is described in the next chapter, "Working with Outlines and Fills." Note, however, that you can specify the color and fill before or after drawing an object.

Drawing Closed Shapes

When you start Presentations, the Closed Shape Object tool looks like a shaded rectangle. Clicking and holding the mouse button on this tool reveals a palette of shapes you can select from (see fig. 12.2). The Rectangle, Rounded Rectangle, Circle, Ellipse, and Arrow tools are fairly self-explanatory. The Irregular Polygon tool enables you to draw many-sided, irregular shapes. The Closed Curve tool enables you to draw irregular, rounded shapes. And, you can use the Regular Polygon tool to draw many-sided shapes with sides of equal lengths, like hexagons.

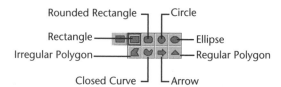

Rounded Rectangle — — Circle
Rectangle — — Ellipse
Irregular Polygon — — Regular Polygon
Closed Curve — — Arrow

Fig. 12.2
The closed shape objects you can draw.

Using the Rectangle, Rounded Rectangle, Circle, and Ellipse tools is a straightforward process of clicking-and-dragging. Here are the steps for creating these closed shapes:

1. Click and hold the mouse button on the Closed Shape Object tool on the Tool Palette to reveal the palette of shapes.

2. Drag until the red selector surrounds the shape you want.

3. Point on the slide to one corner of the area that you want to contain the shape. The mouse pointer becomes a crosshair. Press and hold the left mouse button. Pressing Alt while moving the mouse draws the

Tip
If you begin drawing a shape and decide that you started in the wrong location, press Esc to cancel the shape you started.

shape from the center out (or from edge to edge in the case of the Circle tool). Pressing and holding Shift while drawing constrains the rectangle, rounded rectangle, and ellipse shapes to perfect squares or circles.

4. Drag to create the shape, as shown in figure 12.3.

Fig. 12.3
Dragging to create an ellipse.

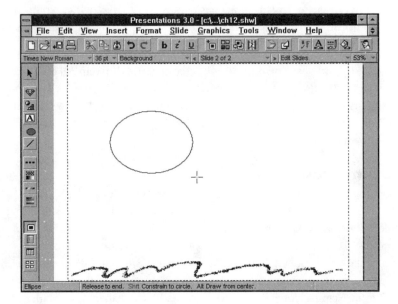

5. Release the mouse button when the shape has reached the size you want.

Using the other Closed Shape tools also requires clicking-and-dragging, but creating each shape requires some special techniques:

Tip
Pressing Backspace removes the last anchor point created.

■ To create an irregular polygon or closed curve after selecting the appropriate tool, click to establish the first angle or curve anchor point (*anchor points* define the point of an angle or apex of a curve; you can move the anchor points to change the shape). Click again for each subsequent anchor point (see fig. 12.4). To finish the shape, double-click the last angle or curve point.

■ To create the arrow, you have the option of clicking to start a straight arrow, or dragging to draw a curved arrow. If you want to constrain the angle perfectly in a particular direction (in increments of 45 degrees), you can press and hold Shift while creating the arrow. Finally, to anchor the head of the arrow in a particular location but curve the arrow tail, click to establish the point of the arrow, move the mouse pointer to draw the arrow head, and press and hold Alt to lock the arrow head in place. Then move the mouse pointer to position the tail and click to finish the arrow.

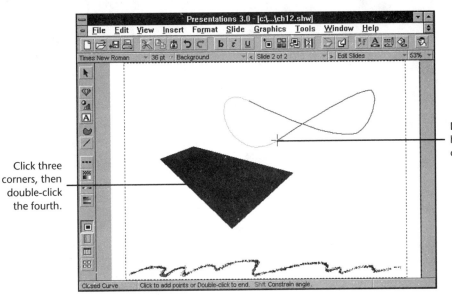

Fig. 12.4
Creating an irregular polygon or closed curve.

Double-clicking here finishes the closed curve.

Click three corners, then double-click the fourth.

- To complete a regular polygon after clicking that tool, first enter how many sides you want the polygon to have in the Regular Polygon dialog box that appears (see fig. 12.5). Then drag to create the shape, shifting the mouse pointer to the left and right to adjust the rotation of the shape.

Troubleshooting

I pressed Shift while dragging to draw a perfect square, but when I released Shift and the mouse button, the shape snapped to an irregular rectangle. Why didn't it work?

When you're using Shift to constrain a line or shape that you're drawing, you need to make sure that you release the mouse button before you release the Shift key. Otherwise, the results may be unpredictable.

Fig. 12.5
Use this dialog box
to specify how
many equal sides
you want a
polygon to have.

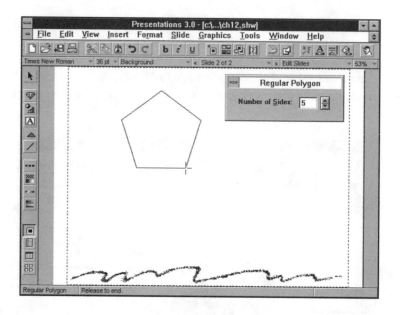

Drawing Lines

As with the Closed Shape Object tool on the Tool Palette, clicking and holding the Line Object tool displays a palette of tools you can choose from to create several types of lines, as shown in figure 12.6.

Fig. 12.6
Presentations
offers tools for
creating several
kinds of lines.

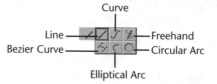

To select a particular Line tool from the palette, click on the Line Object tool and hold the mouse button to display the palette of choices. Drag until the red selector surrounds the Line tool you want. From there, you need to use a different method to create each line type:

■ To draw a single straight line, click one end, move the mouse pointer to the position of the other end, and double-click. Pressing Shift while dragging constrains the line to 45-degree increments. To draw a line with angles, click the first end and move the mouse pointer to the first angle; click and move the mouse pointer to the location of the next angle. Repeat to create additional angles, and double-click to complete the line.

IV

Drawings and Graphics

■ To draw a curve, click one end, move the mouse pointer to the position of the peak of the curve and click to anchor it, and then move the mouse pointer to the other end of the curve and double-click. Pressing Shift while dragging constrains the current side of the curve to 45-degree increments. To draw a curve with multiple bends, click one end, move the mouse pointer to the position of the peak of the first curve, and click to anchor it. Then move the mouse pointer to the location where you want the curve to change direction, and click again. Continue clicking to change the curve direction and double-click to end the curved line (see fig. 12.7).

■ Use the Freehand tool like a pencil. Click to start one end of the line. Hold the mouse button and drag. The line appears wherever you drag. Release the mouse button to end the curve. Figure 12.8 shows an example outline drawn with the Freehand tool.

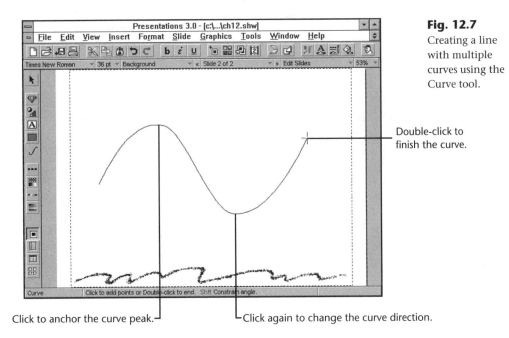

Fig. 12.7
Creating a line with multiple curves using the Curve tool.

Double-click to finish the curve.

Click to anchor the curve peak.   Click again to change the curve direction.

Fig. 12.8
The outline of a banana, drawn with the Freehand tool.

■ The Bezier Curve is a special smooth curve that you can reshape using control points that enable you to define the size and sweep of the curve. As opposed to curved lines, which are composed of multiple connected arcs, the Bezier line itself is curved. Creating a Bezier curve is somewhat tricky once you select that tool. Click to start one end of the curve. Move the mouse pointer to the area where you want to create a curve in the line. Click-and-drag to create a pair of control handles connected by a dashed blue outline (see fig. 12.9). While still holding the mouse button, drag to curve the line. When the curve appears as you want it to, double-click to end it. Or, to extend the line and curve it back in the other direction, release the mouse button, point to another area where you want the line to curve, and click-and-drag to display control handles again. Repeat the process as needed, and double-click to finish the curve.

Fig. 12.9
Creating a Bezier
curve.

Click to start.

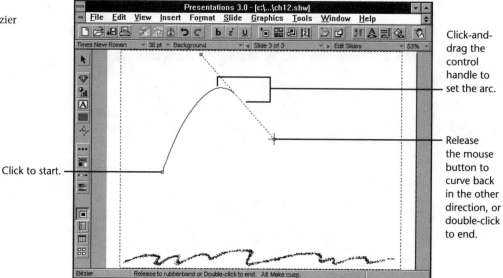

Click-and-
drag the
control
handle to
set the arc.

Release
the mouse
button to
curve back
in the other
direction, or
double-click
to end.

■ To draw an elliptical arc, select that tool. Then point to one end of the arc and drag to create the arc; release the mouse button when it's the length you want. Pressing Shift while dragging makes the arc symmetrical, and pressing Alt while dragging reverses the curve of the arc.

(If you want to change an arc into a wedge after you draw it, click the selection arrow and then double-click the arc. Point to one end of the arc, press the left mouse button, and drag to create the wedge.)

■ The last Line tool, the Circular Arc, enables you to draw perfect portions of a circle. After selecting this tool, drag to set the width of the arc; then release the mouse button and move the pointer to "rubberband" the arc into shape. When it's shaped the way you want, click to complete the arc.

Adding Text

Chapter 6, "Adding and Editing Text," provides a detailed look at how to create text areas and text lines on a slide. Even though those objects are contained in boxes, the boxes containing them are transparent. You therefore can lay text areas and text boxes over drawn objects to add text to your graphics, as in the medallion shown in figure 12.10. Like drawn objects and lines, the text can be selected and reshaped, or combined with other objects as explained in "Grouping and Ungrouping Objects," later in this chapter.

Using the Grid

In Chapter 4, "Adjusting the View," you learned to use the **G**rid/Snap submenu of the **V**iew menu to turn on a **G**rid (or to press Alt+Shift+F8) to identify regular measured intervals on the slide and to have objects **S**nap to Grid (by pressing Alt+F8), or to automatically line up to the nearest grid line whether or not the grid is displayed. The grid can bring great precision to your drawing, enabling you to line up objects or create symmetrical shapes (see fig. 12.11). If you're using the grid while drawing objects, note that a tiny box appears as part of the crosshair pointer. This box indicates the nearest grid interval that your object would snap to if you started drawing from that pointer location.

Tip

Whether you have **S**nap to Grid on or not, you can use the crosshair pointer to align objects to the displayed grid by carefully aligning the vertical and horizontal pointer lines and bullseye center with the displayed grid.

Fig. 12.10

This simple drawing combines two circles with some text to create a medallion.

Fig. 12.11
Displaying the grid
and having objects
snap to it enables
you to perfectly
draw and position
objects.

Symmetrical curve created by clicking alternate grid intersections

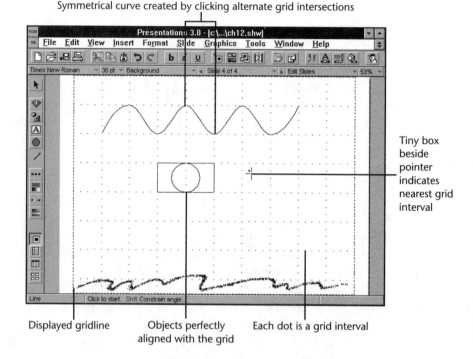

Tiny box
beside
pointer
indicates
nearest grid
interval

Displayed gridline   Objects perfectly   Each dot is a grid interval
                            aligned with the grid

Selecting and Editing Objects

Individual shapes that you have drawn may be attractive, but to really create
drawings that impress your audience (or to edit the QuickArt that comes with
Presentations), you need to be able to select and manipulate the drawn objects. This part of the chapter focuses on the techniques you need to effectively manipulate drawn objects. You learn not only how to select and size
objects, but also how to copy, group, and add special effects to them.

Tip
To select multiple
objects quickly,
click the Select
tool and drag to
create a dotted
outline box
around all the
objects to select
them. Release the
mouse button, and
the objects are
selected.

Troubleshooting

*I'm trying to select an object, but I get a crosshair pointer instead of the arrow. How can I
select the object?*

After you draw an object, you need to click the Select icon (it's the top one on the
palette that looks like the regular arrow mouse pointer) on the Tool Palette to be able
to select objects for editing.

Selecting Objects

As with text and various chart elements, before you can move or change an object in any way, you need to select it. You can perform a regular selection on an object to display its selection handles for basic operations, or you can select it for editing (shape changing) as described in "Editing the Object Shape," later in this chapter.

To display an object's *selection handles*, which are small black boxes that appear around the object, click the Select or Pointer tool on the Tool Palette, and then simply click the object. You can select more than one object at a time for operations that require it. If you want to resize several objects simultaneously to ensure that they stay in proportion with each other, for example, you can select all the objects before resizing. To select multiple objects, click on the first object, and then press and hold down the Ctrl key and click each subsequent object to select it. When multiple objects are selected, only one set of selection handles surrounds the collection of selected objects, as shown in figure 12.12.

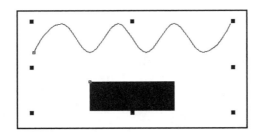

Fig. 12.12
Selecting multiple objects collects them within one set of selection handles.

To remove the selection handles, press Esc or click on a blank area away from the selected object(s).

The Select submenu of the Edit menu also enables you to select objects. Choose the All command from that submenu to select all the objects on a slide. Select one object and then choose the Like command on that submenu to select all objects of that type.

Resizing and Moving Objects

The selection handles enable you to resize the object by dragging to the shape you want, or by displaying dialog boxes that enable you to size or stretch the object by designated intervals. To resize an object proportionally, use one of these procedures:

- Point to a corner handle until the mouse pointer turns into a double-headed arrow. Press the left mouse button and drag until the object is the size you want.

Tip
Pressing and holding Ctrl while you move or resize an object creates a copy of the object and moves or resizes the copy.

- Point to a corner until the mouse pointer turns into a double-headed arrow. Right-click to display the Size dialog box. Enter a Size Ratio in the **M**ultiplier text box, and specify whether you want the object to be resized from the center point, or whether you want a copy of the object to be created and then resized.

To stretch an object when you resize it, follow one of these procedures:

- Point to a side, top, or bottom handle until the mouse pointer turns into a double-headed arrow. Press the left mouse button and drag until the object is the size you want.

- Point to a corner until the mouse pointer turns into a double-headed arrow. Right-click to display the Stretch dialog box. Enter a Size Ratio in the **M**ultiplier text box, and specify whether you want the object to be resized from the center point, or whether you want a copy of the object to be created and then resized.

To move an object when it's selected, simply point to it, hold down the left mouse button, and drag it to a new location.

Deleting and Duplicating Objects

When an object is selected, you can remove it from the slide or copy it using methods described earlier in this book. Opening the **E**dit menu and choosing **D**elete (Del) removes the object from the slide. Use Undo to reinstate the object. You can cut the object from the slide and place it on the Windows Clipboard by opening the **E**dit menu and choosing Cu**t** (or pressing Ctrl+X), or by clicking the Cut icon on the Toolbar. To create a duplicate of the object, copy it to the Clipboard, and then paste the copy of the object onto the slide. First select the object, and then open the **E**dit menu and choose **C**opy (or press Ctrl+C) or click the Copy icon on the Toolbar. Then open the **E**dit menu and choose **P**aste (or press Ctrl+V) or click the Paste icon on the Toolbar to place the copy on the slide. The copy is selected when pasted, so you simply can drag it to a new location on a slide.

Rotating and Flipping Objects

Despite the angle at which you originally placed an object, you can rotate it or skew it to change its position. Figure 12.13 illustrates rotated and skewed objects. *Rotating* an object simply turns it around an axis; the object shape remains perpendicular to the axis. *Skewing* the object turns it around an axis and simultaneously tilts the shape relative to the axis.

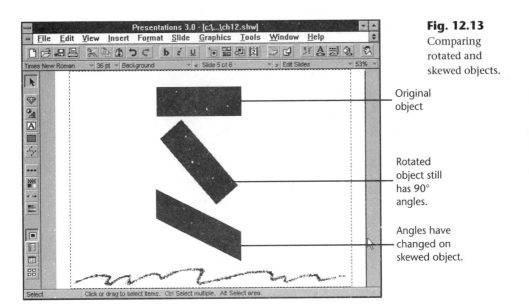

Fig. 12.13
Comparing rotated and skewed objects.

Original object

Rotated object still has 90° angles.

Angles have changed on skewed object.

To rotate or skew an object, follow these steps:

1. Select the object or line you want to rotate.

2. Open the **E**dit menu or QuickMenu and choose R**o**tate. The object changes to have rotation handles and a rotation axis, as shown in figure 12.14.

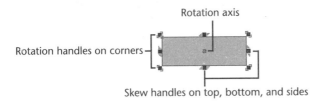

Rotation axis

Rotation handles on corners

Skew handles on top, bottom, and sides

Fig. 12.14
The rotation and skewing handles appear.

3. Drag the rotation axis to a new location if needed.

4. Drag a rotation or skew handle to a new location. Pressing Ctrl while dragging creates a copy of the object and rotates or skews it.

Note

To rotate or skew by precise intervals, point to a rotate or skew handle and right-click. Use the settings in the Rotate or Skew dialog box that appears and click OK.

You can flip an object you add vertically or horizontally. Click to select the object. Then open the **G**raphics menu and choose **F**lip; from the submenu, choose **L**eft/Right or **T**op/Bottom.

Reordering Objects

When you're layering multiple objects to combine effects or to add depth to an image, Presentations actually does perceive the objects as being on different drawing layers. Suppose that you create a text line, then a straight line, and then a square. If you tried to move the square over the text line (thinking that you want it to look like the square is surrounding the text line), the square would cover your text because it was drawn last and therefore is on the top drawing layer. Planning your drawings so that you create all the pieces on the precise layer needed would be unwieldy and frustrating. Therefore, Presentations has the capability of reordering objects—moving them forward or back to arrange layers appropriately.

Look at figure 12.15, for example. It contains three objects: some text and two triangles, drawn in order from left to right. To create a Yield sign from these objects, you obviously would need to have the largest, colored triangle in back, the white triangle in the middle, and the text on top so that you can read the sign. When you move the objects into the correct positions for this sign, however, the text is covered by the white triangle (drawn second), which is covered by the large triangle (drawn last).

Fig. 12.15
Three objects,
drawn from left to
right.

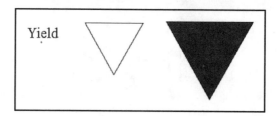

To fix this, first select the large triangle. Open the **G**raphics menu and the **O**rder submenu, and choose **B**ack. This command sends the large triangle to the very back drawing layer, as shown at the top of figure 12.16. This leaves the text between the two objects, even though it needs to be on top. You therefore need to select the white object, open the **G**raphics menu and the **O**rder submenu, and choose Bac**k**ward One. This command sends the selected object back one drawing layer, as shown at the bottom of figure 12.16.

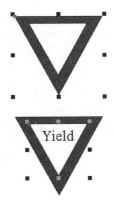

Fig. 12.16
Sending the large object all the way back and the white object back one layer to reveal the text.

Use the **G**raphics **O**rder submenu to rearrange selected objects on drawing layers as just described in the example. Here are the four commands and their function:

- *Front.* Moves the selected object to the front layer.

- *Back.* Moves the selected object to the back layer.

- *Forward One.* Moves the selected object forward one layer.

- *Backward One.* Moves the selected object back one layer.

Grouping and Ungrouping Objects

After you create a drawing like the Yield sign shown in figure 12.16, you probably will want to work with it like any other object—moving it around, copying it, resizing it, and so on. You can perform these operations, but selecting the multiple objects that are part of the drawing can prove tedious and troublesome. If you fail to select an object and move or resize the drawing, the unselected object remains unmoved or unsized, creating a problem that you have to fix.

Luckily, you can *group* multiple objects in a drawing into a single object that you can conveniently move and resize. (The QuickArt drawings are made of grouped objects.) Each of the objects in the group retains its own attributes and formatting, but you can copy, resize, move, and otherwise alter the grouped objects as a unit. To group and ungroup objects, use these steps:

1. Click the Select (Pointer) tool on the Tool Palette.

2. Select the object(s) to group or ungroup by clicking the first object and Ctrl+clicking the rest, or by dragging to create a dotted outline box around the objects and releasing the mouse button.

3. Open the **G**raphics menu or QuickMenu and choose **G**roup to group objects, or S**e**parate to break the drawing back down to its original pieces.

> **Caution**
>
> You cannot group objects if one of the objects is a text area or text line. In that case, your only option is combining, but note that combining may remove desirable attributes from some objects.

Combining Objects

Combining resembles grouping in that it enables you to treat multiple objects as a single unit. However, individual objects keep their original attributes when *grouped*, but individual objects take on the attributes of the object on the bottom (**B**ack) drawing layer when *combined*. Look at figure 12.17, for example. The top dolphin consists of grouped objects, and the bottom dolphin was made by combining. When the objects in the bottom dolphin were combined, they took on the attributes of the very back layer, which had a dark foreground color.

Fig. 12.17
The top dolphin has been grouped and the bottom dolphin has been combined.

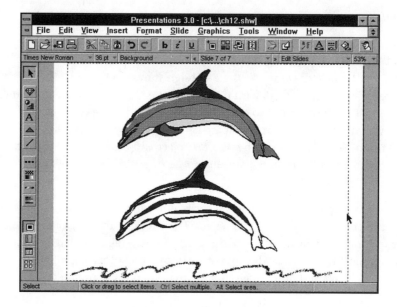

You therefore should use combining whenever you want a drawing to have an attractive, monochromatic look. Combining also is a good choice if you will be printing your slide show and your printer has limited capabilities for handling various shades of gray. To combine or separate objects, follow these steps:

1. Click the Select (Pointer) tool on the Tool Palette.

2. Select the object(s) to combine or separate by clicking the first and Ctrl+clicking the rest, or by dragging to create a dotted outline box around the objects and releasing the mouse button.

3. Open the **G**raphics menu or QuickMenu and choose **C**ombine to combine objects or S**e**parate to break the drawing back down to its original pieces. Note that when you separate a combined drawing, the separated objects revert back to their original attributes.

Aligning Objects

When you have several objects and you select them, there are some shortcuts available for aligning the objects within the selection area bounded by the selection handles. The **G**raphics menu offers the **A**lign and **S**pace Evenly submenus, each of which provide options for changing the alignment of a collection of objects, such as the one shown in figure 12.18.

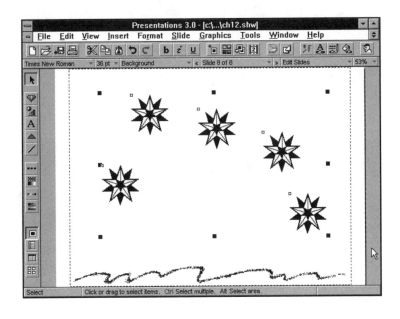

Fig. 12.18
A collection of selected objects ready for alignment.

The **A**lign submenu aligns objects relative to the boundaries of the selection area. Simply choose one of the following options from this submenu to align the selected objects:

- *Left.* Aligns the objects along the left boundary of the selection area.

- *Right.* Aligns the objects along the right boundary of the selection area.

- *Top.* Aligns the objects along the top boundary of the selection area.

- *Bottom.* Aligns the objects along the bottom boundary of the selection area (see fig. 12.19).

- *Center Left/Right.* Moves the objects horizontally to center them between the left and right boundaries of the selection area.

- *Center Top/Bottom.* Moves the objects vertically to center them between the top and bottom boundaries of the selection area.

- *Center Both.* Combines Center Left/Right and Center Top/Bottom, moving all objects to the center of the selection area.

Fig. 12.19

The objects from figure 12.18 aligned by opening the **G**raphics menu, choosing **A**lign, and then choosing **B**ottom.

Tip

Combining the effects of **G**raphics **A**lign and **S**pace Evenly on a group of objects as shown in figures 12.18 through 12.20 is a good way to create a border made of small objects.

The **S**pace Evenly submenu commands align three or more objects relative to each other within the area bounded by the selection handles, adjusting the objects to appear at regular intervals. Figure 12.20 shows the objects from figure 12.19 after the **G**raphics **S**pace Evenly **L**eft/Right command has been applied, inserting equidistant spacing between objects from left to right. **S**pace Evenly **T**op/Bottom spaces the objects at regular vertical intervals.

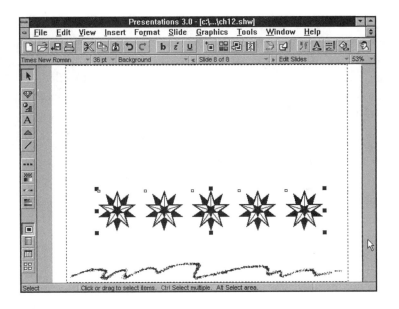

Fig. 12.20
Space Evenly
positions the
objects at regular
intervals within
the selection area.

Note that spacing the objects does not align them. If you have one object that is one inch from the left margin, one that's two inches from the left margin, and one that's three inches from the left margin, for example, **G**raphics **S**pace Evenly **T**op/Bottom might move each object up or down slightly, but it will not adjust them horizontally; they will remain one, two, and three inches from the margin respectively.

Troubleshooting

I tried to use Graphics Space Evenly on two objects, but nothing happened. What's wrong?

Graphics **S**pace Evenly must be used on three or more objects, because this command measures the average distance between objects and moves the objects so they're all separated by that average distance. You need three or more objects to create two distances to average.

I applied Graphics Space Evenly to a collection of objects, but they came out overlapping instead of having space between them. What's the problem?

Space Evenly spaces the objects within the selection area, which is defined by the far left and far right or top and bottom objects in the selected collection. If that distance is less than the sum of the widths or heights of all the objects, the result of a Space Evenly operation is to create equally overlapping objects. In other words, the selected objects must have ample space between them to begin with if you want space between them after spacing them evenly. So, an easy fix is to move one object far away from the others (horizontally for a left/right space and vertically for a top/bottom space) and then select them to Space Evenly.

Adding Quick3-D and QuickWarp

Chapter 7, "Enhancing Text," introduced you to Quick3-D and QuickWarp, two neat Presentations features that enable you to add quick special effects to a selected object. Figure 12.21 shows an example of each of these effects. For an in-depth look at the dialog boxes for creating each of these effects, see Chapter 7. To see the steps for applying each of these effects, read on.

Fig. 12.21
Applying Quick3D and QuickWarp gives a professional touch to drawn objects.

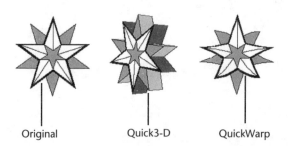

Original   Quick3-D   QuickWarp

As opposed to perspective, which makes a flat shape appear to have perspective, Quick3-D adds 3D depth and shading to the object, as well as tilting the text. Here's how to use Quick3-D:

1. Click on the Select (Pointer) tool in the Tool Palette, and then click to select the object you want to add 3D to.

2. Open the **G**raphics menu and choose Quick**3**-D. The Quick3-D dialog box appears.

3. Click to choose a predefined rotation from the **R**otation area, or change the X, Y, and Z rotation values.

4. From the Perspective area, click a type of perspective and change the **D**epth, if needed.

5. Drag to change the Color **A**djustment for the depth area of the object.

6. Click OK to inspect your results.

To shape a text line or text area to fill a specialized curve or wave, Presentations offers the QuickWarp feature. Here's how to use it:

1. Click on the Select (Pointer) tool in the Tool Palette, and then click to select the object you want to warp.

2. Open the **G**raphics menu and choose Quick**W**arp to display the QuickWarp dialog box.

IV

3. Click the shape you want from the choices at the left side of the dialog box. The preview area shows what effect that choice will have on your object.

4. Click OK. Your object warps on the slide to the shape you selected.

Editing the Object Shape

When you have a simple drawn object, or one that has been separated so that it consists of a collection of objects, you can edit the object to change its shape and make it more simple or more complex. Selecting an object for editing is the second type of selection mentioned earlier in this chapter. When you select an object to edit its shape, *editing points* or *handles* appear at line ends, angles, and curve changes to enable you to edit the object (see fig. 12.22). As opposed to regular selection handles, these handles are hollow and can appear in many locations around an object's perimeter. The line between two editing handles is called a *line segment*.

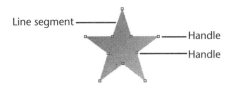

Fig. 12.22
Editing points or handles enable you to reshape drawn objects.

To display the editing handles for an object, use one of the following two methods:

- Click on the Select (Pointer) tool in the Tool Palette, and then click to select the object. Double-click the object to make the editing handles appear.

- Click on the Select (Pointer) tool in the Tool Palette, and then click to select the object. Open the **E**dit menu or QuickMenu and choose Ed**i**t Points.

Selecting and Moving Points

To select an edit handle, click on it to make it turn black. Once it's selected, you can move it, delete it, and more. Right-clicking the selected handle displays a QuickMenu that enables you to perform these and other operations. To move an edit handle, simply select it and then drag it to a new location, as shown in figure 12.23.

Fig. 12.23
Dragging an edit
handle to reshape
this drawn object.

Adding and Deleting Nodes

To create more angles or curve points in a shape, you need to add *nodes* (editing handles) that you can move to reposition the object outline. Conversely, if you want to immediately remove an angle or straighten out a curve, you can delete a node. Figure 12.24 shows an example of an angled shape and a curved shape with the results of nodes being added and deleted.

Fig. 12.24
Changes you can
make by adding
and deleting
nodes.

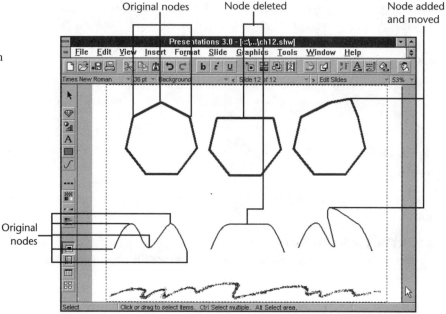

To add or delete a node, click the object and then double-click it to display the editing handles. Click the handle to delete or the handle beside which you want to add a node. Right-click to display the QuickMenu and then choose **A**dd or **D**elete as appropriate.

Opening and Closing Shapes

When you display the edit handles, you also can choose to close a shape by drawing a connecting segment between the nodes at the ends of a line, or to open the shape by removing one of the segments. Click the object and then double-click it to display the editing handles. Click the handle at one end of a line or beside the line segment to delete. Right-click to display the QuickMenu and choose **O**pen or **C**lose as appropriate.

Changing Lines to Curves and Back

When you have an edit handle separating curved line segments, you can choose to change those two line segments to straight segments and vice versa. Click the object and then double-click it to display the editing handles. Click the handle at the angle or curve you want to change to select it. Right-click to display the QuickMenu and then choose To Cur**v**e or To **L**ine as appropriate.

> **Note**
>
> Changing straight line segments to curves makes them Bezier curves, which you can work with as described in the next section.

Working with Bezier Curves

For the most part, working with Bezier curve editing handles is the same as working with editing handles for straight lines. You can move, add, or delete the Bezier curve editing handles, change open shapes to closed shapes, and so on. In addition, the QuickMenu for Bezier curve edit handles supplies two additional options: **S**ymmetrical, which evens the lines on either side of the editing handle; and **S**mooth, which softens the curves of the adjoining segments.

There is one significant difference in working with the editing handle on a Bezier curve, however. When you click the handle to select it, in addition to it turning black, two control handles separated by a dashed line appear (see fig. 12.25). These control handles enable you to easily adjust the shape and size of the curve without having to create and drag around multiple editing handles.

As indicated on figure 12.25, dragging a control handle toward or away from its pivoting edit handle shrinks or stretches the adjoining curve segments, making the curve softer or sharper, respectively. Dragging a control handle clockwise or counterclockwise skews the curve, twisting it on itself or even creating a loop. You can rotate a control handle a full 360 degrees.

Fig. 12.25
Selecting an editing handle on a Bezier curve displays its control handles.

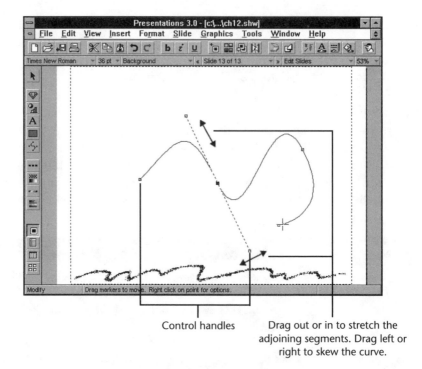

Control handles

Drag out or in to stretch the adjoining segments. Drag left or right to skew the curve.

From Here...

Drawing can be a pleasurable creative process, especially when you have the right tools in hand. This chapter introduced you to the drawing tools offered by WordPerfect Presentations 3.0 for Windows, explaining the basics of using all the tools, as well as giving you guidance for modifying and combining objects to create professional results. To explore additional ways to unleash your creative impulses, see these chapters:

■ Chapter 13, "Working with Outlines and Fills," provides information on editing the fills for vector images and more.

■ Chapter 14, "Working with Bitmap Images," explains how to use the Presentations paint tools to create and edit bitmap images, pixel-by-pixel if needed.

■ Chapter 15, "Working with Masters, Templates, and Backgrounds," addresses how to create custom slide show designs by using your own artwork and text for every slide in a slide show.

Chapter 13

Working with Outlines and Fills

Remember that person in high school who always mixed stripes, plaids, and the loudest color choices possible? That person may not have looked attractive, but he or she at least avoided looking plain and nondescript.

Although you shouldn't aspire to throw every stripe and pattern possible into your text and drawings, tasteful applications of colors, outlines, and fill patterns can add interest and appeal to your slide show, and enable you to create drawings with realism and depth. WordPerfect Presentations 3.0 for Windows provides you with great flexibility in applying colors and patterns to object outlines and fills. You learn how to add a little flair to outlines and fills in this chapter, including these topics:

- Specifying an outline, color, and thickness

- Setting interior fill colors

- Choosing a fill pattern

- Creating solid, gradient, and transparent fills

- Adding shadows to objects

- Blending objects

- Copying outline and fill attributes

Defining the Outline

As is obvious, the outline for an object or text is, well, the outline. Whether you want an outline that's actually visible, one that blends into your object or text, or no outline at all, you have to choose what type of outline you want. In Presentations, you also can add a pattern to an outline for a really unique effect.

You have two opportunities to specify the outline for an object. You can choose the outline before you draw the object or after you create the object (draw it and then select it).

> **Note**
>
> For a realistic effect on many of the drawings you create, try creating objects without outlines or with outlines that match the fill of the objects. You don't see thick black outlines around everything, do you?

Changing the Color

The outlines for objects and text have a foreground color and a background color (these colors are used as the top and bottom layers in a pattern). Unless you're specifying a pattern for your outline, it is unnecessary to worry about any color but the foreground color. There are two ways to change the outline color for a selected object. A quick-and-dirty method enables you to change the outline foreground or background color if that's the only attribute you intend to change. The second method, described later in the section "Changing All Line Attributes at Once," displays a dialog box where outline color is one of several elements that you can change.

> **Note**
>
> Any color palette you see in Presentations is conveniently organized to help you easily pick complementary gradient colors. Each horizontal line in a palette (except for the top line) contains different tones of the same color, from darker on the left to lighter on the right. Click a darker value on one palette line for the background color and a lighter value on the same palette line for the foreground color.

To quickly specify an outline foreground or background color, use these steps:

1. With the Select tool on the Tool Palette active, click the object or text you want to change the outline for to select it. Or simply go to step 2 to preset the outline color for an object you haven't drawn yet.

> **Note**
>
> If the text you want to change the outline for is in a layout area for a pre-
> defined slide type, you have to double-click the text area, and then drag to
> highlight the text you want to change. To apply your change to all similar text
> in the slide show or to detach the slide's master to change the text, see Chap-
> ter 15, "Working with Masters, Templates, and Backgrounds."

2. Click the Line Color tool on the Tool Palette to display a Line Color palette, shown in figure 13.1.

Current foreground color ⎯⎯⎯⎯ ⎯⎯Current background color

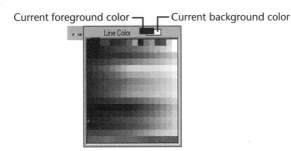

Fig. 13.1
Use the Line Color
tool on the Tool
Palette to apply a
foreground or
background color
to the outline for
the selected text or
object.

3. To specify a foreground color, point to the color you want and click the left mouse button.

4. Repeat step 2 to redisplay the palette.

5. To specify a background color, point to the color you want and click the right mouse button.

Changing the Thickness and Style

Presentations enables you to make object and text outlines thick or thin, and to add patterns to the outlines as your design needs dictate. The *line thickness* is its width or weight. The *style* indicates whether a line is solid; dashed, dot-ted, or a combination of dots and dashes. You can specify a line thickness before creating text or an object, or after you have created and selected the text or object. As for line color, you quickly can select a line thickness and style, or use the Fill Attributes dialog box as described later in this chapter.

Here's the fastest way to choose a new line thickness or style:

1. With the Select tool on the Tool Palette active, click the object or text you want to change the outline for to select it. Or simply go to step 2 to preset the outline thickness or style for an object you haven't drawn yet.

> **Note**
>
> If the text you want to change the outline for is in a layout area for a pre-defined slide type, you have to double-click the text area and then drag to highlight the text you want to change. To apply your change to all similar text in the slide show or to detach the slide's master to change the text, see Chapter 15.

2. Click the Line Style tool in the Tool Palette to display a Line Style palette, as shown in figure 13.2.

Fig. 13.2
Use this palette to choose a new line thickness or style.

3. To specify a thickness, click on one of the thickness choices from the left side of the palette. Or, select the None check box to turn off the outline display.

4. Repeat step 2 to redisplay the palette.

5. To specify a style, click on one of the style choices from the right side of the palette.

Changing All Line Attributes at Once

The Line Attributes dialog box enables you to set the outline foreground and background colors, thickness, and style for selected objects and text. In addition, this dialog box enables you to apply patterns and different line endings. With effects like these, you painlessly can create such elements as the frame shown in figure 13.3.

Use these steps to display the Line Attributes dialog box and use it to design an outline:

1. With the Select tool on the Tool Palette active, click the object or text you want to change the outline for to select it. Or simply go to step 2 to preset the outline for an object you haven't drawn yet.

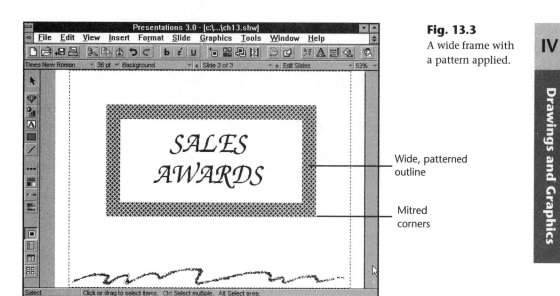

Fig. 13.3
A wide frame with
a pattern applied.

IV

Drawings and Graphics

Wide, patterned
outline

Mitred
corners

Note

If the text you want to change the outline for is in a layout area for a predefined slide type, you have to double-click the text area and then drag to
highlight the text you want to change. To apply your change to all similar
text in the slide show or to detach the slide's master to change the text, see
Chapter 15.

2. Open the Format menu and choose Line Attributes, or click the Line
Attributes icon on the Toolbar. The Line Attributes dialog box appears
(see fig. 13.4).

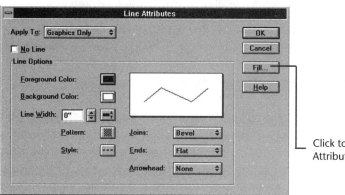

Fig. 13.4
The Line
Attributes dialog
box offers another
method of setting
line foreground
and background
colors.

Click to go to the Fill
Attributes dialog box.

3. If you didn't select an object in step 1, the Apply **T**o pop-up menu is available to you. Use this pop-up menu to specify what kind of new objects you create to apply the new outline selections to—**G**raphics Only, **T**ext Only, or Gr**a**phics and Text.

4. If you want to turn off the outline, turn on the **N**o Line check box and go to step 13.

5. To choose a new **F**oreground Color, click the color button for that setting to display a color palette, and click the color you want.

6. To choose a new **B**ackground Color, click the color button for that setting to display a color palette, and click the color you want.

7. To choose a Line **W**idth, enter a new setting in the text box, or click the pop-up button beside it and click a line width.

8. To choose a line **P**attern, click the pop-up menu beside it and click the pattern of your choice.

9. Choose a **S**tyle by clicking the pop-up menu and clicking your choice.

10. You can specify how a line **J**oins with another line by clicking to display that pop-up list. Choose from **B**evel, **M**itre, and **R**ound joins. (A *mitred corner* joins like a picture frame corner; the joined pieces each have a 45-degree cut so they match up to form a perfect 90-degree angle.)

11. You can choose an appearance for the line **E**nds. **F**lat, **R**ound, and **S**quare are the choices. Click the pop-up menu and then click the choice you want.

12. To choose an **A**rrowhead, click the pop-up menu and then click one of the choices: **N**one, **B**eginning, **E**nding, or **B**oth Ends.

13. Click OK to close the dialog box and implement your changes.

Defining the Interior Fill

The *fill* for text and objects is the color or pattern within an outline. Used effectively, fills add necessary color and texture to your text and drawings. Exercise restraint when choosing patterns and colors; trying to emphasize every item usually has the opposite impact. You also need to ensure that your slide text is clear and readable. Figure 13.5 compares two examples: the top item shows how an object fill interferes with text, and the bottom item shows how a fill enhances text. Even though the same fill pattern is used in both rectangles in the figure, the bottom example is more readable because a lighter color was chosen for the pattern. This section describes how to choose a fill color and pattern for your text and objects, which you can do before or after creating them. You also learn how to create gradient and transparent fills.

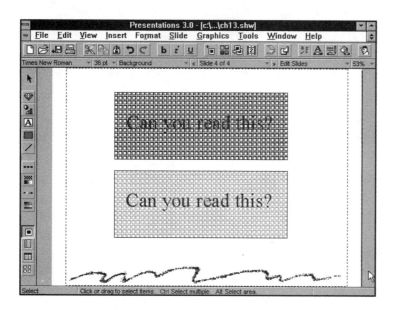

Fig. 13.5
Be careful when choosing fills and fill colors, especially if it interferes with the readability of text.

Setting Fill Colors

Foreground and background fill colors create the patterns in a fill. If no pattern is specified, the object or text normally is filled with the foreground color. The process of choosing fill colors is nearly the same as choosing fills for lines:

1. With the Select tool on the Tool Palette active, click the object or text you want to change the fill color for to select it. Or simply go to step 2 to preset the fill color for an object you haven't drawn yet.

2. Click the Fill Color tool in the Tool Palette to display a Fill Color palette, as shown in figure 13.6.

3. To specify a foreground color, point to the color you want and click the left mouse button.

4. Repeat step 2 to redisplay the palette.

5. To specify a background color, point to the color you want and click the right mouse button.

Current foreground color ⌐ Current background color

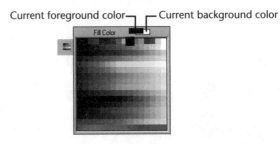

Fig. 13.6
Use the Fill Color tool on the Tool Palette to apply a foreground or background color to the fill for the selected text or object.

Troubleshooting

I changed the foreground color to white so that I could create an outline object, but my outline disappeared.

Changing the foreground color automatically changes the outline color as well. Use the Line Attributes tool on the palette to adjust the outline color.

Creating Pattern Fills

Presentations provides several predefined fills you can apply to objects or text to add interest. You can apply these patterns with the Fill Attributes dialog box. Use these steps to display the Fill Attributes dialog box and use it to design a fill:

1. With the Select tool on the Tool Palette active, click the object or text you want to change the outline for to select it. Or simply go to step 2 to preset the outline for an object you haven't drawn yet.

Caution

If the text you want to change the outline for is in a layout area for a pre-defined slide type, you have to double-click the text area and then drag to highlight the text you want to change. To apply your change to all similar text in the slide show or to detach the slide's master to change the text, see Chapter 15.

---

2. Open the Format menu and choose Fill Attributes, or click the Fill Attributes icon on the Toolbar. The Fill Attributes dialog box appears (see fig. 13.7).

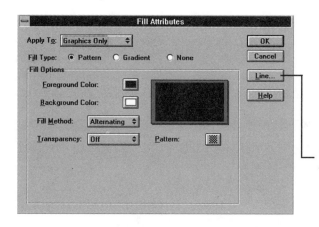

Fig. 13.7
This dialog box
offers another
method of setting
fill foreground and
background colors.

IV

Drawings and Graphics

Click to go to the Line
Attributes dialog box.

3. If you didn't select an object in step 1, the Apply **T**o pop-up menu is
made available to you. Use this pop-up menu to specify what kind of
new objects you create to apply the new outline selections to—**G**raphics
Only, **T**ext Only, or Gr**a**phics and Text.

4. To choose a new **F**oreground Color for the pattern, click the color
button for that setting to display a color palette, and click the color you
want.

5. To choose a new **B**ackground Color for the pattern, click the color
button for that setting to display a color palette, and click the color you
want.

6. Click the Fill **M**ethod pop-up menu and choose between Alternating
(fills alternate areas) and **W**inding (fills overlapping areas).

7. Click the **P**attern pop-up menu, and then click the pattern you want.

8. Click OK to close the dialog box and apply your selected fill.

Tip
Use the None
button in the Fill
Attributes dialog
box to remove the
selected fill.

If you don't need to change the foreground and background colors, there's a
quick way to choose a new fill color. Simply click the Fill Attributes icon on
the Tool Palette to display a variety of fill pattern choices (see fig. 13.8). Click
the choice you want, or click None to remove the current fill pattern.

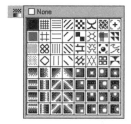

Fig. 13.8
A palette of
patterns you can
apply to objects
and text.

Creating Gradient Fills

A *gradient fill* blends one color into another. In Presentations, you can select the colors to gradate together and the angle or blending shape. Figure 13.9 shows examples of how you can use gradations to add realism, creating the illusion of distance (as in the sky) or fullness (as in the sun).

Fig. 13.9
Gradations can help objects look realistic and three-dimensional.

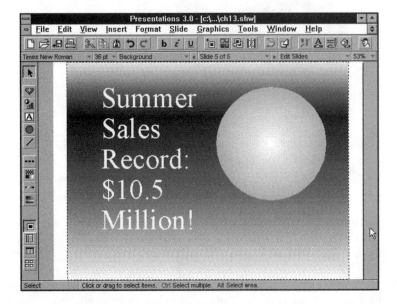

To create a gradation in text or an object, follow these steps:

1. With the Select tool on the Tool Palette active, click the object or text you want to change the outline for to select it. Or simply go to step 2 to preset the outline for an object you haven't drawn yet.

> **Note**
>
> If the text you want to change the outline for is in a layout area for a pre-defined slide type, you have to double-click the text area, and then drag to highlight the text you want to change. To apply your change to all similar text in the slide show or to detach the slide's master to change the text, see Chapter 15.

2. Open the Format menu and choose Fill Attributes, or click the Fill Attributes icon on the Toolbar. The Fill Attributes dialog box appears.

3. Click the Gradient button to display the options shown in figure 13.10.

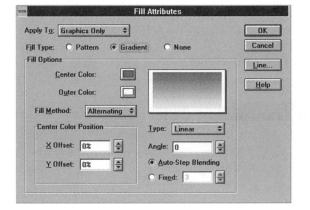

Fig. 13.10
The Fill Attributes
dialog box options
for gradations.

4. If you didn't select an object in step 1, the Apply **T**o pop-up menu is
   made available. Use this pop-up menu to specify what kind of new
   objects you create to apply the new outline selections to—**G**raphics
   Only, **T**ext Only, or Gr**a**phics and Text.

5. To choose a new **F**oreground Color for the pattern, click the color button
   for that setting to display a color palette, and click the color you want.

6. To choose a new **B**ackground Color for the pattern, click the color button for that setting to display a color palette, and click the color you
   want.

7. Click the Fill **M**ethod pop-up menu and choose between **A**lternating
   (fills alternate areas) and **W**inding (fills overlapping areas).

8. If you want the gradient to originate from somewhere other than the
   upper lefthand corner of the screen, enter new values in the **X** Offset
   (controls left-to-right position) and **Y** Offset (controls top-to-bottom
   position) boxes. Legal values range from 0 to 100, with 50 being the
   screen midpoints.

9. Click the **T**ype pop-up menu to indicate a new fill type: **L**inear, Circular, or **R**ectangular. This dictates whether the colors blend along a
   straight line, in a curve, or at an angle.

10. Enter an An**g**le value of 1 to 359 to rotate the gradient.

11. Leave **A**uto-Step Blending selected if you want Presentations to specify
    the number of blending steps between the gradient colors, or click
    Fix**e**d and enter a value to specify the number of blending steps.

12. Click OK to close the dialog box and apply the gradient fill.

If you don't need to change the gradient, there's a quick way to adjust the gradation angle. Simply click the Fill Attributes icon on the Tool Palette to display a variety of gradient choices near the bottom of the palette (refer to fig. 13.8). Click the choice you want, or click None to remove the current fill pattern.

Creating Transparent Object Fills

Even though you create transparent fills using the Fill Attributes dialog box, they bear a bit of separate explanation. The Transparency feature enables you to layer objects and see through them, as in figure 13.11. Specifying a transparent background color lets objects behind show through the object areas normally occupied by the background color. A transparent foreground color lets objects behind show through areas normally occupied by the foreground color. To specify a transparent foreground or background, go to the Fill Attributes dialog box, click the **T**ransparency pop-up menu, and click one of the fills to make it transparent.

Fig. 13.11
The side petals of this *fleur-de-lis* have a transparent foreground color, and the middle petal has a transparent background color.

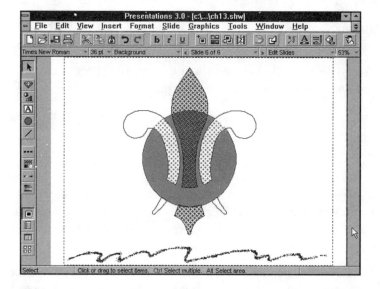

Troubleshooting

I specified a transparent foreground color, with just a flat fill (no pattern), and the object disappeared. What happened?

Specifying a transparent foreground makes the object look the same as specifying None for the fill. Place an object behind the transparent object, or specify a new fill.

Creating Shadows

Drop shadows give the illusion that an object is floating over the slide. They're very easy to add to your selected objects. Follow these steps:

1. Click the text container for the text you want to change to select it.

> **Note**
>
> The template masters don't enable you to add a drop shadow for text created by one of the slide types.

2. Open the Format menu and choose **S**hadow Attributes, or right-click and choose **S**hadow Attributes from the QuickMenu. You also can click the Shadow button on the Toolbar. The Shadow Attributes dialog box appears.

3. Click the **S**hadow On check box. This displays a preview of the shadow (see fig. 13.12).

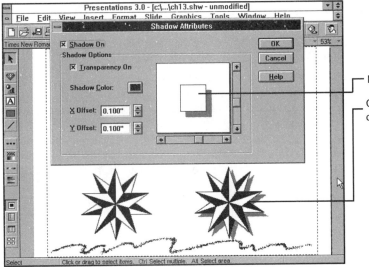

Fig. 13.12
Adding a shadow to the selected object.

— Preview

— Object with drop shadow

Tip
Use opaque drop shadows only if you choose a much lighter color for the shadow; otherwise, you create a "seeing double" effect rather than a shadowed effect. In general, lighter colors create more subtle drop shadows.

4. To make the shadow opaque rather than transparent, click to deselect the **T**ransparency On check box.

5. Click the Shadow **C**olor button to display a palette of colors. Click a color to select it for the drop shadow.

6. If you want to reposition the drop shadow, enter new values in the **X** Offset (controls left-to-right position) and **Y** Offset (controls top-to-bottom position) boxes. Legal values range from -0.500 to 0.500. You also can change the drop shadow position by using the scroll bars at the bottom and right side of the drop-shadow preview.

7. Click OK to close the dialog box and apply the drop shadow.

To remove a drop shadow, follow steps 1 through 3 of this procedure. Clicking the **S**hadow on check box toggles it off (removes the x from the check box) in this case. Click OK once again to close the Shadow Attributes dialog box.

Blending Objects into Each Other

Have you ever seen objects morphed so that one object turns into another? You can accomplish that same effect on a slide using Presentations' **B**lend capability. **B**lend morphs two objects over a series of steps, so that one object evolves to have the shape and attributes of another. Here's how to blend two objects that you have drawn and formatted:

1. With the Select tool on the Tool Palette active, click the first object to blend.

2. Press and hold Ctrl, and click the second object to blend.

3. Open the **G**raphics menu and choose **B**lend. The Blend dialog box appears (see fig. 13.13).

4. If needed, change the Number of **S**teps in the blend. This is the number of interim objects Presentations will create from the first object to the second object.

5. Click OK to close the dialog box and create the blend (see fig. 13.14).

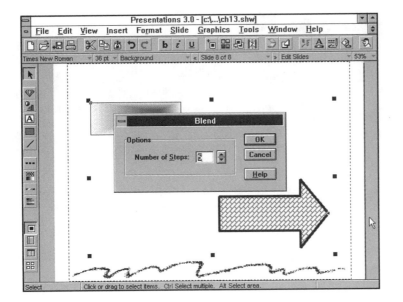

Fig. 13.13
The Blend dialog box enables you to specify how many interim steps there will be in the blend.

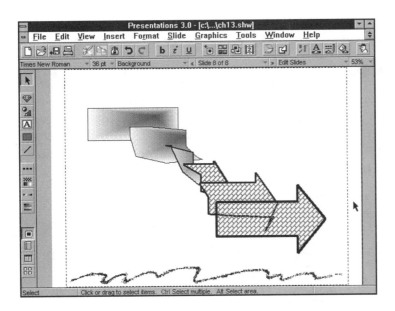

Fig. 13.14
Blending one object into another.

IV

Drawings and Graphics

Copying Attributes

If you want to create a group of similar-looking objects, you don't have to format them one by one. The **G**et Attributes and Appl**y** Attributes commands on the Fo**r**mat menu enable you to copy the attributes you select and apply those attributes to other objects. Here's how to use those commands:

1. Apply the attributes you want to an object.

2. Click the object to select it.

3. Open the Fo**r**mat menu and choose **G**et Attributes. The Get Attributes dialog box appears.

4. Choose whether you want to copy the attributes for **G**raphics Only, **T**ext Only, or Gr**a**phics and Text by clicking the appropriate option. Click OK.

5. Select the text you want to copy the attributes to.

6. Open the Fo**r**mat menu and choose Appl**y** Attributes.

Working with Color Palettes in Presentations

If you want to use a consistent set of colors when editing a bitmap or drawing, or simply to have a consistent set of colors to use when you create a slide show, you need to create and save a color palette. When you create and then retrieve a color palette, you can apply those colors in your slide show. Use these steps to create a color palette:

1. Open the Fo**r**mat menu and choose **C**olor Attributes. The Color Attributes dialog box appears (see fig. 13.15).

Fig. 13.15
The Color Attributes dialog box enables you to create and retrieve custom color palettes in Presentations.

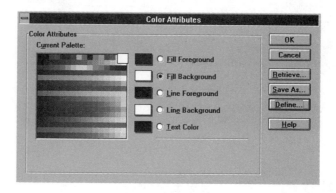

2. Click one of the radio buttons to select a color to change (such as the Fill Background button). Then click a color in the Current Palette at the left side of the dialog box to choose it for that element.

3. Repeat step 2 to change the color for other elements.

4. If you want to change a color on the Current Palette, click the Define button. In the Define Color Palette dialog box, click the color to change in the Current Palette list. Then click on the color wheel in the upper left corner of the dialog box to change the color. Click other palette colors and redefine them as needed before clicking OK to close the dialog box.

5. Click the Save As button to display the Save Color Palette dialog box.

6. Type a Filename, and then click the Save button to save the palette.

To reload the palette, open the Color Attributes dialog box as described in step 1 and click the Retrieve button. Then use the Retrieve Color Palette dialog box to select the color palette you want.

From Here...

WordPerfect Presentations 3.0 for Windows gives you great flexibility in adding different outlines, fills, and patterns to your objects so that you can achieve any effect you want—from realistic to abstract and from serious to whimsical. This chapter introduced you to the menu commands, Toolbar icons, and Tool Palette icons you can use to work with outlines and fills. For more information on adding elements to slides and using fills, see these chapters:

- Chapter 7, "Enhancing Text," provides guidance on changing the outlines and fills for text on your slides.

- Chapter 12, "Using the Presentations Drawing Tools," explains how to draw vector objects directly on a slide.

- Chapter 14, "Working with Bitmap Images," explains how to use the Presentations paint tools to create and edit bitmap images, pixel-by-pixel if needed.

- Chapter 15, "Working with Masters, Templates, and Backgrounds," addresses how to create custom slide show designs by using your own artwork and text for every slide in a slide show.

Chapter 14

Working with Bitmap Images

Bitmap images, commonly created in paint programs, are composed of numerous pixels with different colors assigned to them; as opposed to *vector images*, which are composed of mathematically defined shapes. The different shapes you draw to create a vector image remain as distinct objects that you can move and resize. Bitmap shapes, however, become indistinguishable from the rest of the drawing once you add them; you cannot click to select an object later. This makes editing bitmap objects much more tedious; in some cases, you might have to edit them pixel by pixel.

Why, then, would you even use bitmap images in WordPerfect Presentations 3.0 for Windows? First, there are some effects you can create with paint tools that you cannot create with drawing tools—for example, a spray-can effect that spritzes the selected color where you want it, and an eraser effect with which you can remove selected parts of images. Second, you can create much more subtle and natural gradations of colors in bitmaps; you aren't limited to the mathematically defined drawing tool gradations. Third, scanning images to an electronic format creates bitmap files like TIFF or PCX images. To add these images to your slide show (and certainly to edit them), you need to be familiar with the techniques and tools for working with bitmap images.

This chapter explains how to use bitmap images in a slide show. The techniques you learn about here follow:

- Drawing your own bitmaps

- Modifying bitmaps you create or import

- Using the paint tools, including the shape tools, line tools, selection tools, and more

- Modifying or removing parts of the bitmap image

- Working with fill colors

- Using bitmap text

- Moving and sizing a bitmap image on a slide

- Converting bitmaps to vectors

- Scanning your own bitmaps directly into a slide show

Adding Original Bitmaps to a Slide

Chapter 16, "Inserting Objects into Slides," explains how to use the File Command from the Insert menu to place a pre-existing bitmap image from another source on a slide. That process is a simple matter of using the command, selecting the type of file to insert, and then selecting the file. After you insert a file in this way, you can use any of the techniques described in the rest of the chapter to modify and work with the file.

You also can create your own bitmaps from scratch, much as you would in Windows Paint Brush or another paint program. You use a three-step process: first you insert the bitmap into the slide, you use the paint tools as described later in this chapter to create the image, and then you exit the Bitmap Editor. The next section, "Modifying a Bitmap," explains how to use the paint tools in the Bitmap Editor. Here's the overview for inserting and exiting the bitmap:

1. Go to the slide where you want to insert the bitmap.

2. Open the Insert menu and choose Bitmap. Or, point to the QuickArt icon on the Tool Palette and press and hold the left mouse button to display a small palette. Drag to move the red highlight around the icon that looks like a painter's palette and release the mouse button. The mouse pointer changes to look like a hand holding a dotted outline.

3. Drag to define the size of the bitmap. Presentations takes you to the Bitmap Editor screen, shown in figure 14.1. This screen provides modified menus, a Toolbar, a Tool Palette, and a Power Bar with special paint tools for creating and working with bitmap images.

Tip
Click on the slide after selecting the Bitmap tool to create a full-slide size bitmap.

IV

Drawings and Graphics

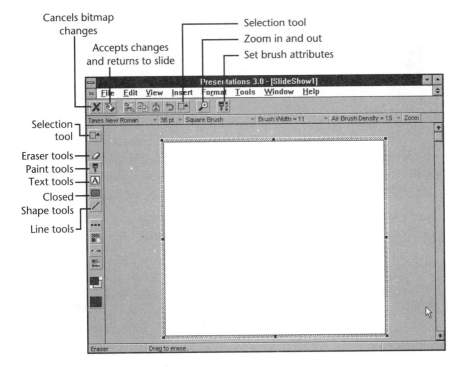

Cancels bitmap changes

Accepts changes and returns to slide

Selection tool

Zoom in and out

Set brush attributes

Selection tool

Eraser tools

Paint tools

Text tools

Closed

Shape tools

Line tools

Fig. 14.1
The Bitmap Editor provides special paint tools not available in the normal Presentations window.

4. Use the tools and menus as needed to create your bitmap image. The various tools are described in the next section, "Modifying a Bitmap."

5. When you're finished creating the bitmap image, open the **F**ile menu and choose **R**eturn (or press Ctrl+F4), or click the Toolbar icon for accepting changes and returning to the slide. (It's the second icon from the left, which looks like a hand pointing left.) This action closes the image and inserts it into the slide in the area you defined, as shown in figure 14.2.

Fig. 14.2

A hand-drawn
bitmap inserted
into a slide.

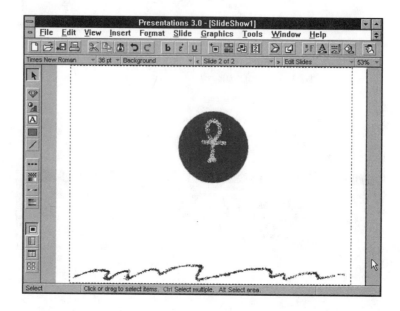

To return to the slide without accepting the changes made to the bitmap,
open the **F**ile menu and choose **C**ancel, or click the Cancel icon at the far left
on the Bitmap Editor Toolbar.

> **Note**
>
> When you're in the Bitmap Editor and want to create a custom Toolbar, menu, or
> keyboard (as described in Chapter 20, "Customizing with Macros, Toolbars, and
> Menus"), the default for each of these items is named <bitmap> instead of <slide>.
> Although you cannot edit the <bitmap> Toolbar, menu, or keyboard, you can copy it
> and add custom tools for use in the Bitmap Editor.

Modifying a Bitmap

As for many other charts and objects you add to a slide, there are two ways
to "select" a bitmap on a slide. The first method is selecting it in the strict
sense of the term: you click on the bitmap to make selection handles appear
around it. When you do so, you also can right-click to display a QuickMenu
for the bitmap, as shown in figure 14.3.

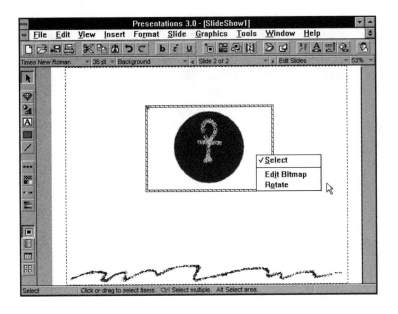

Fig. 14.3
You can right-click
a bitmap to display
its QuickMenu.

IV

Drawings and Graphics

The other way to "select" a bitmap is to open it in the Bitmap Editor to make changes to it. To select a bitmap for editing, use one of the following two methods:

■ Click to select the bitmap. Open the Edit menu or QuickMenu and choose Edit Bitmap.

■ Double-click the bitmap.

After you display the Bitmap Editor, you can make the changes you want to the current bitmap and then return to the slide as described earlier. Right-click on the painting area to display a QuickMenu. Bitmap editing techniques are described next.

Drawing Elements

The Paint Tools icon, Closed Shape Tools icon, and Line Tools icon each display a palette of different tools when you point to them and hold down the left mouse button. You basically drag to select the tool you want and then use the tool in the drawing area. Many of these tools are available on the Insert menu as well.

One significant difference between the paint tools and the drawing tools that you learned about in Chapter 12 is that with the paint tools, you must select all colors and attributes after selecting the tool and before drawing the shape. After the shape is drawn, it's no longer an individual object that you can select and edit. It's a series of individual pixels with color applied. There are some limited changes you can make at that point, but it's much more time-consuming than doing it right the first time. Changing brush attributes and making color selections is described next.

The Closed Shape and Line tools in the Bitmap Editor are virtually identical in operation to those on the drawing palette, which were described in Chapter 12. To learn how to use these tools see Chapter 12, "Using the Presentations Drawing Tools."

The paint tools, however, are unique to the Bitmap Editor and need explanation. To display these tools, point to the Paint Tools icon on the palette and press and hold the left mouse button. The palette shown in figure 14.4 appears.

Fig. 14.4
The Bitmap Editor paint tools.

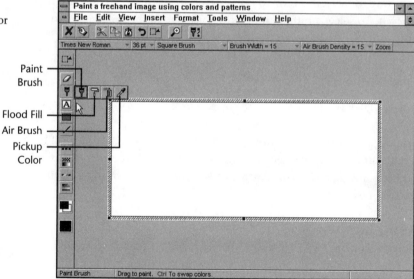

Drag to select the tool you want and then use it in the painting area, as in the following procedures:

- After selecting the Paint Brush icon (by clicking it or opening the **Insert** menu and choosing Paint **B**rush), select attributes and colors if needed, and then point to the painting area. Press and hold the left mouse button and drag to create any freeform shape you want. Pressing Ctrl and holding it while clicking-and-dragging draws in the background color rather than the foreground color. Release the mouse button when your line is finished.

- The Flood Fill tool enables you to fill with colors and patterns. It doesn't fill a draw shape, however. When you select Flood Fill (by clicking the tool or opening the **I**nsert menu and choosing **F**lood Fill) and click on a pixel, it fills that pixel and any adjoining pixels of the same color with the new color or pattern you specify. Figure 14.5 shows a new fill applied with the Flood Fill tool to the background of a bitmap. The new color flowed only to adjoining pixels. Select this tool, select the fill color or pattern, and click on the area to fill.

Tip

If you're creating your own bitmap and want a colored or patterned background rather than plain white, use the Flood Fill tool to create a background by selecting the tool, selecting the attributes you want, and clicking the white background area.

Adjoining pixels filled with a new color

Fig. 14.5
The flood fill roller fills adjoining pixels of the same color with a new fill (original image from Corel Corporation).

- The Air Brush tool (which you select by clicking it or opening the **I**nsert menu and choosing **A**ir Brush) spritzes color where you specify, much like spray paint. You control the density and color of the spray. Select the Air Brush tool and then press the left mouse button and drag wherever you want spray to appear.

■ The last tool, the Pickup Color tool (which looks like an eyedropper), picks up a color and makes it the foreground or background color. This is a useful tool if you want to match a color on a bitmap image and you cannot readily pick the color from the palette. Select this tool (by clicking it or opening the **I**nsert menu and choosing Pickup **C**olor) and click on the color you want to pick up. Pressing Ctrl and holding it while clicking makes the picked up color the background color.

Changing Brush Attributes

The Paint Brush and Air Brush tools offer attributes you can change. The shape of the brush affects the appearance of the line it creates, especially at the line ends. The density of the air brush spray (as well as how quickly you drag that tool) affects the line, too. Figure 14.6 shows some examples. For both of these tools, you can specify a new thickness.

Fig. 14.6
Different brush shapes and spray densities affect the results of the Paint Brush and Air Brush tools.

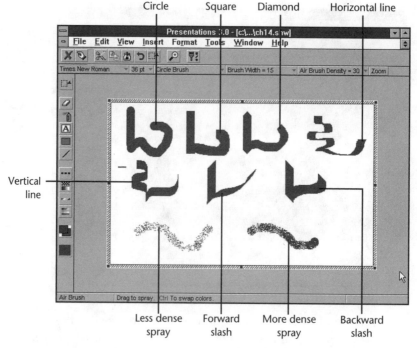

You must change the attributes for the paint brush or air brush before you draw the shape. To change the attributes, open the Fo**r**mat menu or QuickMenu and click **B**rush, or click the Attributes button on the Toolbar. The Brush Attributes dialog box appears (see fig. 14.7). To select a new paint

IV

brush **S**hape, click that pop-up button and click your choice from the list that appears. To paint a wider stroke, increase the entry in the **B**rush Width text box. And, to color more pixels per stroke with the air brush, increase the **A**ir Brush Density setting. Click OK to close the dialog box when you finish changing the settings. Note that the Power Bar also provides buttons for changing all three of these settings.

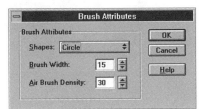

Fig. 14.7
The Brush Attributes dialog box enables you to change attributes for the Paint Brush and Air Brush tools.

Changing Colors, Lines, and Fills

As noted earlier in this chapter, you need to specify colors, lines, and fills before you draw elements with any of the paint tools. Most of the tools for selecting colors and fills are the same as those used for drawing tools. The Tool Palette offers commands for changing line style, fill pattern and gradient, line color, and fill color. In addition, the Fo**r**mat menu offers **C**olor Attributes, Li**n**e Attributes, F**i**ll Attributes, and **T**ext Attributes commands for setting fills and colors. Using these Tool Palette tools and Fo**r**mat menu choices is covered in detail in Chapter 13, "Working with Outlines and Fills."

> **Note**
>
> When you load a bitmap from another source, such as a scanned-in image, the color palettes are adjusted to represent the tones already available in the image. Continue using those tones if you want your edits to have a natural, subtle impact. If you want to make wild color changes to the image, you need to load another color palette, as described in Chapter 13.

Selecting Specific Areas

A Select tool appears on both the Toolbar and Tool Palette, as well as the painting area QuickMenu. This tool selects a rectangular area on which you can perform Cut, Copy, and Move operations. Click the Select tool, and then drag on the bitmap to define the selected area. A dashed rectangle appears to indicate the selected area, as shown in figure 14.8.

Tip
Before pasting, select an area with the Select tool to paste specifically to that area. Make sure that you select an area large enough to paste to so that your shape isn't cut off. If you don't select an area before pasting, the paste puts the new shape precisely over the old one, and you must drag it into place.

Fig. 14.8
Dragging creates a
selected area.

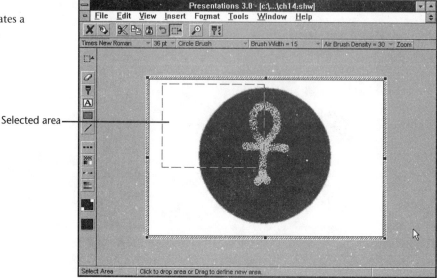

Selected area—

Tip
After choosing the
Select tool, click
on the painting
area to select the
entire area.

Note that if you want to move an entire shape on the painting background,
you should be sure that the selection area fully contains it. If you didn't select
quite the right area the first time, click outside the selected area, and then
drag again to select a new area.

Erasing Part of the Image

The most obvious way to erase is to perform a Cut operation on it. Select the
area to erase. Then open the **E**dit menu and choose Cu**t** (or press Ctrl+X), or
click the Cut icon on the Toolbar. The selected area is cut, as shown in figure
14.9. You can open the **E**dit menu and choose **P**aste (or press Ctrl+V) to paste
the cut material into another bitmap. Similarly, opening the **E**dit menu and
choosing **C**opy (or pressing Ctrl+C) and **P**aste enables you to copy bitmap
selections.

A special bitmap tool, the Eraser tool, enables you to perform more specialized erasing. You control the shape of the erased area by dragging and by
setting eraser attributes (see "Changing Brush Attributes," earlier in this chapter). There are two types of erasers. Here's a description of each eraser and
how to use it:

■ The *regular eraser* is the one that's visible by default on the Tool Palette.
   It erases both the foreground and background colors in the area you
   specify. Select this eraser by clicking it in the Tool Palette or by opening
   the **I**nsert menu and choosing **E**raser. Click on the area that you want
   to start erasing and drag to erase the areas you want.

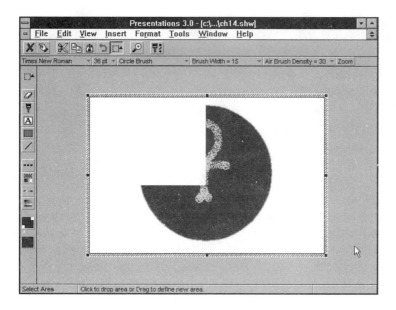

Fig. 14.9
Cutting the area
that was selected
in figure 14.8.

■ The *selective eraser* removes the foreground color only, revealing the background color where you want (see fig. 14.10). Select this eraser by clicking it in the Tool Palette or by opening the **I**nsert menu and choosing **S**elective Replace. Click on the area that you want to start erasing and drag to erase the areas you want.

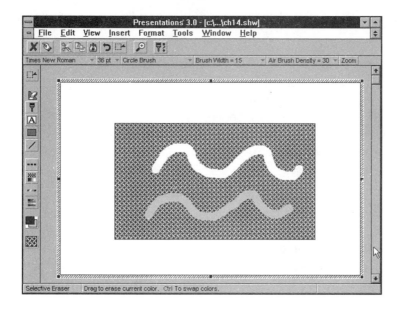

Fig. 14.10
Erasing the
foreground and
background colors
(top) and the
foreground color
only (bottom).

Caution

The **E**dit menu also offers a Cle**a**r (Ctrl+Shift+F4) command. Use this command sparingly, because it deletes everything in the painting area (not just the selection) and doesn't place the deleted contents on the Clipboard.

Troubleshooting

I tried to perform a selective erase, and it didn't work at all. Did I do something wrong?

If you were trying to perform a selective erase on an image from another source, such as an image you scanned or a bitmap you imported, selective erase doesn't work because these bitmaps generally only have one layer of color; there is no foreground color to erase. Selective erase also doesn't work with gradient fills, presumably because the "foreground" and "background" colors are really mixed on one layer to create the opaque gradient effect.

Moving Portions of the Image

When you have selected a portion of the image with the Select tool and want to move it to a new location, click in the center of your selection and drag the selection to a new location. The moved section remains selected until you click elsewhere to deselect it; don't do so until you're sure that you have correctly placed the section, because reselecting precisely the same area could prove difficult.

Editing Pixels

In some situations, you will need to edit your image pixel by pixel, such as when you're cleaning up a bitmap you scanned directly into Presentations. To edit the pixels, you need to zoom in on the image, as shown in figure 14.11. To zoom in, open the **V**iew menu and choose **Z**oom (or press Shift+F5), click the Zoom icon on the Toolbar, or click the Zoom button on the Power Bar.

Select the new colors you want, and then use the Paint Brush tool to change individual pixels or the Flood Fill tool to change multiple adjoining pixels. Drag the red box in the FULL BITMAP or ACTUAL SIZE display to change the area you're zoomed in on. To zoom back out, open the **V**iew menu and choose **Z**oom (or press Shift+F5), click the Zoom icon on the Toolbar, or click the Zoom button on the Power Bar.

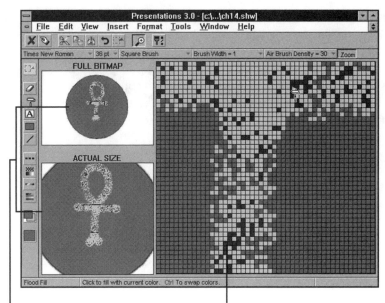

Fig. 14.11
Zooming in on an
image enables you
to edit pixels.

IV

Drawings and Graphics

Drag the red box to change   You can flood fill adjoining pixels.
the zoomed area.

Adding and Editing Bitmap Text

You can create text areas and text lines in a bitmap using the tools described
in Chapter 6, "Adding and Editing Text." However, once you click outside
the text you've added to a bitmap, it ceases being an independent object and
becomes a series of colored pixels. If you select the text and try to move it, for
example, any surrounding background is moved with it, unlike text drawn on
a slide (see fig. 14.12).

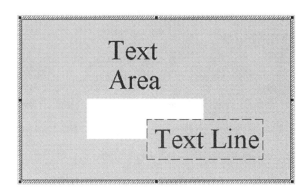

Fig. 14.12
Bitmap text is fully
integrated in the
image. Moving it
moves its back-
ground as well.

While you're creating text in the Bitmap Editor, as long as the insertion point is visible, you can drag over the text to highlight it and change its font, outline, fill, and so on. Once you click on the painting area to deselect the text, you have to edit it as you would any other bitmap shape—pixel by pixel, or by using flood fills. This process does give you the opportunity to experiment with letters as artistic shapes. Figure 14.13 shows a text line where a different flood fill color has been applied to every letter, for example.

Fig. 14.13
In the Bitmap Editor, text is treated as shapes with pixels, so you can apply a different flood fill to each letter.

Applying Special Paint Effects

Many high-end painting programs such as Corel PHOTO-PAINT and Adobe Photoshop offer special effects that you can apply to selected areas of bitmap images to make uniform changes quickly. Presentations now offers some similar effects in its Bitmap Editor. Here are the effects you can apply to all or part of your bitmap image:

- *Blur.* Blends the edges of objects into the background.

- *Brightness.* Makes the image darker (low percentages) or lighter (high percentages) by the percentage you specify.

- *Contrast.* Makes an object more distinct from the background by a high percentage for high contrast or a low percentage for low contrast.

- *Emboss.* Makes an object appear raised from the background.

- *Equalize.* Reduces contrast between objects and the background.

- *Mosaic.* Breaks an image into colored squares.

- *Rain.* Makes the image appear as if it's smeared by raindrops.

- *Saturation.* Enables you to adjust how vivid the image appears by specifying a higher or lower percentage.

- *Sharpen.* Makes edges crisper.

- *Smooth.* Makes edges smoother.

- *Spike Removal.* Removes pronounced flaws from the edges of objects.

- *Stereogram.* Converts the image to a black-and-white "stereogram," which reveals a 3D image when you view it correctly.

- *Trace Contours.* Removes object colors, leaving the outlines.

- *Wind.* Makes an image look windblown, or smeared horizontally.

Figure 14.14 shows some examples of the special effects available in Presentations. In addition to these effects, you can rotate a bitmap and add perspective to it when it's placed on a slide.

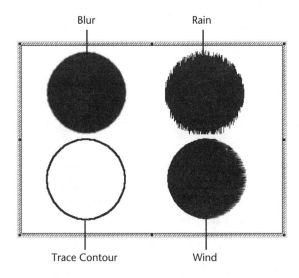

Fig. 14.14
Some of the special effects you can apply to bitmaps in Presentations.

Here are the steps for applying a special effect:

1. Select the area to apply the special effect to using the Select tool.

2. Open the **T**ools menu or the QuickMenu and choose Special E**f**fects. The Special Effects dialog box appears (see fig. 14.15).

3. Click to open the **E**ffects drop-down list, and then click to select the effect you want. Your selection here determines what appears in the Options area of the dialog box.

Fig. 14.15
The Special Effects
dialog box supplies
options for
applying the
specified effect to
the bitmap
selection.

Move to specify the preview area.

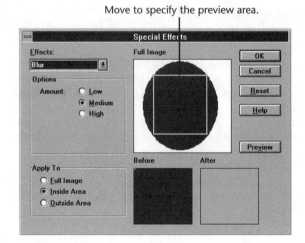

4. Make your choices in the Options area. For the Blur effect, for example, you can select a **L**ow, **M**edium, or Hi**g**h amount of blur.

5. In the Apply To area, choose an option. **F**ull Image applies the effect to the entire bitmap, regardless of whether you have made a selection. **I**nside Area applies the effect to the inside of the selected area. **O**utside Area applies the effect to everything outside the area you selected in step 1.

6. You may want to preview your choice. If necessary, drag the square box within the Full Image area to ensure that the edge of a shape appears within the Before box, because the effect will be visible primarily at the edge of the image. Then click the Pre**v**iew button.

7. Click OK to apply the special effect.

Troubleshooting

I made a change to a bitmap that I don't like, but Undo won't let me undo it. How do I revert to my original image?

Open the **F**ile menu and choose **C**ancel, or click the Cancel icon at the far left end of the Toolbar. When Presentations asks whether to discard the changes you have made, click **Y**es. Note that this action does undo ALL changes you have made during the current Bitmap Editor session—not just the change you weren't happy with.

Moving and Sizing a Bitmap

You can size a bitmap both on the slide and in the Bitmap Editor. Resizing it on the slide merely changes the shape and size of the image; it does not affect how the image appears, except to contract or expand the image, possibly making it look a bit jaggie.

To move or size a bitmap on the slide, click on it to make black selection handles appear around it. To move a bitmap, click on it and drag to a new location. To size the bitmap, point to one of the selection handles until the mouse pointer becomes a double-headed arrow, and click-and-drag to resize. Dragging a corner resizes the image proportionally, and pressing Ctrl while dragging creates a copy of the image and resizes the copy. Right-click a corner or side selection handle to display the Size and Stretch dialog boxes respectively, which you can use to resize the image by entering a ratio.

When you're in the Bitmap Editor, you also can resize the image by dragging the selection handles on the hatched outline. Dragging the handles to increase the size of the image simply adds more room to the bitmap painting area. You can fill up that area with additional shapes. When you return to the slide, those shapes will be visible as part of the bitmap.

In contrast, when you make the boundaries of the hatched outline smaller or move some of the contents of the bitmap so that they're "cut off" at the hatched border, you are *cropping* the image. When you return to the slide, the cropped portions are not visible. For example, figure 14.16 shows a photo of a valley. Suppose that you only want to use the top third of the image, the mountain skyline, as a backdrop for your slide. Start by double-clicking the bitmap to enter the Bitmap Editor. Then point to the bottom hatched boundary until you see the double-headed arrow, and drag the boundary up to the size you want, releasing the mouse button when you're satisfied (see fig. 14.17). Until you return to the slide, you can continue resizing and recropping the bitmap as you want. Once you return to the slide, however, the bitmap cropping becomes permanent. When you restart the Bitmap Editor and move the hatched outlines, the cropped portions of the bitmap no longer exist.

Caution

Always ensure that you have a bitmap image saved elsewhere to disk before cropping it. You may need to use the full image again in Presentations or in another application.

Fig. 14.16
A full-size bitmap
scene.

Fig. 14.17
Dragging the
bottom hatched
boundary to crop
the bitmap.

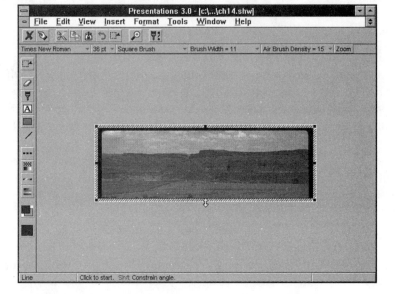

Changing Bitmaps into Vector Images

Because not all special effects are available for bitmap images, there may be instances where you want to convert a bitmap image to a vector. In some cases, this also can enable you to make edits you weren't able to make before. Always be sure that you have another copy of a bitmap on hand before tracing, because tracing cannot be undone. To convert a bitmap image to a vector image, click on the bitmap to select it on the slide. Right-click to display the QuickMenu, and choose T**r**ace Bitmap. Your image is converted to a bitmap, which could take some time if it's complex. Figure 14.18 shows a traced bitmap and a QuickWarped version of it on the right.

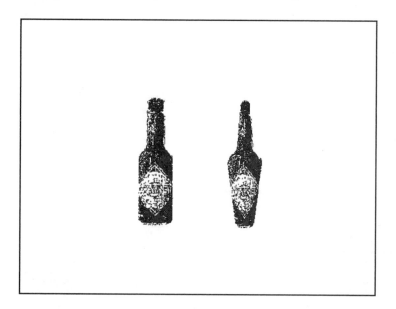

Fig. 14.18
Tracing a bitmap converts it to a vector so that you can apply QuickWarp (right) and more.

Note that this process works best for very simple bitmaps. Scanned bitmaps may not work as well, because if the edges of the objects are less than clean, tracing creates a million little objects instead of a few simple ones.

Scanning Images into Presentations

A new feature to this version of Presentations is *TWAIN compliance*—the capability to send an image from your scanner (which you must have attached to your system to scan) directly onto a slide, provided that you have the correct TWAIN software as well, of course. The TWAIN software is the intermediary between your scanner and the Presentations software. You launch the TWAIN application from within Presentations, set a few options, and scan; the software then places the scanned bitmap directly on the current slide. You then can select and edit it as you can any other bitmap.

The TWAIN software I use is Logitech's ScanMan TWAIN Image Source, which was specially developed for Logitech's ScanMan line of scanners. Because the scanning process hinges somewhat on the software you're using, your steps may vary slightly. Here's how to acquire (scan) an image into a Presentations slide:

1. Go to the slide you want to add the image to.

2. Open the **I**nsert menu and choose **S**elect Image Source. The Image Source dialog box appears.

3. Click the scanner you want to use in the Sources list and click Select.

4. Open the **I**nsert menu and choose Ac**q**uire Image, or click the Acquire Image icon on the Toolbar. The Acquire Image dialog box appears, presenting various scaling options.

5. Click a scaling option and then click OK. The dialog box for the TWAIN software appears (see fig. 14.19).

Fig. 14.19
The TWAIN software tells you it's ready for scanning.

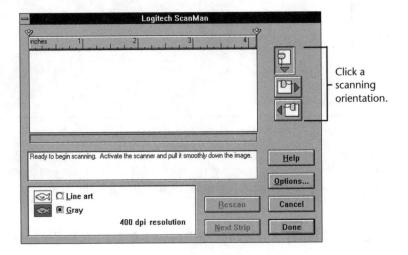

Click a scanning orientation.

6. Scan the image.

7. Click Done or the equivalent when scanning is complete. Your image appears on the current slide. Move, edit, and resize it as needed. Figure 14.20 shows a scanned image on a slide.

Fig. 14.20
I scanned this mug shot directly into the current slide. (My brother's gonna kill me!)

There are a few things to note about scanning images before jumping into it. The first and foremost is to BE PATIENT! Even though scanning seems like a straightforward process, it takes practice and judgment. Here are a few things you need to consider to ensure that you have the best success possible when scanning:

- Your results are limited by the scanner you're using. A hand-held scanner with a maximum resolution of 400 dpi will never perform like a 1200-dpi flatbed scanner. Know the limitations of your hardware.

- If you need a super high-quality image (such as when you're including photos of your product in a sales presentation), consider taking the images to a service bureau for scanning if you're not a confident and experienced scanner user, or if your scanner doesn't have the resolution you want. Service bureaus are listed in the Yellow Pages under "Printers," "Copiers/Duplicators," or "Typesetters." The fees for these services usually are reasonable, and some of these companies may provide capabilities that you don't have, such as scanning 35-mm slides.

- Start off scanning simple images, like very simple logos or clear, simple line art. You soon will see that the little things count—like making sure that the original is absolutely straight so that the bitmap isn't skewed, or making sure that you use a steady, smooth motion when dragging your hand-held scanner.

■ Pay attention to and make notes about the scanner settings that work best for different kinds of images. If setting the scanner to scan a little darker gives crisper outlines for simple shapes, take note of it. If a lighter setting works better for certain kinds of photos, remember that, too.

■ Be aware of copyright laws and other legal issues for scanned images and images from other sources that you use in a slide show. You generally cannot use the likenesses of celebrities to promote your products, and you cannot use works that are copyrighted by others. Likewise, you should be aware that not all stock image and stock clip-art collections give you free use. In some cases, you need to include a permission line. In others, you need to pay to use the image. Use common sense, and don't steal other people's work. A good rule of thumb is *if in doubt, leave it out.*

From Here...

This chapter picked up where the preceding two chapters left off, explaining how bitmap images differ from vector images, and how you can create or scan your own bitmaps, or work with those from other sources. For related topics, see these chapters:

■ Chapter 13, "Working with Outlines and Fills," provides information on editing the fills for vector images and more.

■ Chapter 15, "Working with Masters, Templates, and Backgrounds," addresses how to create custom slide show designs by using your own artwork and text for every slide in a slide show.

Part V

Fine-Tuning and Finishing the Show

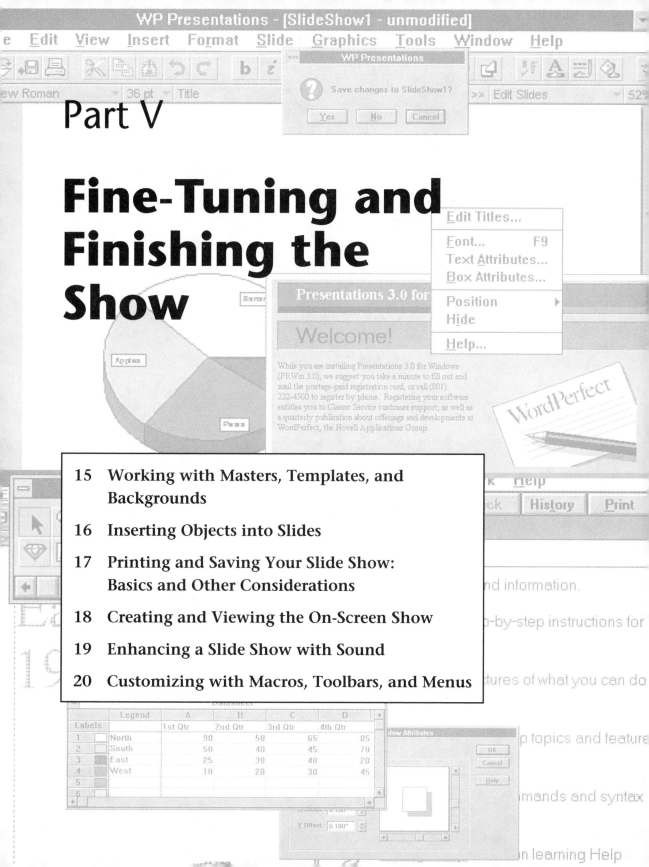

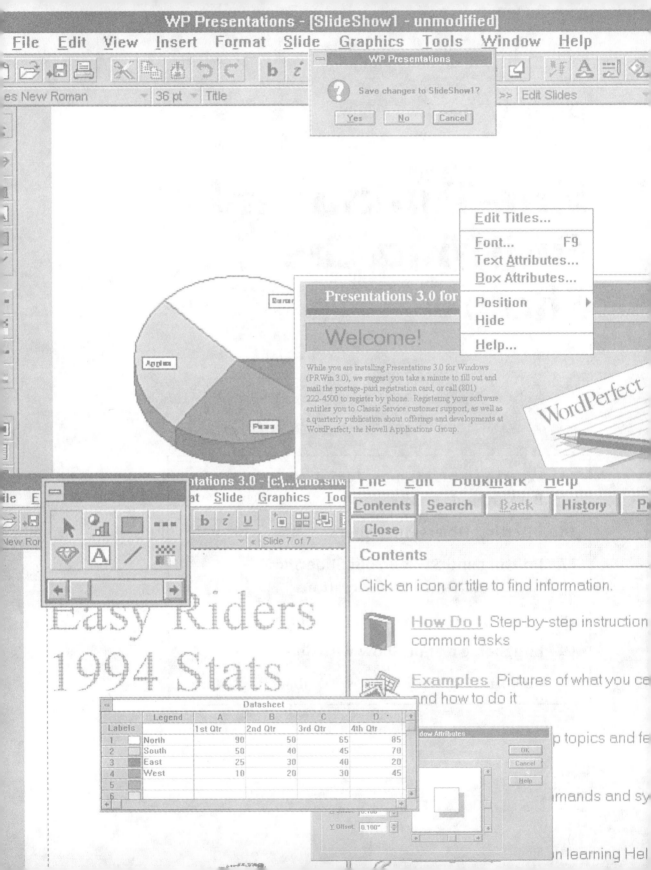

Chapter 15

Working with Masters, Templates, and Backgrounds

The Master Gallery and default slide templates in WordPerfect Presentations 3.0 for Windows provide you with numerous attractive, interesting layout possibilities for your slide shows. You can use any of these layouts and masters to focus on the information in your slide show rather than the design. Eventually, most users of presentations graphics programs encounter a situation where the predefined layouts and designs don't work. Even something as simple as showing a company logo on every slide would require placing the graphic on each and every slide—unless you could edit the master design.

Presentations does enable you not only to change the layout and backgrounds for particular slide templates, but also to save new layouts and backgrounds to build your own masters. This chapter explores how masters, templates, and backgrounds interact. You also learn how to do the following:

- Save changes to an existing master or a new master file

- Display and make changes to backgrounds

- Save and rename backgrounds

- Display and make changes to templates

- Add a new background to a template

- Change the show master or import masters

- Add a new master file to the Gallery

- Work with the master and background on a single slide

Understanding Masters, Templates, and Backgrounds

The *background* for a slide is a layer containing the slide's fill color, pattern, and any default graphics (such as the curving line displayed at the bottom of many of the example slides seen in this book). The background serves as a foundation layer for you to build your slide on. A *slide template* consists of a background plus predefined layout areas for text. Slide show *masters* contain multiple slide types and one or more slide backgrounds; all slide templates (which include layouts) and backgrounds must be stored in a master file. The background and template are the bottom layers on your slide. The top layer is the layer where you normally work to add your graphics and text.

Within the master, you can create new slide templates and backgrounds and assign different backgrounds to templates. The master applies to the entire slide show. Although you can add slides that don't have any background or template to a slide show (by choosing **N**one from the **T**emplate pop-up menu) to build a slide from the ground up, you also can detach the master from an individual slide to edit all the layout and background elements for that slide, or specify a different background for an individual slide. You learn how to perform all these operations in this chapter.

Saving New Template Layouts and Backgrounds in a Master

Whenever you create new backgrounds and layouts that you want to use again in other slide shows, you should save them to the slide master file. Otherwise, those changes are saved only within the slide show where you made them. All the slide master files are stored in the \OFFICE\PRWIN\ GALLERY directory, and they all share the MST file-name extension. You can save the changes to an existing master file or create a new master file that you even can add to the Master Gallery.

Here are the steps for saving changes to a slide show master:

1. Open the **F**ile menu and choose Save **A**s (or press F3). The Save As dialog box appears.

2. Double-click the Master/Galleries Directory choice in the **Q**uickList, or use the Dri**v**es and **D**irectories lists to go to the \OFFICE\PRWIN\ GALLERY directory.

3. Click to pull down the Save File as **T**ype list. Scroll to the MST 3.0 - Master File (*.mst) choice, and double-click it to put `*.mst` in the File**n**ame list box.

4. Press Enter to accept *.mst. The Save As dialog box now should look something like figure 15.1, listing the names of the master files presently in the \OFFICE\PRWIN\GALLERY directory.

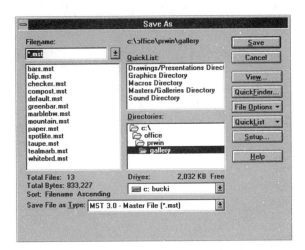

Fig. 15.1
Saving your background and layout changes to a master.

5. To save your changes to an existing master file, click on its name in the File**n**ame list. Or, to save the changes as a new master file, type an eight-letter name in the File**n**ame text box.

6. Click **S**ave. When you're saving a new master, Presentations simply saves the file. If you're saving the changes to an existing master file, Presentations displays a dialog box asking you to confirm whether you want to change the master. Click **Y**es to complete the save.

Editing Backgrounds

The slide *background* holds the graphics and colors that serve as the backdrop for your slide text. You can create backgrounds to do the following in a slide show:

■ Add a company name, logo, or QuickArt that you want to appear in slides of a particular type or in all slides in a slide show (see fig. 15.2).

V

Fine-Tuning the Show

■ Create a *watermark* effect, where you place a pale graphic that appears behind text (see fig. 15.2).

Fig. 15.2
A slide with a custom background.

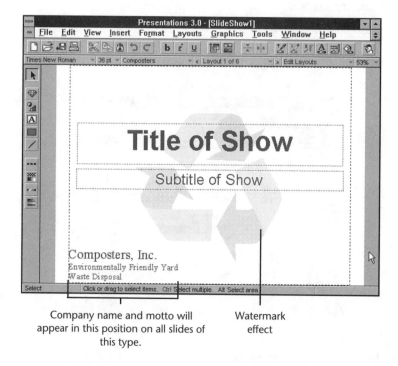

Company name and motto will appear in this position on all slides of this type.

Watermark effect

■ Use a scanned scenic photo as a background to set or emphasize a particular mood.

■ Change the colors used to fill a background.

To edit a background, you first must display it. Once you've moved to the background layer, you can draw on it, add text to it, open the Format menu and choose **P**age **C**olor to fill it with a new color, add QuickArt, and more, as described in the earlier chapters of this book. You also can add, delete, and rename the backgrounds in the current master.

Moving to the Background Layer

Edit Slides

You can choose to edit backgrounds from any view, but you most often will do so from Slide Editor view. To edit backgrounds, open the **S**lide menu and choose Edit **B**ackgrounds, or click the next-to-last button on the Power Bar (which says Edit Slides most of the time) and click Edit Backgrounds from the list that appears. When you choose to edit backgrounds, the Presentations screen changes slightly, as shown in figure 15.3. The **B**ackgrounds menu appears on the menu bar, and some new tools appear on the Toolbar and Power Bar to facilitate background editing. Notably, the Power Bar adds a button you can click to select which background in the current master to edit. Click this button, and then click the name of the background you want to go to.

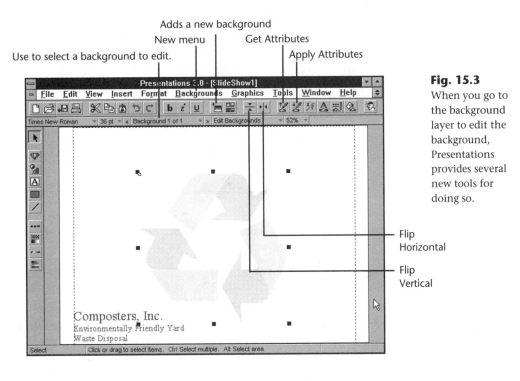

Fig. 15.3
When you go to the background layer to edit the background, Presentations provides several new tools for doing so.

To discontinue editing the background and return to the slide layer, open the **B**ackgrounds menu and choose Edit **S**lides, or click the Edit Backgrounds button on the Power Bar and click Edit Slides.

Note

Don't forget to save the background changes to the master file.

Adding and Deleting Backgrounds

The **B**ackgrounds menu, when available, enables you to add or delete backgrounds in a master. Having multiple backgrounds in a master gives you flexibility in deciding which master to use for a particular slide template. You could assign a flashy, graphic-filled background to title slides (because they have little text) and a plain background to slides where you want your viewers to focus on the content, such as data slides, for example.

To create the look of a new background, you first must add it to the master using these steps:

1. Make sure that you have moved to the background layer.

2. Open the **B**ackgrounds menu and choose **A**dd Background (or press Ctrl+Enter). Or, you can click the Add Backgrounds tool on the master background Toolbar. The Add Background dialog box appears (see fig. 15.4).

Fig. 15.4
Use the Add background dialog box to specify a name for the new background you're adding.

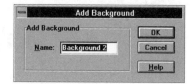

3. If you want to, type a new name for the new background (which will appear on the drop-down list on the Power Bar).

4. Click OK to add the new, blank background to the master.

To delete any background, select it using the Power Bar, and then open the **B**ackgrounds menu and choose **D**elete Background. When Presentations asks you whether you're sure you want to delete the background, click **Y**es.

Renaming Backgrounds

After you have created any background, you can rename it at any time. To do so, follow these steps:

1. Make sure that you have chosen the background layer and the background to rename using the Power Bar.

2. Open the **B**ackgrounds menu and choose **N**ame. The Background Name dialog box appears (see fig. 15.5).

Fig. 15.5
The Background Name dialog box enables you to rename a background.

Use to choose another background if needed.

3. Choose a different background by clicking the buttons at the left side of the dialog box, if needed.

4. Type a new **N**ame for the Background.

5. Click OK to close the dialog box.

Editing Layouts

The slide *layout* is the middle layer that determines where the text appears on a slide and what fonts, colors, and fills it uses. Changing the layout for a slide template applies the changes you make to all slides using that template within the slide show. You also can create new layouts in addition to the six that come with most of Presentations' preset masters. You might create a layout that consists of a title and two subtitles, for example. Editing the layout also enables you to change the default attributes for bullet charts, data charts, and organization charts, and to choose a new background for the slide type. Earlier chapters described how to make those kinds of changes.

To edit a layout, you first must display it. After you move to the layout layer, you can create new text and chart areas on it and change attributes, as described in the earlier chapters. You also can add, delete, and rename the layouts; and apply a new background to a layout in the current master.

> **Caution**
>
> When you change the layout, it changes all the slides to which that layout has been applied. To change the placement of elements on only one slide, detach its master, as described in "Detaching the Master to Edit a Single Slide," later in this chapter.

Moving to the Layout Layer

You need to move to a special view to edit layouts. To edit layouts, open the **S**lide menu and choose Edit **L**ayouts, or click the next-to-last button on the Power Bar (which says Edit Slides most of the time) and click Edit Layouts from the list that appears. When you choose to edit layouts, the Presentations screen changes slightly, as shown in figure 15.6. The **L**ayouts menu appears on the menu bar, and some new tools appear on the Toolbar and Power Bar to facilitate layout editing (resembling those you saw for background editing). Notably, the Power Bar adds a button you can click to select which layout in the current master to edit. Click this button, and then click the name of the layout to which you want to go.

Edit Slides

Fig. 15.6
When you choose to edit layouts, Presentations provides several new tools for doing so.

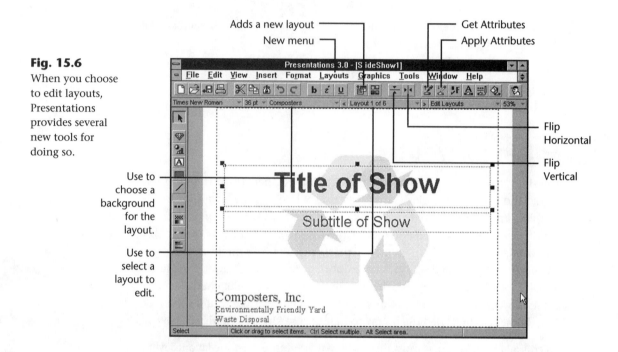

To discontinue editing the layout and to return to the slide layer, open the **L**ayouts menu and choose Edit **S**lides, or click the Edit Layouts button on the Power Bar and click Edit Slides.

Adding and Deleting Layouts

You can add and delete layouts in a master with the **L**ayouts menu, just as you can add and delete backgrounds. To create the contents of a new layout, you first must add it to the master using these steps:

1. Make sure that you have chosen the layout layer.

2. From the list of layouts to edit on the Power Bar, select the layout after which you want to insert the new layout.

3. Open the **L**ayouts menu and choose **A**dd Layout (or press Ctrl+Enter). Or, you can click the Add Layouts tool on the master layout Toolbar. The Add Layout dialog box appears (see fig. 15.7).

Fig. 15.7
Use the Add Layout dialog box to specify a name for the new layout you're adding.

4. If you want to type a new name for the new layout (which will appear on the drop-down list on the Power Bar), do so.

5. Click OK to add the new, blank layout to the master.

To delete any background, select it using the Power Bar, and then open the **L**ayouts menu and choose **D**elete Layout. When Presentations asks you whether you're sure you want to delete the layout, click **Y**es.

Renaming Layouts

You can rename any layout you create to be able to easily identify it later. Follow these steps:

1. Make sure that you have changed to the layout layer and have chosen the layout to rename using the Power Bar.

2. Open the **L**ayouts menu and choose **N**ame. The Layout Name dialog box appears (see fig. 15.8).

Use to choose another layout, if needed.

Fig. 15.8
The Layout Name dialog box that enables you to rename a layout.

3. Choose a different layout by clicking the buttons at the left side of the dialog box, if needed.

4. Type a new **N**ame for the layout.

5. Click OK to close the dialog box.

Adding Layout Placeholders

When you create a slide layout, you need to create *placeholders* that appear when you add a slide using the layout. In Chapter 3, "Using the Various Slide Templates," you double-clicked placeholders to add text to the layouts that come with Presentations. You add placeholders to the layout, and then format them as you want them to appear in the actual slides. When you add a slide to your show and specify a layout with a placeholder you created, it displays a dotted outline and a message to double-click to add your real data (see fig. 15.9).

V

Fine-Tuning the Show

Fig. 15.9
An org chart slide
with a layout
placeholder
created.

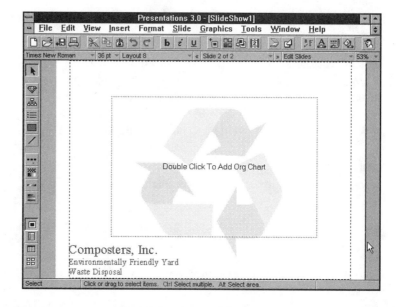

Use the **I**nsert menu to add placeholders to a slide. Choose **D**ata Chart or **O**rg Chart from that menu, drag to create the placeholder area, and then specify the attributes for the chart (you don't need to edit the data).

Tip
Use Fo**r**mat **D**efine Bullets/ Fonts Bo**x**/Frame to add a frame to the Title, Subtitle, or Body place-holder.

Creating the Title, Subtitle, and Body or Bullet List layout placeholders is a bit quirky. To add any of these to a layout, open the **I**nsert menu and choose B**u**llet Chart. Drag on the layout to define an area, and the dialog box shown in figure 15.10 appears. Click **T**itle, **S**ubtitle, or **B**ody, and click OK. A hatched outline appears. Type some sample text so that you always will be sure where the placeholder appears on the layout. To change the attributes for Title, Subtitle, or Body text, click on the placeholder, open the Fo**r**mat menu or QuickMenu, and choose **D**efine Bullets/Fonts and use the Font **C**olor button to change the text attributes of the placeholder. Also change the size and location of the placeholder as needed.

Fig. 15.10
The Create Text
Chart dialog box
enables you to add
Title, Subtitle, and
Body text place-
holders to slide
layouts you create.

Choosing a New Background

In addition to creating new layout placeholders and reformatting the other
placeholders on a layout, you can choose a new background to be part of a
layout you create. Follow these steps:

1. Make sure that you have changed to the layout layer and have chosen
   the layout to add a new background to using the Power Bar.

2. Open the **L**ayouts menu and choose Assi**g**n Background to display the
   Assign Background dialog box (see fig. 15.11).

Currently assigned backgrounds

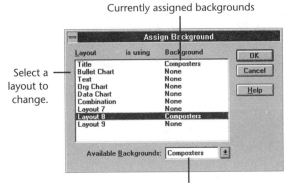

Select a
layout to
change.

Backgrounds to choose from

Tip

If you have se-
lected the layout
you want to
change the back-
ground for, you
simply can click
the third (from
the left) Power Bar
button to display
a list of available
backgrounds, and
then click the
background you
want.

Fig. 15.11
Part of creating a
layout includes
specifying the
background you
want for the
layout using the
Assign Background
dialog box.

3. Choose the **L**ayout to change if you didn't do so in step 1.

4. Choose the background you want from the Available **B**ackgrounds list.

5. Repeat steps 3 and 4 to change the backgrounds for other layouts.

6. Click OK to close the dialog box and return to the layout layer.

V

Fine-Tuning the Show

Troubleshooting

*I made changes to my master, adding backgrounds and layouts, and chose **S**ave from the **F**ile menu to save them, but the changes didn't appear in the master the next time I used it. What happened?*

Choosing **S**ave from the **F**ile menu only saved the master changes to the slide show you were working on—not to the master itself. To save those changes to the master now, open the slide show, and then open the **F**ile menu and choose Save **A**s to save the changes to the MST file, as described earlier in this chapter.

Changing the Master for a Slide Show

After you've created a slide show, you're not stuck with the master you origi-nally selected. You can select another master to apply to the slide show. Pre-sentations automatically applies the background and layout formatting for the new master to the slides in your slide show.

Note

Changing the master does not change the attributes for any text areas, text lines, drawn objects, or graphics you have added to a slide; it only changes the attributes for defined slide layouts. You need to change the attributes for added objects indi-vidually.

To select a new master for the current slide show, follow these steps:

1. Open the **S**lide menu and choose **M**aster Gallery, or click the Master icon on the Toolbar. The Master Gallery dialog box appears, with the current master selected (see fig. 15.12).

Fig. 15.12
Use the Master Gallery to select a new master for the current slide show.

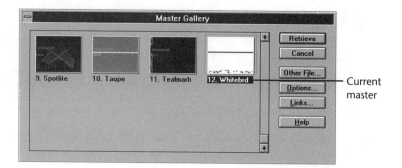

2. Use the scroll bars to display the master you want, if needed.

3. Click to select the master you want.

4. Click Retrieve to apply the new master.

Importing Masters

If you previously created and saved a master but didn't add it to the Master Gallery, you can use the Import feature of the Master Gallery to apply it to the current slide show. To import a master and apply it to the current slide show, use these steps:

1. Open the **S**lide menu and choose **M**aster Gallery, or click the Master icon on the Toolbar. The Master Gallery dialog box appears, with the current master selected.

2. Click the Other F**i**le button to display the Insert Master dialog box (see fig. 15.13).

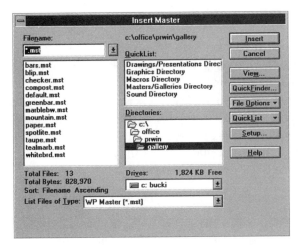

Fig. 15.13
Use this dialog box to apply masters you haven't added to the Master Gallery.

3. Use the Dri**v**es and **D**irectories lists or QuickList if needed to display master files in other directories.

4. Click the name of the file you want in the File**n**ame list and then click **I**nsert, or simply double-click the file name. Presentations closes the Insert Master and Master Gallery dialog boxes, and applies the master you selected.

Changing the Master Gallery Display

You can customize the Master Gallery display by clicking the **O**ptions command button in the Master Gallery dialog box. The Gallery Options dialog box shown in figure 15.14 appears. Change the **N**umber of Columns setting to specify how many columns of thumbnails to display in the Gallery. You can display one to nine columns. The Create **Q**uick Files option is a bit more complicated. When this option is enabled, Presentations saves the master you view in special bitmap files on the hard drive, which speeds up the display of the master images. There are downsides to enabling this option, however. Doing so takes up more hard drive space and memory (RAM), so if you're low on either of those commodities, turn off this option. Click OK after you make your choice to close the Gallery Options dialog box.

Fig. 15.14
Changing how many columns appear in the Master Gallery dialog box.

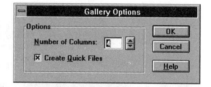

Adding a Master to the Master Gallery

As you can for QuickArt Gallery files, you can add the masters you create to the Master Gallery to make them easy to access. You already learned in this chapter how to save new master files with the MST extension in the \OFFICE\PRWIN\GALLERY directory on your computer. Adding a master to the Gallery after saving the file is a matter of adding a cover slide for the new category to the list of title slides for the Gallery, and then linking the title slide in the Gallery to the master file.

Follow these steps to add a new Master Gallery category:

1. Create a new master file and save it as described in "Saving New Template Layouts and Backgrounds in a Master" at the beginning of this chapter.

2. Change to the layout layer (by opening the **S**lide menu and choosing Edit **L**ayouts), and use the list displayed by clicking the fourth button from the left on the Power Bar to choose the layout type you want to use as the cover slide for the master in the Gallery.

3. Open the **F**ile menu and choose Save **A**s (or press F3). The Save As dialog box appears.

4. Use the **Dri**ves and **D**irectories lists to specify the directory to save the cover slide to.

5. Click to pull down the Save File as **T**ype list. Scroll to the WPG 2.0 - WordPerfect 6.0 Graphics (*.wpg) choice, and double-click it. This puts *.wpg in the File**n**ame list box. Press Enter.

6. Type a name for the file in the Filename text box and click **S**ave to save the file where you specified.

7. Open the **F**ile menu and choose **O**pen (or press Ctrl+O) or click the Open icon on the Toolbar, and open the MASTRGAL.SHW slide show from the \OFFICE\PRWIN\GALLERY directory.

8. Now you need to copy the cover slide for your slide show to the MASTRGAL.SHW slide show, which organizes the cover slides for all the slide show categories. With MASTRGAL.SHW open, press Ctrl+End to move to the last slide in the show. Then open the **S**lide menu and choose **A**dd Slides or click the Add Slides button on the Toolbar. This action inserts a new, blank slide into MASTRGAL.SHW.

9. Open the **I**nsert menu and choose F**i**le. In the Insert File dialog box, choose the WPG file you saved in steps 3 through 6. Click **I**nsert to paste your image into MASTRGAL.SHW.

10. Open the **V**iew menu and choose **O**utliner or click the Outliner View tool on the palette to change to Outliner view. You now can add a title for your cover slide, which you just copied to MASTRGAL.SHW (see fig. 15.15). There should be an icon for your cover slide, with a blank Title line beside it. Click in the Title line and enter a name for your master. If you skip this step, your cover slide will be named "Untitled" in the Master Gallery.

11. Save MASTRGAL.SHW by opening the **F**ile menu and choosing **S**ave (or pressing Ctrl+S). Open the **F**ile menu and choose **C**lose (or press Ctrl+F4) to close the file.

12. Open the **S**lide menu (or **L**ayouts or **B**ackgrounds menu) and choose **M**aster Gallery, or click the Master Gallery tool on the Toolbar. This action displays the Master Gallery dialog box. Scroll to the cover slide for your new master. Click it to select it (see fig. 15.16).

Fig. 15.15
Use the outliner view in MASTRGAL. SHW to add a title for your cover slide.

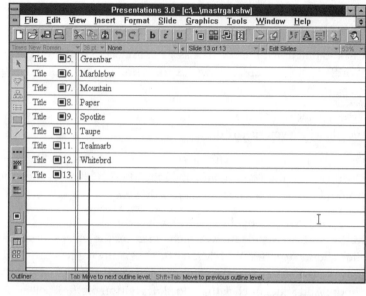

Enter a title for the new master.

Tip
While you're in Outliner view, you also can drag cover slides to new locations to change the order that the categories appear in within the Master Gallery.

Fig. 15.16
The cover slide you added to MASTRGAL.SHW now appears in the Master Gallery. You need to link it to the master file you created for the category.

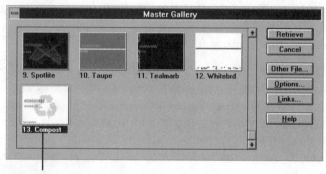

New cover slide

13. Click the **L**inks button. Presentations displays the Edit Gallery dialog box. You need to specify the file name of the new master, as shown in figure 15.17. Type the file name in the **F**ilename list or use the File icon beside the text box to browse for the file. Click OK after you specify the file name.

14. Clicking OK linked the master file to the cover slide. You can apply the new master using the Master Gallery dialog box.

Your cover slide title

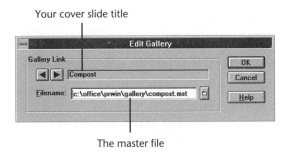

Fig. 15.17
Linking the master file with your images to the cover slide title.

The master file

Detaching the Master to Edit a Single Slide

If you want to be able to change the positioning of layout elements on a slide without redesigning the template layout, you need to detach the master from the slide. This action takes all the objects and text on the slide—background layer objects, layout layer text placeholders, and slide layer objects—and places them on a single layer. It gives you complete freedom to edit all the elements—even the layout placeholders—independently. The changes you make don't affect any other slides in the slide show. To detach the master from the current slide, use these steps:

1. Select the slide in your slide show.

2. Open the **S**lide menu and choose Apply **T**emplate to display the Apply Template dialog box (see fig. 15.18).

Choose a new background for the slide(s).

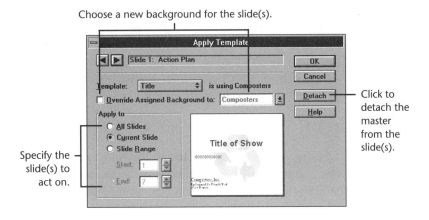

Fig. 15.18
Use this dialog box to apply a new slide template or to detach the master from the slide(s) indicated.

Click to detach the master from the slide(s).

Specify the slide(s) to act on.

3. If desired, use the Apply To settings to specify more than one slide from which to detach the master.

4. Click **D**etach. The Detach Template dialog box appears.

5. Click **Y**es to complete detachment and return to your slide. You now can select any element directly on the slide layer—even the elements that once were on the background and layout layers.

Changing the Current Slide's Background

The Apply Template dialog box also enables you to apply a new background to the indicated slides. Doing so applies the new background layer without disturbing the layout or any other elements you added. Display the Apply Template dialog box (open the **S**lide menu and choose Apply **T**emplate), and then choose the slides you want to change the background for in the Apply To area. Click to turn on the **O**verride Assigned Background To check box, and then use the drop-down list beside the check box to choose the new background. Click OK when finished.

From Here...

Masters, templates, and backgrounds not only provide convenience by enabling you to apply global formatting changes and even save them for later use, but also flexibility in terms of choosing and changing the design elements you apply. This chapter explained how to create, edit, and save masters, backgrounds, and layouts. In addition to learning how to work with the background and layout layers, this chapter explained how to save your changes to a master file and add the master to the Master Gallery. To review how to add elements like text and graphics to your backgrounds, see these earlier chapters:

■ Chapter 6, "Adding and Editing Text," explains how to work with text in slide template layout areas and how to add text wherever you want on a slide. The chapter also explains how to use built-in proofreading features such as the Spell Checker, QuickCorrect, and more.

■ Chapter 7, "Enhancing Text," explains how to add colors and patterns to text, as well as how to create numerous special effects that lend a professional appearance to your slide show.

■ Chapter 8, "Adding QuickArt to a Slide," explains how to add a graphic touch to any slide using the QuickArt provided with WordPerfect Presentations 3.0 for Windows, as well as giving you the basic steps for importing other types of graphics files.

■ Chapter 12, "Using the Presentations Drawing Tools," explains how to use the tools on the Tool Palette to draw vector images on a slide and how to edit objects. You can save these kinds of images in your own QuickArt categories.

■ Chapter 13, "Working with Outlines and Fills," teaches you to apply attributes to vector objects on a slide. You can use the techniques described here to edit QuickArt images.

■ Chapter 14, "Working with Bitmap Images," describes how to create bitmap images in Presentations, and how to scan bitmap images directly into Presentations for use in slides or for saving in a QuickArt category.

V

Fine-Tuning the Show

Chapter 16

Inserting Objects into Slides

One of the beauties of WordPerfect Presentations for Windows is that even though it gives you a lot of guidance in placing information on slides, it puts few limitations on where you place the information, or the source from which you draw the information. You can redesign a slide to deliver more information and reuse information you have created in other applications.

This chapter explains how you can add more information to slides. You learn to add more charts to files, to create speaker notes for slides, and to apply different techniques for using information from other sources. Specifically, you learn about the following:

- Inserting charts into a slide

- Inserting entire files into a slide

- Creating links between slides and information sources

- Using OLE to add objects to a slide

- Adding speaker notes to a slide

Inserting Charts

At times, the basic chart types—even the combination chart—may not provide information in the way you want them to. You might need to show two bullet charts on a slide to present the pros and cons of an issue, for example. Or, you might have a reason to display two bar charts on a slide, perhaps to make a side-by-side comparison that wouldn't be possible otherwise.

You might want to display an organization chart beside a bullet list. You might even want to present paragraph text along with a data chart, as shown in figure 16.1.

Fig. 16.1
A data chart has been added to a text slide.

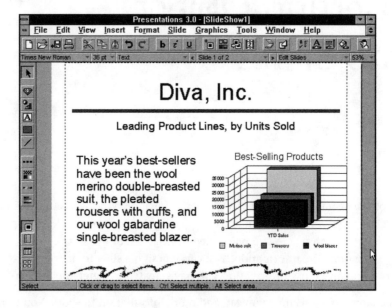

After you place another chart on a slide, you can move it around and resize it as you can other chart objects. The **I**nsert menu in Presentations offers a few commands for inserting additional charts on a slide (see fig. 16.2).

Fig. 16.2
Commands for inserting additional charts on a slide.

Choose to insert a chart on a slide

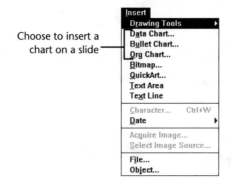

To insert an additional chart on a slide, use these steps:

1. Open the **I**nsert menu.

2. Choose D**a**ta Chart, B**u**llet Chart, or **O**rganization Chart. Or, click the Chart tool in the Tool Palette and use it to insert a data or organization chart.

3. Complete the chart by entering data as required for the chart type you selected.

4. Move and resize the chart as needed to fit with other data on the chart.

Inserting Files

The process of inserting a file into a slide show takes a copy of the file and incorporates it into the slide at the location you designate. You learned in Chapter 6, "Adding and Editing Text," how to import text by inserting an ANSI, ASCII, or WordPerfect file into a slide show. You can use the same basic process to insert a graphics file or another slide show file into a slide show. If you created a sales slide show that covers only two product lines, for example, and you're in the process of creating a slide show covering all your product lines, you can insert the smaller slide show file into the current slide show file to save yourself the trouble of re-creating all those slides.

When you insert a slide show file into the current slide show, Presentations inserts the text and data only; the inserted information adapts the formatting of the master selected for the current slide show. Here are the steps for inserting a graphic or slide show file into a slide show:

1. Select the slide onto which you want to insert the graphics file or after which you want to insert the slides from another slide show.

2. Open the **I**nsert menu and choose F**i**le. The Insert File dialog box appears (see fig. 16.3).

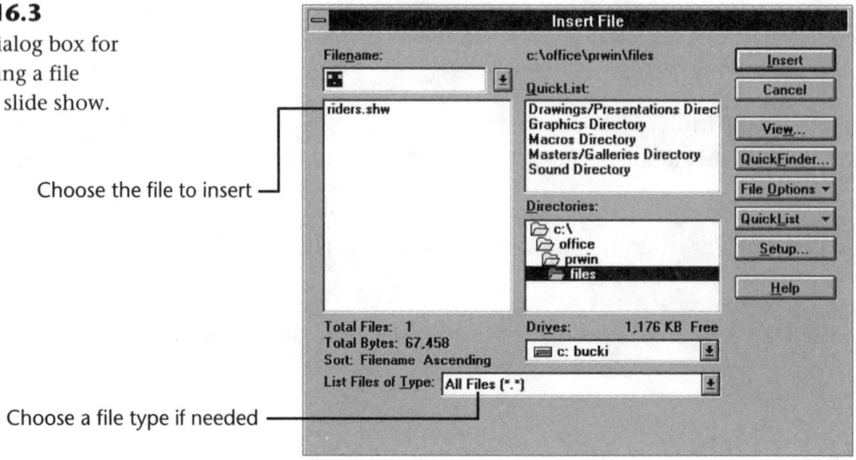

Fig. 16.3

The dialog box for inserting a file into a slide show.

Choose the file to insert ⎯

Choose a file type if needed ⎯

3. Choose a file type from the List Files of **T**ype drop-down list, if needed.

4. Use the Dri**v**es and **D**irectories lists to change to the drive and directory that contains the file, if needed.

Tip

You can double-click a file in the File**n**ame list to select it.

5. Choose a file from the File**n**ame list.

6. Click the **I**nsert button to complete the procedure.

Creating Links

Object Linking and Embedding (OLE) is special technology that enables you to link to Presentations graphics, text, spreadsheets, and sound clips created in another application. The linked material is called an OLE *object*. You use the Paste **S**pecial command from the **E**dit menu to create a link. You copy the data from the original application and use Paste **S**pecial to place the copy in the slide show; that copy remains linked to the source application. There are three advantages to linking data. First, you eliminate errors and mistakes because you aren't re-creating the information from scratch. Second, you can update the linked copy whenever you edit the information in the original application, if desired. And, finally, you save time because you don't have to re-create information in two different applications.

If you created and specially formatted a colorful spreadsheet table that you would need to update frequently, for example, it would be much more expedient to link it to Presentations, as shown in figure 16.4.

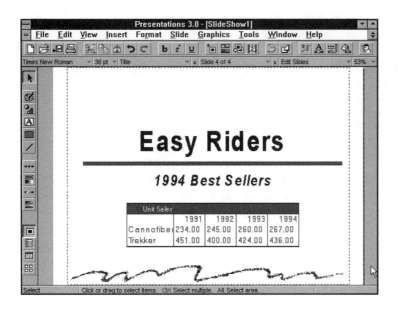

Fig. 16.4
Excel spreadsheet
information
linked in a slide
show.

To create a link, follow these steps:

1. Create and save the material you want to link in the original application.

2. Select the object by clicking on it or by dragging to highlight it. Open the **E**dit menu and choose **C**opy (or press Ctrl+C).

3. Open Presentations and the slide show in which you want to insert the object. Move to the slide that you want to contain the object.

4. Open the **E**dit menu and choose Paste **S**pecial.

5. Select Paste **L**ink and choose a format from the **A**s list, if needed (see fig. 16.5).

Fig. 16.5
Pasting a link into
a slide show.

6. If you want an icon to appear rather than the selected data, turn on the **D**isplay As Icon check box.

7. Click OK to paste the linked object into a slide.

Troubleshooting

*When I changed to Presentations to create the link, Paste **S**pecial wasn't available. What happened?*

If you closed the application in which you created the object before pasting the link, the link cannot be completed because you're creating a link to the application. Make sure that you leave the original application open when you switch to Presentations.

Now, your link is saved in your slide show. When you edit and save the object in its original application (leaving that application open) and then reopen the slide show to which the object is linked, the updates appear in the linked copy in the slide show. If you're working on the slide show and want to edit the object, you can double-click it to open it in its original application. After you make the changes you want, choose the **S**ave or **U**pdate command from the **F**ile menu to preserve your changes.

To change the characteristics of the link or to sever the link, use these steps:

1. Open the **E**dit menu and choose Lin**k**s. The Links dialog box appears (see fig. 16.6).

Fig. 16.6
The dialog box for updating and changing links.

Choose a link from this list.

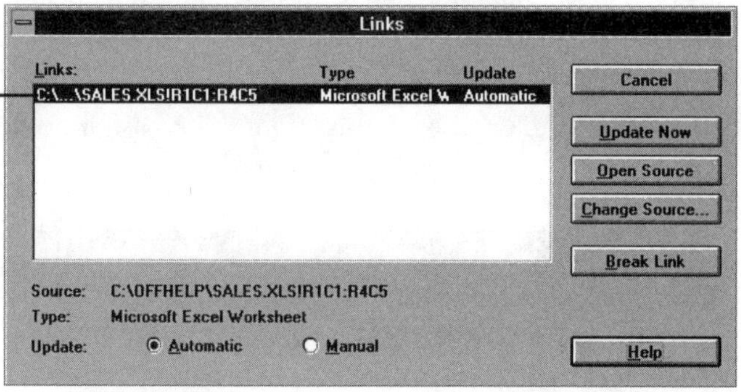

2. Choose a link to edit from the **L**inks list.

3. At the bottom of the dialog box, choose an Update option. **A**utomatic updates the object automatically whenever you open the slide show. Choose **M**anual to update the object only when you choose **U**pdate Now in the Links dialog box.

4. Click the **U**pdate Now button to update manual links.

5. Click the **O**pen Source button to open the original application to edit the object.

6. Use the **C**hange Source button to choose another object to use for the link.

7. Click **B**reak Link to terminate the link.

8. Click Close to close the Links dialog box.

Inserting OLE Objects

You can create objects directly in a slide show without first creating the object and saving it in the original application. *Embedding* an OLE object places that object in the slide show only, but uses another application to create the object. When you edit the embedded object, the tools of the other application appear so that you can make your changes. You can embed a copy of an already created object as well. When you do so, editing the object in the slide show doesn't change the original in the source application. The updated data for the object is stored in the slide show file, not in the original application.

Use these steps to create an embedded object in a slide show:

1. Go to the slide where you want to embed the object.

2. Open the **I**nsert menu and choose Ob**j**ect. The Insert Object dialog box appears, as shown in figure 16.7.

Other OLE applications on your system

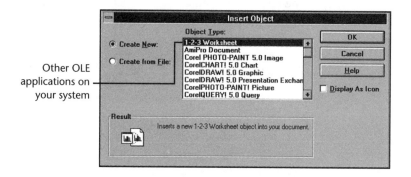

Fig. 16.7
Use the Insert Object dialog box to choose what kind of object to insert into your slide show.

3. Specify whether to Create **N**ew or Create from **F**ile.

4. Choose the type of object you want to embed, select Display as Icon to display the object as an icon, and then click OK.

5. Depending on your choice in step 4, you will be able to choose either an Object **T**ype or a Fil**e** to insert.

6. Click OK. If you're inserting a new object, the application for creating the object appears. Figure 16.8, for example, shows the Microsoft ClipArt Gallery as it appears when you choose to insert an object from it.

The title bar tells you that
the object is being inserted.

Fig. 16.8

Inserting an object
into a slide show.

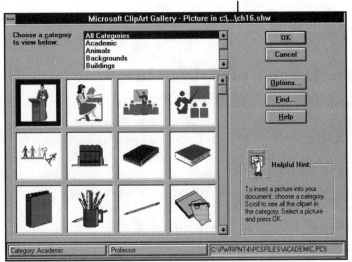

7. Create or select the object.

8. Click OK to close the application. Or, open the **F**ile menu and choose **U**pdate, and then open the **F**ile menu again and choose E**x**it & Return to return to the slide show. You can move and resize the inserted object as needed.

Double-clicking the embedded object displays its source application so that you can edit it. Use the **U**pdate and E**x**it & Return commands from the **F**ile menu to save your changes.

Creating Speaker Notes

One feature you can add to a slide show that is not always readily available to your audience is speaker notes. If you add speaker notes for the slides in a slide show, you can print them and use them as you deliver the slide show presentation to your audience. Figure 16.9 shows an example printout of speaker notes. You learn more about printing these notes in Chapter 17, "Printing and Saving Your Slide Show: Basics and Other Considerations."

Fig. 16.9
Using speaker notes to remind yourself of remarks you want to make during a slide show.

Tip
You also can print the slides with speaker notes for your audience to spare them the trouble of having to take detailed notes during a presentation.

V

Fine-Tuning the Show

To add speaker notes to a slide show, follow these steps:

1. Go to the slide to which you want to add notes.

2. Open the **S**lide menu and choose Speaker **N**otes. The Speaker Notes dialog box appears (see fig. 16.10).

Fig. 16.10

The Speaker Notes dialog box.

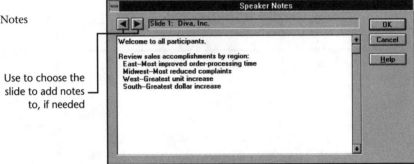

Use to choose the slide to add notes to, if needed

3. Use the arrow buttons at the top of the dialog box, if necessary, to choose the slide to which to add notes.

4. Type your notes in the text area.

5. Repeat steps 3 and 4 for other slides, as needed.

6. Click OK when finished.

From Here...

Enhancing your slides with extra charts or information from other applications can make your slide show even more informative and effective. The **I**nsert menu provides several options for adding objects from Presentations and other applications to your slide. In addition, you looked at how to add speaker notes to a slide show, which you can use to help you with your presentation or to provide notes to your audience to save them the trouble of taking detailed notes. For related topics, refer to these chapters:

■ Chapter 6, "Adding and Editing Text," explains how to import text into a slide show using the **F**ile command from the **I**nsert menu.

■ Chapter 8, "Adding QuickArt to a Slide," presents another alternative for inserting a graphics file into a slide: using the QuickArt gallery.

■ Chapter 17, "Printing and Saving Your Slide Show: Basics and Other Considerations," explains how to print speaker notes, among other topics.

V

Fine-Tuning the Show

Chapter 17

Printing and Saving Your Slide Show: Basics and Other Considerations

Slide shows you create with WordPerfect Presentations 3.0 for Windows are meant to be viewed—on-screen, as overhead transparencies or slides, or as hard copies—and to be saved for repeated and different uses. Although basic printing and saving are straightforward operations, there are other techniques you should be aware of to ensure that you always get the results you expect—and the result that is appropriate for your presentation needs.

This chapter covers what you need to know about printing and saving, explaining the following tasks:

- Selecting the printer
- Choosing what parts of the slide show to print
- Previewing and then printing
- Outputting 35-mm slides
- Saving a slide show in the format of your choice

Printing a Slide Show

When printing a file, you can choose to output the whole slide show, part of the slide show, slides, speaker notes, and so on. Those options are available no matter what printer you're using. However, the particular printer you want to print to does limit or enhance the kind of output you want to create. You can preview printing and specify numerous other options.

If you have a printer with a low resolution, the printouts will have a low resolution. If you have a color printer, you can have color printouts. With a film recorder, you can create 35-mm and larger slides and film.

The printers available to Presentations are determined by the printers you have installed to work with Windows. Each printer is controlled by a *printer driver file* in the \WINDOWS\SYSTEM directory. (See your Windows documentation or "Installing the Correct Driver," later in this chapter, to learn how to install additional printer drivers for Windows.) To begin the printing process, you need to select the correct printer, what to print, and other options, as described next.

Selecting a Printer and Printing Options

To print correctly, you need to select a printer that currently is enabled for your computer system. The dialog box that enables you to do so, the Print dialog box, also is where you specify options for printing. To begin the printing process by selecting a printer, use these steps:

1. Open the slide show file you want to print.

2. Open the **F**ile menu or QuickMenu and choose **P**rint (or press Ctrl+P), or click the Print icon on the Toolbar. The Print dialog box appears (see fig. 17.1).

3. The top part of the dialog box displays the Current Printer. If this is not the printer you want to use to print the slide show, click the **S**elect button to display the Print Setup dialog box, shown in figure 17.2.

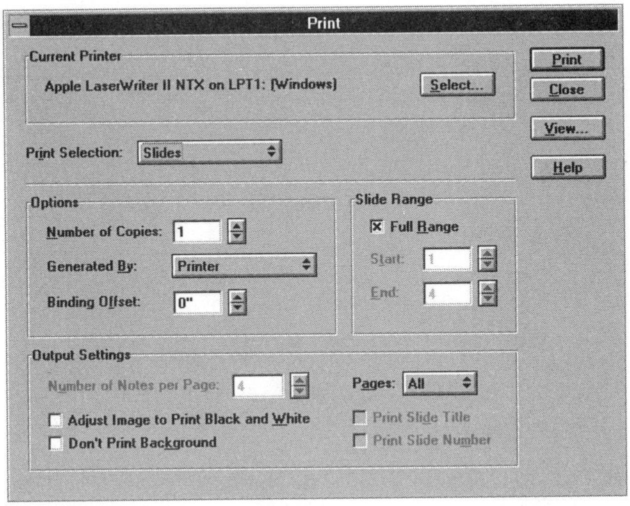

Fig. 17.1
The Print dialog box enables you to choose options for printing your slide show.

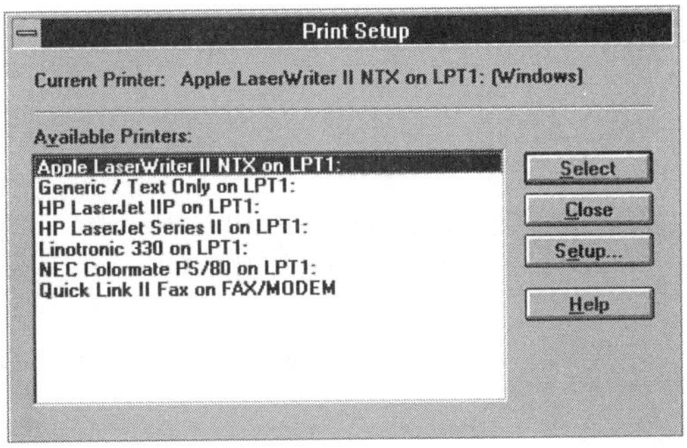

Fig. 17.2
The Print Setup dialog box displays all the printers that presently are installed with Windows.

4. To select another printer, click it in the Available Printers list.

5. If you need to change the available options for that printer (such as paper source or default number of copies printed), click the Setup button, specify the options you want, and click OK to return to the Print Setup dialog box.

6. Click Select to finish your printer selection and return to the Print dialog box.

The remainder of the settings in the Print dialog box enable you to specify what to print and how to print it.

After you specify which printer to use as just described, use these steps to tell Presentations what to print:

1. Use the Print Selection pop-up list in the Print dialog box to specify the format you want to print. Here are your choices on that pop-up menu:

   ■ *Full Page*. Outputs only the current drawing or slides.

   ■ *Current View*. Prints only what appears in the current view in Presentations.

   ■ *Slides*. Prints all or a range of slides.

   ■ *Slide List*. Prints the title of each slide and other options, as organized in Slide List view.

   ■ *Handouts*. Prints multiple slide thumbnails to provide to an audience; you specify how many slides to print per page—up to 16 (see fig. 17.3).

   ■ *Speaker Notes*. Prints multiple slide thumbnails and their speaker notes on a single page; you specify how many slides to print per page—up to 16 (see fig. 17.4).

   ■ *Selected Objects*. Prints objects you had selected on the slide before displaying the Print dialog box.

Fig. 17.3
A handout printout with four thumbnails per page.

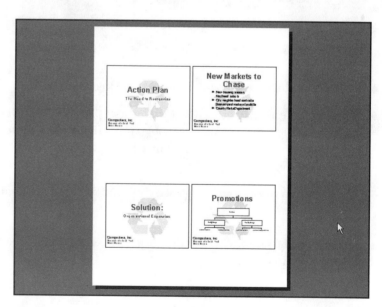

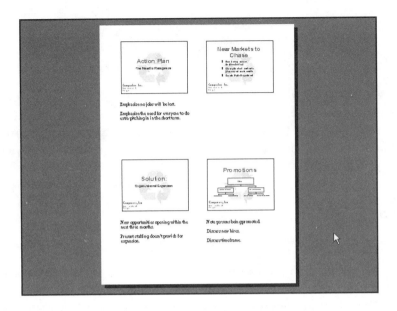

Fig. 17.4
A printout with
four thumbnails
and speaker notes.

2. In the Options area, specify the **N**umber of Copies to print.

3. Use the Generated **B**y pop-up to choose whether your printer or WP Print Process (Presentations **3**.0) generates the output.

4. Specify a value for Binding O**f**fset if you want extra white space to be left along the left margins so that the printed pages can be bound.

5. If you chose to print **S**lides, **H**andouts, or Speaker **N**otes, you can specify the Range of slides to print. To print less than the whole slide show, turn off the Full **R**ange check box, and specify S**t**art and **E**nd slides.

6. If you chose to print **H**andouts or Speaker **N**otes, use the N**u**mber of Slides or Number of Notes per page setting to change how many thumbnails appear per page. Also use the P**a**ges pop-up menu to specify whether to print **A**ll, **E**ven, or **O**dd pages only. Turn on the appropriate check boxes to Print Sli**d**e Title and Print Slide **N**umber for each slide.

7. To adjust the images to print more clearly on a black-and-white printer, turn on the Adjust Image to Print Black and **W**hite check box.

8. If your slide master has a colored background that you believe will print too dark, turn on the Don't Print Bac**k**ground check box to suppress printing of the background.

Now you have chosen a printer and have specified the options you think you want. Don't click **P**rint yet, however. Consider previewing what will be printed.

Previewing Printing

WordPerfect Presentations 3.0 for Windows has a preview feature that enables you to check what the printed output will look like after you have specified print options. Figures 17.3 and 17.4 show printing previews. To preview what your printed output will look like, click the **V**iew button in the Print dialog box. If the printout consists of more than one page, use the space bar to move through the pages. Press Esc to return to the Print dialog box to adjust the options or continue printing.

Printing

Tip

If you're printing your slides on transparency film, check the printer manual to see whether you need to adjust your printer for the film. Hewlett-Packard PaintJet printers, for example, need a few adjustments prior to printing transparencies.

After you specify all the options in the Print dialog box, you simply can click Print to send the print job to the printer. The printer you selected for the print job remains in effect; there's no need to reset the printer for each subsequent print job, unless you want to change the selected printer.

Troubleshooting

*I clicked the **P**rint button and got a message that my printer is off-line or not selected. What's wrong?*

First, check to ensure that your printer is turned on and all the cables are connected firmly to your system, and that there is plenty of paper for the print job. If those items check out, use the steps for selecting a printer described earlier in this chapter to ensure that the printer connected to your system is the one selected in the Print dialog box.

Printing Multiple Files

You learned in earlier chapters that numerous dialog boxes perform file-related operations such as opening, saving, and more. Within those dialog boxes, the File **O**ptions pop-up menu displays a list of commands you can perform on the files selected in the File**n**ame list of the dialog box (see fig. 17.5).

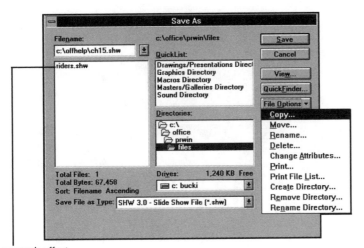

Commands affect
files selected in
this list.

Fig. 17.5
File-related dialog
boxes like the Save
As dialog box
provide a File
Options pop-up
list of commands
you can execute
directly.

Depending on the dialog box you started from, the File **O**ptions pop-up list
will contain a **P**rint command (which isn't available from the Open File dialog box) and/or a Print File **L**ist command. The **P**rint command prints the
selected file in the File**n**ame list without opening the file. Click the name of
the file to print, click the File **O**ptions button, and click **P**rint. The dialog box
shown in figure 17.6 appears. You can change the file name, if needed, and
then click **P**rint to send the slide show to the printer.

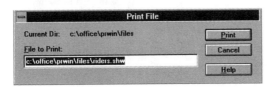

Fig. 17.6
When you print a
file from a file-
related dialog box,
this dialog box
enables you to
confirm the file to
print.

When you choose the Print File **L**ist option from the File **O**ptions pop-up
menu, you see the dialog box shown in figure 17.7. Use this dialog box to
print a list of files in the current directory selected in the file-related dialog
box. The Options area enables you to choose whether to print only the
names of the file(s) you selected in the File**n**ame dialog box, or all files (Print
Entire List) in the current directory. Turn off the **I**nclude Subdirectories check
box to tell Presentations to not print the names of files in subdirectories of
the current directories. If you want, use the **S**etup button to set up the current printer or to choose another printer. Also use the **C**hange button to
change the font that will be used to print the list. After making your choices,
click the **P**rint button to send the list to the printer.

Fig. 17.7
The Print File List dialog box enables you to print a listing of files from a file-related dialog box.

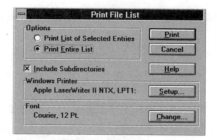

Working with a Service Bureau to Print 35-mm Slides

Unless you're fortunate enough to have a *film recorder* (the device that outputs images to various sizes of film such as 35-mm film) attached to your computer system, it's likely that you will have to use a service bureau to create 35-mm slides of your slide show. *Service bureaus* are printing companies—sometimes highly specialized printing companies—that provide typesetting, printing, and specialized file output services such as color printing, printing to slides and transparencies, and more. In return for a reasonable fee, the service bureau outputs your image on the media of your choice—you have just accessed thousands of dollars worth of equipment for a very modest cost!

> **Note**
>
> To take any file to a service bureau for output, you need to confirm what kind of output device the service uses and add the driver file for that device to your system. If you want 35-mm slides and the service bureau uses a Genigraphics device, for example, you have to use the Genigraphics driver, not the Stingray driver, in Presentations to prepare the slide show for slide output.

As for printing to a printer, printing to a film recorder requires a special driver file that needs to be installed with Windows (one of these drivers is a Genigraphics driver; another 35-mm driver, the Stingray SCODL driver, comes with Presentations). You specify this printer driver in the Print dialog box. Then, when you click the **P**rint button, Presentations outputs the slide show to a disk file that you can take to the service bureau to have the actual slides output.

Installing the Correct Driver

Some presentations graphics and graphic layout programs come with a driver
file for Genigraphics devices, which are common devices used by service
bureaus to generate 35-mm slides. If this driver is already on your system,
you can choose it by clicking the **S**etup button in the Print dialog box.

WordPerfect Presentations 3.0 for Windows comes with a driver for
35-mm slide output. This driver is the Stingray SCODL driver. When you
installed Presentations, the Setup program copied this driver file to the
\WINDOWS\SYSTEM directory on your hard drive. To use this driver to
prepare a slide show for output by a service bureau, you must use the Windows Control Panel to install the driver to work with Windows.

To install a driver to work with Windows (such as the Stingray driver), follow
these steps:

1. Go to the Windows Program Manager.

2. Double-click the Main program group icon to open the Main group
   window.

3. Double-click the Control Panel icon to open the Control Panel window.

4. Double-click the Printers icon to display the Printers dialog box.

5. Click the **A**dd button to expand the Printers dialog box as shown in
   figure 17.8.

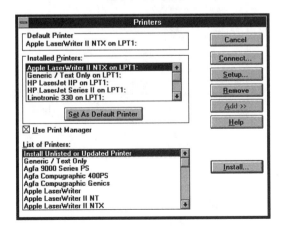

Fig. 17.8
Installing a new
printer driver to
work with
Windows.

Tip
When installing
most Windows
drivers, you would
insert the Win-
dows disk holding
the printer drivers
into drive A for
step 7 and click
OK rather than
specify your Win-
dows directory.

6. Make sure that Install Unlisted or Updated Printer is highlighted in the **L**ist of Printers, and then click the **I**nstall button. The Install Driver dialog box appears.

7. Type **C:\WINDOWS\SYSTEM** in the text box, because that's where Setup copied the Stingray SCODL file, and then click OK. The Add Unlisted or Updated Printer dialog box appears.

8. Scroll in the **L**ist of Printers to display the Stingray SCODL driver, and click to highlight it as shown in figure 17.9. Click OK. The Stingray driver appears in the Installed **P**rinters list in the Printers dialog box.

Fig. 17.9
Selecting the
Stingray driver.

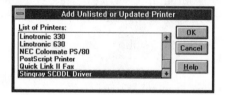

9. Click the **C**onnect button to display the Connect dialog box (see fig. 17.10). In the **P**orts list, click to select a port that is not used on your system, like LPT 3 or COM 4. You want to choose a port that's not in use, because Stingray outputs to a disk file that you can take to the service bureau. Click OK.

Fig. 17.10
Connecting a
printer to a
particular port, or
specifying to print
to a file.

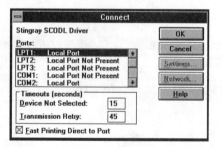

10. Click Close to close the Printers dialog box.

Once you've installed the printer driver to use with Windows as just de-scribed, you can return to Presentations and use it to create an output file to take to a service bureau, as described next.

Creating the Output File

Before you create the output file for 35-mm slides or a particular film size (such as 8×10 for overheads), you should change the page format first to ensure that elements don't end up scrunched or misplaced in the final file. You do have the option to select 35mm as a page size (the actual slide size is 24mm×35mm or 7.33×11", which is a 2 to 3 ratio). When you change the page format, Presentations automatically reformats the layouts of individual slides to conform to the new orientation, margins, and so on.

Use these steps to select the correct page size for your slide or film output:

1. Open the Format menu or QuickMenu and choose **P**age **S**ize/Margins (or press Ctrl+F8). Presentations displays the Page Format dialog box.

2. Click the Si**z**e pop-up list and click **3**5mm for slides. Or, click the Si**z**e pop-up list and choose **O**ther from the bottom of the list. Then use the Wi**d**th and He**i**ght text boxes below the Si**z**e pop-up list to enter 8"×10" or 4"×5" dimensions for film sizes (type a value or click the incrementor arrows to increase/decrease the values).

3. Specify new margin widths, if needed, in the Margins area. Type a value for each margin or click the incrementor buttons to increase and decrease the values as needed.

4. Choose **P**ortrait or **L**andscape orientation, if needed.

5. Turn on the **U**se as Default check box if you want Presentations to use your new page format settings as the default for all new slide shows.

6. Click OK to close the dialog box and apply the new settings. As already noted, Presentations reformats all slides in the open slide show to conform with the new settings.

At this point, you may want to review the slides in your slide show to ensure that the change in page size hasn't created any errors or squeezed any information. Then, you can initiate the process for actually outputting the slide show to a file (setting up the Stingray driver along the way) by using these steps:

1. Open the **F**ile menu or QuickMenu and choose **P**rint (or press Ctrl+P), or click the Print icon on the Toolbar. The Print dialog box appears (see fig. 17.1).

2. Click the **S**elect button to display the Print Setup dialog box, shown in figure 17.2.

Tip

If you want to print a file to disk using a certain printer driver (such as when you want to have color printouts made by a service bureau and the service bureau uses an HP color printer), select the printer in the Printers dialog box, click the **C**onnect button, and select the FILE choice in the **P**orts list.

Tip

To save yourself the most time and aggravation, choose the appropriate page size immediately after starting the slide show. Doing so ensures that you will create slides correctly the first time.

V

Fine-Tuning the Show

3. Click on the Stingray SCODL driver in the Available Printers list.

4. Click the Setup button to display the configuration dialog box shown in figure 17.11.

Fig. 17.11
Use this dialog box to set up the Stingray driver for slide file output.

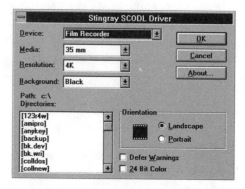

5. Use the **D**evice drop-down list to choose another kind of output device specified by your service bureau, if needed.

6. Pull down the **M**edia drop-down list if you want to choose 4×5 inch or 8×10 inch film output rather than 35-mm slides.

7. Use the **R**esolution drop-down list to choose **8**K if your service bureau uses an Agfa Forte and can handle it. Otherwise, don't change this setting.

8. Specify a different **B**ackground color, if desired.

9. Use the **D**irectories list to specify a directory in which to output the file.

10. Choose the Orientation that matches the page setup you chose for the slide show.

11. Choose to Defer **W**arnings or use **24** Bit Color, if needed.

12. Click **O**K to close the driver setup dialog box.

13. Click **C**lose to close the Print Setup dialog box.

14. Click the **P**rint button in the Print dialog box.

15. The Stingray dialog box appears. Click **O**K to print the file to disk. Presentations creates a file with the SCD extension in the location you specified. This is the file you should take or send to the service bureau.

Note

After you use the Stingray driver to output a slide show to disk, don't forget that you have to choose another printer (in Presentations or using the Printer Setup feature in another Windows application) to return to using your regular printer.

Troubleshooting

I tried to print my slide show file to disk so I could take it to a service bureau, but I got an error message that there was an error writing file*. What happened?*

The disk you tried to print the file to doesn't have enough space available. Delete other unneeded files from the disk to make room for the output file, or print the output file to your hard drive rather than a floppy, and then use a disk compression program like LHARC or PKZIP (available in local software stores or via online services) to compress the file so that it will fit on a floppy disk.

Finding a Service Bureau

To find service bureaus in your local area, look in the Yellow Pages under "Copying & Duplicating Services," "Printers," "Typesetting," and similar entries. Check for companies that provide "computer output services," "35-mm slide shows," and "overheads" as their services. As when shopping for any new service you plan to purchase, call a few different vendors to check their capabilities, ensuring that they can output files created with the Stingray driver.

If you cannot find a service bureau in your area to create 35-mm slides from your Presentations file, try calling some of the following services. Many will turn around your slides in 72 hours or less:

AIM
Attention: Imaging
823 East A. Street
Moscow, ID 83843
Phone: (208) 885-5955
Fax: (208) 885-5555

Beekman Group Inc.
Phone: (212) 509-1817

V

Fine-Tuning the Show

Brilliant Image
Seven Penn Plaza
New York, NY 10001
Phone: (212) 736-9661
Fax: (212) 736-9879

Graphexec Visuals Inc.
1991 Highway 54 West
Fayetteville, GA 30214
Phone: (404) 487-2165
Fax: (404) 631-8620

Graphicsland
17730A South Oak Park Avenue
Tingley Park, IL 60477
Phone: (708) 532-8224
Fax: (708) 614-1974
BBS: (708) 532-4060

MAGICorp
50 Executive Blvd.
Elmsford, NY 10523
Phone: (800) 367-6244

Slide Effects
262 Thatcher Road
Rockport, MA 01966
Phone: (508) 546-9207
Fax: (508) 546-3603

Slide Imagers
Phone: (800) 232-5411
Fax: (404) 873-1517
BBS: (404) 874-48043

Saving a Slide Show in Different Formats

Chapter 2, "Developing a Slide Show," explained the basic procedure for saving your slide show. Chapter 15, "Working with Masters, Templates, and Backgrounds," explained how to use the Save File As **T**ype pop-up list in the Save As dialog box to save changes to a master file. That pop-up list also can be used to save all or parts of slide shows in different formats, for use in other applications.

When you choose to save the slide show in a graphics format like EPS (Encapsulated PostScript) or WPG (a WordPerfect graphics file format), only the contents of the current slide are saved to the file. When you choose to save the file as a WPD file, the slide show contents are saved in a generic WordPerfect outline format. Table 17.1 reviews all the file formats you can choose from the Save File As **T**ype pop-up list in the Save As dialog box.

Table 17.1 Formats You Can Save Your Slide Show in

Extension and Type	Description
BMP - Windows Bitmap (*.bmp)	Saves the current slide as a Windows Bitmap file
CGM - Computer Graphics Metafile (*.cgm)	Saves the current slide as a vector metafile, a common graphics format
EPS - Encapsulated PostScript (*.eps)	Saves the current slide as a PostScript graphic, which can be output only on a PostScript printer
MST 2.0 - Master File (*.mst)	Saves background and layout changes to a master file in Presentations 2.0 format
MST 3.0 - Master File (*.mst)	Saves background and layout changes to a master file in Presentations 3.0 format
PCX - PC Paintbrush (*.pcx)	Saves the current slide as a bitmap file in the common PCX format
SHW 2.0 - Slide Show File (2.0)	Saves the entire slide show as a WordPerfect Presentations 2.0 for Windows file
SHW 3.0 - Slide Show File (3.0)	Saves the entire slide show in a normal Presentations 3.0 file
TIFF - Tagged Image File Format (*.tif)	Saves the current slide as a bitmap file in the common TIF format commonly used for scanned grayscale images
WMF - Aldus Windows Metafile (*.wmf)	Saves the current slide as a vector image in the metafile format defined by Aldus

V

Fine-Tuning the Show

(continues)

Table 17.1 Continued

Extension and Type	Description
WMF - Microsoft Windows Metafile (*.wmf)	Saves the current slide as a vector image in the metafile format defined by Aldus.
WP 5.1 - Text Outline (*.doc, *.wpd)	Saves the entire slide show as a text outline that's backward compatible with WordPerfect 5.1.
WP 6.0 - Text Outline (*.wpd)	Saves the entire slide show as a text outline.
WPG 1.0 - WordPerfect 5.1 Graphic (*.wpg)	Saves the current slide as a WordPerfect graphic that's backward compatible with WordPerfect 5.1.
WPG 2.0 - WordPerfect 6.0 Graphic (*.wpg)	Saves the current slide as a WordPerfect graphic.

From Here...

This chapter reviewed some important issues relating to slide shows—namely creating the output for your finished show and saving all or parts of it in various formats for reuse. In addition to covering all the saving options, this chapter explained how to have 35-mm slides or overheads created. For additional information on finishing and rounding out your slide show, see these chapters:

■ Chapter 2, "Developing a Slide Show," explains how to create a new slide show file; open an existing slide show; navigate in Presentations; add slides, text, and charts; and save the slide show.

■ Chapter 18, "Creating and Viewing the On-Screen Show," explains what you need to do to create a presentation to run on a computer screen, including how to adjust some of the options found in Slide List view (described in this chapter).

■ Chapter 19, "Enhancing a Slide Show with Sound," explains how to add sounds to make your computer slide show a multimedia production.

■ Chapter 20, "Customizing with Macros, Toolbars, and Menus," explains how to create macros and customize Toolbars and menus.

Chapter 18

Creating and Viewing the On-Screen Show

Before presentation graphics programs, the only options for delivering a presentation were to use actual slides or overhead transparencies. Presenters were required to lug unwieldy projectors to on-site presentations (a particularly fun thing to do when you're flying) or to call an equipment-rental company and hope that the equipment arrived where and when it was needed.

Programs like WordPerfect Presentations 3.0 for Windows have opened up another, more convenient way to deliver a slide show—on the computer screen. Taking a slide show on the road can be as simple as carrying a laptop computer—which many business travelers routinely carry, anyway. You even can create employee training presentations and make them available on computers in a training center; by viewing such slide shows, employees can train themselves. In Presentations, any collection of slides can be played as a slide show, but there are some tools you can use to increase the automation of the on-screen show and make it more effective.

This chapter explains how to use the features in Presentations to enhance your on-screen show, including how one slide transitions to the next and what tools are available for running the on-screen show. You learn about the following tasks:

■ Running a slide show on-screen

■ Setting the transitions from slide to slide

■ Creating links to jump quickly between slides

■ Adding animations to the slide show

■ Rehearsing the slide show and using the pointer while running it

■ Creating a slide show you can run outside the Presentations program

Adding Transition Effects

If you have watched any television, you have seen transitions in shows and commercials. When one image fades out and another fades in, that's a *transition*. The transition can appear along a straight line, or in a shape like a box or jigsaw puzzle pieces.

When you view your slide show as an on-screen show (rather than working in the Presentations application window), the normal transition when you move between slides is instant: the contents of one slide disappear and the contents of the next appear. You are not limited to this simple kind of transition, however. Presentations offers a variety of different transitions that add interesting and attractive movement from one slide to the next. Adding a transition to a particular slide controls how the slide *appears* when it's displayed in the show; when you move to the next slide, the current slide simply disappears. Table 18.1 lists the kinds of transitions you can specify for your slides.

Table 18.1 Slide Transitions in Presentations	
Type	**Makes the Slide Contents**
Wipe	Roll onto the screen in a straight line from the direction you specify
Open	Appear from the center of the slide out, in vertical or horizontal lines
Close	Appear from the edges of the slide in, in vertical or horizontal lines
Box	Appear in a box shape from the edges in or from the center out
Spots	Appear in random spots on-screen in the size you specify
Blinds	Appear in vertical or horizontal strips
Jigsaw	Appear randomly as interlocking puzzle pieces in the size you specify
Snake	Fill the screen in a back-and-forth pattern from the direction you specify

Type	Makes the Slide Contents
Diagonal	Appear from the corner you specify to fill the screen
Overwrite	Appear with the background shown first, with the contents overwriting the background

Rather than adding a transition, you can choose to skip displaying a slide in the on-screen show. You can specify whether you have to manually initiate transitions, or whether transitions occur after specified time periods. You also can add sounds to transitions (described in Chapter 19) and keys that enable you to jump from the present slide to any other slide in the slide show. Some of these topics are described later in this chapter.

For now, here are the basic steps for adding a transition to a slide:

1. Choose the slide to add a transition to.

2. Open the **S**lide menu and choose Trans**i**tion, or click the Transition icon on the Toolbar. The Slide Transition dialog box appears, as shown in figure 18.1.

Use to choose different
slides to add transitions to.

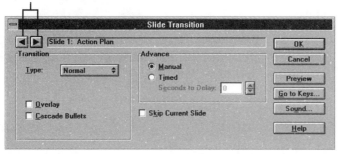

Fig. 18.1
The Slide Transition dialog box enables you to add transitions to slides.

3. If you need to, use the buttons at the upper left corner of the Slide Transition dialog box to choose a different slide to add the transition to.

4. In the Transition area of the dialog box, click the **T**ype pop-up list and choose a transition type from the list.

5. If the type of the transition you selected makes a **D**irection or Si**z**e pop-up list appear, use it to choose precisely what kind of transition you get.

6. By default, **M**anual is selected in the Advance area. This setting means that you have to press a certain key to advance to the slide. Choosing T**i**med means that the slide advances automatically after the time you specify in the S**e**conds to Delay text box (or by using the incrementor buttons). If you want to specify a T**i**med transition, do so.

7. If you want to skip the current slide and transition directly to the slide following it, click to turn on the S**k**ip Current Slide check box.

8. Repeat steps 3 through 7 to add transitions to other slides.

9. Click OK to close the Slide Transition dialog box when you're finished using it.

Previewing a Transition

To see the results of the transitions you have applied, you can view the slide show as described later in this chapter. Although this method works, it can be quite time-consuming to switch back and forth between the slide show and the Slide Transition dialog box. The Slide Transition dialog box enables you to preview the transition you have specified on the spot, so you can immediately make a change if you're not satisfied. When you're using the Slide Transition dialog box, assign the transition you want, and then click the Pre**v**iew button to display the Preview Transition window that displays the transition, as shown in figure 18.2.

Fig. 18.2
This window enables you to preview the transitions you have designed.

Double-click to close the window.

The Preview Transition window remains open until you close it so that you can test other transitions. Each time you specify a new transition, click the Preview button to view it in the Preview Transition window. When you are finished previewing transitions, double-click the Control menu box on the Preview Transition window to close it.

Using the Slide List

You learned in Chapter 4, "Adjusting the View," how to work with your slide show in the various views provided in Presentations. One of the views discussed there was Slide List view (see fig. 18.3). As shown in the figure, by default this list shows the Transition and Advance assigned to the slide. You also can add the Go To keys and sound assigned to the slides by adding those categories to the list heading bar as described in Chapter 4. To work with the transitions from Slide List view, highlight the slide you want to change the transition for in the list, and then right-click the Transition or Advance column to display the Slide Transition dialog box with the transition for that slide chosen.

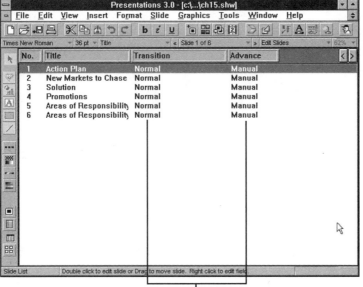

Fig. 18.3
The Slide List view displays Transition and Advance information.

Right-click either column to
display the Slide Transition
dialog box.

With Slide List view, you can assign the same transition to several slides or change the transition for more than one slide at once. To do so, you need to select the slides you want in the list before displaying the Slide Transition dialog box. To select multiple slides, click the first slide in the list to select it. Then press Shift and click on the last slide to select the range (see fig. 18.4). Then, you can right-click the Transition or Advance column to display the Slide Transition dialog box and select a transition to apply to all the selected slides.

Click on the
first slide...

Fig. 18.4
You can select
multiple slides in
Slide List view to
apply transitions
to all the slides at
once.

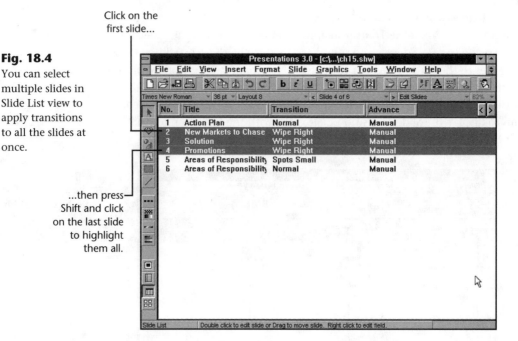

...then press
Shift and click
on the last slide
to highlight
them all.

Creating a Build Slide

A build effect applied to a bullet chart slide provides a very dramatic way to present multiple points to your audience. The build effect helps you "build" your argument; Presentations reveals the first bullet item only, then the second, and so on. There are two ways to create a build type effect in a slide show: using the *overlay* feature and using the *cascade bullets* feature. Using the first method enables you to display one slide and then add text or graphics as you choose. The second method takes a bullet chart slide and displays the bullet items one by one.

To create an overlay build effect, you have to create multiple slides in the correct order in the slide show, carefully placing the elements as you want them to appear. Then you apply the overlay transitions to the involved slides to create the build. When you run the slide show, a slide appears, and then the contents of the next slide are layered over the first slide, the contents of the next slide are layered over the first two slides, and so on. Figure 18.5 shows an example of three slides created for a build effect. The build starts with a title only and ends with the title, subtitle, and graphic (see fig. 18.6).

First slide with title; no overlay needed

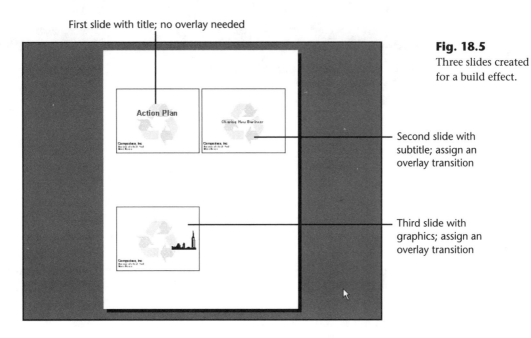

Fig. 18.5
Three slides created for a build effect.

Second slide with subtitle; assign an overlay transition

Third slide with graphics; assign an overlay transition

V

Fine-Tuning the Show

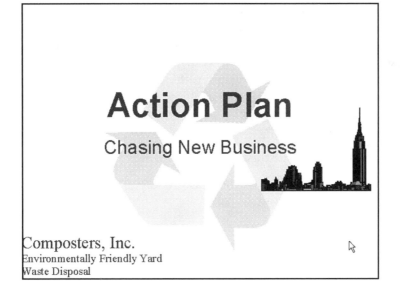

Fig. 18.6
The three slides shown in figure 18.5, combined in an overlay build.

After creating the slides you want to combine with an overlay build, you need to assign the overlay transitions. You do not choose the overlay build for the first slide in the group; you only assign it to the second and subsequent slides in the build. To assign an overlay transition to a slide so that its contents are laid over the previously displayed slide, open the Slide Transition dialog box, select the slide, and turn on the **O**verlay check box.

> **Note**
>
> When you're creating a build effect, the Transition **T**ype also applies in addition to the build you specify. You therefore can have a slide **W**ipe when it **O**verlays, for example.

When you create a bullet chart slide, Presentations can create a special kind of build when you play the slide show that doesn't require you to create multiple slides. When you choose to **C**ascade Bullets and play the slide show, Presentations displays the title for the bullet slide, then the first bullet, then the second bullet, and so on to build the full slide. To add a build effect to a bullet chart slide, display the Slide Transition dialog box, select the slide using the buttons at the top of the slide, and then click to turn on the **C**ascade Bullets dialog box. Doing so displays an additional check box labeled Transition **B**ullets Only. Clicking to turn on this check box means that other transition effects apply to the slide bullets only; the title and subtitle appear with a normal transition.

Creating Links with Go To Keys

Another type of transition enables you to jump from one slide to another slide when you're running the slide show, skipping the interim slides. This makes the slide show interactive. You can have the viewer press different keys to answer questions, for example, with each key press jumping to a particular slide show slide. To create a transition like this, called a *link*, you assign a Go To key that jumps from the current slide to the specified slide elsewhere in the slide show.

To create a Go To key, use these steps:

1. Open the **S**lide menu and choose Go To **K**eys. The Slide Go To Keys dialog box appears (see fig. 18.7).

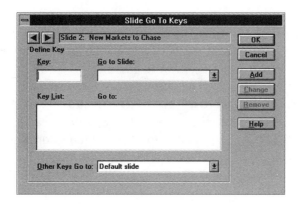

Fig. 18.7
The Slide Go To Keys dialog box enables you to create a transition to jump from one slide to another in the show.

2. Use the buttons at the top of the dialog box to define what slide to jump from.

3. In the **K**ey box, type the key you want to use to jump to the other slide. You can type any letter in the alphabet or a number from 1 to 9.

4. Click the down arrow to display the **G**o to Slide list. Click the slide you want to advance the show to when the **K**ey is pressed.

5. Click the **A**dd button to add the Go To key you just defined to the Key **L**ist in the dialog box.

6. You can set up an either/or transition if you want. In this situation, pressing the Go To key would jump to the Go To Slide you specified. Pressing any other key (except space bar) would jump to a different slide you specify. To specify a slide that other key presses jump to, open the **O**ther Keys Go To list and choose the slide you want other key presses to jump to.

7. (Optional) Repeat steps 3 through 6 to define other Go To keys for the specified slide. If you have a quiz with four questions, for example, and you want three of the answers (the wrong ones) to take you to the same slide, you would add multiple Go To keys for the same slide.

8. (Optional) Repeat steps 2 through 7 to define Go To keys for other slides.

9. Click OK to close the Slide Go To Keys dialog box. You now can play your slide show and use the Go To Keys to navigate the slide show.

To remove any Go To key, start by displaying the Slide Go To Keys dialog box. Use the buttons in the upper left-hand corner of the dialog box to select the slide that has the Go To key you want to delete. Click on the key to delete in the Key **L**ist, and then click the **R**emove button. To change the key assignment for a key chosen in the Key **L**ist, click the **C**hange button, change the key assignment, and then click the **A**dd button.

Overriding Transitions and Advances

If you want to select temporarily one kind of transition or advance for all slides in the slide show without deleting assigned transitions and advances one by one, you can do so by opening the **S**lide menu and choosing the **O**verride command. This command displays the Slide Override dialog box, shown in figure 18.8.

Fig. 18.8
Use the Slide Override dialog box to assign temporarily one transition or advance type to all the slides in a show.

Turn on the **O**verride Transition or Override **A**dvance check box to override transitions or advances in the current slide show. Then, choose the transition or advance type you want to use by specifying options as you did in the Slide Transition dialog box. Use the **C**ascade Bullets check box to create build slides from bullet chart slides. Click OK to close the dialog box.

To turn off the Override feature, simply display the Slide Override dialog box and disable the **O**verride Transition or Override **A**dvance check box, and then click OK.

Adding Animations

Animations are video-like clips you can add to incorporate moving pictures into your slide show on playback. These animations are in the form of media clips in the Microsoft Video for Windows format (AVI files). Presentations comes with some animation files in the \OFFIC\PRWIN\GRAPHICS directory, but you can insert any media clip in the AVI format into your slide show. When you insert an animation into a slide show and then play the slide show, you can run the animation by clicking it, or you can specify that the animated sequence run a designated period of time after the transition to the slide holding the animation.

Animations are inserted into a slide show as OLE objects. Inserting and working with OLE objects are described in more detail in Chapter 16, "Inserting Objects into Slides." Here are the steps for inserting an animation:

1. Go to the slide where you want to embed the object.

2. Open the **I**nsert menu and choose Ob**j**ect. The Insert Object dialog box appears.

3. Make sure that Create from **F**ile is selected.

4. Specify a Fil**e** to insert, using the File Folder icon to display the Select File dialog box.

5. Click OK. The animation is inserted into the current slide in its own window that you can drag and resize as needed.

You need to make some adjustments to control how the animation appears and plays back when you play your slide show. Here are the steps for setting animation options:

1. On the slide where it appears, click the animation to display its selection handles.

2. Open the **E**dit menu or QuickMenu, choose Media Clip **O**bject, and choose **E**dit from the submenu that appears.

3. The Media Player window appears. Open its **E**dit menu and choose **O**ptions (or press Ctrl+O). The Options dialog box appears (see fig. 18.9)

Tip
To play the animation in the Presentations window, click to select it. Then open the **E**dit menu or QuickMenu, choose Media Clip **O**bject, and choose **P**lay from the submenu that appears.

V

Fine-Tuning the Show

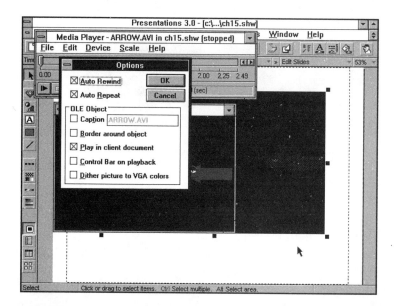

Fig. 18.9
Controlling how an animation appears on playback.

4. Turn on the **A**uto Rewind check box to have the clip automatically return to the start after it plays.

5. Turn on the Auto **R**epeat check box to have the animation replay until you transition to the next slide.

6. Specify a Cap**t**ion if you want one to appear for the animation on the slide.

7. Specify whether you want a **B**order around the object.

8. Turn on the **P**lay in Client Document check box to play the animation within the slide show, not in a separate application window.

9. Check to display a **C**ontrol Bar on Playback.

10. Check to **D**ither Picture to VGA Colors to optimize the display.

11. Click OK to close the Options dialog box.

12. Open the **F**ile menu and choose **U**pdate *filename*.

13. Open the **F**ile menu again and choose E**x**it & Return to Filename.

In addition to changing appearance settings for the media clip, you need to change the playback settings. Follow these steps:

1. Click the animation to display its selection handles.

2. Open the **S**lide menu or the QuickMenu and choose OL**E** Play Settings. The Play Settings dialog box appears (see fig. 18.10).

Fig. 18.10
Specifying the Play settings to control playback of the OLE object when you play the slide show.

3. Click the Hide While **N**ot Playing check box to hide the animation on the slide until it's needed.

4. Choose a Start Play option—When Click on **O**bject or When **T**ransition Ends (specify a delay in the Plus text box).

5. Click OK to confirm your selections.

Adding Visual Cues for Your Audience

When you play the slide show on-screen, especially if the slide show is being run as a stand-alone show for use by others who did not create the show, you should include reminders on slides when Go To keys are available or when a reader needs to click to run an animation. Add these reminders in the form of text boxes or text areas added to the slide. Figure 18.11 shows a cue added to a slide telling viewers to press a Go To key to jump to another show slide.

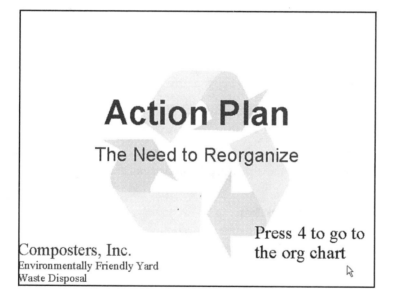

Fig. 18.11
Add text to remind slide show viewers of Go To keys.

Viewing a Slide Show

And now for the moment you've all been waiting for... playing your slide show on-screen rather than looking at the slides in the Presentations window. Playing the slide show removes the Presentations menu bar, Toolbar, Tool Palette, and so on from the screen, displaying the slides as full-screen images. To start playing the slide show, open the **S**lide menu and choose **P**lay Slide Show. The Play Slide Show dialog box appears (see fig. 18.12).

Fig. 18.12
When you play
your slide show,
you first see this
dialog box.

Tip
Press Esc at any
time to discontinue viewing the
slide show and
return to the
Presentations
window.

Specify a **S**tarting Slide, turn on the **R**epeat Slide Show check box if you want
the slide show to replay continuously until you stop it, and then click **P**lay.
Presentations displays the first slide of the show.

Advancing the Slides

Unless you specified **Ti**med advances in the Slide Transition dialog box, you
need to manually advance the slide show by pressing keys or using the
mouse. Here are the techniques you can use to move through the slide show:

- Press the space bar to move to the next slide.

- Use the down-arrow or right-arrow key to move to the next slide; use
  the up-arrow or left-arrow key to move to the preceding slide.

- Use the PgUp and PgDn keys to move forward and backward through
  the show.

- Click the left mouse button to move to the next slide; click the right
  mouse button to move to the preceding slide.

Using the Highlighter

One of the beauties of using a slide projector or overhead projector is that the
presenter can point to pertinent data. Overhead projectors even enable you
to mark on the transparency to underline or circle information. You have the
same capability whenever you play a slide show.

To annotate a slide when it appears on-screen, point to the area you want to
annotate, hold down the mouse pointer, and drag to write as if you're writing
with a pencil (see fig. 18.13). The annotations you make with the highlighter
are temporary. Once you move to another slide in the show, they disappear.

You can change the **C**olor and **W**idth of the highlighter line using those
settings in the Play Slide Show dialog box.

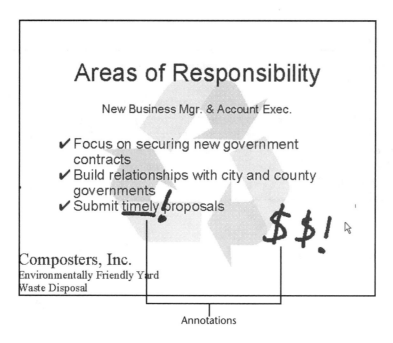

Fig. 18.13
Using the pointer to emphasize information during a slide show.

Annotations

Choosing Faster Playback

The Play Slide Show dialog box also enables you to create a special file called a Quick File, which you can choose to play back when you view your slide show by turning on the **U**se Quick File check box. The Quick File runs much more quickly and is much more responsive on-screen. Before you can run the Quick File, however, you have to create the Quick File and store it on disk. When a Quick File is created, it's saved to the same directory that contains the slide show file, and is given the same name as the slide show, with a PQW extension.

To create a Quick File, follow these steps:

1. To start playing the slide show, open the **S**lide menu and choose **P**lay Slide Show. The Play Slide Show dialog box appears.

2. Click the Create **Q**uick File button. The Create Quick File dialog box appears, telling you the slide show will be played as the Quick File is created on-disk.

3. Click OK to continue. Presentations plays the slide show, automatically advancing through the slides to create the Quick File. When the process is finished, you're returned to the Play Slide Show dialog box, so that you can select the **U**se Quick File option and then play the show.

V

Fine-Tuning the Show

Troubleshooting

I created a Quick File to view, but it looks grainy and the text looks bad. Did I do something wrong?

No, you didn't do anything wrong. Creating the Quick File takes the text and graphics from the slide show file—even smooth clean vector graphics—and converts them to specially stored bitmap images. Because bitmap images are created by colored on-screen pixels, they look jaggier than the original vector images. If appearance quality is more important in your slide show than its speed, do not run your slide show from the Quick File.

Creating a Stand-Alone Slide Show

You may want to run Presentations slide shows on numerous computers in your business—from the laptops your sales people carry to the computers in your training center. Even if you cannot afford to purchase Presentations for every machine, you can run slide shows from as many machines as you want by creating runtime versions of slide shows. Creating a runtime version of a slide show copies a Quick File version of it and the files you need to run it to a special directory, so you can copy the files in that directory to a floppy disk to copy to other computers as needed.

Here are the steps for creating a runtime show:

1. Create and save your slide show.

2. Open the Slide menu and choose Make **R**untime. The Make Runtime dialog box appears (see fig. 18.14).

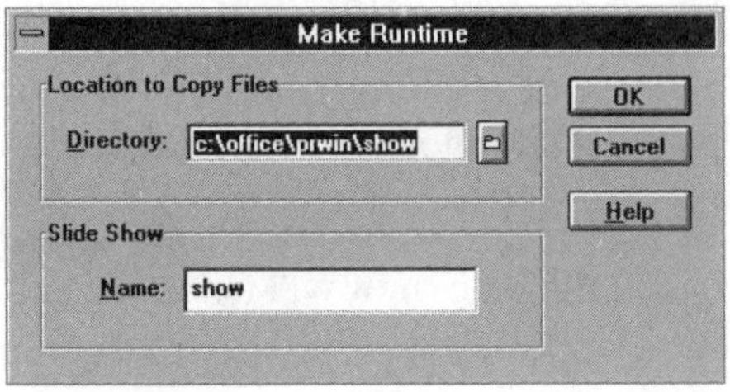

Fig. 18.14
Specify where you want Presentations to store the runtime files.

3. Choose a location in which to store the runtime files using the **D**irectory text box, or click the File Folder icon beside it to display the Select Directory dialog box, and choose a directory. You also can simply accept the default selection, \OFFICE\PRWIN\SHOW.

Caution

When creating your runtime show, choose an empty directory to save it to. The process of creating the runtime show creates several files. It is easier to copy these files to another computer if you don't have to pick them out from a long list of files.

---

4. Enter a **N**ame for the slide show. Presentations takes the name you specify and creates a file with that name and an EXE extension. This is the file that will execute the runtime slide show.

5. Click OK. If the directory you specified in step 3 doesn't exist yet, click **Y**es at the message that appears to create it.

6. If Presentations asks whether you want to copy sound drivers, click OK.

7. Click OK to close the dialog box telling you that the runtime show is created.

When you want to play the runtime show on another computer, you need to copy all the files from the directory holding the show (the one you specified in step 3) to a floppy disk. Copy the files to the disk, and then copy them to another computer in their own directory. Then use these steps to run the show:

1. Go to the Windows Program Manager.

2. Open the **F**ile menu and choose **R**un. The Run dialog box appears.

3. Click the **B**rowse button to choose the slide show file from the directory you specified in step 3 of the preceding procedure. The show will have the name you specified in step 4, plus the EXE extension. Click OK to return to the Run dialog box.

4. Click OK to close the Run dialog box. The WP Presentations Runtime dialog box appears.

5. Make sure that the **R**un Show File text box lists the name of the show to display. If not, use the Other **F**ile button to select a different runtime file.

Tip
In place of steps 1 through 3, you simply can double-click the Runtime icon in the PRWin 3.0 program group window in Program Manager.

6. Click OK to run the runtime file. You can use the same techniques to move through the runtime show as through a regular slide show. You also can use the highlighter.

From Here...

This chapter explained how you can display an on-screen slide show and control that display. You learned how to create transitions between slides in a show, how to have the slides advance automatically at timed intervals, and even how to create a runtime show that you can play on other computers— even if Presentations isn't installed on them. To review some final issues in working with a slide show, see these chapters:

- Chapter 19, "Enhancing a Slide Show with Sound," explains how to add sounds that play when you play back your slide show on-screen.

- Chapter 20, "Customizing with Macros, Toolbars, and Menus," explains how you can create tools to make WordPerfect Presentations for Windows even more convenient to use.

Chapter 19

Enhancing a Slide Show with Sound

Multimedia has been a big buzzword in the computer industry for a few years now. Only recently has the mainstream business world embraced multimedia as a necessary part of business communication. To enhance results in today's competitive business environment, presentations need to stimulate an audience in a variety of ways: with text, graphics, moving animations, and *sound*.

Chapter 18 mentioned briefly that you can add sounds to the transitions in your slide shows. This chapter rounds out that discussion, explaining how to attach sounds in various formats to slide transitions so that the sounds play when you play the slide show. This chapter does not explain how to edit or mix sounds. That discussion is beyond the scope of this book; the documentation for the utilities that came with your sound card should give you more information on these topics.

WordPerfect Presentations 3.0 for Windows offers enhanced capabilities for dealing with sound. This chapter discusses those features and the following:

- Understanding the basics of sound, including terminology, hardware, and copyright

- Adding digital (WAV) sounds to a transition

- MIDI—what it is and how to use it

- Including tracks from your favorite audio compact disc in a slide show

- Setting sound options

- Recording your own WAV sounds

A Sound Technology Primer

Sounds are really waves crashing through the air around us. When the waves hit your eardrums, the vibrations cause you to perceive sounds. The sound waves are *analog* in nature, meaning that they vary in a continuous, unbroken fashion. The original sound recording and playback devices—for records and various kinds of tapes—also "spoke analog." They read and recorded tiny waves to echo the actual sound waves.

Sound had to be digitized for use with computers, because computers can work only with digitized data. As opposed to analog waves, *digitized sound* is composed of discrete values. As a result, digitized sound can specify that a specific pitch play for a specific interval at a specific volume. Generally, sounds recorded digitally can come out cleaner because noises easily can be eliminated, unwanted variations in the voice can be cleaned up, and so on. This is why audiophiles went nuts when audio compact discs were introduced several years ago.

But, the main advantages to digitized sound have to do with storage and retrieval. Analog sounds took a lot of space to record; if you tried to cram them on smaller or thinner tape, you lost sound quality. And, to get to the sound sequence you wanted, you had to fast forward or rewind reams of tape. Digital formats remove these limitations; as technology improves and digitized data can be stored in smaller and smaller spaces, vast amounts of sound can be stored with little loss of quality. And, with digital sound you can jump precisely to the segment you want, just as you can retrieve almost instantly any computer file you have stored on a disk. To sum it up, compare the old 12-inch LP with an audio compact disc. It took both sides of a 12-inch vinyl disk to hold the equivalent (or less) of one side of a 5-inch compact disc.

Some Basic Definitions

Although you don't need to know much about sound to work with it in Presentations, you should understand the names of the file formats you will be working with and how they differ.

WAV (wave) files are basic digitized (digital) sounds that are used commonly in a variety of Windows applications such as Sound Recorder. When you record sounds, they're very often stored as WAV files. You can edit WAV files in a variety of ways, from changing the volumes, to adding portions of other files, to adding special effects like echo.

MIDI stands for *Musical Instrument Digital Interface.* MIDI is actually a communications protocol (language) enabling a computer to exchange information with a MIDI instrument such as a synthesizer. Because MIDI is a language, it provides much more flexibility in capturing and editing sounds. It also is a very compact format, taking very little disc space to store a great deal of music. These files generally are identified with a MID extension.

Compact discs are read on computers by CD-ROM (Compact Disc Read-Only Memory) drives. While audio CD players can recognize only audio data, CD-ROMs read data optically (with a laser) and can recognize a variety of digitized data, as long as you have the software and any other needed hardware to do so. CD-ROMs are optimized for extremely fast data retrieval. The individual songs on the disc are called *tracks.*

Hardware Considerations

To use sound in any practical way with Presentations, you need to add a sound card to your system. A *sound card* is an adapter card that enables you to record and play back sounds in a variety of formats, and usually provides jacks for speakers (output), a game joystick and microphone (input), and MIDI devices. Here are the buying considerations for multimedia hardware for use with Presentations:

- The sound card should be MPC (Multimedia PC) 2 compliant. This is a standard that ensures that the card is up to date and compatible with current applications that use sound. This standard also helps identify other compatible multimedia components. If you're buying a new card, buy one that's 16-bit; 8-bit cards are fast becoming dated.

- Spend the extra $30 to get higher quality speakers. You should look for ones that are at least 5 watts, but choose 10 watts or more if you will be playing your slide show in front of a large audience.

- If you want to record at all, buy a microphone.

- If you want to include CD audio in a slide show, you must have a CD-ROM drive. Make sure that you purchase a double-spin drive that's MPC 2 compliant.

- Consider buying a multimedia upgrade kit if you don't have any multimedia components (Creative Labs offers a good one with the best-selling SoundBlaster 16 sound card). These are value priced, and you know the components you will be getting are compatible.

Tip
To learn more about updating your PC for sound and multimedia, see *Upgrading Your PC to Multimedia,* also published by Que.

V

Fine-Tuning the Show

Copyright Considerations

"Consider the source," advises a bit of folk wisdom; this wisdom applies very well to using sound in slide shows. Music can be copyrighted. Presentations provides numerous WAV and MID files for your use in the \OFFICE\PRWIN\SOUND directory. These files are yours to use as you like in Presentations, free of charge. There also are sound-clip collections widely available through computer dealers; these may or may not be used royalty-free. Check the information that comes with the collection to understand the usage agreement. Many sound-clip files are found on on-line services like CompuServe or the Internet. If the sound clip is from a well-known source (like a clip of a hit song) or is an original MIDI composition, make sure that you get permission from the appropriate parties before using the sound for any commercial purposes.

If you plan to use audio CD tracks in a slide show, proceed with extreme caution. These songs have owners who collect royalties whenever they're used. (Nike had to pay someone a heck of a lot of money to include John Lennon's *Revolution* in a TV commercial.) If you're using sounds from an audio clip collection on CD, see the usage agreement to understand what rights you've purchased. If you want to work with popular songs on CD, never consider doing so for commercial purposes without obtaining permission. If you get caught using a celebrity's music to promote your product to a trade show with 50,000 attendees, you may encounter legal problems.

Working with Digital Sounds

You can attach a WAV sound to a transition from virtually any view in Presentations. Start by following these steps:

1. Open the **S**lide menu and choose **S**ound to display the Sound dialog box, shown in figure 19.1. You also can display this dialog box by clicking the So**u**nd button in the Slide Transition dialog box.

Select the slide to
add the sound to.

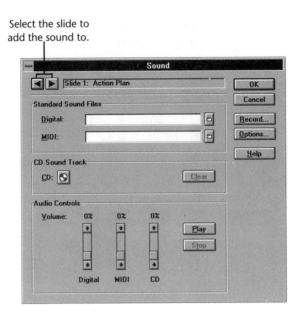

Fig. 19.1
Use the Sound
dialog box to
attach sounds to
transitions.

2. Use the buttons at the upper left corner of the dialog box to select the
   slide to add the sound to.

3. Click the File Folder icon at the right end of the **D**igital text box. This
   displays the Select File dialog box, shown in figure 19.2.

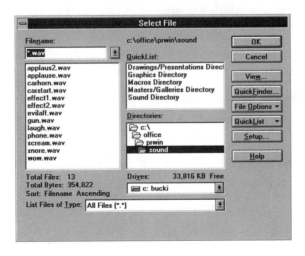

Fig. 19.2
Selecting a sound
file to insert into a
slide show is
similar to selecting
other kinds of files.

V

Fine-Tuning the Show

4. By default, the Select File dialog box should open with the WAV files in the \OFFICE\PRWIN\SOUND directory displayed. If it doesn't, or if the file you want is in another directory, use the Dri**v**es, **D**irectories, and List Files of **T**ype lists to display the appropriate file.

5. Click the name of the file you want in the File**n**ame list.

6. If you're not sure that a file is the one you want, and you want to pre-view it, click the Vie**w** icon. The Viewer window appears and plays the sound file (see fig. 19.3). You can use the buttons at the bottom of the Viewer window to replay the sound file, if necessary.

Fig. 19.3
The Viewer window isn't just for graphics; use it to preview sounds, as well.

Double-click to close Viewer window.

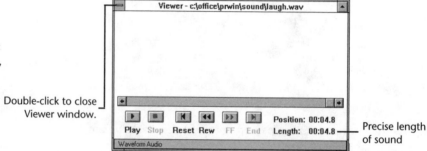

Precise length of sound

7. Double-click the Viewer window's Control menu box to close it.

8. Repeat steps 4 through 6 to preview other sounds if needed.

9. Click the OK button to choose the file presently selected in the File**n**ame dialog box and to return to the Sound dialog box. The sound file name appears in the **D**igital text box.

10. Click the **P**lay button in the Audio Controls section to check the sound volume. If needed, drag the Digital **V**olume slider (scroll box) up or down to increase or decrease the volume.

11. Repeat steps 2 through 10 to change the transitions for other slides, if needed.

12. Click OK to close the dialog box and add your sound(s) to the specified transition(s).

Adding MIDI Sounds

The process for adding MIDI sounds to a transition is virtually the same as for WAV files. Here are the steps:

1. Open the **S**lide menu and choose **S**ound to display the Sound dialog box. You also can display this dialog box by clicking the So**u**nd button in the Slide Transition dialog box.

2. Use the buttons at the upper left corner of the dialog box to select the slide to add the sound to.

3. Click the File Folder icon at the right end of the **M**IDI text box. This displays the Select File dialog box.

4. By default, the Select File dialog box should open with the MID files in the \OFFICE\PRWIN\SOUND directory displayed. If it doesn't, or if the file you want is in another directory, use the Dri**v**es, **D**irectories, and List Files of **T**ype lists to display the appropriate file.

5. Click the name of the file you want in the File**n**ame list.

6. If you're not sure that a file is the one you want, and you want to preview it, click the Vie**w** icon. The Viewer window appears and plays the sound file (see fig. 19.4). You can use the buttons at the bottom of the Viewer window to replay the sound file, if necessary.

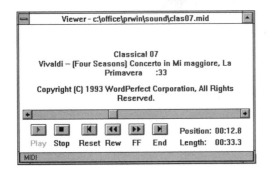

Fig. 19.4

This is how the Viewer window appears when it's playing back a MIDI file.

7. Double-click the Viewer window's Control menu box to close it.

8. Repeat steps 4 through 6 to preview other sounds if needed.

9. Click the OK button to choose the file presently selected in the File**n**ame dialog box and to return to the Sound dialog box. The sound file name appears in the **M**IDI text box.

Tip
If you intend to talk over a sound file (that is, if it's used for background atmosphere only), make sure that you choose a relatively low volume for it. When you want a sound to stand alone or really emphasize a point, choose a higher volume. Be sure to play the slide show a time or two to check all the volume levels you set.

10. Click the **P**lay button in the Audio Controls section to check the sound volume. If needed, drag the MIDI **V**olume slider (scroll box) up or down to increase or decrease the volume.

11. Repeat steps 2 through 10 to change the transitions for other slides, if needed.

12. Click OK to close the dialog box and add your sound(s) to the specified transition(s).

Including CD Audio with a Presentation

The process for using audio CD tracks is similar to the process for other sounds, but you have a few additional options with CD audio. You can add a name for the track, specify which track to play, start at the beginning of the track or a specified location, stop at the end of a track or a specified location, and more.

> **Note**
>
> When you assign WAV and MID files to transitions in a slide show and create a runtime version of the slide show, Presentations automatically copies the sound files to the directory holding the runtime show, so you can conveniently copy everything you need. When you use CD sounds, however, you always must have the CD you need in the CD-ROM drive, whether you're playing the original slide show or a runtime version. Also, you're limited to the tracks on one CD; you could swap them in and out during the course of the show, but your audience would find this disruptive and distracting.

Here are the steps for assigning CD audio tracks to transitions:

1. Insert the audio CD with the tracks you want to use into the CD-ROM drive.

2. Open the **S**lide menu and choose **S**ound to display the Sound dialog box. You also can display this dialog box by clicking the So**u**nd button in the Slide Transition dialog box.

3. Use the buttons at the upper left corner of the dialog box to select the slide to add the sound to.

4. Click the **C**D icon in the CD Sound Track area of the dialog box to display the Slide CD-Audio dialog box (see fig. 19.5).

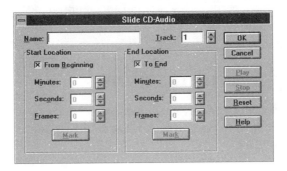

Slide CD-Audio

Fig. 19.5
Use this dialog box to assign CD tracks to a transition in a slide show.

5. (Optional) Type the name for the track in the **N**ame text box.

6. Use the **T**rack setting to specify the number of the CD track you want to use for the transition.

7. If you want to start playing the track from a location other than its beginning, click to turn off the From **B**eginning check box in the Start Location area. Enter the number of **M**inutes, Sec**o**nds, and **F**rames into the track that the play should start. Alternatively, after turning off the From **B**eginning check box, click the **P**lay button at the right side of the dialog box to play the track. When it reaches the point where you want play to begin, click the **M**ark button in the Start Location area of the dialog box.

8. If you want to end track play at a location other than its ending, click to turn off the To **E**nd check box in the End Location area. Enter the number of Min**u**tes, Secon**d**s, and Fr**a**mes into the track that the play should stop. Alternatively, after turning off the To **E**nd check box, click the **P**lay button at the right side of the dialog box to play the track. When it reaches the point where you want play to end, click the Mar**k** button in the End Location area of the dialog box.

9. **R**eset the settings whenever you need to.

10. Click the OK button to return to the Sound dialog box. The CD track number appears beside the **C**D icon. (Click C**l**ear to remove this track at any time.)

11. Click the **P**lay button in the Audio Controls section to check the sound volume. If needed, drag the CD **V**olume slider (scroll box) up or down to increase or decrease the volume.

V

Fine-Tuning the Show

12. Repeat steps 3 through 11 to change the transitions for other slides, if needed.

13. Click OK to close the dialog box and add your sound(s) to the specified transition(s).

Setting Sound Options

The Sound dialog box contains an **O**ptions button that enables you to make changes to the current transition sound. The Sound Options dialog box appears in figure 19.6.

Fig. 19.6
Sound options apply to the transition sound you're presently assigning.

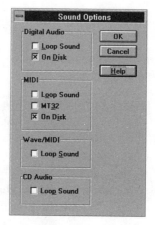

Each of the areas explain what type of sounds the choices there apply to. **L**oop Sound check boxes always play the sound from a single disc file, no matter how many slide shows you use it in. On **D**isk ensures consistency in how the sound files are stored on disk. Turn on the MT **3**2 check box to continuously play the selected sound in the background until a new sound is encountered; this option is available for MIDI sounds only.

Recording Sounds

You may want to record unique sounds or voice annotations to include with your slide show. Presentations enables you to do so when you have a microphone attached to your sound card. Presentations takes advantage of *Sound Recorder*, an applet that comes with Windows 3.1, to record sounds, as explained in the following steps:

1. Open the **S**lide menu and choose **S**ound to display the Sound dialog box. You also can display this dialog box by clicking the So**u**nd button in the Slide Transition dialog box.

2. Use the buttons at the upper left corner of the Sound dialog box to select the slide to add the sound to.

3. Click the **R**ecord button. The Sound Recorder applet appears, as shown in figure 19.7.

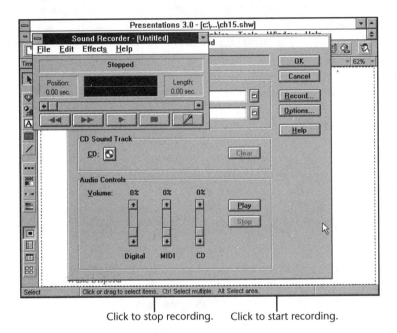

Click to stop recording.   Click to start recording.

Fig. 19.7
This Windows 3.1 applet enables you to record a sound using your sound card and micro-phone.

V

Fine-Tuning the Show

4. Ensure that your microphone is positioned properly to capture the sound you want to record.

5. Click the button to start recording in the bottom right corner of the Sound Recorder window.

6. Speak or otherwise project the sound to record into the microphone.

7. Click the button to stop recording.

8. Open the Sound Recorder **F**ile menu and choose the **S**ave command. The Save As dialog box appears.

9. Use the Dri**v**es and **D**irectories list to save the file to the location you want. It is a good idea to save it to the \OFFICE\PRWIN\SOUND directory along with your other sound files.

   10. Click OK to close the Save As dialog box.

   11. Repeat steps 4 through 10 to capture and save additional sounds.

   12. Open the Sound Recorder File menu and choose Exit to leave the
   Sound Recorder.

Once you've recorded sounds as just described, you can proceed with using
the Sound dialog box to assign those sounds to transitions. If you checked
out any of the other menu options in Sound Recorder, you have seen that it
does offer some basic tools for editing and enhancing sounds. Working with
these tools might be your next step in customizing sounds. Most sound cards
also come with programs (utilities) for working with sound. Explore the
capabilities of those programs, as well.

From Here...

This chapter helped you add the last multimedia component to your
WordPerfect Presentations 3.0 for Windows slide show—sound. You learned
how to add sounds of three formats to slide show transitions, how to set
sound options, and how to record sounds. If you're using sounds, you must
be fairly advanced in your use of Presentations. These other chapters might
be of interest to you:

■ Chapter 18, "Creating and Viewing the On-Screen Show," explains how
   to create slide transitions, add animations, and play back your slide
   show, annotating it with the highlighter if you want.

■ Chapter 20, "Customizing with Macros, Toolbars, and Menus," explains
   how you can create tools to make WordPerfect Presentations for
   Windows even more convenient to use.

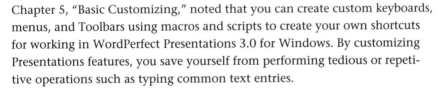

Chapter 20

Customizing with Macros, Toolbars, and Menus

Chapter 5, "Basic Customizing," noted that you can create custom keyboards, menus, and Toolbars using macros and scripts to create your own shortcuts for working in WordPerfect Presentations 3.0 for Windows. By customizing Presentations features, you save yourself from performing tedious or repetitive operations such as typing common text entries.

Macros are a feature common to many kinds of programs. These mini programs replay specified keystrokes and commands to save you time. This chapter explains how to create macros and other customized timesavers. When you create a macro or new menu, Toolbar, or keyboard from one slide show, those changes are available in all other slide shows. Read on for information about the following:

- Recording, playing, stopping, and pausing macros

- Making changes to the default Presentations Toolbar, including adding and deleting buttons

- Creating new Toolbars

- Editing menus and creating new menus

- Creating custom keyboards that execute macros and other shortcuts

Working with Macros

When you create a macro, you store your keystrokes and command selections in a special file that you can replay to execute those commands and keystrokes again. Basically, you can think of macros as your own custom Presentations commands. Presentations makes macro creation easy by enabling you to *record* the keystrokes and commands as you issue them—you don't have to learn any exotic or complex programming language. You create a name for your macro, and Presentations stores it in the \OFFICE\PRWIN\MACROS directory, adding the WCM extension to the file name you specified.

Macros in Presentations are fairly versatile. Although some applications don't enable you to record mouse actions in macros, Presentations does. Here are some examples of situations in which you can create a macro to automate:

- If you have a logo and want to use the QuickArt Gallery to place it on selected slides in different slide shows with different backgrounds, you can write a macro to import and place the file in a specified size and location.

- If you have a particular color you want to apply to selected text in different locations in the slide show, you can write a macro to apply that color.

- If you have a long title or subtitle that you will need to enter in numerous locations in the slide show, you can create a macro to type those keystrokes.

Tip

Before you record your macro, plan out the steps on paper or run through the steps a few times, particularly if you're recording a long or complex operation. This step ensures that you don't record wrong or unneeded steps to clutter up your macro.

Recording Macros

Recording a macro is just like recording audio tape. You start the recorder, play what you want to record, and then stop the recorder. The **M**acro submenu on the **T**ools menu provides the tools for recording and working with macros in Presentations. The **R**ecord command on this submenu enables you to initiate macro recording. Here are the steps for creating a macro:

1. Do anything you need to do to lead up to the steps you want to record. If your macro will apply formatting to selected text, for example, you must create and select some text to prepare for the formatting steps.

2. Open the **T**ools menu, choose **M**acro, and then choose **R**ecord (or press Ctrl+F10). The Record Macro dialog box appears (see fig. 20.1).

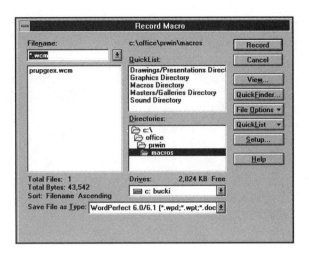

Fig. 20.1
The dialog box for naming the macro you're recording.

3. The Filename box should be selected by default. Type a name (up to eight characters) for your macro. There's no need to type the WCM extension. Presentations adds that for you automatically.

4. Use the Drives and **D**irectories lists, if desired, to specify another location to save the macro file to.

5. Click the Record button. The Record Macro dialog box closes and Presentations begins recording your every keystroke and mouse click.

6. Perform all the actions you want Presentations to record.

7. When you open a dialog box during macro recording, you see that a special check box has been added to the right side of the dialog box title bar (see fig. 20.2). Turn on this check box if you want the macro to display the dialog box during playback so that you can specify options in it.

8. Open the **T**ools menu and choose **M**acro, and then choose **S**top (or press Ctrl+Shift+F10). This discontinues the macro recording and stores the steps in the file name you specified.

Tip
Give your macros memorable names so you can remember what they're for. (After all, a month from now, MAC001.WCM might not be too meaningful.) If needed, create a slide show file listing the names of the macros you've created and what they're for.

V

Fine-Tuning the Show

Click if you want the dialog box to appear for
you to set options during macro playback.

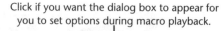

Fig. 20.2
When recording a
macro, specify the
options you want
when you open
dialog boxes.

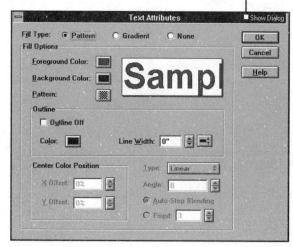

Playing Macros

When you want a macro to perform the steps recorded in it, you have to play
the macro. Playing the macro is as straightforward as recording it. Here's how
to play back a macro:

1. Do anything you need to do to lead up to the steps the macro will perform. If your macro will apply formatting to selected text, for example,
   you must create and select the text to prepare for the formatting steps.

2. Open the Tools menu, choose Macro, and then choose Play (or press
   Alt+F10). The Play Macro dialog box appears (see fig. 20.3).

Fig. 20.3
Playing back a
macro.

Select the macro
to play.

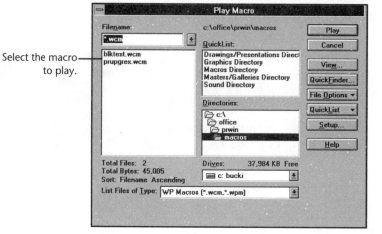

3. If necessary, use the Dri**v**es and **D**irectories lists to change to the location where the macro you want to play is stored.

4. Click on the name of the macro to play in the File**n**ame list.

5. Click the Play button. Presentations replays the steps you recorded.

6. If a dialog box appears during playback, specify the options you want in it, and then click OK or the appropriate button to close the dialog box. The macro continues and plays until it's finished.

Tip

In place of steps 4 and 5, you simply can double-click the macro name in the File**n**ame list.

Pausing and Stopping Macros

Playing a macro isn't an irreversible action. You can discontinue the macro or pause it temporarily. To pause or stop the macro, follow one of these steps:

■ Open the **T**ools menu, choose **M**acro, and then choose Pa**u**se (or press Shift+F10). To resume macro playback, choose Pa**u**se again.

■ To stop the macro, open the **T**ools menu, choose **M**acro, and then choose **S**top (or press Ctrl+Shift+F10).

If the actions performed by a macro are undoable, you can undo the macro immediately after running it.

Editing Toolbars

Tools are useful only if you have a way to use them. A lawnmower generally is useless if you live in an apartment, for example. Similarly, if you don't usually use particular Toolbar tools, you can remove them from the Toolbar, adding others that you find more useful. If you like the default Toolbar, but also would like to temporarily display different tools for particular operations, such as when you're working with graphic objects, you can create completely new Toolbars to suit your purposes. This section focuses on editing Toolbars and creating custom Toolbars. Chapter 5 explains how to select the custom Toolbars you create.

> **Note**
>
> You cannot edit the default <Slide> Toolbar that comes with Presentations. If you attempt to edit this Toolbar, Presentations asks whether you want to make a copy of it for editing.

V

Fine-Tuning the Show

Copying Toolbars to Add New Ones

A safe way to begin working with Toolbars is to copy an existing Toolbar so that you can feel free to make changes to the copy. To copy a Toolbar, use these steps:

1. Open the **E**dit menu and choose Preferences. The Preferences dialog box appears.

2. Double-click the Toolbar icon. The Toolbar Preferences dialog box appears (see fig. 20.4).

Fig. 20.4

You do most of your work with Toolbars in this dialog box; choose the Toolbar to work with from the Toolbars list.

3. Click the Toolbar to copy in the Toolbars list to select it.

4. Click the Co**p**y button. The Copy Toolbar dialog box appears (see fig. 20.5).

Fig. 20.5

Creating a copy of a Toolbar.

5. Type a name for the Toolbar in the To list. The name can be descriptive in nature and can include spaces, as in "Lisa's tools."

6. Click OK to finish the Toolbar copy. (If you want, you can edit the new Toolbar at this point as described in the next section, "Moving, Deleting, and Adding Buttons.")

7. Click **C**lose to close the Toolbar Preferences dialog box.

8. Click **C**lose again to close the Preferences dialog box.

Note that you can use the **C**reate button in the Toolbar Preferences dialog box to create a new Toolbar. The Create button bases the new Toolbar on the Toolbar selected in the Tool**b**ars list. As opposed to Co**p**y, **C**reate doesn't immediately list the name of the new Toolbar until you click OK to leave the Toolbar Preferences dialog box.

Moving, Deleting, and Adding Buttons

One of the simplest ways to change a Toolbar is to move its buttons around. If you're right-handed and move the mouse with your right hand, for example, you may be able to work more quickly if key icons like the Save icon appear at the right side of the Toolbar. Similarly, if you don't have a TWAIN-compatible scanner attached to your system, you may want to replace the Acquire Image icon with another that's more useful to you; that requires deleting one icon and adding another. To lead up to performing all three of these operations—moving, deleting, and adding icons—you display the same dialog box. Follow these steps:

1. Open the **E**dit menu and choose Prefere**n**ces. The Preferences dialog box appears.

2. Double-click the Tool**b**ar icon. The Toolbar Preferences dialog box appears.

3. Click the Toolbar to alter in the Tool**b**ars list to select it.

4. Click the **E**dit button to display the Toolbar Editor dialog box, as shown in figure 20.6. From this point, you can make all the edits you want to the Toolbars, as described in the following paragraphs.

Moving and deleting Toolbar icons doesn't involve actually working in the Toolbar Editor dialog box. Instead, when that dialog box is on-screen, you can drag icons around on the Toolbar to move them, as shown in figure 20.7. Position the mouse pointer over the icon you want to move, and then press the left mouse button to make the pointer change to a hand shape. Drag the icon to the new location you want on the Toolbar. Drag the tool to the icon that you want it to precede (to be to the left of), and then release the mouse button. You also can drag the separators around on the Toolbar.

V

Fine-Tuning the Show

Separators

Fig. 20.6
Displaying the
Toolbar Editor
dialog box enables
you to make edits
to the selected
Toolbar.

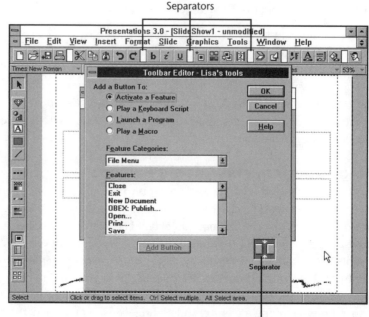

Drag a separator onto the Toolbar at
the top of the screen to add it in.

Fig. 20.7
Drag a Toolbar
tool to a new
location.

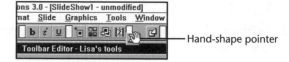

Hand-shape pointer

Deleting icons from the Toolbar is a simple matter of dragging, as well. Position the mouse pointer over the icon you want to delete, and then press the left mouse button to make the pointer change to a hand shape. Drag the icon down off the Toolbar until the pointer changes to a waste basket, as shown in figure 20.8. Then release the mouse button to make the icon disappear. Alternatively, you can point to the icon you want to delete, click the right mouse button to display the QuickMenu, and choose Delete.

Fig. 20.8
Dragging an icon
or separator off
the Toolbar
trashes it.

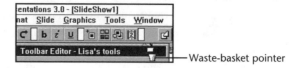

Waste-basket pointer

Adding new icons to the Toolbar does require you to use the Toolbar Editor dialog box shown in figure 20.6. As you can see at the top of the dialog box, you can add buttons for four different actions. Choosing the kind of icon to add makes different options appear in the Toolbar Editor dialog box. Here's how to create each type of icon:

- Figure 20.6 shows the options available to create an icon to Acti**v**ate a Feature. The F**e**ature Categories drop-down list displays the feature categories, or menus. Choose the menu you want from this list by clicking it. Then, in the **F**eatures list, scroll to the command you want and click to select it. Doing so displays a predrawn icon and description at the bottom of the dialog box. Click **A**dd Button. Presentations adds the new button to the right end of the Toolbar; you can drag it to the position you want.

Tip
The F**e**ature Categories list offers more commands than actually shown on the Presentations menus of the same names.

- Click Play a **K**eyboard Script to display a large text box titled **T**ype the Script This Button Plays. In this area, type text you use often; clicking the icon you create with this method inserts that text at the insertion point location on a slide. Type the text and click the **A**dd Script button. The script button is added to the right side of the Toolbar, and pointing to it displays a Quick Tip listing the first word of the script text (see fig. 20.9).

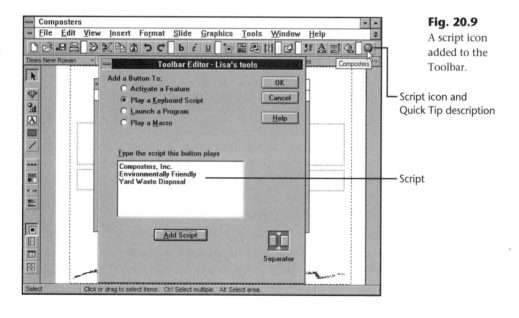

Fig. 20.9
A script icon added to the Toolbar.

Script icon and Quick Tip description

Script

- Click **L**aunch a Program if you want to create an icon that launches another program, such as Quattro Pro for Windows or a sound-editing application. Click the **S**elect File button that appears to display the Select File dialog box. Use this box to select the executable (EXE) file that starts the application and then click OK. Presentations adds a new button (which looks like a sphere) to the right side of the Toolbar.

■ Click Play a **M**acro to create a button that plays back a macro you have recorded. This choice displays an **A**dd Macro button; click it to display the Add Macro to Toolbar dialog box (see fig. 20.10). Move to the location where your macro is stored, if needed, and click the macro you want to add a tool for in the File**n**ame list. Click Add. Presentations asks whether you want to save the macro with the full path. Click **Y**es, and Presentations adds the macro to the Toolbar. Its icon looks like a cassette tape, and the Quick Tip description is the name of the macro file.

Fig. 20.10

The Add Macro To Toolbar dialog box enables you to add a Toolbar button that executes a macro you have created.

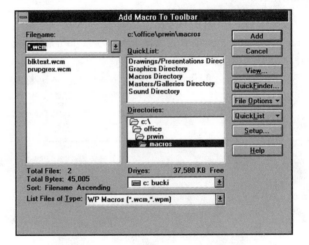

After you use the various methods just described to add all the icons you want to the selected Toolbar, you can click OK to return to the Toolbar Preferences dialog box.

Customizing Buttons

Working with the Toolbar Editor dialog box also enables you to customize Toolbar buttons. You may have noticed, for example, that adding both script and program-launch tools creates icons displaying a gray sphere. To tell these icons apart, you have to point to them to display the Quick Tips. The Quick Tips might not say what you want them to say, however. You can change both the icon and the Quick Tip Help label; you also can change the script, macro, launch program, or feature attached to the macro.

To customize a Toolbar tool, follow these steps:

1. Open the **E**dit menu and choose Preferences. The Preferences dialog box appears.

2. Double-click the Tool**b**ar icon. The Toolbar Preferences dialog box appears.

3. Click the Toolbar with the icons to alter in the Tool**b**ars list to select it.

4. Click the **E**dit button to display the Toolbar Editor dialog box.

5. Right-click on the icon you want to edit to display its QuickMenu.

6. Click Customize. The Customize Button dialog box appears (see fig. 20.11).

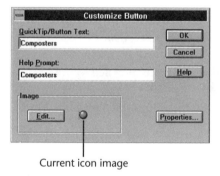

Current icon image

Fig. 20.11
The Customize Button dialog box enables you to change the icon's name and image, as well as the script, macro, and so on attached to it.

7. Type new **Q**uickTip/Button Text (the name that you can display as a Quick Tip or icon text) and Help **P**rompt (the description that appears in the Presentations title bar when you point to the icon) labels, if needed.

8. Click the **E**dit button in the Image area to display the Image Editor dialog box (see fig. 20.12).

9. Edit the image using the techniques explained in figure 20.12. Note that you can **C**opy an entire image, go to the Image Editor dialog box

for another icon, and **P**aste the image there to make a big change. Click OK to finish editing and return to the Customize Button dialog box.

Fig. 20.12
Editing the
appearance of an
icon.

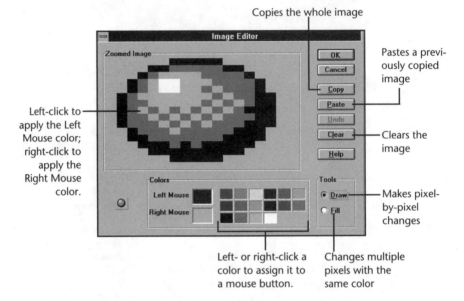

Copies the whole image

Pastes a previ-
ously copied
image

Clears the
image

Makes pixel-
by-pixel
changes

Left-click to
apply the Left
Mouse color;
right-click to
apply the
Right Mouse
color.

Left- or right-click a
color to assign it to
a mouse button.

Changes multiple
pixels with the
same color

10. Click the **Pr**operties button in the lower right corner of the Customize Button dialog box to display a dialog box to change the script, macro, program, or feature attached to an icon. The dialog box that appears varies depending on what is attached to the icon. Make your new selections in the Properties dialog box, and then click OK to close it and return to the Customize Button dialog box.

11. Click OK to finish customizing that button.

12. Repeat steps 5 through 11 to edit other buttons on the same Toolbar as needed.

13. When finished, close the Toolbar Editor, Toolbar Preferences, and Preferences dialog boxes.

Renaming or Deleting Toolbars

After you create a Toolbar, you can rename or delete it at any time, using these steps:

1. Open the **E**dit menu and choose Prefere**n**ces. The Preferences dialog box appears.

2. Double-click the Toolbar icon. The Toolbar Preferences dialog box appears.

3. Click the Toolbar to delete or rename in the Toolbars list to select it.

4. Click Rename or Delete.

5. Depending on your selection in step 4, choose the appropriate course of action:

   ■ Enter a new name for the Toolbar in the Rename Toolbar dialog box and click OK.

   ■ Click Yes to finish deleting the Toolbar.

6. Repeat steps 3 through 5 to edit other Toolbars as needed.

7. When finished, close the Toolbar Editor, Toolbar Preferences, and Preferences dialog boxes.

Setting Toolbar Options

There are several more Toolbar display features that you can control to ensure that the Toolbars are as easy as possible for you to use. You can display descriptive text with the Toolbar icons, display multiple rows in the Toolbar, and more. Figure 20.13 shows a few examples of changes you can make to the display of your Toolbars.

Two rows

Scroll bar appears when there are more rows of icons to display.

Fig. 20.13
Displaying Toolbars with text and picture (top) and text only (bottom).

To change the options for the displayed Toolbar, use these steps:

1. Open the Edit menu and choose Preferences. The Preferences dialog box appears.

2. Double-click the Toolbar icon. The Toolbar Preferences dialog box appears.

3. Click the Toolbar to display and change the options for in the Toolbars list to select it.

4. Click the **O**ptions button. The Toolbar Options dialog box appears (see fig. 20.14).

Fig. 20.14
Controlling the
Toolbar display
with the Toolbar
Options dialog
box.

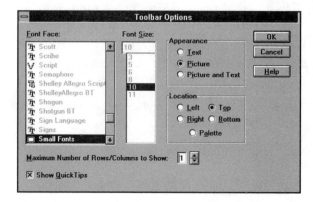

5. Choose an Appearance option. You can display the tool icons with **T**ext only, **P**icture only, or **P**icture and Text. The two options with text display the **Q**uickTip/Butt**o**n Text you saw in the Customize Button dialog box (see fig. 20.11).

6. If you have chosen to display text with the icons, you can choose a new **F**ont Face or Font **S**ize for the text using those lists.

7. Choose a default Location for the Toolbar. The P**a**lette option displays the tools in a floating palette window you can move around on-screen. The other options are self-explanatory. Note that choosing one of the top four options does not preclude you from dragging the Toolbar to a new on-screen location.

8. Specify the **M**aximum Number of Rows/Columns to Show on-screen in the Toolbar. If more rows/columns exist than you choose to display, Presentations adds a scroll bar to the end of the Toolbar so that you can display the other icons when needed.

9. Use the Show **Q**uickTips check box to control the display of those tips.

10. When finished, close the Toolbar Editor, Toolbar Preferences, and Preferences dialog boxes.

Editing Menus

Editing and creating menus resembles the process for editing and creating Toolbars. The Menu Bar Editor dialog box greatly resembles the Toolbar

Editor dialog box, offering all the same command buttons (with the exception of the **O**ptions button, which does not appear in the Menu Bar Editor dialog box). You use all those buttons just as described for editing and adding Toolbar tools, so those buttons aren't described in depth with regard to menus.

As for Toolbar icons, you can add menu bar commands that execute a Presentations feature or macro, replay scripts, or launch other applications. The dialog boxes for attaching these elements resemble those you saw for creating Toolbars, too. The main difference between creating Toolbar icons and menu commands lies in how you drag elements onto the menu bar. The techniques for doing so are described next.

> **Note**
>
> You cannot edit the default <Slide> menu bar that comes with Presentations. If you attempt to edit this menu bar, Presentations asks whether you want to make a copy of it for editing.

Adding Menu Bars

You can add a new menu by copying an existing one or creating a new one. Copying a menu immediately places the name of the copy in the **M**enu Bar list. To copy a menu bar, use these steps:

1. Open the **E**dit menu and choose Prefere**n**ces. The Preferences dialog box appears.

2. Double-click the **M**enu Bar icon. The Menu Bar Preferences dialog box appears (see fig. 20.15).

Fig. 20.15
You do most of your work with menu bars in this dialog box; choose the menu bar to work with from the **M**enu Bars list.

3. Click the menu bar to copy in the **M**enu Bars list to select it.

4. Click the Co**p**y button. The Copy Menu Bar dialog box appears.

5. Type a name for the menu bar in the To list. The name can be descriptive in nature and can include spaces, as in "Lisa's menus."

6. Click OK to finish the menu bar copy. (At this point, you can select the menu and edit it as described next in the section, "Editing Existing Menus.")

7. Click **C**lose to close the Menu Bar Preferences dialog box.

8. Click **C**lose again to close the Preferences dialog box.

Note that you can use the C**r**eate button in the Menu Bar Preferences dialog box to create a new menu bar. The C**r**eate button bases the new menu bar on the menu bar selected in the **M**enu Bar list. As opposed to copy, C**r**eate doesn't immediately list the name of the new menu bar until you click OK to leave the Toolbar Preferences dialog box.

Troubleshooting

I created a new menu bar and then used the Cancel button in the Menu Bar Editor dialog box to cancel some changes I made. When I reopened that dialog box to continue to edit my menu bar, it didn't appear. How did I lose it?

The menu bar you create isn't stored until you choose the OK button to close the applicable Menu Bar Editor dialog box. (This is true when you're creating Toolbars, too!) To immediately store a new menu bar, use the **C**opy button instead of the C**r**eate button.

Use the Re**n**ame and **D**elete buttons in the Menu Bar Preferences dialog box to rename or delete a menu bar selected in the **M**enu Bars list.

Editing Existing Menus

After you create or copy a menu bar, you can make a variety of changes to the menu bar. You can add and delete commands and dividers in particular menus. You can move menus to a new location. And, you can remove menus and add completely new menus. Many of these operations are accomplished with dragging.

Moving and deleting menus and menu commands doesn't involve actually working in the Menu Bar Editor dialog box. Instead, when that dialog box is on-screen, you can drag menus around on the menu bar to move them to a new location. Position the mouse pointer over the menu you want to move, and then press the left mouse button to make the pointer change to a hand shape. Drag the menu to the new location you want on the menu bar. Drag the menu to the menu that you want it to precede (to be to the left of), and release the mouse button.

Deleting menus from the menu bar is a simple matter of dragging, as well. Position the mouse pointer over the menu you want to delete and press the left mouse button to make the pointer change to a hand shape. Drag the menu down off the Toolbar until the pointer changes to a waste basket. Then release the mouse button to make the menu disappear.

When you move the mouse pointer over the menu name, the menu contents appear as in figure 20.16. Drag the hand pointer down (without pressing a mouse button) to move the highlight over a command or separator line you want to move or delete. Press the left mouse button to close the hand around the mouse or separator. Drag the command or separator to a new location on the menu, or drag it off the menu to delete it.

Tip

Dragging a selected command up to the menu bar and then left or right opens other menus so that you can move the command to another menu.

Drag down without pressing the mouse button to
highlight a command to move or delete.

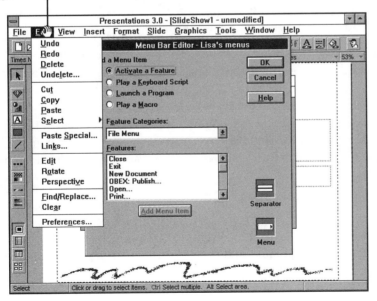

Fig. 20.16
Opening a menu
to edit it.

Adding separators to a menu or commands to a menu bar is slightly different. To add a separator, move the mouse pointer over the Separator icon in the

Menu Bar Editor dialog box until the pointer changes to a hand. Press the left mouse button to grab a separator. Drag up to the menu bar, drag left or right to open the menu you want to add the separator to, and then drag the separator into place. To create a menu, use the same process, dragging from the Menu icon to the menu bar. This process puts a new menu titled "Menu" on the menu bar. Then, to name the menu, double-click it to display the Edit Menu Text dialog box (see fig. 20.17). Type a new name for the menu (such as **Extras**) in the **M**enu Item text box, and type new Quick Tip text in the Help **P**rompt text box. Click OK to finish your change.

Fig. 20.17
Naming a new menu you have added.

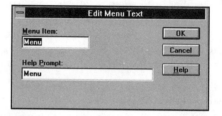

Creating new menu commands requires using the Menu Bar Editor dialog box and dragging. As you can see at the top of the dialog box, you can add commands for four different elements. Choosing the kind of menu command to add makes different options appear in the Menu Bar Editor dialog box. Here's how to create each type of command:

- Figure 20.16 shows the options available to create a command to Acti-**v**ate a Feature. The F**e**ature Categories drop-down list displays the feature categories, or menus. Choose the menu you want from this list by clicking it. Then, in the F**e**atures list, scroll to the command you want and click to select it. A description appears at the bottom of the dialog box. Click **A**dd Menu Item. Presentations adds the new command to the right end of the menu bar; you can drag it to the menu and position you want.

- Click Play a **K**eyboard Script to display a large text box titled **T**ype the Script This Menu Item Plays. In this area, type text you use often; choosing the command you create with this method inserts that text at the insertion point location on a slide. Type the text in the text box, and then click the **A**dd Script button. The script command is added to the right side of the menu bar, with the first word of the script text as the script name. Drag the script command to the menu and position you want.

- Click **L**aunch a Program if you want to create a command that launches another program, such as Quattro Pro for Windows or a sound-editing application. Click the **S**elect File button that appears to display the Select File dialog box. Use it to select the executable (EXE) file that starts the application, and then click OK. Presentations adds a new command to the right side of the Toolbar, using the name of the EXE file as the command name. Rename the command if needed (by double-clicking), and then drag it to where you want it to appear.

- Click Play a **M**acro to create a command that plays back a macro you have recorded. This choice displays an **A**dd Macro button; click it to display the Add Macro to Toolbar dialog box. Move to the location where your macro is stored, if needed, and click the macro you want to add a command for in the File**n**ame list. Click Add. Presentations asks whether you want to save the macro with the full path. Click **Y**es, and Presentations adds the macro to the menu bar. Rename and move the icon as needed.

After you use the various methods just described to make all the changes you want to the selected menu bar, you can click OK to return to the Toolbar Preferences dialog box.

Creating Custom Keyboards

The words of wisdom imparted earlier in this chapter in regard to creating custom Toolbars and menu bars apply to creating custom keyboards as well. The Keyboard Preferences dialog box greatly resembles the Preferences dialog boxes for Toolbars and menu bars (see fig. 20.18). Select a keyboard to edit from the **K**eyboards list. Then use the C**r**eate, **E**dit, Co**p**y, Re**n**ame, and **D**elete buttons, which function the same as in the other dialog boxes.

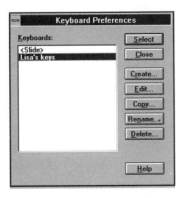

Fig. 20.18

Use the Keyboard Preferences dialog box to create and edit custom keyboards.

The only button that works slightly different is the **E**dit button. Clicking this button displays the Keyboard Editor dialog box shown in figure 20.19.

Fig. 20.19

Assigning new functions to keys in a custom keyboard.

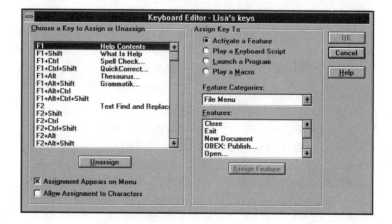

To make a key assignment using the Keyboard Editor dialog box, follow these steps:

1. (Optional) Turn on the All**o**w Assignment to Characters check box in the bottom left corner of the dialog box to assign functions to the alphabetic keys rather than key combinations.

2. In the **C**hoose a Key to Assign or Unassign list, scroll to display the key or combination you want to alter, and then click on it to select it.

3. To simply remove the current assignment from the key, click the **U**nassign button.

4. To add a new function to a key or change its existing function, use the Assign Key To choices. These choices work the same as for editing Toolbar tools and menus (see "Moving, Deleting, and Adding Buttons" and "Editing Existing Menus," earlier in this chapter).

5. Repeat steps 2 through 4 to change assignments for other keys.

6. Use the Ass**i**gnment Appears on Menu check box to specify whether the keyboard combinations appear on menus beside the commands they activate.

7. Click OK to close the Keyboard Editor dialog box. You then can close the Keyboard Preferences and Preferences dialog boxes.

> **Note**
>
> When you're working with a custom keyboard in a slide show, you can press Ctrl+Shift+Alt+Backspace to return to the default <slide> keyboard.

From Here...

This chapter concludes coverage of the features available in WordPerfect Presentations 3.0 for Windows. I hope you find this book useful in creating your own stunning slide shows, particularly while using the customization features described in this chapter. For more information on preferences, see this chapter:

- Chapter 5, "Basic Customizing," explains how to select which Toolbar, menu bar, or keyboard is presently in use. In addition, it introduces you to other features you can customize in Presentations.

V

Fine-Tuning the Show

Installing WordPerfect Presentations 3.0 for Windows

WordPerfect Presentations 3.0 for Windows is part of the Novell PerfectOffice suite of products. Presentations' Setup facility enables you to specify how to install the program, it creates the \OFFICE\PRWIN and \OFFICE\SHARED directories and additional subdirectories, and it creates a PRWin 3.0 program group and all the necessary program icons in Windows.

You must install Presentations on a Windows-compatible PC with a mouse and 3 1/2-inch, high-density (1.44M) floppy disk drive. In addition, your computer must meet the following requirements:

- 80386, 25 MHz or higher processor, with 4M or more RAM

- VGA or higher monitor and video card

- Windows 3.1

- DOS 5.0 or higher

- 24M hard disk space

Caution

Although the Presentations documentation says that you can run the program on an 80386 20 MHz system with an EGA monitor and video card, there's a good chance that you won't be satisfied with the results if you do so. The program probably would run very slowly, and the images on-screen would look jagged. To really work effectively with a graphics program like this, you need a faster system and better video card. In fact, a good recommendation is an 80486 system with 8M of RAM and VGA or SVGA video.

If you want to use some of the more advanced features of Presentations, you need a TWAIN-compliant scanner (for scanning graphics directly into Presentations) and a MIDI-capable sound card if you want to create on-screen multimedia slide shows.

The Setup program gives you several installation choices. Make your selection based on the hard disk space you have available, the parts of the program you want to use, and whether you plan to use Presentations on a network. The four install options are **S**tandard, **C**ustom (which enables you to select which features to install), **N**etwork, and **M**inimum (which installs the minimum files necessary, if you're short on disk space or running Presentations on a laptop). The last choice, **O**ptions, displays a dialog box asking whether you want to view README files for the stand-alone and network versions of Presentations.

Because the standard installation is the process that will be used most often, it's described next. Information about the other installation methods follows.

Standard Installation

You can install Presentations for the first time or over a previous version of Presentations with Setup. To start the install process, follow these steps:

1. If you're installing over an old version of Presentations, make sure that you create a new directory (named \BACKUP, perhaps) and save any graphics, slide shows, and master files there. This step ensures that none of your data gets overwritten. Make sure that you have 24M of free disk space before you start the setup process.

2. Start Windows and go to the Program Manager.

3. Insert the Install 1 disk into drive A or B.

4. Open the **F**ile menu and choose **R**un. The Run dialog box appears.

5. Type **a:setup** or **b:setup** (see fig. A.1). Click OK.

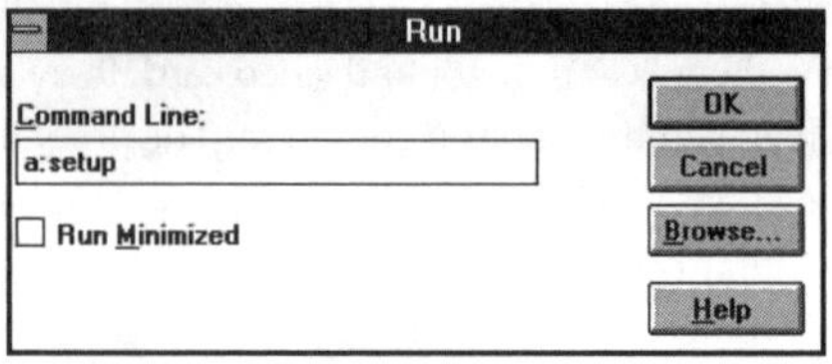

Fig. A.1
Running the Setup program.

6. Setup copies some working files to your hard drive, and then displays the Presentations Setup screen (see fig. A.2). Click **I**nstall or press Enter.

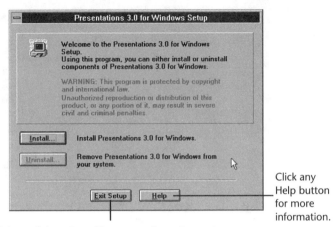

Fig. A.2
Choosing to install
Presentations.

Click any Exit or Cancel button to discontinue setup.

Click any
Help button
for more
information.

7. In the Registration Information screen, enter your Name, Company, and License Number, pressing Tab after each entry (see fig. A.3). Then click **C**ontinue or press Enter.

Fig. A.3
Entering your user
name, company,
and product
license number.

Tip
You need your
License number to
apply for a PIN
number so that
you can get tech
support when you
need it. To update
your license num-
ber and PIN num-
ber after installing
the program, open
the **H**elp menu
and choose **A**bout
Presentations 3.0.

8. At the Installation Type screen, click **S**tandard (see fig. A.4). This installation requires 24M of hard disk space.

9. In the Select Drive dialog box, type the hard drive to which you want to install (such as drive C), or click the drive in the list and click OK. Setup starts copying files to your hard drive, displaying information messages as shown in figure A.5.

Fig. A.4
Choose the
installation type.

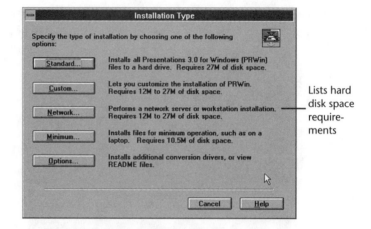

Lists hard
disk space
require-
ments

Fig. A.5
Setup starts
copying files to
your hard drive.

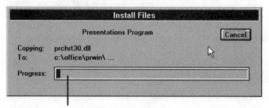

Setup shows how much progress it has made.

10. Setup prompts you for disks as needed (see fig. A.6). Insert the requested disk into the specified drive and click OK or press Enter. Continue swapping disks when prompted.

Fig. A.6
Presentations asks
you to insert
another disk.

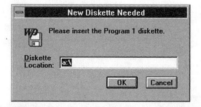

11. When finished asking for disks, Setup installs some fonts, and then creates the PRWin 3.0 group and program icons in Windows. A README Files dialog box appears, asking if you want to view the README files. Click **Y**es, and then click the file you want to read. When you're finished reading the file, double-click the Control menu box for the file to close it, and click **C**lose.

12. Next, you see the Presentations 3.0 for Windows Installation Complete dialog box. Click OK to complete the installation.

13. Store the original program disks in a safe place where they won't be exposed to heat, dirt, dampness, or light.

Custom Installation

If you want to install some parts of Presentations but not others, you can use the **C**ustom setup option. You can choose whether to install such items as WAV sound files or additional TrueType fonts. Custom installation also is useful if you want to reinstall select portions of the Presentations program. To perform a custom setup, use these steps:

1. Begin the Setup process as described in steps 1 through 7 of the standard procedure just described.

2. At the Installation Type screen, click **C**ustom (refer to fig. A.4). This installation requires 12M to 24M of hard disk space.

3. The Custom Installation: Presentations window appears (see fig. A.7). Click a check box at the left to deselect a whole category of files, if desired. You may be warned that the files you're deselecting are necessary for the program. For the category that remains selected, click its Files button at the right to move to another dialog box where you select specific files.

Click a check box to deselect an option.

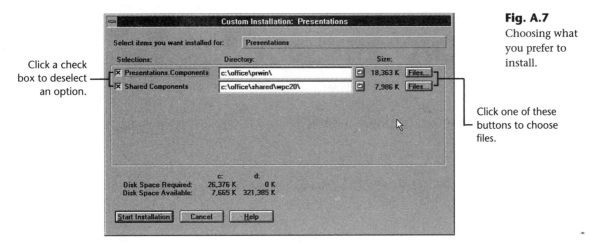

Fig. A.7

Choosing what you prefer to install.

Click one of these buttons to choose files.

4. At the Custom Installation: Presentations Components dialog box, as shown in figure A.8, click check boxes at the left to deselect categories of files to install, or use the files buttons at the right to narrow the files that will be installed for selected categories (click OK when you're finished doing so).

... or, if a Files button is active, click it to choose files.

Fig. A.8
Deselecting files
that you don't
want to install.

Click to
deselect
files...

Scroll
bar

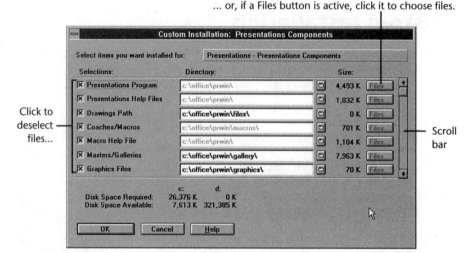

5. Click OK to close the Custom Installation: Presentations Component dialog box.

6. Click Start Installation to continue the Setup procedure. Setup asks you to swap disks and continue much like the standard setup procedure.

Network Installation

If you are a system administrator and need to install Presentations on a network, you will want to read this section to guide you through the installation process, which is similar to installing other types of applications. Basically, there are two stages to setting up Presentations on a network. First, you need to install the software itself on the network server. Then, you need to set up icons for individual users. Before you begin installing Presentations, you need to ensure that you have at least 24M of hard disk space available on the server. Keep in mind that your Certificate of License specifies how many copies of Presentations can be in use at once. You may need to purchase additional licenses from WordPerfect/Novell. The following procedure assumes that you have system administrator privileges and can copy, rename, write, delete, read, and create files and directories on the server.

To set up Presentations on a network server, follow these steps:

1. Make sure that you can access the drive to which you intend to install Presentations.

2. Follow steps 1 through 7 of the standard setup procedure described earlier in this appendix. Make sure that when you start Windows, no other applications are running.

3. At the Installation Type screen, click **N**etwork (refer to fig. A.4). This installation requires 12M to 24M of hard disk space. The Network Installation dialog box appears.

4. Choose **S**erver. Presentations prompts you to continue the installation process. Make sure that you specify Setup to install the program to a drive that's available on your server.

5. When the server installation is complete, set up individual workstations. To do so, go to the workstation you want to set up, follow steps 1 through 3 of this procedure, and continue to the next step.

6. When the Network Installation dialog box appears, choose **W**orkstation, and follow the on-screen prompts to finish creating the icons for using Presentations.

As for any application on a network, you should protect key program files so that they can't be edited, deleted, and so on by unauthorized users. See Appendix I of the documentation or the README.NET file in the \OFFICE\PRWIN directory for more information on protecting key files and changing network-wide settings after Presentations is installed.

Minimum Installation

The **M**inimum setup option takes only 10.5M of disk space, making it the ideal installation choice if you're low on hard disk space or are using a laptop (refer to fig. A.4). This option copies only the necessary files to run WP Presentations 3.0. Minimum setup does not install these files:

■ Spell Check, Thesaurus, and QuickFinder

■ Color palettes

■ Sound files

■ Help files

■ Conversion DLL files (for converting other graphic formats)

In addition, this option only installs eight of the master templates, including Default (blue background), World, Purple Bar, Diagonal 2, Grid, Boxes 1, Slash, and Stripes.

If you choose the **M**inimum setup the first time you install Presentations, and you want to install more files, such as the sound files, later, use the **C**ustom setup option.

Uninstalling Presentations

You may have noticed in the initial Presentations 3.0 for Windows Setup screen that there's also a button to **U**ninstall Presentations (refer to fig. A.2). Choosing this option enables you to determine whether you want to perform a **S**tandard uninstall to delete all the Presentations program files, or a **C**ustom uninstall to select the files you want to remove. Before uninstalling, you should be careful to preserve any slide show and drawing files you created or edited if you want to use them again. Do this by copying them to a special directory on your hard drive or to floppy disk files as needed.

Index